Village
England

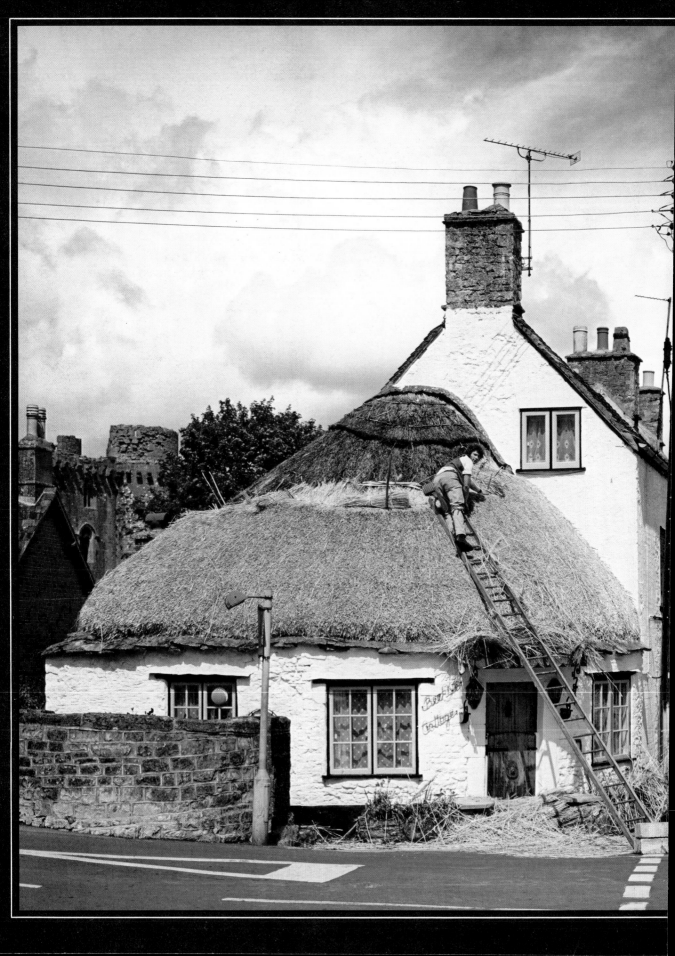

Village
England

Edited by
Peter Crookston

HUTCHINSON
London Melbourne Sydney Auckland Johannesburg

Hutchinson & Co. (Publishers) Ltd

An imprint of the Hutchinson Publishing Group

3 Fitzroy Square, London W1P 6JD

Hutchinson Group (Australia) Pty Ltd
30–32 Cremorne Street, Richmond South, Victoria 3121
PO Box 151, Broadway, New South Wales 2007

Hutchinson Group (NZ) Ltd
32–34 View Road, PO Box 40–086, Glenfield, Auckland 10

Hutchinson Group (SA) (Pty) Ltd
PO Box 337, Bergvlei 2012, South Africa

First published in book form 1980

Set in Monophoto Ehrhardt by Tradespools Ltd

Printed and bound in Great Britain
by Morrison & Gibb Ltd, Edinburgh

British Library Cataloguing in Publication Data

Village England.
  1. England – Description and travel –
  1971–
  I. Crookston, Peter
  914.2′04′857   DA632

ISBN 0 09 142320 1

**Research for Village England
organised by SARAH HOWELL
and PAMELA BROWN
Maps by DICK LEDBETTER.**

Half-title page:
The church at Coates, near Cirencester

Title page:
**Thatching at Nunney: the Wright brothers trace
their family business back 200 years**

Contents

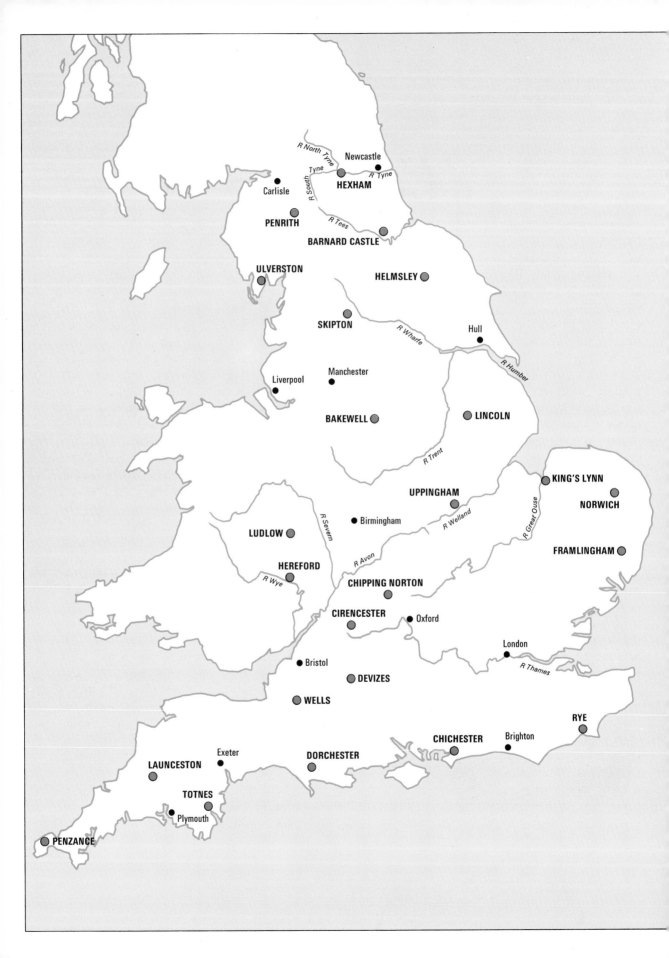

Introduction

Most of us have a mind's-eye view of the perfect English village, and it would be safe to wager that each of them includes at least a green, a duck pond, a church and an inn. To everyone's delight it is easy to find all of these elements in dozens of English villages. But most of us stumble over them as we travel somewhere else, and have only the vaguest idea about the role that a particular village has played in the wider historical or economic context of its nearest city or town – to which we are now heading – or its surrounding countryside – in which we are soon about to disport ourselves. We may decide to stay a while and explore; satisfy our thirsts at the inn and our minds in the quiet of the churchyard – but we seldom learn very much about the village: why it came into being, what 'village Hampdens or mute, inglorious Miltons' may have lived there, or what treasures of historical interest lie within its boundaries. This book, we hope, will go some way towards providing that knowledge.

We cannot claim to give information about every interesting or pretty town in the country, for that would outdo the Domesday Book and would be of unmanageable proportions. We have consciously tried to avoid the obvious – the villages and towns that are so well known it's hard to see the green because of bumper-to-bumper cars or shoulder-to-shoulder people. Thus, you will not find Stratford-upon-Avon, or Windsor, Berkshire, or Broadway, Worcestershire, in this guide, because they are such well-trodden tourist attractions that there are other guidebooks aplenty to tell you all you wish to know about them. We also left out the Home Counties on the grounds that they, too, are so well known that further investigation was unnecessary.

We were inspired, to a great extent, by the lessons we learned from Professor W. G. Hoskins in his pioneering books and his marvellous BBC television series *Landscapes of England*. So we looked for villages, towns and landscapes which have contributed to the social and cultural development of England. With this in mind to help us select our areas, we then decided to choose the most interesting county town or market town in each one as our bases for exploring the surrounding villages. Our next, and most important, decision was to have each place introduced to the reader by someone who had intimate knowledge of it, who lived there or was a frequent visitor, could write lovingly about it and provide genuinely inside information. In this endeavour we were assisted by Geoffrey Grigson, the distinguished poet and writer about the English countryside, and we are indebted to him for the many suggestions he gave us about writers who should be asked to contribute.

Village England was originally an 11-part series in *The Observer Magazine* in the summer of 1979, and it proved to be as popular as our earlier successful series, *Village London*, which was published in 1977, and later became an Arrow paperback.

The information following the introductory text on each section is provided by members of *The Observer Magazine* research team, and we have tried to ensure its accuracy. All dates, opening times and other information in the 'Where to go', 'Where to stay', etc, sections were as far as possible correct at the time of going to press. Where telephone numbers are given it would be wisest to check before making your visits in case of changes. Most of all, we hope this book helps you, in these busy times, to find a corner of England that you may feel is, for a little while, all your own.

PETER CROOKSTON

Penzance

Penzance is at the end of the line. One has made the joke before – that, if the buffers at Penzance station don't stop the train from Paddington, it will glide right on to Grand Central, New York: there's absolutely nothing in between. It's Penzance that's the centre (from which all roads radiate northwards, like the spokes of half a wheel) of Penwith. And Penwith is the last, westernmost knob of the mainland of England: only the Scillies lie still farther out to the west.

The West. I've always had the feeling, when driving home, or even in the train, that once you're over the Tamar, and in Cornwall therefore, then somehow the earth curves over and down: you're definitely going on over the edge – the edge of England, certainly; perhaps the edge of Europe (and Asia). This last 70 miles always seems downhill: you hardly use the accelerator at all as you fly past Bodmin, Truro, Redruth into Penwith; even the train, after Saltash, seems to be using its brakes half the time.

And when you jam on your own car brakes, in the dusk, at the end of the 300-odd-mile drive from London (and you're already farther from London than Paris or the Scottish border), you have the distinct impression that you're lucky not to have fallen over the rim of the land into the glowing, iridescent Atlantic – the Atlantic *Ocean*, that is: it's so different from the opaque English Channel or the even muddier North Sea. And perhaps the enormous disc of the dilated sun, pale orange-gold, is just about to slide behind an incandescent yellow-green knife-edge horizon that seems always *curved*, by the way; a horizon below which one actually senses the towers of the World Trade Center in Lower Manhattan (another joke).

But this feeling of space, of oceanic space, dominates everything in Penwith. If you stand on any rock near my house on the silhouetted skyline of the moors at Zennor, four miles further west along the north coast, towards Land's End, beyond St Ives, and about eight miles due north of Penzance in Mount's Bay, you'll see the rock-strewn ridges of the high ground lying in wave-like formation. Each treeless crest seems a frozen wave of solid land which, in itself, only just succeeds in keeping its position above the vast plain of the surrounding ocean; and which, in all its streamlined shapes (of individual rocks, of clifftops, of head-land profiles), patently registers the same great movements of weather, the same elemental forces that push the ocean itself against the land's edge, against the rocks and sand of the jagged coastline.

To stand on the top of the central heights of the moorland spine of Penwith, and to see the sea on both sides of Cornwall, is to feel most definitely exposed. Exposed to all the elements. Both sea and land seem to be falling away all around you and below you. The space of the

Zennor and, beyond, the Atlantic Ocean

sky seems disproportionately enormous – far greater than the earth's surface, whether sea or land. Penwith feels an island. And its light, as I've frequently explained, is unique for its whiteness – the surrounding mirror of the sea is responsible: this has been the decisive factor in St Ives's magnetism for painters and sculptors.

Where artists lead, the tourists inevitably follow. And nothing threatens the indigenous culture, the local life and character of any place, more effectively than its emergence as a centre of tourist attraction. Whole towns and villages can be destroyed, their inhabitants demoralized utterly, by this fate. An example: a few years ago the revival of fishing from St Ives harbour was actually discouraged on the grounds that the smell of fish being landed would be offensive to the 'visitors'.

There is a deadly culture gap of, say, 20 years when the inhabitants of any remarkable region can save their native landscape if – and only if – they've woken up to the realization that their wobbly 400-year-old kerbstones, or their narrow irregular streets or lanes or footpaths, or their winding field walls and hedges, and indeed their tiny irregular fields, are indigenous to their particular parish; that it is precisely the

St Michael's Mount: 'the view that launched a thousand postcards'

unstreamlined, non–suburban characteristics of such landscapes as the Penwith moors and cliffs and coasts and coves and beaches and inlets that hypnotize and attract the visitor from virtually any other place. How to stop St Ives trying to turn itself into a mini-Blackpool – how to make it realize that in so doing it destroys the very things it's famous for – this is the problem.

St Ives is not quite destroyed. It is still unique. The vulgarity is still largely a surface accretion, in the old part of the town: it could be tailored away. But Penzance and Newlyn still have chances to attract just because they appear, by comparison with St Ives, to be 'working' towns.

Penzance, especially, seems uncelebrated. Perhaps it has to be discovered on foot; and it's true that it's always surprising: terrace after terrace of exquisite Regency stucco houses of all shapes and sizes and colours lie hidden away down granite-paved footwalks and pedestrian alleys. The temperate warmth of the gardens, tucked away in front of all these hidden terraces, public and private, is such a contrast to the windswept, sandblown, treeless and gardenless passages and flights of steps of old St Ives, out on its isthmus of sand and rock. Not that

Penzance shows any more conscious care of its inheritance. Some years ago thousands of tons of waste from a local quarry were spewed into Penzance's handsome granite-walled harbour, filling up half its enclosed space to make – yes, you've guessed it – a mammoth car park. And, at the time of writing, historic houses and a hotel are due for demolition – more car parks. In passing, though, one can truthfully say that the conservationist cause has become much more respected, if not understood entirely, in Penwith in recent years.

The most extraordinary thing about this final toe of Cornwall is the extreme contrasts it contains. All along the very high north coast from St Ives through Zennor, Morvah, Pendeen, St Just and Sennen to Land's End nothing could be bleaker, nothing more barren, despite the famously rich and emerald grass in the hundreds of tiny irregular clifftop fields – fields outlined by the wobbly calligraphy of Bronze Age granite walls and hedges. Yet drop down any of the miniature ravines leading to any cove, and the lush growth suddenly abounds, once you are out of the destructive reach of gale-force winds.

The bony moorland crests above and the severe granite farms and hamlets are as bare as the Outer Hebrides – though without feeling gaunt, if only because blue sea, hot sun and an amazing all-the-year-round patchwork of wild flowers are so benign. But cross over to Mount's Bay, to the south coast, and the descent registers immediately: sub-tropical mesembryanthemum may fall like a curtain down a cliff's rocky face anywhere between Porthgwarra and The Lizard; palm trees mix with magnolia in the cottage gardens; succulents and cacti sprout from crevices in loose granite walls; small fields of narcissi and anemones, hedged in by fuchsia or escallonia windbreaks, run down to the coastal rocks.

So temperate is this south coast. Yet turn inland and north from almost any of the almost claustrophobically enclosed valleys such as Lamorna, dense with Cornish elms and sycamores, and rise up a mere hundred feet, and there again are the rippling lines of the wind-blasted moors, littered by ancient sculpture, most of it natural – the extra-ordinarily elaborate collections of granite on every skyline are natural: the wind and rain, over the millennia, have carved out these outcrops. But, if you know where to find them, there are also numerous ancient man-made 'sculptures' – the Men-an-Tol, its vertically balanced ring of granite aligned between two verticals; the Lanyon Quoit, a sort of gigantic granite three-legged milking stool, a triangular slab balancing on its three supporting stones; various stone circles, quite magical in their mysteriously affecting power; or Chysauster, a whole settlement of circular huts still remarkably intact apart from their missing wooden roofs.

So go to Penwith. But don't expect it to offer the amenities of a South Coast Channel resort. It is a remarkable and ancient land. Walk into it, over it, round it. Discover it all for yourself.

PATRICK HERON

Penzance

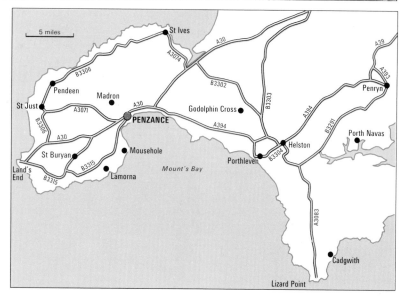

WHERE TO GO

Market Jew St: Penzance's commercial centre, a row of elevated shops next to old Market House – an imposing granite building with Renaissance dome and Ionic portico. Now that the market has moved to newer buildings up the hill, portico is used as craft shop selling pottery. In front of Market House stands a statue of Sir Humphry Davy – scientist, poet, a founder of the London Zoo and inventor of the safety lamp for miners: you can see lamp in his hand.

Chapel St: the Bond Street of Penzance – Regency and Georgian town houses now given over to antique and other specialized shops. Unusual for Cornwall – many Chapel St buildings are of brick. Alison Hodge at No 5 specializes in books on Cornish subjects, Laity's Bakeries at No 56 has been making old-style crusty bread for over 60 years, while next door the Little Gallery sells exclusive hand-made Cornish or historical dolls. Further down at the Admiral Benbow restaurant you can drink in the Lady Hamilton Bar, where not long ago thousands of pottery fragments were processed on their way from Sir William Hamilton's shipwreck to the British Museum. Or sit at the windows and watch diving for treasure near the harbour. Maria Branwell lived at 25 Chapel St before she moved to Yorkshire and bore four Brontë children. It is said her tales of the ghost of Chapel St and other Penwith legends inspired the Brontës to come up with their own versions.

Barbican building: Quay St, looking out towards the Battery Rocks: once a warehouse and granary, now converted into stalls where you can watch craftsmen work in leather, hand-painted silk and silver. The coffee shop serves good cake. Open summer months only.

St Michael's Mount: the view that launched a thousand postcards. Open June–Oct Mon–Fri, May Mon, Tue, Wed, Fri, Nov–Mar Mon, Wed, Fri, 10.30–4.45. Ferry boats to Mount (incl weekends) if tide in, walk if out.

Morrab Gardens: palm trees line one pathway to this beautifully landscaped park. Circular beds burst with exotic vegetation and elaborate fountain of seal with spouting fish. Sunday concerts in the blue and wrought iron bandstand; bring a picnic.

Bolitho Gardens: a park following harbour curve with views of St Michael's Mount.

Penlee House: museum with exhibitions on the fishing industry, tin mining and the area's rich collection of prehistoric sites, set in 15 acres of gardens (greenhouse sells a new variety of the Penwith myrtle). Open all year Mon–Sat (not bank hol) 12.30–4.30.

Nautical Museum: 19 Chapel St: built on four decks to scale of an 18th c man-o'-war. Hundreds of articles from local shipwrecks; see the beautiful silver tray with prancing seahorses. Open May–mid-Sept. 10.00–1.00, 2.00–4.00, also some summer evenings.

Causeway Head: ticky-tacky street full of tiny shops and the Savoy movie theatre. Great bargains in navy surplus from Bill's Market or from Daphne's lace oasis, secondhand bookshops, several shops for good souvenirs like photos of Cornish shipwrecks made from original negatives.

Newlyn Art Gallery: towards end of promenade, featuring one-man shows of local artists to outside exhibitions. Also houses one of best poetry bookshops in Cornwall. Open Mon–Sat 10.00–6.00 (5.00 in winter).

Drift Reservoir: situated two miles west just off the A30, a 65-acre lake which was formed by flooding the Drift Valley. Quiet and secluded with good supplies of brown and rainbow trout. Angling details: Chyandour Estate Office, Chyandour, Penzance, tel Penzance 3021.

ACTIVITIES

Fishing: flounders and mullet from the promenade, conger eel after dark from the pier. Tackle, bait and permits available from Lanxons, 18 Causeway Head. Shark-fishing: information from Albert Pier.

SHOPPING

Market day: Sat (cattle market Tue).
Early closing: Wed.
Egyptian House/National Trust Shop, Chapel St: sells gifts and local delicacies such as smoked mackerel pâté and scallop soup.
Nautifacts, Old Anchor Court, Chapel St: an age-old trading house which deals in such nautical antiques as pieces of eight.
Cornish Candy Shoppe, Market Jew St: 12 types of full cream fudge, hand-cooked on an open gas fire.
Arcade Dairies, Alverton St: home-made clotted cream, ice cream, plus cheeses and pâtés. Bright and clean building used to be public house, pleasant courtyard with metal sculptor working in old stables.
Harvey's Crab Factory, by Newlyn roundabout: the freshest crabs in town.

FOOD AND DRINK

Egon Ronay's Lucas Guide recommends **Bistro One**, New St, for meat dishes and sauces. Pubs include: **Turk's Head Inn**, Chapel St – 300-year-old pub, Penzance's oldest. Low-beamed, chintzy, with a friendly feel and cellar bar. Devenish bitter. **Union Hotel**, Chapel St: where the victory of Trafalgar was first announced. Pleasant hotel bar and traditional bar at back: draught Bass. **Yacht,** on promenade: splendid Mount's Bay view, plenty of outdoor seating and parking space. Two St Austell favourites – Hicks special bitter and St Austell XXXX, a dark, fruity mild.

WHERE TO STAY

Egon Ronay recommends **Lesceave Cliff Hotel**, Praa Sands (about eight miles east), tel Germoe 2325. Stylish and Mediterranean with friendly staff.

TOURIST INFORMATION

Alverston St, tel Penzance 2343 or 2207. Open daily (including evenings) June–Sept, Winter Mon–Fri.

Villages and country towns

Cadgwith

Diminutive, unspoilt, a fisherman's toy town nestling among The Lizard's steep cliffs: inaccessibility is Cadgwith's crowd control (park at top near weather-beaten entrance posts). A cluster of thatched cottages in palest pink, stony granite and white with blue trim; its pub serves two traditional beers – Devenish bitter and Devenish Cornish. On hill's edge is the Cadgwith Hotel, Mediterranean and jaunty with green-striped awning, plenty of seats outside; its restaurant lies so close to the water you can almost watch dinner swim by.

Fishing, not tourism, is Cadgwith's main concern: there are now 15 boats on the tiny beach – not long ago there were three. At water's edge a cliff bisects the cove; a pathway to the tip reveals perilous steps descending to black rocks called the Todden. Another path near waterfall leads to the Devil's Frying Pan,

The Egyptian House, built *c*. 1830

now a National Trust yawning hole with sides 200 feet deep.

Best place, though, is Sharky's café, an old pilchard cellar on the harbour – note grooves along floor which used to catch oil. Draped fishing nets, tables on the cobbled courtyard near a boat's-eye view of the sea. Fresh crab sandwiches in the afternoon, at night the day's shellfish catch.

Godolphin Cross

Small village grouped around crossroads, has strong feudal feeling about it: a manor house, a hill, a tin mine, a chapel and several pubs all named Godolphin. In 1584 most workers in surrounding area employed in tin mines owned by Godolphin family. Sidney Godolphin was Lord High Treasurer at time of William and Mary, Sir Francis Godolphin was governor of Scilly Islands. Margaret, Sidney's wife, died in London at an early age; her funeral procession back to Cornwall included a regiment of cavalry and cost £1000. She is buried in Godolphin Chapel in next village, Breage. It was from Godolphin tin mines that many infamous wreckers emerged to plunder ships stranded in the vicinity. William Godolphin and friends accused of accepting stolen goods worth £10,000 – about £150,000 by today's standards. Wrecking continued well into 19th c.

Godolphin village is a group of dark stone buildings around Godolphin

Cross, church nestled to one side. Clean, unpretentious pub called Godolphin Arms, also 15th c, with handsome brass bed-warmer near open fire. Half a mile down lane is Godolphin Hall – Tudor and Hanoverian mansion with Tuscan columns. Some of *Poldark* TV series filmed here. To left of large circular driveway is the old cider house where pottery is now made. Inside west wing of house is the 'King's Room' where the future Charles II stayed during his escape to Scilly Islands. Open May–June Tue, July–Sept Tue, Thur 2.00–5.00.

Lamorna

A flower valley near rugged moorland. Marconi is said to have sailed across Mount's Bay to visit his lady love in Lamorna which abounds in ivy-covered rendezvous.

The old village school is now home of the Lamorna Singers – full Cornish programme on various summer dates. The Wink pub is decked out with maritime instruments of mahogany and brass. Perched on a cliff is the Lamorna Hotel and Restaurant, recommended by *Egon Ronay's Lucas Guide* for its seafood and views. Above hotel is a house once used as convalescent home for suffragettes just out of prison.

Cove a disappointment with its granite quarry and great chunks of rock. The Toby Cafe sells snacks, but better to have a picnic in the flower fields above.

Madron

Village 380 ft up with spectacular views of St Michael's Mount and Atlantic Ocean five miles west. Streets follow slopes towards sea, then make an abrupt right-angle to form sheltered enclave from chilly ocean gales. Architectural blend of Victorian houses, granite cottages and church built on early Celtic settlement *c* 500 A D. Mother church of parish built when Penzance was still a fishing port and contains many antiquities, including an 8th c inscribed stone and the finest set of musical handbells in Cornwall. Protruding from one corner is the King William IV pub, with vaguely Western ambience of wagon wheels and horseshoes, Courage best bitter.

Uphill road heading north passes signposted lane to Madron's Holy Well and baptistry, romantically described in Daphne du Maurier's book *Vanishing*

Cornwall. Track to the baptistry is scenic but swampy, choked by brambles and a brook with floating wildflowers. Serene and demure, baptistry is enclosed by six-foot-high mossy walls – small spring nearby. Perfect for a picnic. A search to the right unearths the well, small and undistinguished. Du Maurier wrote that long ago a piece of clothing was strung on the shrubs as a votive offering. Subsequent visitors have adopted the practice over-enthusiastically and the place now looks like a rubbish dump.

Mousehole

Pronounced 'mao-zel': popular artists' haunt and former smuggling village overlooking Mount's Bay. More tourists than fishermen, but winding streets and postcard-pretty harbour have survived with dignity; Harbour Commission clock tower a handsome focus. Village is said to be named for gaping cavern – now collapsed – south of village which was once breeding ground for rare birds and 36 kinds of ferns.

17th c Ship Inn, near the quay with low-beamed ceilings, slab floor and intimate atmosphere is ideal for discussing smuggling strategy. Ship is the hang-out of Mousehole's native son and most celebrated artist Jack Pender. Lots of cafés for fresh crab sandwiches.

Village sacked by Spanish in 1595; it was a Mousehole man who first sighted the Armada seven years earlier. Only surviving building of this period is Keigwin Arms – now private – perched on granite pillars above courtyard where Squire Keigwin slew six Spaniards defending his home. It's Mousehole's most famous event; celebrated annually in July at splendidly situated Cairn Dhu Hotel with a commemorative dinner where names of dishes tell the story. Festivities and carnival the previous day.

The winding backstreet which houses Keigwin Arms was birthplace of Dolly Pentreath, last-known speaker of Cornish, whose funeral was interrupted for a whisky break. Along Raginnis Hill stands the Wild Bird Hospital, started by two ladies and managing to survive on private donations.

Convalescing crows share a property developer's dream view over St Clement's Island, and against a mossy wall is a bell with a sign issuing the gentle command, 'Please ring the bell if you have a bird'.

Pendeen

Mining village dominated by Geevor tin mine, one of only two still producing ore. Mine's external workings loom large – but provide much-needed employment for over 300 people. Guided tours of surface treatment plant Easter–Sept Mon–Fri. Models and relics in the mining museum next door chronicle the area's industrial past. Open April–Sept 10.00–5.00 daily. After rain be sure to notice Pendeen's puddles – they turn red from the tin in the ground.

Best bakery about is the attractive blue and white building; Mr Butters gets up at 3.15 am to bake pasties and scones from traditional Cornish recipes. Delicious when straight out of the old-fashioned oven: be sure to try the 'hevvy cake'. Road to Pendeen Watch, a white-latticed lighthouse, passes 13th c Manor Farm, burnt by Cromwell, later the birthplace of William Borlase – the 'Cornish Godfather of Archaeology' – who was most responsible for documenting Penwith's rich collection of prehis-

Penzance – 'terrace after terrace of exquisite Regency stucco houses'

toric sites. His interest was probably generated by 2000-year-old fougou (multi-roomed chamber) in the yard of Manor Farm. Permission to view from current owner, but avoid milking time.

The Radjel pub, unpretentious with bare floors and St Austell bitter, is kept by Willie Warren, described by the *Cornishman* as 'the oldest licensee in the county' – he was born in a room upstairs.

Porthleven

'Village for sale' is how this west Lizard fishing community hit national headlines a few years ago. Although only the harbour and seafront area were auctioned, most of the community's industry is at stake and local concern is high (a consortium raised £300,000 but were outbid by a mere £100,000).

Certainly Porthleven could do with a facelift – the decline of net-making and pilchard industries has left economic scars, and the impressive double harbour is in need of repair. But visitors love its shabby ambience. The Granary restaurant specializes in locally caught fish and has extensive wine list; tortoise-shell jewellery is made in craft shop on the harbour – watch the work. 400-year-old Ship Inn – a shocking pink sentinel on edge of harbour – has Courage best bitter and smuggling connections, while the more modern Atlantic Inn serves Devenish Cornish. Quaint but 'foreign' is the Oven Door bakery; a local man runs the modest bakery up the hill and it is the only place for a cup of tea on early closing day (Wed). Good pollack, bass and conger fishing, boats for hire.

But the best surprise is hidden. Walk to edge of pier with its Men's Institute and 'Big Ben' clock tower lashed by the sea (summer art exhibitions inside). Look left – 2½ miles of shingle beach, ¼ mile wide, called Loe Bar; it separates the sea from calm, collected Loe Pool, the largest freshwater lake in Cornwall. Pink samphires and yellow poppies blow in the breeze – makes a lovely wildflower walk.

Porth Navas

Definitively du Maurier. First glimpse from an elevated ridge lane of elms and beech trees – below, estuary is a quicksilver ribbon and Porth Navas a collage of bright cottages, and matching sailing boats. Rich smell on the drive down – a mixture of flowers and fish. Nearest pub is Ferry Boat Inn in Mawnan Smith (own beach and cream teas), in Porth Navas the yacht club welcomes temporary members and has counters laden with lobster, mullet and home-made pizza. Or sit on the quayside with a loaf of bread and oysters from oyster farm next door.

A meander through lush fields can end at Glendurga Gardens, National Trust. Open March–Oct Mon, Wed, Fri 10.30–4.30, with hillside maze and sub-tropical grounds of Chinese rhododendron and ancient tulip trees. House is owned by the Fox family, not open to public. This garden-valley stops at the lovely National Trust cove of Durgan. Demure and secluded – note double-doored 'donkey cellars'. At Durgan, estuary curves, then widens. Spindly trees drape the water at oblique angles and Frenchman's Creek is only a short boatride away. Ask a fisherman.

St Buryan

A 92ft church tower on plateau visible from land and sea. Village named after resourceful saint, Burianna, who floated from Ireland on a granite plinth. Bloody battle fought here between the Cornish and English, *c* 935 AD. Church part of an endowment made by King Athelstan after his final Celtic conquest. Lawsuits, laconic letters and disputes over English/Cornish jurisdiction continued centuries later. On wall of church is carved screen depicting a hunting scene between good and evil. Birds with human heads fly about; whether they are Cornish or English is hard to say. Certainly the church is curious in itself, rising from a small mount and guarded by the spookiest tombstones in all Cornwall. Tall, unnaturally thin and tumbled into eerie postures by fierce winds, this burial ground has prompted at least one ghost story. An 11th c Celtic cross stands by the south gateway.

Near the forge is a hardware shop and the Farewell Restaurant is good for cream teas. In the St Buryan Inn there's a picture of Dustin Hoffman playing the pub's piano, taken when Sam Peckinpah's *Straw Dogs* was filmed nearby. Two popular agricultural events: a gala in July when old farm machinery takes to the roads amidst much drinking and merry-making, and the 'crying the neck' harvest ceremony in early autumn.

Merry-making was supposedly the cause of two of area's best prehistoric sites – Merry Maidens Stone Circle and the Pipers Standing Stones across road, both visible from B3315. The musicians were providing tunes for 19 village girls out dancing – but on the Sabbath. God didn't approve, and turned them all to stone.

St Just

Busy tin-mining town in area of harsh, abandoned beauty. A good place for shopping, particularly fruit and fish; a hardware shop stocks everything necessary for the beach, but, unlike other nearby villages popular with tourists, St Just makes no concessions: all shops close for lunch 1.00–2.30.

In the Star pub men occasionally still chew tobacco twists instead of smoking cigarettes, which might have been dangerous underground. The Star, highly regarded by locals, is pleasant, with courtyard at back, children's room with shelves of toys, and accommodation spotless enough for John Wesley when he came to stay two centuries ago.

Cape Cornwall lies 1½ miles down gorse-covered slopes. The atmosphere is wild and brooding, old tin mines litter the hills like melancholy castles. This is the area of 'wreckers' who lured ships on to rocks by tying lanterns to horses' necks.

—*Places to visit*—

Land's End: the first, the last and the most crowded. Best to go at sunset after the hordes have left.

Lizard Point: alternatively, go at dawn.

Lizard Lighthouse: open to the public after 1 pm most clear days. Wonderful panorama, but long queue during the high season.

Trengwainton Gardens: near Madron, off the B3312. In Cornish Trengwainton means 'the farm of the spring'. Possible to see plants growing in the open air which cannot be cultivated anywhere else in England. A meandering lane to Trengwainton House – private – beside a small brook, views of St Michael's Mount. Profusions of colour and floral exotica like Japanese magnolias and Himalayan poppies. Open March–Oct Wed–Sat, also bank hol 11.00–6.00.

Disused tin mine near Penzance: mines litter the landscape like melancholy castles

Suttons Gulval Trial Grounds: a must for anyone with botanical interests. A testing ground for seeds from all over the world, wander freely through 500 different varieties. Open Mon–Fri, 8.00–5.00. Near Gulval, off the A30.

Minack Theatre: spectacularly situated open-air theatre presenting different shows, June–Sept. Theatre hewn from rugged cliffs with a backdrop of sky and sea. Natural scenery sometimes overshadows productions but nobody cares. Aim for a full moon, bring blankets and coffee. Near Porthcurno off the B3315.

Cornish Seal Sanctuary: 'Hospital and five large pools for the care of the "orphans of the sea".' Plus dolphins, whales, and a £1000-a-month fish bill. Open daily 9.30 to sunset. Near Gweek on Lizard Peninsula on the B3291.

Marconi Memorial, Poldu: an obelisk on the cliffs commemorating the first wireless transmissions across the Atlantic, c 1901. Visitors to site will have to vie with those digging and diving for treasure left by shipwrecks and a 17th c pirate named Avery. On west side of Lizard Peninsula. Take B3296 past Mullion to Poldu Cove, then walk.

Antiquities: the Penwith peninsula is rich in natural antiquities (stone circles, prehistoric villages, fougous etc) – there are almost 50 within a five-mile radius of the village of Sancreed. Some are in remote fields – wear sturdy shoes – some are easily reached by road, some are in farmers' back gardens, so knock at door for permission to view. We suggest the booklet published by the Cornwall Archaeological Society, easily obtainable in bookshops and with grid references taken off the 1:50,000 Ordnance Survey map (Sheet 203). Here are a few of the best.

Chysauster Roman Iron Age Village: large, and beautifully preserved; numerous courtyard houses complete with yards, living rooms and narrow side rooms. Possibly was once a prehistoric 'university' for astronomers. Detailed guide from custodian. Signposted, take the footpath from road linking B3311 to Penzance/Zennor road at New Mill.

Men-an-Tol holed stone: colourful and atmospheric doughnut-shaped rock between two standing stones. Children were passed through hole to cure rickets. Further up same track is Men-Scryfa inscribed stone, 6th c. East of Penzance/

Madron/Morvah road down track in field.

Lanyon Quoit: impressive megalithic chamber tomb, very tall, visible from Penzance/Madron/Morvah road. Nimble photographers should set camera to include remains of Ding Dong tin mine ½ mile north.

Boscawen-Un stone circle: cosiest stone circle in Britain, nestled in rich agricultural ground behind Boscawen Farm – knock on the door for permission to view. 19 stones with tilted centre pillar; Gorsedd of the Bards of Cornwall inaugurated here in 1928. Just south of A30 at Crows-an-Wra.

Lizard Peninsula: heathland unique in Britain, owing to climate, flat topography and geology, especially the famous crimson-veined serpentine rock. Around the Goonhilly Downs Earth Station is the rare heather Cornish Heath, usually found with Purple Moor Grass and Black Bog Rush. There have

Kynance cove on the Lizard Peninsula

Prehistoric Lanyon Quoit – ancient man-made sculpture

been damaging fires here recently – please be careful. Footpaths around the pretty if overrun coves of Kynance and Mullion offer still different and unusual vegetation.

St Ives: famous town of artists, smugglers, crooked streets and seafood. The Museum of Cinematography and the Barbara Hepworth Museum are well worth a visit, as is the headquarters of Leach Pottery. 'Park and ride' is a new scheme to make it easier in summer for motorists to visit the town's congested streets. Park at Lelant Staltings, just off the A30, three miles away and take train to St Ives and back. Tickets include all-day parking.

Land's End Airport: do five to eight minute 'quickie trips' in a Cessna 172 around Land's End area. Great way to study Penwith's unusual topography. Airport on B3306 towards St Just.

Cornwall Aero Park: put together by two ex-naval pilots, includes Concorde flight deck, novelty aerogolf. Open daily Easter–5 Nov 10.00–5.00 (July 7.00). Located on Helston side of Culrose Air Station at Penboa (A3083).

Bird Paradise and Children's Zoo: rare birds like the Cornish choughs, free-flying macaws and a miniature railway.

Open daily 10.00 to one hour before dusk. Near Hayle on the A30.

World of Entertainment: pier equipment – penny coin machines, magic lantern shows, etc. Open May–end Sept weekdays 10.30–5.30, Sun 2.00–5.30. At Goldsithney on B3280, off the A394.

Age of Steam: free steam train rides for children, self-drive trains, 18-acre site. Open daily Easter–Oct 10.30–6.00 (last admission 5.00). At Crowlas on the A30.

ACTIVITIES

Hang-gliding: off the cliffs at Sennen. Bring own equipment, nerve.

Beaches: most accessible are at Marazion and Porthcurno on the south coast; Sennen and Porthmeor on the west. There has been a recent crack-down on nude bathing, so find intimate coves yourself.

Surfing: Sennen and Gwynver beaches on the west coast. Can rent sub-professional boards on Sennen beach.

Walking: all clifftop walks lovely, but of special interest is the walk from Mousehole to Lamorna, a pilgrimage of mysterious origin made by hundreds each Eastertime. Also, around the serpentine caves near Kynance Cove, beautiful with its black rocks flecked golden and crimson, or try walking from St Just to St Ives – sea to the left and dozens of abandoned tin mines at water's edge, protruding from craggy hills or silhouetted against the sky.

FOOD AND DRINK

Egon Ronay's Lucas Guide recommends **Riverside**, Helford (Lizard Peninsula), tel Manaccan 443. Star rating, delightful restaurant, French cooking. **Outrigger**, St Ives, tel St Ives 5936. Attractive presentation, emphasis on fish.

TOURIST INFORMATION

Publications: the *Cornishman*, published every Thur has entertainments page, also useful for things like auctions. *South West Arts Diary*, published every two months has separate arts diary for Cornwall. Free from newsagents.

Tourist information offices: at St Ives and Falmouth.

Research: Martha Ellen Zenfell.

Launceston

My home-town of Launceston is on Cornwall's freshwater shore, midway between north and south on the river line that almost severs the rough triangle of the county from England. Standing at my front door, on the ancient track once called Old Street that stretches from Land's End to London Bridge, I sometimes feel I can touch the Devon tors of Dartmoor where they begin to rise on the other side of the river Tamar.

Launceston was once a Norman garrison town, and still encloses – even for Cornwall – a particularly secret and inward-looking community. If an eye is cast beyond itself at all, it is in the direction of England: half-marooned from the rest of Cornwall as we were until a century ago by the dangerous barrier of Bodmin Moor. But those who travel west over our border in an unstoppable rush by way of the hard spine that is the A30, or the rail and road bridges to the south, leave behind them what I believe to be the loveliest and least-spoilt region in the county: a green strip, perhaps 15 miles wide, from Morwenstow to Saltash. It is the landscape of a people's last, and nearly lost, paradise.

Launceston is a twin-humped market town; a stone camel squatting comfortably on the Cornish side of the Tamar. About 5000 inhabitants occupy its seven steep hills, its ridges and valleys. The approach from Lifton over Polson Bridge shows it, unforgettably, as a child's cut-out, laid against the Cornish sky: castle, thin pointer of chapel spire, thicker fingers of church towers, houses huddled and heaped as if one on top of the other. One begins to realize, slowly, why Betjeman described Launceston as the most beautiful inland town in Cornwall.

Riverside, where I was born, is at its deepest point, a local Jericho, sunk between the hills of St Thomas and St Stephen, by the clattering river Kensey (Cornish, 'first' or 'foremost') near the end of its 10-mile dash to the Tamar. Our house echoed with the sweet sound of water. The old priory boundary of Harper's Lake ('lake' here signifying 'stream') bubbled against the wall and sometimes came in the window.

But we were water babies, and normally the river was thin. We fished for minnows from the fifteenth-century pack-bridge and, without exception, all fell in. The tiny church of St Thomas-the-Apostle, by the bridge, seemed our personal property. It was cleaned by my grandmother, who also supplied bread for holy communions and warmed water for christenings. I was christened in its square font, the largest in Cornwall, with the bearded Norman faces at each corner. One of the few glories to survive the rather over-zealous church restoration in the 1870s is the delicate and faded wall painting of a winged angel in close conversation with the fourteenth-century St Roche the healer, who is accompanied by the faithful hound responsible for the saint's recovery from plague while travelling in Italy.

Tintagel Castle on the headland of Tintagel

Hidden behind the churchyard's eastern wall are the stone bones of an Augustinian priory church: the remaining visible sign of a religious community which flourished in this valley before 1539.

The castle was, and is, ever intrusive. It is impossible to escape that baleful bluestone-and-shale eye. Perched on an artificial, conical hill by the iron-nosed Normans, its summit, in my boyhood, oozing ivy, it looked perpetually in danger of slithering sideways into the Town Square: a crumbling, two-tier stone wedding cake the rats had been at. Today, under the scrupulous hand of the Department of the Environment, it has regained much of its original visual authority, and even menace.

In its heyday it was dubbed Castle Terrible and was famous for the filthiness and squalor of its jail, as – among many others – the Quaker George Fox (imprisoned here in 1656) and the Roman Catholic seminary priest, St Cuthbert Mayne, executed in the Square in 1577, discovered.

From the topmost castle wall you may gaze west over Bodmin Moor, the peaks of Brown Willy (1375ft) and Rowtor (1312ft) becalmed like granite whales on its surface. Immediately below the castle, and all around, is a warm, grey muddle of sharp roofs, narrow streets, cracks and alleys, houses mailed top and side with Delabole slates against the needling Atlantic rains.

Here, the line between fact and fancy is blurred. When the black-faced quarterjacks on the mock-Gothic town hall beat midnight, Britannia, with trident, descends from her Georgian roof-ridge in Castle Street and guides the leaden eagles that guard the house-entrance down to the Kensey to drink. By the time the jacks strike the hour of one, any Launceston child will tell you, they have all *flown* back. A pebble lodged on the back of the recumbent figure of St Mary Magdalene on the east wall of the town church (every square foot of its granite exterior cut by Tudor craftsmen into the shapes of fruit and flower, minstrel, beast and bird) will bring you good fortune and a new outfit of clothes within a twelvemonth. Below The Walk, a delightful promenade commanding the Kensey valley, is the five-gabled, cob-walled Dockacre: reputedly haunted, scene of the mysterious death of the wife of a high sheriff in 1714, and the Dolbeare of Sabine Baring-Gould's Victorian romance-novel *John Herring*.

The whole town presents an astonishing variety of architecture. A medieval gate, splendidly preserved, stands a few yards from the Georgian birthplace of Philip Gidley King, sometime Governor of New South Wales, for whom Launceston, Tasmania, is named. Round the next corner, a magnificent market-house (1840), its rise of roofs as elegant as that on a Chinese pagoda, lies next to the battlemented tower of a 1930s cinema.

Thomas Hardy, then a young architect working on church restoration, was in Launceston in 1870 on his way to St Juliot, about 16 miles to the north-west, where he was to meet his first wife.

Below St Juliot, where the river Valency slides down a stairway of pure rock to Boscastle and the sea, is what is for me the most romantic spot in Cornwall: where, in the 1870s, Hardy picnicked with Emma Lavinia. In his celebratory poem, written years later, a woman's voice tells of a wine-glass lost in the fold of the river bed:

> By night, by day, when it shines or lours,
> There lies intact that chalice of ours,
> And its presence adds to the rhyme of love
> Persistently sung by the fall above.
> No lips has touched it since his and mine
> In turns therefrom sipped lovers' wine.

North-east of St Juliot, a mile or so from the source of the Tamar, is the coastal parish of Morwenstow. To stand on Hennacliff (over 450ft sheer from the sea and, next to Beachy Head, the highest perpendicular cliff in England) is to recognize the once-fearful truth of the ancient rhyme, 'From Padstow Point to Lundy Light/Is a sailor's grave by day and night,' and of how many such vessels as 'the Caledonia came ashore/To feed the hungry and clothe the poor.' The valiant, white figurehead of the Caledonia still faces the seas that ride in from Labrador, and marks the grave of her crew. It is also a reminder of all the drowned seamen buried here by the poet Robert Stephen Hawker (vicar here 1834–75) and his parishioners. Hawker – whose poem *The Quest of the Sangraal* is described by John Heath-Stubbs, I think rightly, as 'the most successful poem directly inspired by the Arthurian legend in English since the Middles Ages' – wrote much of his verse in the sturdy hut built of salvaged ships' timbers and still fixed firmly under the terrible brow of the cliff above Lucky Hole: the headland of Tintagel – 'grim Dundagel: throned along the sea!' – thrusting into the ocean to the west.

Five miles south of St Juliot is Cornwall's perhaps most mysterious site. A few hundred yards upstream from Slaughter Bridge, over the river Camel (Cornish, 'crooked'), is the spot where – according to strong local oral tradition – King Arthur met his death after despatching his treacherous nephew Mordred. A simple piece of slate by the roadside, incised with the image of a pair of crossed swords, marks the battle-ground of Briton and Saxon. Crossing a small field and slithering down an intensely Pre-Raphaelite brake of bushes and briars to the river bed will reveal a written, granite stone, heeled over in the rattling water, its message almost obliterated.

What, specifically, it says, and whom (if anyone) it commemorates are, to me, beside the point. It is, simply, a celebration of the power of folk-memory: of the deep, human need to associate the fabled hero or god with a particular place. I find it easy, then, to imagine that from here Tennyson's Sir Bedivere carried Arthur's sword Excalibur back to Dozmare ('a drop of the sea') on the high moor.

Just off the main road from Dozmare to Launceston is Altarnun: its noble church rising like a mini-cathedral from a grey and green setting of granite and slate, trees and water. The village is the birthplace (marked) of Cornwall's greatest native-born sculptor Nevil Northey Burnard (1818–78). Slate gravestones, carved and signed by him as a

Font of Altarnun Church – 'rising like a mini-cathedral from a grey and green setting'

boy with a six-inch nail, are to be found in the churchyard. The bas-relief head of John Wesley on the wall of the old Methodist meeting house is also an early work. Burnard became a successful London sculptor but, badly affected by the death of a favourite daughter, returned to Cornwall as a tramp and to a pauper's grave in Camborne. The sights and stories that inform Cornwall's river-line, that land within a land, are without number. One day, I must search Launceston Town Square for the bullet holes that mark the Sunday evening battle between black and white American troops in September 1943.

Meantime, five miles south, I savour for the hundredth time the beauty of the great Tudor hall and chapel (subject of an exquisitely melancholy painting by John Piper in 1943) at Trecarrell Manor: the building of the remainder was abandoned by Sir Henry Trecarrell on the accidental death of his infant and only son. The stone was used, finally, for the rebuilding of Launceston's St Mary Magdalene church, begun in 1511.

Farther south again, a mile and a half from Callington, is another jewel: the Holy Well of Dupath, its flowing bath of water large enough for total immersion, its roof ornamented with a gleaming granite crown: the whole building reminiscent of a Hindu or Thai temple. From here, the land falls in a gentle slope to the Tamar's cliffs, where the river moves, now stronger and deeper, to the already visible sea.

When I was still teaching, I brought a class of young children to Dupath Well. Some lines in a poem written by a girl of nine have lodged in my memory ever since.

> I did not want to go away . . .
> It made me feel like
> I lived there.

This, perhaps, is the secret motivation, the half-conscious aim, of all our journeys.

CHARLES CAUSLEY

Launceston

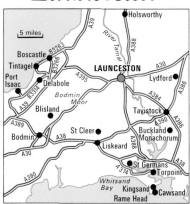

WHERE TO GO

The Guildhall: has a splendid clock on which two quarterjacks strike the time, and an equestrian portrait of Charles I. Fearing retribution after the collapse of the King's cause, the owner disguised it as a fake wall. Two centuries later a distraught local discovered the staring eye of the horse while doing rudimentary brickwork. Open by appointment, apply caretaker or ask at town hall.

Launceston Castle: there were once three circular walls, now two remain, Norman-built and 12ft thick. Inner tower was added in 13th c by Richard, Earl of Cornwall. The green was the site of public executions, the last in 1821. Now it is the subject of annual archaeological investigations, with plans for an exhibition of articles found. If in summer, see them dig. Already visible are foundations of the Assize Hall, its 13th c plaster intact. View from castle is magnificent, overlooking fertile fields, moorland hills and the town itself. Open May–Sept daily 9.30–7.00, April daily 9.30–5.30, March, Oct weekdays 9.30–5.30 Sun 2.00–5.30, Nov–Feb weekdays 9.30–4.00 Sun 2.00–4.00.

Castle St: remains of old cobbles can still be seen; has two well-preserved Georgian houses, one a lovely hotel, the other **Lawrence House**, town museum by north gate of castle. Stylish rooms with moulded ceilings, one the mayor's parlour, others contain military exhibitions and intriguing oddities such as an old wooden bier used to push coffins. Open April–Sept Mon–Fri 2.30–4.30; also Mon, Wed, Thur, Sat 10.30–12.30.

Spectacular White Lady waterfall at the foot of lush, green Lydford Gorge

Coronation Park: public swimming pools, tennis courts, putting green and excellent views: Dartmoor to the east, the Cornish Heights to the west and, below, the distinctive and charming roofscape of the town and castle.

St Mary Magdalene Church: truly remarkable 16th c church – every square inch carved out of granite, Pevsner calls its roses, pelicans and bears a 'barbarous profusion'. Roof inside is impressive – said to contain over $1\frac{1}{2}$ miles of carved oak, 162 figures and more than 400 bosses.

South Gate Gallery, South Gate: Penny Harris has a unique location, her gallery lies up mossy steps in the ancient arch, with a view of steeples and chimneys. She paints on glass – backwards and often using mirrors – to produce rural scenes: Vixens and butterflies are favourite subjects. Penny attributes the discovery of this backwards technique to being left-handed.

Look for: beautiful historical buildings housing very boring shops. The old market-house, pale and graceful, is a furniture store; the hardware shop on Westgate Street once belonged to the town hall and looks like a mock-Gothic church.

SHOPPING

Market day: Tue, Sat (cattle market Tue).

Early closing: Thur.

Folley and Sons, High St: 'traditional grocery' with 60lb cheddar cheese in window; romantic picnic fare such as cooked lobster or crab, fresh churned Cornish butter.

Raddalls, Westgate St: comprehensive sporting goods shop including fishing tackle and golf clubs for hire, a complete stock of saddlery and riding clothes, and information on angling permits, etc.

FOOD AND DRINK

Egon Ronay in *Just a Bite* recommends **Dockies Bistro**, 20 Westgate St, for seafood lunches. Pubs include: **White Hart Hotel** on The Square: this old coaching inn has three bars, main lounge area used to be courtyard. Whitbread best bitter. Note front entrance with its Norman doorway from old priory. **Bell Inn**, Tower St: 17th c with children's room, a cheeky poltergeist and Courage beer.

WHERE TO STAY

Egon Ronay recommends **Arundell Arms** in Lifton (four miles east), tel Lifton 244, a fisherman's paradise with 20 miles of its own water on the Tamar and four of river's tributaries.

Medieval dovecote at Cotehele

Villages and country towns

Blisland
Village on the edge of Bodmin Moor with a large green – unusual for Cornwall – surrounded by moorstone houses. Some of Blisland's fine elm trees were recently ravaged by Dutch Elm disease, but local groups are making efforts to restore the village to its former showpiece status. The Royal Oak Inn has several pub games and is listed in the *Good Beer Guide*. At the St Pratt's Fair in Sept there's all-day drinking, lots of cattle and plenty of pasties. The Fair is part of the Patronal Festival, which includes a procession to St Pratt's Cross where children lay posies of flowers.

Blisland's remaining claim to fame is the Norman and medieval church, its remarkable rood-screen of gold, red and green radiating Byzantine influences. On the north wall is a fine slate carving – too soft for rubbings – of six kneeling figures.

Local blacksmith melts 'a couple of tons' of iron daily. Outside, a five-foot-high sculpture of rusty, abandoned horseshoes.

Boscastle
Two villages, one perched on top of shale cliffs, the other a magnificent harbour – in some of the most beautiful scenery in Britain. Boscastle village is T-shaped, a cluster of hotels on the horizon, and shops and stocky cottages with crooked chimneys running down to the harbour. Each village has its own bakery, its own pub(s), and cast-iron loyalties: the cliff-top free house is the Napoleon, while the 300-year-old coaching inn below is the Wellington. Boscastle is well catered for in the way of restaurants, craft workshops.

Harbour itself is a miniature fjord, eerie, claustrophobic. On far edge is a stunningly situated youth hostel, the old forge is a National Trust information centre, open 10.30–6.00. The Cobweb pub (Whitbread draught, mead on tap) is named for the floor-to-ceiling spider webs which used to hang near the bar, but the harbour's eeriness is best shown in the Witches' Museum, containing magic wands with tiny clenched fists, human skulls mounted as drinking cups: displays for the curious but not – as the warning reads – for children. Open every day during summer.

Buckland Monachorum
Situated in wooded Tavy Valley. Village used to have three pubs, now there is one, timbered by Elizabethan sailing ships, several handsome whitewashed cottages and – courtesy of the Garden House – 12 acres of roses, rhododendrons and camellias. A personal garden gone grand: blossoms grow on steep terraces thought to have been made centuries ago for the cultivation of wine; walk past a 15th c tower and sharply shaven hedge tunnels on your way to a pretty stream at the bottom.

About a mile away is Buckland Abbey ('monachorum' means 'place of monks'), properly imposing with splendid views all along the valley. Its medieval tithe barn contains a huge cider press and an ancient pram; at the abbey visitors can enjoy a cream tea. The abbey was bought after the Dissolution by Sir Richard Grenville, whose grandson sold it to Sir Francis Drake. All four floors are filled with things to see – a naval gallery, the Silver Room, banners and Drake's Drum, ready to sound the warning whenever England is in danger.

The Garden House: open every Wed April–Sept. Buckland Abbey: open Easter to Sept 11.00–6.00 Mon–Sat, Sun 2.00–6.00; Oct–Easter Wed, Sat, Sun 2.00–5.00. National Trust.

Delabole

Home of the Delabole Slate Quarry, mentioned in the Guinness Book of Records as 'the largest hole in England'. Almost everything in Delabole is made of slate. Bettle and Chisel pub (name refers to quarry tools) is friendly and serves St Austell bitter, and good views of Brown Willy on the moor can be had from the large children's playground. The Pengelly Galleries offer everything you never knew could be made out of slate – from clocks to hand-painted pictures.

Quarry itself is over 500ft deep and 1½ miles in circumference. Visitors can stand at a viewing platform and gain entrance to the museum containing photos of horses and carts bringing up the slate, plus local workers giving a slate-splitting and dressing demonstration. In viewing any samples, look out for the 'Delabole Butterfly', a small delicate fossil. Museum open daily Easter–Sept 10.00–6.00.

Holsworthy

Robust farming community near the Cornwall/Devon border. Busy, utilitarian, a good place for pubs, shopping and anything to do with agriculture. Buildings with names like Mole Valley Farmers Ltd lie near a bookstore for buying maps or a pamphlet of local 'recipes, hints and remedies', a rural museum, and an eccentric chemists. The Full Gospel Mission house is a food arcade – butchers and plump fruit within. Bodmin Street is surprisingly sophisticated, a tidy lane of beautifully kept cottages – some still with their original hitching posts.

At Bodmin Street Hill is a plaque commemorating the Great Tree, said to be mentioned in the Domesday Book, from which by Royal Charter given in 1154 the annual proclamation of St Peter's Fair is made. This fair still goes by the old calendar – so is not necessarily held on St Peter's Day but for three days

sometime in July. Thought to have been originally a 'hiring and firing' fair for fieldhands, it still retains agricultural flavour. The contemporary cattle market takes place every Wed and Thur, near the viaduct.

Kingsand/Cawsand

Charming twin villages overlooking Plymouth Sound. The Halfway House marks the border between the villages and until 1835 it divided Devon and Cornwall. Of the two, Cawsand has the

Church of St Juliot, the village where Hardy met his first wife

better smuggling reputation – brandy kegs were floated underwater and away from the eyes of the law – while Kingsand specializes in activities such as sailing and fishing. The Boatel on Kingsand harbour rents everything from dinghies to speedboats.

The communities share colourful history – Drake took his ship into the bay to meet the Spanish Armada, and in 1815 HMS Bellerophon anchored off nearby Rame Head where Napoleon was handed over en route to St Helena. Garrett Street is a long curving lane connecting Kingsand to Cawsand, a lovely walk past pastel houses of surprising sophistication, and the Criterion Hotel, serving first-rate meals and teas. Sea and sound on the left. The Halfway House is at one end of street (a free house, with accom-

modation and pleasant fireplace), with 200-year-old Smugglers Inn at the other, Courage best bitter. Lord Nelson and Lady Hamilton are said to have slept at the Old Ship Inn.

A fabulous four-mile hike to Rame Head and back. Rame Church was mentioned as long ago as 981 AD and contains a 'leper squint', a solitary aperture in the south wall through which lepers could watch the service. Buried in the churchyard, it's said, is the last person in England to die from the Black Death. Rame Head is breathtaking: on a clear day Lizard Point can be seen 44 miles away. At the summit is a small slate chapel dedicated to St Michael with path, steps and water on three sides. Perfect for a picnic, best to bring one as there's no place for tea between here and Cawsand.

Lydford

A single-street village situated on a promontory with a castle, a famous gorge and a moorland skyline. Castle dominates a small hill lying on the far edge of the street, a roofless, ivy-covered structure with Norman foundations and stonework dating to 1195. During the Middle Ages the keep was a prison; the Stannary Court met upstairs to dispense 'Lydford Law', the notoriously rough justice dealt out to errant tin-miners – one had three spoonfuls of molten tin poured down his throat. Castle open at any reasonable hour. 16th c Castle Inn, free house, has pristine accommodation (fresh flowers in every room) and very good evening meals served in a cosy low-beamed room: home-made soup or pâté, roast Devon duckling and extensive wine list. Obviously a favourite with discerning locals, best to book. Tel Lydford 242. Egon Ronay in *Just a Bite* recommends tea at the post office, more accurately the Chantry Tea Rooms which are part of it. Good for snacks, special prices for children. Also in post office – a light, bright souvenir shop with lots of brass, and corn dollies in the shape of horseshoes.

200 yards down winding lane is the Lydford Gorge – lush, green and scary. Bring rubber-soled shoes. A 1½-mile steep-sided wooded valley with a riverside walk, ending at the 90ft White Lady waterfall. Open daily Easter–Oct 9.00 to one hour before sunset. Nov–March daily from Manor Farm entrance to waterfall only.

Port Isaac

Name in Cornish means 'corn port'. Hills so steep that bread used to be baked at top and transported to harbour on donkeys, and such a complicated labyrinth of alleyways and narrow crossings even an Ordnance Survey attempt got it wrong. Squeezibelly Alley is only 20in wide and actually bisects a house. This town was built for walking, so park at the top beyond the two garages. Cross 'the stream at side of Middle St to the butcher's shop for best meat for miles around, or go to Stanley House on Fore St for good groceries and delicatessen. Try the post office for anything else – gumboots to Guernsey sweaters.

Port Isaac has history of fishing dating back to 16th c: see shellfish in the tidal ponds on the left-hand side of the harbour, stored live on way to restaurant tables of Paris and London. Crabs, lobsters, mackerel or Camel River salmon can be bought in fish cellars near the lifeboat slipway. Better bet is catch all the fish yourself, boats can be hired from the Platt, equipment supplied. Dancing up the narrow streets on some summer evenings when a brass band plays on the harbourside platform where John Wesley used to preach. Nearby is the Golden Lion pub, with St Austell Hicks special bitter and on the wall a map as the village used to be. Golden Lion was once called Red Lion and in 18th c had cellars for storing contraband – one, named 'Bloody Bones', with a tunnel to the beach. Best for pub lunches is the Port Gaverne Hotel in adjoining village, where you can sit outside and see the sea.

A two-mile walk west starting at the clifftops passes a chapel haunted by a restless monk, then to Portquin, a tiny ghost cove of cottages and pilchard cellars. Legend has it the entire fishing fleet was wiped out by a storm; cynics say they emigrated to Australia. Now restored by the National Trust, hamlet is a tranquil picnic site with wild flowers and cows that look as if they are standing in the sky. Further on is Doyden Castle. Built in 1830 by Mr Samuel Symons, this magnificent folly was erected solely for the purpose of drinking and gambling.

St Cleer

Quiet village 700ft up, just under Bodmin Moor, emerging fast into 20th c: modern bungalows crowd the famous holy well. Farther up the hill lies a 15th c church. St Cleer parish festival – usually in July – lasts several days with floats, football matches and concerts. The unpretentious Market Hotel offers clean accommodation and Courage beer.

More important is village's proximity to the wealth of antiquities scattered around Bodmin Moor. King Doniert's memorial is the most accessible, a 9th c inscribed stone by the roadside, signposted. A lovely mile walk can end at the impressive Trethevy Quoit – take earthen alleyway across from Tremar Potteries to emerge directly below the 4000-year-old burial chamber.

Near the moorland hamlet of Minions stand The Hurlers stone circles, remains of three rings said to have been men playing a forbidden sport: note one running away. In the distance is the famous Cheesewring, its mysteriously balanced top stone reputed to turn around whenever a cock crows. Also the home of the eccentric stone-cutter Daniel Gumb – see his hut near the quarry – who in 1735 lived with his wife and family in a rock house, beds, tables and benches entirely of granite.

St Germans

An aristocratic-looking village on the banks of the river Lynher. St Germans was first a Celtic settlement, later a borough, with a history of political events and river traffic that lasted until the railway boom. Fine Norman church with windows by Burne-Jones and William Morris; try to be there on Thursday evening for bell-ringing practice. Next to it is Port Eliot, a privately owned Regency mansion built on site of ancient priory. Rest of village is stately but subdued. The row of almshouses has been carefully restored, an extremely elegant ironmongers has agricultural implements hanging from the ceiling.

Ripe, delicious home produce available from the Port Eliot garden shop with its attractive glass portico, and John Smith's Yorkshire bitter from the pub.

The walk to the quay is a pleasant one – eyes firmly left to avoid the hideous new town – leading to a small harbour under the sweeping arches of a viaduct. A footpath back to the church grounds follows the curves of the estuary. On his side of the viaduct Lord Eliot is building a maze.

Places to visit

Tintagel: If King Arthur ever returned home he'd probably get knocked down by a tour bus. Souvenir shops, hotels and ice-cream stands have obliterated whatever magic there was, although the castle with its beautiful cliffs and navy blue water can never entirely change. More interesting is Merlin's Cave lying directly below, or Tintagel Old Post Office, a 14th c miniature manor house with great hall, used 100 years ago as the letter-receiving office for area. Egon Ronay in *Just a Bite* says the Cottage Tea Shop is 'just like taking tea in a private house', four tables plus garden and cucumber sandwiches. If too crowded take a picnic and any number of wonderful walks – to Barras Head with its earthworks even older than the castle, or the plunging, zig-zag route to Boscastle, arguably the best scenery in the UK. Castle: Open May–Sept daily 9.30–7.00, April daily 9.30–5.30, March, Oct weekdays 9.30–5.30 Sun 2.00–5.30, Nov–Feb weekdays 9.30–4.00 Sun 2.00–4.00. Old Post Office: April–Oct 11.00–1.00, 2.00–6.00 or sunset if earlier, Sun 2.00–6.00. Information centre in the old blacksmith's forge, Boscastle harbour. Open April–Sept 10.00–6.00.

Cotehele: Medieval house of grey granite, built 1485–1627. Original furniture, tapestries and a fairytale garden: medieval dovecote, a working water-mill adjoining a cider press, Cotehele Quay on the river Tamar with 18th and 19th c buildings, a shipping museum and a sailing barge. One of the loveliest country homes in England, the bedrooms are the best, warm and cosy. Shop and good restaurant. Open April–Oct every day 11.00–6.00, with last admission at 5.30 (National Trust). House closed Mon except bank holidays, everything else open. Five miles from Gunnislake.

Antony House: early 18th c house of silver stone and red brick. A sombre staircase, lovely 'lived-in' library, Chippendale chairs and Waterford china. Landscaped park contains fine cedar, ginkho and oak trees, with a Bath Pond House beside the estuary. Open April–Oct Tue–Thur, Bank Holiday Mon 2.00–6.00 (last tour 5.30). Five miles west of Plymouth via Torpoint car ferry.

Mount Edgcumbe House and Park: the Commander of the Spanish Armada was said to have vowed to live here after he won the war. Tudor house almost entirely destroyed by stray German bomb but much has been rebuilt. Handsome hexagonal towers contain six-sided rooms, several pretty mullioned windows. Open May–Sept Mon, Tue 2.00–6.00. Tea-room in the orangery. Enormous park – 864.4 acres – open all the time, with peacocks, deer, other animals and thousands of flowers.

Bodmin Moor: approx 100 square miles – wild, lonely and beautifully desolate. Legends and eccentrics everywhere, like the weird vicar of Warleggan who supplemented his diminishing congregation with cardboard cut-out figures. Too many tors, stone formations and moody pools to mention, best to arm yourself with supplies and a large-scale Ordnance Survey map. If driving – look out for cattle grids and stray animals. Don't forget Dozmare Pool. Riding on the moor:

nish 'hevvy cake'?) and a Wedgwood-type Victorian loo. Plus comprehensive selection of books on bygone farming techniques, friendly girl director who put it all together herself. Open April–Sept Mon–Sat 10.30–5.00.

Siblyback Lake: 140-acre reservoir set on south edge of Bodmin Moor. Members can enjoy fishing competitions, sailing regatta, table tennis, fly-fishing for trout. Plus bird-watching, access to clubhouse and information on all necessary permits, etc. For further details write to Fisheries & Recreation Information Office, 3–5 Barnfield Road, Exeter, Devon or tel Liskeard 42410.

Dobwalls Forest Railway: miniature railway that 'pounds up the grades, through the canyons and tunnels and along the ridges of the Forest Trail'. Admission includes a free ride on train. Open Easter, then May–Oct 10.30–6.00 daily. A38 west of Liskeard.

at Alder Quarry Pond, Dutson Water, Stone Lake, Stowford Pond. Details from South West Water Authority, 3–5 Barnfield Road, Exeter EX1 1RE, tel Exeter 31666. Sea fishing: near Portquin the occasional shark; bass and flat-fish, dog-fish and mullet at Bude; on south coast pollack, wrasse and conger off Rame Head.

Walking: north coast – almost entire coastline is under care of National Trust and is exceptionally beautiful; long but spectacular walk from Boscastle north to the 700ft cliffs of Crackington Haven; south coast: all around Rame Head offers far-reaching views, but cliffs can crumble – be careful; Bodmin Moor: anywhere, take sturdy shoes. Plenty of wild flowers, including thrift and wild carrot.

Scenic boat trips up the River Tamar, lovely way to arrive at Cotehele. Contact Millbrook Steamboat Co, tel Plymouth 822202.

Brent Tor: on the edge of Dartmoor between Lydford and Tavistock

Tall Trees Stables, tel Otterham Station 249. Beginners on the edge, experienced riders go towards Roughtor. All-day ride every Friday in summer, explore for miles.

Monkey Sanctuary, near Looe: first protected breeding colony of Amazon woolly monkeys in the world. Open Eastertime, then May–Sept 10.30–6.00 daily.

St Endellion, near Port Isaac: hard-working committee produces two annual music festivals at Easter and Aug of high professional standard. For information send sae to Mrs Holden, Rock House, Delabole, Cornwall.

North Cornwall Museum and Gallery, The Clease, Camelford: this museum of rural life won the Pilgrim Trust Award in 1978 for best small museum in England. Interesting and spacious, far superior to the usual folk collection, with bizarre household things like a two-man vacuum cleaner, a slate rolling-pin and pastry-board (for Cor-

Musical Instrument Museum, The Old Mill, St Keyne: organs from fair, cafes, player pianos and all sorts of 'automatic music'. Open May–Sept 10.30–1.00, 2.30–5.00, plus Easter week. Oct, March, April Sun 2.30–5.00.

ACTIVITIES

Best beaches: north coast – Trebarwith Strand nr Tintagel, Widemouth Sand, and Summerleaze and Crooklets beaches at Bude; south coast – Downderry, Seaton beaches, Whitesand Bay (can be dangerous – watch for signs).

Surfing: best is Crooklets at Bude, also Widemouth, Trebarwith Strand.

Sailing: north coast too dangerous except at Bude or further down at Padstow, so it's best to stick to calmer waters of Plymouth Sound.

Angling: Bude – rudd, tench, carp on the canal and Lower Tamar Lake. Launceston – salmon and trout on river Tamar; tench, carp, bream, some perch

FOOD AND DRINK

Egon Ronay's Lucas Guide recommends **Horn of Plenty,** Gulworthy, tel Gunnislake 832528. Three-star restaurant, speciality is sweetbreads *en brioche* with marbled two-sauce effect. Also venison marinated in wine with fir-cone sauce. Very good wine list. **George Hotel Restaurant,** Hatherleigh, tel Hatherleigh 454. Menu changes daily, treats like goose pie. **Woodford Bridge Hotel Restaurant,** Milton Damerel, tel Milton Damerel 252. Steaks and chicken dishes.

TOURIST INFORMATION

Local papers: *Cornish and Devon Post* – large offices at Launceston. *Cornish Guardian* – published on Thur.

Tourist information centres: at Plymouth, Looe and Bude.

Guidebooks: Bossiney Books, published locally in Bodmin, are good personal guidebooks about Tintagel, Bude Canal etc. Buy them in Smiths at Launceston or large bookshop in Holsworthy.

Car ferries over Plymouth Sound: check points at Cremyll and Torpoint; journey takes minutes and only a nominal charge. No set times; ferries run when full (every few minutes).

Research: Martha Ellen Zenfell.

Totnes

Behind the popular resort of Tor Bay in south Devon, there lies to the west a quiet almost unspoilt countryside stretching for mile after mile called the South Hams. Anywhere in Devon in summer has its traffic problems – wise natives stay indoors or in the garden for weeks on end – but it is possible to summon up courage and a one-inch map and to venture out on the lesser roads.

On the edge of the South Hams stands the little town of Totnes, one of the most delightful towns in England. It is crowded, of course, in the season but there seem to be adequate car parks, and it is anyway the sort of town where one needs to get rid of the car and stroll about looking at things. Daniel Defoe, the creator of Robinson Crusoe, is less well known for his *Tour through England and Wales*, which he made between 1719 and 1724. Much of the Totnes he saw still stands, and on the whole the town council have treated it better than many places one could name.

Of Totnes he writes: 'This is a very good town; of some trade, but has more gentlemen in it than tradesmen of note.' Actually, though he did not know it, the gentry were descended from the Royalist gentry who backed the wrong side in the Civil War. They were heavily fined by the Parliamentarians, their estates sold off or confiscated, and thus impoverished. Defoe indeed notes that Totnes was a very good place to live in, 'especially for such as have large families and but small estates, and many such are said to come into those parts on purpose for saving money, and to live in proportion to their income'.

The Dart, on which Totnes stands, is still a good salmon river, though, like most of the Devon salmon rivers, less important than in Defoe's time. He relates that the landlord 'of the great inn next the bridge' had just caught a large number of salmon peal with the aid of dogs. Defoe and his fellow-traveller bought for a shilling six salmon which they consumed for their dinner. Defoe remarks that in London these would have cost 6s 6d each and would not have been so fresh, having been brought up from Chichester. What a magnificent start for touring a town!

The inn, now the Royal Seven Stars Hotel, stands at the bottom of the long uphill main street rising from the bridge at the banks of the Dart. Apart from the slope, one must walk slowly as every side-turning calls for a diversion into alleys and the back-gardens of the sixteenth- and seventeenth-century houses on the main street. These are, or were, the houses of the rich Elizabethan cloth merchants – a typical bit of English history but too easily rattled off without thinking. No 70 Fore Street, now an excellent local museum, was carefully rescued by the enlightened town council a few years ago and restored under expert

Dartmouth – perhaps the loveliest estuary in all England

supervision. With its 15 rooms, and its contemporary outbuildings for storage, it shows the scale of the business and also the size of an Elizabethan family. It is a common myth that our forefathers bred like rabbits but that a heavy infant mortality kept the numbers within bounds. Not so: many Elizabethan families had 10 to 15 children, and most of them grew up to marry and reproduce.

The long street (Fore Street flows into High Street) is full of Elizabethan houses and courtyards. Passing through the East Gate there is one house to pick out especially – No 16, now a branch of Barclays Bank. It is dated 1585 and carries the initials N B. The builder was Nicholas Ball, a rich merchant who had made a fortune out of pilchards, which once swarmed round these coasts. He specialized in pressing them down into barrels and exporting them to the Catholic countries of the Mediterranean. He died suddenly a year after his grand house was finished, leaving a rich widow who was rapidly courted by Thomas Bodley, himself the son of a rich Exeter merchant. Bodley gained the widow and the fortune and out of this wealth, or part of it, he founded the Bodleian Library at Oxford about a dozen years later.

Castle Drogo: high above Teign gorge stands the last castle built in England

But Totnes is almost too full of native English architecture, much of it Georgian as well as Elizabethan. Then there is the Butterwalk, a covered walk just like that at nearby Dartmouth, early seventeenth-century, perfect in a solid granite manner. One can only wonder why, in a wet climate like that of Devon, or indeed England generally, every shopping town did not build in this way. Halfway up the street, but set back from it, is the superb parish church of St Mary, built in 1432–60 (we still have all the building accounts) in a brilliant red sandstone from a quarry just down the river. Inside is the lovely rood-screen of Beer stone, brought across Lyme Bay and up the Dart; also the Caroline pews, the medieval pulpit, the remarkable medieval doors. One of the finest churches in Devon.

There is so much besides all this in the delectable little town: wander about it in the cool of the evening, and explore the stone-walled gardens as far as the perimeter of the ancient walls. Totnes was founded by the Saxons, probably to guard the head of the Dart estuary, and its shape as seen from the air is almost a perfect oval. The lines of the ancient burgh have dictated to a great extent the street plan inside. So

much to see – a two-day expedition if possible, for behind the grand church lies the humble little Elizabethan guildhall, and above all (literally) is the splendid shell-keep of the Norman castle on its mound, carefully sited inside the town walls like Rougemont Castle at Exeter. Secondhand bookshops and good eating complete the scene – and the street vistas of slate-hung houses (to keep out the rain again).

From Totnes one can go out into the country and see two more fine castles. Berry Pomeroy Castle, a romantic ruin, was first built by a Pomeroy in the early fourteenth century: the manor has had only two families as lords since the Norman Conquest – the Pomeroys and the Seymours. It is in all its ruin a splendid example of an Edwardian castle, almost buried in deep woods not far from the town.

Rather farther away, hidden in deep lanes that are the despair of the motorist, is a quite different kind of castle – Compton. Probably better described as a fortified manor house, it was first built about 1320 and much enlarged about 1450 in the troubled years of the Wars of the Roses. You come across it suddenly after being convinced that you are completely lost in the lanes, and there it is, standing back and looking for all the world like a child's dream of what a castle should look like.

Up-river and down-river from Totnes are superb things to see. Up the river is Dartington, the most splendid medieval house in Devon, which is not notable for its country houses as a whole. Once allowed to fall into ruin, it was rescued by the Elmhirsts and American money, and now looks like an Oxford college – grey, with wide lawns, built for the Hollands, Dukes of Exeter in the fourteenth century, and now a lively cultural centre for the west of England, with a wonderful great hall.

And down the river is Dartmouth, best reached by the river steamer – a hackneyed trip but never to be missed. I have done it many times with visitors, and it never palls. The wooded banks of the Dart sweep down to the very water's edge, the deep river winds from one view to another with Georgian country houses far above, down to perhaps the loveliest estuary in all England, down to the ancient port of Dartmouth, which, like the woods, climbs up steep hills.

If Totnes were not so near I would say that Dartmouth was the place to stay, the home of Chaucer's 'schipman', the gathering-place for two Crusades (in 1147 and 1190), and for part of the Normandy invasion fleet in 1944. To stroll along the waterfront at Dartmouth in the evening light, to see an original of Newcomen's engine (he was a Dartmouth-born man) now at rest in the park, and to wander round the old town with its good bookshops and pubs – all this is a fitting end to this lovely part of Devon.

Sometimes I think that it is a misfortune to be born in Devon as I was, and my ancestors back to the 1580s, for where else in England is so deeply beautiful and appealing? Let others argue for their counties, but Devon is unsurpassable. It is a pity it inevitably rhymes with Heaven, as so many full-chested baritones at local concerts have found, but one can bear it and believe it in the general euphoria.

W. G. HOSKINS

Totnes

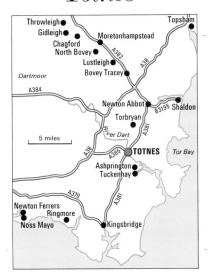

WHERE TO GO

River Dart: gentle stretch of water bordered by quays and old warehouses, now used by the timber trade. In the middle, Vire Island, where you can fish or sun yourself with the ducks. Bridge built 1826–28 by Devon-born architect Fowler.

The Plains: over bridge and to the left, wide early 19th c square with statue of William Wills, intrepid explorer of the Australian outback, born at No 3.

East Gate: with Gothic battlements and cupola, divides the steep hill on which Totnes is built into Fore St and High St. Saxon eastern boundary of the town.

Fore St and High St: bright and bustling, shops and houses with slate-hung and painted fronts, lots of Georgian, some Elizabethan. Look out for Gothic House (antique shop) in Bank Lane just off Fore St – pointed bay windows and castellated roof; a little further up, No 36, former King Edward VI Grammar School – late 18th c with handsome hooded porch and Corinthian pillars; No 16 High St, Nicholas Ball's house, with heavy studded door and inside richly decorated plaster ceiling.

Butterwalk and Poultrywalk: on either side at top of High St – shops under covered piazzas with granite pillars.

Elizabethan House: Local museum in fine merchant's house c 1575. Exhibits include weaving and agricultural implements, fascinating collection of children's toys and a room devoted to Charles Babbage, 19th c Totnesian inventor of the analytical engine – forerunner of the computer. Weekdays 10.30–1.00 and 2.00–5.30, March–Oct.

St Mary's Church: red sandstone, handsome pinnacled tower with niches high up and carved statues. Lovely ornate stone rood screen c 1459. Eye-catching monument in north aisle to Christopher Blackhall, 1633, and his four wives.

Guildhall: some steps by East Gate take you up and along the ramparts to the pretty pillared 16th–17th c Guildhall. See ancient Saxon coins minted in Totnes. List of mayors dates from 1359. April–Sept Mon–Fri 9.30–1.00 and 2.00–5.00. As you come out, look up at gargoyles on church – fat-tongued men and monstrous beasts.

Castle: not a lot remaining – a deep moat that used to be filled with water, and motte or mound crowned with circular keep. From the walls you look down over River Dart and rooftops of Totnes. Open all year May–Sept daily 9.30–7.00; winter daylight hours, Sun from 2.00.

Motor Museum: collection of vintage and racing cars on Steamer Quay. Open daily Easter–mid Oct 10.00–6.00.

ACTIVITIES

Elizabethan day: every Tue May–Sept locals dress up in Elizabethan costume. In the morning a Pannier Market at the Civic Place, at 2.30 a guided walk around the town sets off from Vire Island with Elizabethan guide, followed in the evening by lively folk dancing in the Seymour Hotel. It's all taken quite seriously.

Walking: there are lots of lovely walks all around Totnes to villages such as Cornworthy, Ashprington, Harberton and Dartington.

SHOPPING

Market day: Fri – clothes, veg and good junk stalls, Civic Place.

Early closing: Thur.

The Bookshop, 72 Fore St: very good wide-ranging secondhand bookshop which will 'buy, sell and exchange books'.

Collards Bookshop, 4 Castle St: some very collectable editions.

Troika Toyshop, 9 High St: great array of toys, games, crafts and inexpensive knick-knacks that would keep most children engrossed for hours on a rainy day.

The Taste Bud, 22 High St: exceptional delicatessen with customers from miles around. Pâtés, cheese, and everything for the gourmet picnicker from Urchfont mustard to quails' eggs.

FOOD AND DRINK

Egon Ronay's Lucas Guide recommends the **Elbow Room,** 6 North St, country-style restaurant with imaginative dishes; and **Ffoulkes,** 30 High St, for good traditional English and French cooking; and *Just a Bite* suggests **Beans Jacky's Bistro** for soups, salads, pasta etc. Pubs include: **Kingsbridge Inn,** Leechwell St, Totnes's oldest pub – 13th c – free house serves traditional draught beers and good range of food. **Steam Packet Inn,** St Peter's Quay: romantic Whitbread pub tucked away up the river past the warehouses. Sit outside in the garden on summer evenings. **Royal Seven Stars Hotel,** Fore St: real ale and a good restaurant.

Totnes: looking up Fore Street towards East Gate

Hood Fair: medieval midsummer's day tradition

Villages and country towns

Ashprington

Sleepy Devon village with dogs basking in the road on a sunny day. Built on a hill rising up from the Dart. Short but wide main street with well-kept stone houses, bright white paintwork and lacy gables. Odd bits of topiary in the gardens. Halfway up, road divides with simple war memorial standing in the centre. St David's Church stands at top overlooking the village. Tricky bolt on the lychgate – it opens outwards rather than inwards – but inside there's a large Norman font and late 13th c chalice. No shops other than the village post office and store, but a welcoming pub, the Durant Arms.

Chagford

Small market town on edge of Dartmoor ('chag' old dialect word meaning gorse). Whitewashed shops and houses grouped around the square at odd angles, with octagonal Victorian market cross at centre. One of four original stannary towns where miners brought their tin for assaying. In 19th c an enterprising vicar helped bring the tourist trade to Chagford by introducing a modern drainage system, library and Handel on Sundays.

Good centre for exploring the wild moors and valley of the Teign. Local guide suggests some walks. James Bowden and Webber's have everything for the angler and walker – compasses, rods, knives, gumboots etc. Early closing day Wednesday. Excellent open-air swimming pool 200yds past the Teign bridge on the Sandy Park–Rushford road. Several good pubs – Ring o' Bells, free house, has good array of home-made food. Beautiful 13th c Three Crowns Hotel, originally built as a manor house, also has a restaurant.

Information office at 13 The Square has details of all that's happening in the area. Big event is the Chagford Pony Fair in early Oct when the Dartmoor ponies are bought and sold.

Lustleigh

Flower-filled Devon village. Thatched stone cottages, some washed lemon, pink and white, cluster round the church and village green. Mentioned as a bee-keeping area in Domesday Book when the manor was held by the king's kitchen master. 13th–16th c church has three very early effigies set in recesses in the walls, two knights and a medieval lady, a luxuriantly carved screen, and a curious Latin-inscribed stone used as a door-sill in the south porch, thought to be a 5th–6th c memorial.

A general store, dairy and post office; and the Primrose Cafe serves cream teas with home-made cakes and scones, omelettes, salads and soups at lunchtime. 15th c pub Cleave Hotel, one of the best buildings in the village, serves Whitbread traditional draught beer, snacks and salads.

Bustling activity on August Bank Holiday Monday when there's the annual Horticultural Society Show, gymkhana and goat show. Marvellous walks and scenery, especially along Lustleigh Cleave. About three miles on are mossy boulders of Becka Falls.

Newton and Noss

Newton Ferrers and Noss Mayo, names invariably linked together, lie on either side of thickly wooded creek of River Yealm. Best seen when the tide's high, a yachting haven full of brightly painted boats and tiers of cottages with gardens coming down to the water. Lovely coastal walk around the creek. Noss is on the south bank, but Newton has the sun in the afternoon and makes for a good evening stroll. Uncommercialized with very

WHERE TO STAY

No Egon Ronay recommendation in Totnes itself, but Defoe's 'great inn next the bridge' is now the **Royal Seven Stars Hotel**, tel Totnes 864686, prides itself on its freshly caught salmon.

TOURIST INFORMATION

In summer: The Plains, tel Totnes 863168; in winter: The Guildhall, same tel no.

Coombe Cellars Inn at Combinteignhead near Shaldon

few shops, but a sprinkling of pubs. In Noss, the Swan, a trim blue and white Courage pub serving bar meals and real ale. Old Ship Inn right down by the river also has restaurant, as does Yealm Hotel, over in Newton. Yachting activity reaches its peak with the annual regatta. Set according to the tides – end July or beginning Aug. Noss Mayo's Church of St Peter has art nouveau chancel, built 1882, but public footpath takes you to ancient parish church 1½ miles to southeast at Revelstoke, built on cliffside as landmark for sailors. Abandoned in 1870s, now a beautiful and remote ruin with wonderful view of Bigbury Bay and Dartmoor to the north.

North Bovey
Small unspoilt moorland village tucked away down long winding road. Thatched granite and cob cottages grouped around a large hillocky green, studded with oaks. Pump and stone trough in the middle, and opposite church lychgate an old Dartmoor stone cross. No shops but medieval inn, Ring of Bells, has a secluded garden where you can eat and drink – real ale, cold meats, pies and traditional English roasts.

In the 13th–15th c church of St John the Baptist, fascinating wooden bosses on the chancel roof. Three have heads thought to represent Edward I and his two queens Margaret and Eleanor. Delicately carved rood screen and take a look at the old carved bench-ends – one has a bearded Renaissance man with feather in his hat.

Some good walks in the area. Bowerman's Nose, not too far away, is a 39ft pile of granite rocks with distinctly human-looking features. From Hound and Easdon Tors some superb views out over the moors. Look out for old workings of tin mines.

Ringmore
Very pretty village down steep slope surrounded by lovely coastal scenery of Bigbury Bay, the sea about 15 minutes walk away. Droopy thatched roofs and lots of roses – peace and quiet interrupted only by odd bleat of a sheep. Delightful inn, Journey's End, so-called because R. C. Sherriff wrote part of his play here; serves Theakstons beer, home-made soup and crab salads at the bar, and in the restaurant local shellfish and exotic dishes such as quail stuffed with pâté.

Bar billiards, darts and a garden. Leave your car up at the top by the signpost, because once down there's not much room for parking or turning. Little 13th c church has lancet windows.

The way is signposted across the fields to Ayrmer Cove with its secluded beach. Good area for diving and beachcombing.

Shaldon
On other side of river from Teignmouth, much smaller and less crowded. Set between steep red hills and estuary dotted with fishing boats, yachts and seagulls – used to be an excellent cockling ground. A good place to wander in through narrow lanes and down The Strand running along the waterside. Lots of Georgian strawberry-pink seaside houses and gardens full of fuchsias and palms. Most striking building, the Hunters Lodge – a restaurant specializing in locally caught fish. Cream teas to be had at the Shaldon

A la Ronde: (top) the fantasy house of two 18th-century cousins, Jane and Mary Parminter, who filled it with every conceivable craft, including (bottom) feathered friezes

Tea Rooms nearly opposite, and one or two of the hotels along The Strand have riverside tea gardens. To swim or sunbathe, climb up to the wooded headland, the Ness, and then down to Ness Cove.

Throwleigh and Gidleigh
Tiny moorland villages about two miles apart. The cottages of Throwleigh, the larger of the two, form a sort of triangle around a cross commemorating Queen Victoria's 60th anniversary and, in the corner, a little walled lily pond. Mostly 16th–17th c granite and thatch – some of the tiny cottage windows a mass of plants. 15th c granite church has a sundial over the south porch (1663) and a fine priest's doorway to the south chancel. Just one general store and off-licence in the old forge. Carry on up and through the village and you're soon out on to the open moorland.

Gidleigh, further south, is romantic and remote. Just a couple of farmhouses, a rose-coloured granite church and the ivy-clad ruins of a 13th c castle. All around, some superb scenery – wild moorland, plunging valleys and swift-running streams. Just over a mile away Scorhill Circle – see Places to Visit.

Topsham
Old port on estuary of the Exe first used in prehistoric times. Pronounced Topsam. A place to wander in, through narrow lanes and along waterside Strand with its lovely 18th c 'Dutch' houses with Queen Anne gables and small courtyards. For centuries a flourishing port. Now yachts tend to have replaced the fishing boats. Fore St is full of good shops: Musica for violins and other instruments; Amadeus, besides antiques, pictures, china and glassware, sells spinning wheels. Evening classes on how to spin, and you should master the basic skill in three lessons.

Good town for eating and drinking. Peter Fender at 6 Fore St is a free vintner and open all day to serve wine, pâtés, outstanding range of cheese and fine turkey pies, recommended by Egon Ronay's *Just a Bite*. Denley's Wine Bar also has good food. 11 pubs to choose from – down by quay, cosy Steam Packet Inn, a Heavitree house, and the Lighter Inn, free house with wine and food bars. The Bridge Inn just outside on Exeter–Exmouth road has best selection of real ales.

Torbryan

Just a hamlet set in a deep hollow between round hills. Well worth a visit, it has one of the most attractive and interesting churches in Devon, an excellent pub, the Church House Inn. Early 15th c church has severe corrugated-looking tower. Inside, a lovely bright light comes in through clear windows. The boxed pews each with brass candle-holder were added in Queen Anne's time. Beautiful medieval screen *c* 1430.

Built a little later, the Church House Inn opposite has rambling roses and wisteria over the doorway, with cosy dark oak-beamed rooms and low ceilings. Free house with real ale and cider, good food, darts and pool room.

Tuckenhay

Close by Ashprington on quiet side creek of the Dart. Deserted quays and warehouses, it was an early planned industrial complex by Abraham Tucker in 1806. Gas-house was built to light the hamlet and first gas mantles tested out. Still a small fish-curing industry – salmon are netted here by about 15 licensed fishermen. Old Victorian paper-mill used to produce hand-made paper and bank notes until about 10 years ago. Now being turned into a very civilized 'holiday centre'. In an idyllic spot by the river, the Maltsters Arms, where landlord David Manning makes his own cider. Real ale, bar snacks and restaurant. In warehouse next door you can go on a wine-making tour and sample the end results at Pepe's Winery.

—Places to visit—

Berry Pomeroy Castle: romantic ruins perched on wooded cliff edge with stream threading through valley below. Massive outer walls honeycombed with narrow stairways and tiny chambers. At present being renovated by Department of Environment. Off A381 or A385 outside Totnes.

Compton Castle: one of the finest fortified manor houses in the country. Great walls and angular towers a mass of projections, castellations and machicolations (jutting-out galleries with holes at the bottom for dropping missiles or boiling oil on heads of invaders). 14th–16th c, earliest part built 1330–40 by Geoffrey Gilbert, whose adventurous

seafaring descendants have lived there ever since. Full of family treasures. National Trust one mile north of Marldon off A381. Open April–Oct Mon, Wed, Thur 10.00–12.00 and 2.00–5.00.

Castle Drogo: last castle to be built in England, 1910–30 by Sir Edwin Lutyens for Julius Drewe, founder of Home and Colonial Stores. Gaunt and romantic in dramatic setting high above wild Teign gorge. Inside, 20th c baronial home, all natural wood and bare granite walls hung with tapestries, apart from drawing-room painted a cool stippled green like a bird's egg. Notice everywhere Lutyens's extraordinary attention to detail – octagonal oak table in kitchen matches exactly the skylight above it. He designed everything from plate rack to pestle and mortar. At top of terraced garden, an enormous circular lawn hedged by yews that was used as a tennis court. National Trust. Restaurant using traditional recipes for lunches and teas. Open April–Oct daily 11.00–6.00. Two miles northeast of Chagford, best approach off A382 at Sandy Park.

At nearby Drewsteignton, one of best pubs of all, the Drewe Arms, where Mrs Mudge, 'Auntie' to the locals, has been the landlady for 60 years. Excellent beer, bread and cheese

Powderham Castle: stately home of the Courtenays, Earls of Devon, set in elegant deer park close to estuary of the Exe. Greatly altered in 18th c; not much remains of original 14th c castle. Marble Hall is part of original Great Hall, later rooms have much more ornate decoration. Some impressive ancestral portraits, lavish rococo plasterwork in the Staircase Hall, ingenious book-lined doors in the Library. Home-made teas, refreshments, picnic area. Open Easter Sun, Mon and Sun till mid-May, then daily except Fri, Sat to Sept 2.00–6.00. Off A379 at Powderham Village.

Dartington Hall: don't be distracted by complex of shops at Shinners Bridge. They sell an excellent range of modern crafts, home-made jams and cider but are just a modern off-shoot of Leonard and Dorothy Elmhirst's project to set up a viable rural community. Two miles down turning by church is Dartington Hall; essentially a working agricultural, educational and artistic community founded by the Elmhirsts in 1925. The 14th c great hall, now used for concerts, is a beautiful place. The gardens, a great

grassy well with terraces and backdrop of clipped yews like a Greek amphitheatre. Early Henry Moore sculpture on west bank. Open at any reasonable time provided visitors don't disturb community's activities. Detailed leaflets guide you on walks around vast estate. Two miles north of Totnes off A384.

A la Ronde: 16-sided fantasy house with diamond-shaped windows. Built 1798 by Jane and Mary Parminter, who were inspired after seeing San Vitale, Ravenna. Tiny rooms radiate from high octagonal hall. Totally feminine, crammed with every conceivable Georgian craft which the cousins collected or made themselves. Farther up road, Point in View – chapel and spinsters' almshouses also built by the Parminters, 1811. Open Easter–end Oct Mon–Sat 10.00–6.00, Sun 2.00–7.00. Cream teas. In Summer Lane, off A377 just before Exmouth.

Bradley Manor: in secluded spot in wooded slopes of Lemon valley, 15th c Gothic manor house, roughcast and limewashed, with asymmetrical east front, picturesque windows and pointed gables. Hardly altered over the centuries, the great hall has fine collar-beam roof with arms of Elizabeth I, two screens, one Jacobean and the other early Renaissance. Chapel has carved ceiling bosses and lovely perpendicular window, another room slightly later, decorated with black fleurs-de-lis stencilled on white walls. National Trust. Open mid-April–Sept Wed 2.00–5.00. Off A381 on west edge of Newton Abbot.

Bicton: elegant formal gardens reputed to be by Le Nôtre, with water courses, terraced lawns and temple. Lovely domed early 19th c glass house. Now developed into a popular place for family outings with children's playground, pinetum, miniature woodland railway, picnic area, teas, and excellent countryside museum showing transition from horse to mechanized power.

Just behind the church near entrance to gardens, haunting ruins of an earlier church with mausoleum by Pugin. Open April–Oct 10.00–6.00 daily. On A375 seven miles north-east of Exmouth.

Sharpitor: magnificent view from these gardens out over rocky creeks and coves of Salcombe Bay. Lots of exotic rarities that will delight plant lovers. Most famous of all – deep pink magnolia, planted 1901, said to be finest in the country. Overbeck Museum has natural history gallery, sepia photographs of Edwardian Salcombe and 19th c maritime room with models of Salcombe clippers. From here one of the most beautiful coastal walks in S Devon, Bolt Head to Bolt Tail (see Activities) National Trust. Open April–Oct 11.00–1.00 and 2.00–6.00 daily. 1½ miles southwest of Salcombe. Tortuous track unsuitable for coaches.

Lawrence Castle: strange triangular castellated tower with Gothic windows on high wooded ridge in Haldon Hills. From the top, magnificent view of countryside for miles around. Just outside Dunchideock. Open afternoons May–Sept daily 2.30, Oct–April Sat and Sun only (weather permitting).

Dart Valley Railway: old branch line restored 10 years ago by steam train enthusiasts, seven miles of track alongside river Dart. Nostalgic chocolate and cream carriages. Trains run three–four times daily Buckfastleigh to Totnes, return only (you can't get off at Totnes).

Slapton Ley: the lake is separated from the sea by a shingle barrier

Slapton Ley: vast freshwater lake separated from sea by shingle barrier. Conservation area with many rare plants and birds – on the shingle, yellow horned poppy, viper's bugloss and strapwort (only site in British Isles). Overwintering place for all sorts of wildfowl, the reed beds a nesting place for warblers including new arrival from Continent, Cetti's warbler, just established itself over past five years. In the woodland area, three different sorts of woodpeckers. The South Hams Countryside Unit, next to the Field Studies Centre, has informa-

tion about Slapton and surrounding area and organizes two to three guided walks a week.

Prehistoric remains: Dartmoor is littered with prehistoric relics but they don't always have much meaning for the layman. Worth visiting in this area are: **Spinster's Rock** – megalithic burial chamber, like a Cornish dolmen, two miles west of Drewsteignton at Shilstone Farm. **Grimspound** – Bronze Age hut circle. Remains of 24 huts, some with hearths, enclosed by massive wall. **Scorhill Circle** – Bronze Age stone circle, 23 stones still standing, the largest 8ft high. Thought to have been erected for sacred burial rites. 1¼ miles south-west of Gidleigh, footpath from Berrydown or Batworthy.

ACTIVITIES

Walking: South Devon Coastal Path runs from Plymouth to Lyme Regis, particularly beautiful sections either side of Salcombe. Free leaflet giving more details from Countryside Commission, John Dower House, Crescent Place, Cheltenham GL50 3RA.

On Dartmoor take your Ordnance Survey map and stout shoes. Information and details of walks from National Park Dept, Parke, Haytor Rd, Bovey Tracey, and their information centres at Steps Bridge, nr Dunsford; New Bridge, nr Ashburton; and Postbridge. Dept also organizes guided walks over the moor, almost daily in summer, 1½, 3 or 6 hours long. Leaflets giving details from local

libraries, tourist information offices or the National Park Dept, address as above – please enclose sae.

Angling: so many good rivers in area it's worth getting the South West Water Authority's *Angling and Reservoir Recreation Guide*. From Fisheries and Recreation Information Office, 3–5 Barnfield Rd, Exeter or local tackle shops – in Totnes Blake Sports, 73 Fore St. Along the coast, boats to hire for sea fishing.

Riding: lots of stables offering trekking and riding over Dartmoor. These three are approved by the British Horse Society: The Beacons Riding School, Ivybridge, tel Ivybridge 2260; Blackler Barton Riding Stables, Landscove, Ashburton, tel Staverton 236; Haytor Vale Riding School, Minehayes, Haytor, nr Newton Abbot, tel Haytor 348.

FOOD AND DRINK

Egon Ronay's Lucas Guide recommends –**Nobody Inn**, Doddiscombsleigh, tel Christow 52394. Mostly French menu, above average wines. **Moorwood Cottage**, Lustleigh, tel Lustleigh 341. Fresh local produce, game and seafood. **Pitt House**, Church End Rd, Kingskerswell, tel Kingskerswell 3374. 15th c thatched cottage – grills and tasty specialities. **Carved Angel**, 2 South Embankment, Dartmouth, tel Dartmouth 2465. Star rating, superb fish dishes. **Exeter Inn**, Church St, Modbury, tel Modbury 239. Old pub serving five-course dinner, or lunches and suppers at bar. **Hungry Horse**, Harbertonford, tel Harbertonford 441. Rustic atmosphere, inventive menu: Camembert fritters, Japanese *filet de boeuf* Teriyaki. **Dudley's Brewhouse**, Union St, Kingsbridge, tel Kingsbridge 3232. French-style dishes.

TOURIST INFORMATION

Local papers: *Dartington Hall News & South Devon Scene* is best guide to films, music, theatre and other local happenings. Weekly from newsagents.

Tourist information offices: at Bovey Tracey, Brixton, Dartmouth, Kingsbridge.

Guidebooks: excellent guide to Dartmoor produced by National Park Dept. Crossing's *Guide to Dartmoor* still the most thorough for walkers.

Research: Pamela Brown.

Dorchester

Time slowly accumulates in Dorset: the present settles gently into the past without disturbing it. I stand at the corner of Dorchester's High West Street, scarcely changed since the nineteenth century, and glimpse the portly ghost of Emma Lavinia Hardy whizzing downhill on her bicycle, feet perched on a rest below the handlebars, long green velvet dress ballooning out behind her. Every corner of Dorchester is vivid with people from the past but there are very few great, grand houses in the county and Dorchester itself is a place of pleasant, unassuming Georgian and Victorian architecture. Montacute to the north-west in Somerset, an Elizabethan mansion now housing a marvellous collection from the National Portrait Gallery, is the only really fine house within easy reach of Dorchester itself.

By far the greatest architectural structures in or near Dorchester are the prehistoric hill forts; there must be at least a dozen within a radius of 15 miles, as well as numberless other archaeological sites. They survive because there has been so little development and industrialization; the main threat has been ploughing but around Dorchester is mainly chalk and limestone: good sheep country.

Just outside the town Maiden Castle crowns a hilltop with an almost arrogant tension; the monolithic banks and causeways carve the landscape more incisively than anything built since. Less well known but on a supremely dramatic site, on the spur of a hill falling away to a great bowl with the sea beyond, is Eggardon Hill. It stands 10 miles west of Dorchester at the end of a narrow Roman road which probably covers an even older trackway. One of the pleasures of exploring these ancient sites is that they are often linked by old 'grass roads' along which you can walk through miles of undisturbed countryside, often within sight of the sea, and feel your are part of a tradition of over 4000 years.

The Romans shaped Dorchester and made it into an administrative centre. Law, order and agriculture have remained its chief concerns. One of the most fascinating sights of the town is hardly known. Hidden within the Shire Hall, virtually unchanged since the Tolpuddle Martyrs were sentenced here in 1834, is a perfectly preserved eighteenth-century courtroom. It is small but lofty, crammed with a complicated arrangement of pews and boxes, built up high and threaded at floor level by dark, cramped corridors. The judge is set highest of all. Imagine yourself fetched up from the crepuscular cells below, periwigged lawyers, rat-faced and bacon-faced, glancing contemptuously down at you. Like something out of Cruikshank, this courtroom brings home the oppression of farm labourers and how the eighteenth-century establishment maintained its power.

Dorchester, High West Street

The town is still resonant with the sense of Thomas Hardy and one of the pleasures of staying here is to compare his imaginary Wessex with the reality. Longman's bookshop at the top of South Street has a section devoted to his works and books about him. An awkward, complicated, supremely gifted man, Hardy strove to cover up his past but was locked into it and his surroundings seem extraordinarily significant. He was born at Higher Bockhampton, a clutch of cottages two miles east of Dorchester. Modest but comfortable, his cottage is backed by woodlands which the National Trust has turned into a nature trail, and the wilder heath beyond. From Hardy's own bedroom window (but nowhere else in the cottage) you see the distant sight of a phallic monument to his namesake, Nelson's admiral, which crowns the crest of a stupendous view out to sea and inland across the country.

Nearby, at Moreton Church, Laurence Whistler has recently completed a set of windows in engraved glass. Those who know his work on bowls and goblets, usually not large and almost always shown in circumstances which enhance their mystical and numinous quality, will be amazed to see these great sheets of sunlit glass and through them to the further dimension of the countryside beyond. Worth going many miles to see.

Another new and fascinating venture has been set up 15 miles north-west of Dorchester near the pretty little town of Beaminster (almost all West Dorset towns and villages deserve both adjectives). This is at Parnham House, originally sixteenth-century but rebuilt early in the nineteenth century by Nash. Here at Parnham John Makepeace has established his School for Craftsmen in Wood. You can look into the workshops and see inside the house itself which is furnished with examples of the work: breathtaking in its boldness, sensitivity and authority.

Extraordinary as it may seem, Dorset must thank the army for one of its best beaches. The Dorset coast has remained wonderfully unspoilt with very little of the kind of development that smothers the Hampshire shoreline like candle-grease. This is because most of the beaches are shingle; you can tell where the good ones are because the watering places have grown up beside them. But years ago the army grabbed a slice of Dorset for firing ranges and this included the magnificent stretch of fine sand at Worbarrow.

For years no one was allowed in: the farmhouse decayed, the countryside sank into itself. But now, during the summer months, the army lets you into this almost fossilized landscape, as empty and tranquil as it must have been a thousand years ago. A beach like this is very rare on the South Coast.

You can walk along the cliffs very nearly from one end of the county to the other; much of the land is owned by the National Trust. From Kimmeridge and the Isle of Purbeck in the east you can take the coast walk to Durdle Door and Lulworth Cove and see the rock formations, curious and dramatic. Further west are pebbly beaches which are quite hard to reach, and so peaceful when you get there that you can sunbathe in the nude. Further west still, as at Stanton St Gabriel, you start finding fossils like mushrooms. The most famous fossil beds are at Charmouth and Lyme Regis. You can see collections of fossils at the Philpot Museum in Lyme Regis and the fossil shop opposite.

Driving back from Lyme you will pass through Morecombelake, a village strung along the roadside looking out across a valley to the sea. Dorset knob biscuits are made here, and very good they are. You can go round the small kitchens and watch them being made. But it is all a little secretive and somehow you never see the whole process. Having experimented with them myself, I think it has something to do with double baking. Further along the A35 is Bridport, with astonishingly wide streets. Rope has been made here for more than 800 years and the streets once served as rope walks. A 'Bridport dagger' was the old nickname for a hangman's rope.

Bridport Gundry are now the largest rope and twine makers in Europe, but the factory still has a very human scale. Tucked away behind the main gates is a small shop where you can see and buy their products. A humble ball of Bridport twine makes the best sort of souvenir: something you pick up without thinking, which takes you back in a moment. Then instead of going on to Dorchester by the main road, turn off towards West Bay and then take the B3167 along the coast. This romantic road follows the sea for mile after mile: you can see the whole shoreline from Beer Head to Portland Bill, and gaze down from above on the Chesil Bank. This massive natural barrier of graduated pebbles (large at Portland, small towards Abbotsbury) hems in a lagoon, the home of thousands of swans.

Abbotsbury is virtually a seventeenth-century village with a number of pleasures. The least known – and to me the most magical – takes place from the shore just west of the village. There is no sand here, and the land shelves suddenly and deeply, making it dangerous except for experienced swimmers. However, this sudden deepening allows seine fishing.

The end of a long net is rowed out from the shore by a boat which draws a huge semi-circle before returning to land about 200 yards further on. A team of men and women then take each end and slowly draw inwards and together. With timeless nonchalance they lean upon the weight of the net, let the free arm swing, change hands, take a step. Over and over again they repeat the sequence with exquisitely graceful and peaceful rhythm. They appear to do this every summer evening around seven o'clock, and for many years it has been one of our treats to take the children and some friends, buy fish directly it is caught (mostly mackerel or mullet) and cook it over a driftwood fire we make on the shore. The sun sets and the light of the flames flickers across the water; the stones crack and split with the heat; the waves hiss endlessly combing the shingle; the food is simple, delicious, slightly smoky. You could be back in time 5000 years.

ANN JELLICOE

Dorchester

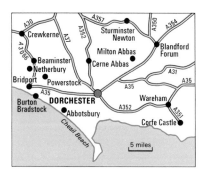

WHERE TO GO

South St: Thomas Hardy was articled to a firm of architects at No 39. The original of Henchard's house in *The Mayor of Casterbridge* is now a branch of Barclays Bank.

High West St: Judge Jeffreys's lodgings are now a restaurant (good for lunch and cream teas). On the other side of the street is the **Crown Court** where the Tolpuddle Martyrs were sentenced. Open Mon–Fri 10.00–4.00.

Maumbury Rings: at the top of Weymouth Avenue, is a fine neolithic ritual monument, later taken over by the Romans as an amphitheatre. It nearly disappeared in the great railway age when philistine Victorians proposed laying Dorchester–Weymouth line through middle of Rings. Company had to settle instead for very tight curve, which still slows trains now.

Roman town house: remains next to County Hall. Open daily.

Grey's Bridge: over River Frome at the bottom of town still bears the warning: 'Any person wilfully injuring any part of this County Bridge will be guilty of felony and upon conviction liable to be transported for life.'

Dorset County Museum, High West St: has big collection of finds from Maiden Castle; also rural craft exhibits and the Thomas Hardy Memorial Collection. Main hall is itself a museum piece, lofty intricate cast iron of the 1880s. Open 10.00–5.00, not Sun.

Dorset Military Museum, Bridport Rd: is stone toytown fort which glorifies the Dorset Regiment, Militia, Volunteers, Yeomanry etc from 1702. Hitler's desk here. Open July–Sept 9.00–1.00 and 2.00–5.00 daily except Sun,

Oct–June Mon–Fri 9.00–1.00 and 2.00–5.00, Sat 9.00–12.00.

Agricultural show: early Sept. Sheep fair in Oct.

SHOPPING

Market day: Wed. Still street barrows on original market place at top of Cornhill, main market has moved to big site near station. Many delightful things and junk of all sorts.

E. Parsons, High East St: is a must. Specializes in tea and coffee which are stored in great japanned boxes, but good for everything and worth a trip for the smell alone.

La Charcuterie, Trinity St: stocks Dorset specialities, Dorset pâté, Dorset blue cheese and, if your teeth are good, Dorset knobs, uncompromisingly hard little rolls. Also good sausages and fillets of smoked mackerel.

H. V. Day, High West St: formerly a church, specializes in old books and prints.

Pancraft, Great Western Rd: is good for stones, fossils and books about them.

Ungaretti, High West St: has lavish selection of home-made sweets and chocolate.

The main hall of Dorset County Museum: it has many finds from prehistoric Maiden Castle

FOOD AND DRINK

Egon Ronay's *Just a Bite* recommends **Nappers Mite**, South St, and the **Horse with the Red Umbrella**, 10 High West St, and **Judge Jeffrey's Restaurant**, 6 High West St.

WHERE TO STAY

Kings Arms in High East St is an agreeable place to adjust to the slower pace of Dorset life. **Antelope** in Cornhill has an old coaching entrance, with trailing vines; original board still proclaims, 'Stagecoaches to all parts.'

TOURIST INFORMATION

Antelope Yard, South St, tel Dorchester 67992.

Villages and country towns

Abbotsbury

Stone and thatch village strung out in a sheltered valley a mile inland from the great sweep of Chesil. Many of the houses built with decorative bits purloined from the old abbey ruins – this stone is whiter than the rest. Best collection at the Old Vicarage, close to the site.

Abbotsbury Castle is an Iron Age hill fort on Wears Hill, roughly triangular, enclosed by ramparts and ditches. The building that looks like a castle standing stark on a steep hill to south of village is St Catherine's chapel, built by 15th c monks. Huge buttresses and gargoyles. Path to chapel leads from West St, next to The Salt Box, but wise to get key from keeper at 3 Back St *before* tackling the steep hill. Open weekdays May–Sept 9.30–7.00, March, April, Oct 9.30–5.30, Nov–Feb 9.30–4.00, Sun from 2.00. The swannery is at the west end of the Fleet, a long salt-water lake trapped behind the high Chesil shingle bank. Biggest swannery in England, founded in 14th c. Open daily May–Sept 9.30–4.30. Abbotsbury Gardens, approached through a long avenue of ilex, sit in a sub-tropical bowl near the sea, 17 acres with magnificent trees, bog garden, rhododendron, hydrangea, informal layout of great beauty, peacock and golden pheasant too. Open daily mid-March–mid Oct 10.00–5.00. Garden ornaments at Ideal Gnome Exhibition, Rosemary Lane, teas at Flower Bowl.

Beaminster

Enchanting overgrown village, Hardy's Emminster in *Tess* and a favourite with William Barnes, Dorset's dialect poet of mid-19th c. Blazes in 1644, 1684, 1781 destroyed many ancient buildings, but excellent Georgian replacements. Handsome Market Cross in charming square, site of an early minster. Church of St Mary dates mainly from 15th c and has tall pinnacle tower, unusual in these parts. Jacobean pulpit and good memorials to the Strode family of Parnham. Next to churchyard are almshouses, gift of Sir John Strode in 1630. Church St and St Mary's St are full of pretty cottages; grander houses are mostly round Whitcombe St.

Beaminster has excellent grocer: Pines, a bow-fronted shop with magnolia grandiflora, just off the square. Next door is Colsons, useful ironmongers, its front decorated with solid cast-iron barleysugar poles and icing. Pickwicks Restaurant in the square is expensive but inventive.

Just outside Beaminster on Bridport Rd is Parnham House, not to be missed. Impressive Tudor mansion, enlarged and embellished by Nash in 1810; 14 acres of garden with peacocks, good topiary, formal terraces, riverside walks. Also home of John Makepeace furniture workshop and School for Craftsmen in Wood. Display of furniture, modern art and woodcraft. Teas available. Open April–Sept Wed, Sun and bank hol 10.00–5.00.

Bridport

Busy, endearing town, full of the sound of seagulls. Wide streets and long, thin gardens are relics of once-dominant trade in rope and nets. Bridport Gundry at the bottom of town on right sell twine at their shop here (not open Sat). The fugitive Charles II stayed at the George Inn (now a chemists) after the battle of Worcester 1651, but his cover was blown and he was chased out of town.

Bridport Museum is 16th c building in South St, with small but interesting collection: ropemaking, town history and old agricultural implements. Upstairs is a huge collection of dolls in national cos-

Abbotsbury swannery: founded in 14th c, it now has about 500 swans

tume and magnificent doll's house. Open all year Mon–Sat 10.30–1.00, June–Sept also 2.30–4.30 Mon, Tue, Wed, Fri. Georgian town hall has East, West and South Streets radiating from it. Underneath the colonnade is good butcher, who has cold meat counter. Bumbles in South St has beach gear and good cheap things for rainy-day bribes. Everything tested on the proprietor's five children. Croft Antiques, East St. occupies one of the town's fine 18th c houses. At West End Dairy, 35 West St, cream

measured out from a gallon jug. Egon Ronay's *Just a Bite* recommends the cafe here. Good street market on Saturday which spills along through the entire town: food, clothes, junk, secondhand books.

Two miles south is Bridport's harbour, West Bay. Noisier pleasures here, candyfloss, trampolines, shellfish stalls, boats for hire, fishing trips. Regatta first week in Aug. Agricultural show last Thursday in Aug.

Burton Bradstock

Picturebook village of thatch and stone, owned by Pitt-Rivers family until 1958. Get away from coast road and wander into the back of the village through Donkey Lane, Darby Lane and Shadrack. 15th c parish church with embattled central tower, unusual carved knobs on 1686 communion rails, charming painted frieze and panelling in green and red. Chesil Beach begins (or ends) here and stretches 15 miles east to Portland with mackerel in quantity in the summer. Village was once famous for its flax and the old mill, shut down in the 1930s, still stands by the stream.

Three Horseshoes inn, with good bar, and Anchor Hotel, both in centre of village. The fishermen's pub is the Dove, on the edge of the village in Southover, draught Worthington, Guinness and cider. You can drink round a table made from the hatch cover of the schooner *Flirt* wrecked under Burton cliffs in

Abbotsbury: stone and thatch village in a sheltered valley

The Dove pub at Burton Bradstock: it has a table made from a shipwreck

1897. Collection of old farming machinery at Bredy Farm. Open Whitsun–end Aug weekdays 10.30–5.00. Antiques at Old Pottery, Cliff Rd, and gifts, exotic shells at Long Barn. Cream teas opposite village hall. Riding at Bucklers Bid Stables. The Hive is the best local beach, with cafe on shore for ices, drinks and shelter if it pours.

Cerne Abbas

Rather a showplace, kept in good order by the higher echelons of the Army and Navy who tend to retire here. Long St, the main village thoroughfare, has pretty houses of orange stone and flint. Fine early 18th c carriage arch at New Inn, stone and flint banding, patched with Georgian brick. Garden at the back, mounting block and old pump, dated 1747. Good food here and bedrooms with stone-mullioned windows. The Singing Kettle opposite does teas. Higher up the street is the smaller stone Royal Oak, Devenish bitter, comfortable bar. The Forge craftshop, hidden away in Duck St, does ironwork, firebaskets, fire irons, chestnut roasters, boot-scrapers.

Abbey St has charming range of timber-fronted houses, two storeys with an overhang, Nos 4 and 5 stripped right down to the bare bones, one with a very pretty decorative door lintel. No 15 has the village stocks. A stone-lined drain brings overflow down from duck pond at the top of street. The abbey now in ruins, but tithe barn and gatehouse with beautiful two-storey oriel window above are open to view.

Cobbled path on left by pink house leads down to pretty walk along the millstream, over a stone bridge and up to the Giant, a rampant Romano-British figure cut into the chalk of the steep hillside. After suffering from drought, he has been reseeded and is temporarily fenced off. Best view is from the A352 on north of village. East and above the Giant is the Trendle, earthwork enclosure, by tradition the spot for maypole dancing.

Corfe Castle

The remains of Dorset's best castle still dominate the huddle of stone houses that grew up under its protection. Fortified by William the Conqueror to control the gap through the Purbeck Ridge, constantly rebuilt and enlarged until finally hammered during a Civil War siege. Parish church on south side of square also badly damaged in siege, lead taken from roof to make bullets, surplices stolen for shirts. The perpendicular tower remained safe, with gargoyles and pinnacles. Tidy little churchyard with interesting early tombs stacked against the walls. Close to the castle is a tiny window display of fossils, the workshop of a local collector, open 'when circumstances permit'. Also under the castle's shadow is the Castle Tea Garden, a pretty stone cottage offering scones and cream teas.

The Ancient Order of Purbeck Marblers, the quarrymen of the neighbourhood, celebrate the enrolment of apprentices by kicking and carrying a bladder through the streets of Corfe. Claimed to be early form of rugby. Small museum in old town jail whips through Corfe history, ending with BBC filming of *The Mayor of Casterbridge*. The Fox, West St, reputed to be oldest pub in Dorset. The Greyhound in the square has an odd little room built out over the entrance on pillars. A walk through the churchyard connects West St to East St and Flowers, an exceedingly pretty shop with a little terrace displaying baskets, earthenware, flowers, and inside, the work of half a dozen Dorset potters. Just off the square is the entrance to the model village of Corfe, on a one-twentieth scale to show the village as it looked in 17th c.

Milton Abbas

Lies in a narrow ribbon along the deep wooded valley of the Milbourne Brook. It was laid out 1771–90 for Joseph Damer, Viscount Milton, who was rebuilding his house and wanted the site of the existing village for his park. This 'unmannerly imperious lord', as his architect called him, destroyed a village, banished the grammar school (to protect his apples) and opened a sluice gate to flood out a particularly argumentative lawyer. But the 'new' village is now charming: identical four-square cottages of cob and thatch with green in front and steep gardens behind.

Tea Clipper craft shop does coffee, lunch and tea. The Brewery Farm Museum is a marvellous collection of local relics, photographs, old inn signs, engrossing details of old village life. Open daily, daylight hours. Short distance to beautiful abbey, the house now a school, in grounds landscaped by Capability Brown. House open daily during summer school holidays 10.00–6.00.

Netherbury

Quiet village of quiet pleasures, several fine large houses with lovely gardens. Church dominates all, rather larger and smarter than most, a memory of the time when village population was twice as big. Beautiful square font (1175) of Purbeck marble, heavy Elizabethan pulpit and oddly rustic Victorian kneelers made with bound hanks of straw, like thick baskets, the tops covered with bits of carpet. Pleasant walk down through the churchyard and then between banks of fern and wild garlic out to the meadow and mill race below. The path crosses the wooden bridge and continues up to a lane the far side of the village.

Another path leads along the box hedge of the churchyard and follows the boundary of fine garden until it comes out in a meadow above the stream. Turn left after the stile at the far end of the field and climb up an old unpaved lane which joins the road back into the village. Mr Warren of Copper Beech Farm, like his father before him, brews cider in a shed beside his orchard.

Powerstock

Much of the present field pattern here was first set out when ancient forest cleared in pre-Roman times. Fine strip lynchets carved into the steep hillsides. Powerstock Castle now just a grassy site, but still good example of motte and bailey. The village, stone and thatch, is scattered in a deep fold, with five lanes meeting at church which has 12th c arch, the most elaborate of any Dorset parish church. Two lengths of spiralled Norman columns have found their way to vicarage garden. Vicar's aesthetic wife of 1860s painted swirling designs of holly, ivy and vine in the nave. Kenneth Allsop buried here. Egon Ronay in *Just a Bite* recommends Three Horseshoes (local steaks and lunchtime pizzas). Footpath near this pub emerges handily across the valley at the Marquis of Lorne, Nettlecombe, fine stone pub. Rising up the east is the stark hill fort of Eggardon, home of the Durotriges tribe, not as grand as Maiden Castle, but much more beautiful.

Sturminster Newton

Originally two villages, Sturminster on the north of the Stour and Newton on the south joined by a fine six-arch stone bridge, late medieval, but widened in the 17th c and pedestrian refuges fitted in at the centre. Sturminster Mill upstream, Fiddleford Mill downstream. Market day Mon with stalls in the old central market place and animals now in new area by Corn Exchange. Auctions, fruit and vegetables in yard of Rivers Arms. Wed early closing. Carnival week in Aug with parish walk, grand procession and bands.

The place is threaded with alleys, several ending up at the church, overlooking the river, which loops round three sides of town. Huge house near is old vicarage. Church lectern commemorates William Barnes, dialect poet. Hardy lived here for a couple of years while writing *Return of the Native*. Market Cross Gallery in the square does copper, brass and other antique bits. Horologists should not miss Tom Tribe's workshop and showroom in Bridge St, filled with grandfather clocks.

Swan Hotel, with red brick facade, has coaching entrance next to the miniature assembly rooms. White Hart (1708) is pretty thatched inn, with beams and inglenooks. Egon Ronay in *Just a Bite* recommends Red Rose and in *Lucas Guide* Plumber Manor Restaurant receives a star. At the bottom of Penny St, footpath on left leads to Fiddleford (about one mile) and mill still working, horizontal wheel. Fiddleford Inn pretty, with garden good food and accommodation.

Milton Abbas: in the 18th century the village was rebuilt to make room for the local landowner's new park

Places to visit

Thomas Hardy's cottage, Higher Bockhampton

Hardy's Cottage, Higher Bockhampton: built by his great-grandfather in 1800. Squint in porch to allow grandfather, an occasional brandy smuggler, to watch the lane for excisemen. Office, where Hardy's father, master builder, paid his men through barred window looking on to Egdon Heath. Hardy wrote *Under the Greenwood Tree* and *Far From the Madding Crowd* here. National Trust. Outside open March–Oct 11.00–6.00 daily; inside by appointment (tel Dorchester 2366). Tea at Mellstock Tea Rooms, Bockhampton Lane. Three miles east of Dorchester, half a mile south of A35.

Maiden Castle: prehistoric hill fort, brilliant piece of military architecture and HQ of the Durotriges tribe. Massive fortifications of ditches and ramparts, the entrance way a complicated maze threaded between them. Later occupied by Romans who built small temple, now excavated. Most of the finds from this site, pots, weapons, jewellery, are in Dorchester Museum. One mile southwest of Dorchester, signposted off A354.

Athelhampton: fine example of 15th c domestic architecture, with king's anteroom and gallery. Most of the present house built by Sir William Martyn, Lord Mayor of London in 1493, who spent his money on great open hall with timber roof and oriel window. Thatched stables and pretty dovecote; 12 gardens in one, with lime walk, cloister, garden, white garden. Teas at the house. Open bank hol, Wed, Thur, Sun Easter–Oct, also Tue, Fri in Aug 2.00–6.00. On A35 east of Puddletown.

Cranborne Manor Gardens: beautiful romantic gardens, laid out in 17th c by John Tradescant, but much embellished this century. Specially good for old roses, unusual Jacobean mount garden and knot garden planted with Elizabethan flowers. Excellent garden centre, specializing in statuary, terracotta pots, open all year. Manor Gardens open first weekend of month, Sat 9.00–5.00, Sun 2.00–5.00 and other times during season, tel Cranborne 248. 18 miles north of Bournemouth on B3078.

Clouds Hill: Lawrence of Arabia rented this cottage when he was serving as 'Private Shaw' in the Tank Corps. The sitting-room upstairs is just as he left it, ascetic and strange. National Trust. Open April–Sept Wed, Thur, Fri, Sun, bank hol 2.00–5.00. Teas at Woolbridge Manor Farm. 9 miles east of Dorchester, 1 mile north of Bovington Camp.

Forde Abbey: resettled by Cistercian monks in 1141. The last abbot, Thomas Charde, built in 16th c a splendid new abbot's lodging and cloister, probably trying to get rid of surplus cash before it could be seized by the Crown. Very little has changed here since Cromwell's Attorney General made it his home in 1650. Garden has huge herbaceous borders, unusual trees, and a beautifully laid out kitchen garden with espaliered fruit and monster vegetables. Pick your own raspberries, currants, loganberries. Open May–Sept Sun, Wed and bank hol 2.00–6.00. Teas at the Abbey. Four miles south-east of Chard off A30.

Sherborne Castle: lots to see in Sherborne: Abbey, Cheap St, almshouses, school and the two castles. Old castle now in ruins, open daily. New castle built in 1594 by Sir Walter Raleigh, enlarged 30 years later by Sir John Digby. Fine furniture, porcelain and pictures, Van Dyck, Gainsborough and others. Newly restored 50-acre lake in landscape laid out by Capability Brown. Open Easter–last weekend in Sept Thur, Sat, Sun, bank hol 2.00–6.00. Teas at the Castle. Five miles east of Yeovil off A30.

Bovington Tank Museum near Wareham: display by the Royal Armoured Corps and Royal Tank Regiment. Over 140 wheeled and tracked vehicles with equipment and weapons from 1915 onwards, including some captured enemy tanks. Open Mon–Fri 10.00–12.30 and 2.00–4.45, Sat, Sun, bank hol 10.30–12.30 and 2.00–4.00.

Worldwide Butterflies, Over Compton, near Sherborne: Compton House is old manor where the owner breeds butterflies. Modern conservatory full of jungle plants where butterflies as big as birds fly free, sipping test-tube nectar from plastic flowers. Good collection of spiders, stick-insects. Silk farm shows end product of silk moths' cocooning. Open daily April–Oct 10.00–5.00.

Brownsea Island, Poole Harbour: owes its wild and beautiful nature to last, eccentric, private owner, Mrs Mary Christie, who lived here for 30 years until 1961. National Trust now look after the beaches, woodlands and 200 peacocks. Notable nature reserve with heronry, ternery and red squirrels run by Dorset Naturalists' Trust. Open daily April–Sept 10.00–7.00. Boats run frequently from Poole Quay and Sandbanks. Guided tours of reserve every afternoon at 2.30.

Poole Pottery, The Quay, Poole: it was at Poole, 1700 years ago, that Dorset ball clay was first used in pottery – Poole Pottery have been here for just 100. Interesting tours of their craft section behind the scenes, also chance to buy 'seconds'.

Fossil Forest, Lulworth

Fossil Forest, Lulworth: amazing formation, millions of years old, halfway down a cliff east of Lulworth. Map in car park shows the only way to get there over army ranges.

Eldridge Pope Brewery, Dorchester: family firm brewing here since premises built in 1880. Beers still made according to recipes in old brewing book. Afternoon tours including brewing process, bottling and the Maltings Museum usually already fully booked, but worth asking. Tel Dorchester 4801.

Wing and Staples Forge, Motcombe, Shaftesbury: watch blacksmiths at work, shoeing horses or forging decorative iron ware. Open Mon–Fri 10.00–4.00. Tel first: Shaftesbury 3104. Visitors also welcomed at Blackmore Vale Forge, Bishops Caundle, Sherborne.

Moores Biscuit Factory, Morecombelake, Bridport: watch baking of Dorset specialities, knobs, butter biscuits, shortbread, gingers, in tiny roadside factory. Open Mon–Fri 9.00–5.30.

Mapperton, Beaminster: terraces and hillside gardens, formal borders, orangery and Georgian fishponds and summerhouse. Open mid-March–early Oct Mon–Fri 2.00–6.00.

ACTIVITIES

Walking: the best thing to do in Dorset. It's a waste to hurry. Lewesdon is a still and strange wooded hill-fort 894ft high with views over Devon, Somerset and the sea. Access to it from Stoke Knapp on the B3162 from Bridport. Golden Cap, highest cliff on south coast of England, offers wonderful walks and views in any direction, along the coast or inland, remains of 13th c chapel in fields at St Gabriel's Farm. There are nature trails in Charmouth Forest (one mile north of Wootton Fitzpaine), Puddletown Forest (two miles east of Dorchester), Thorncombe (one mile east of Dorchester).

FOOD AND DRINK

Egon Ronay's Lucas Guide recommends **Priory Hotel Restaurant**, Wareham, tel Wareham 2772. Inventive menu with a strong French slant.

TOURIST INFORMATION

Local papers: *Western Gazette*, every Fri, has full entertainments guide, also details of markets, auctions.

Guidebooks: *West Dorset Guide* and *Dorchester Town Trail* available from Council Offices, Agricultural House, High West St, Dorchester. Thomas Hardy Society publish tour guides with detailed maps for each of the novels. From local booksellers or Rev J. M. C. Yates, The Vicarage, Haselbury Plucknett, Crewkerne, Somerset.

Tourist information centre: Weymouth.

Research: Anna Pavord.

Chichester

There are few regions in the south of England more fascinating than West Sussex, with its astonishing variety of scenery. It has a wealth of architectural beauty and historical associations; the delights of ancient towns and villages, and the sophisticated and sometimes noisy attractions of modern seaside resorts.

From near Worthing the South Downs, the backbone of the county, march westwards, overlooking on the way the low coastal plain with the holiday towns of Bognor and Littlehampton; the Roman-Saxon-Georgian city of Chichester and the deep sea-inlets of Chichester and Bosham harbours, beloved of sailing-people.

Chichester is the focus of the region, visually as well as socially, for there is hardly a point where you may not stand and see the graceful, pointed spire of its cathedral, even from the sea. The city was the Noviomagus of the Romans. Mosaic pavements and other remains of houses have been found recently under the foundations of the cathedral; otherwise little remains of their occupation but some fragments of the town walls, a few inscriptions and the north-south, east-west layout of the four main streets.

After the departure of the Romans, the Saxons landed in 477 AD at Selsey, a few miles south of the city, and it became Cissa's Coastre (camp) after Cissa, son of the Saxon leader Aella. St Wilfred built the first cathedral near Selsey after he landed in 681 AD, but the bishopric was transferred to Chichester about 1070. Most of the present cathedral was finished by 1123.

The sombre austerity of the Norman interior is dispelled by the fiery glow at the far eastern end of the nave of John Piper's modern Aubusson tapestry representing the Trinity, the four elements and the four Evangelists. It is as though great furnace doors have been opened upon the fire of creation. More colour is added to the interior by Hans Feibusch's mural painting, the *Baptism of Christ*, a window by Marc Chagall and a small painting by Graham Sutherland. Two late-Romanesque sculptured panels representing episodes in the life of Christ are intensely moving; they came from the earlier cathedral at Selsey which now lies under the sea.

Chichester's delightful Market Cross, looking like a Gothic wedding-cake of stone, stands at the junction of the four main streets of the city. Once threatened by a maelstrom of traffic, it is now protected in a pedestrian area. The Council House in North Street is a pleasantly unorthodox Palladian building built in 1731–3 by Roger Morris, a disciple of Lord Burlington. Pallant House is Chichester's most handsome private house, early Georgian in mellow red brick.

Bosham on Chichester Harbour: site of a Roman settlement

Despite its Georgian character, Chichester has some interesting frankly modern buildings. The remarkable Festival Theatre, designed by Powell and Moya in 1961–2, has an Elizabethan open stage and a hexagonal auditorium, with a lot of girders in the roof.

Just off the Chichester-Petworth road is the great Regency mansion of flint and stone, Goodwood House, seat of the Dukes of Richmond and Gordon, and centre for the famous racecourse. James Wyatt, the architect of Hevening ham and Dodington, designed it in about 1800, with an imposing two-storey neo-Greek columnar portico.

Fishbourne Palace: the largest Roman residence yet found in Britain

Guarding the gap of the river Arun through the Downs and the low-lying lands to the sea, is Arundel Castle, whose picturesque skyline is almost as familiar and impressive as Windsor. For centuries it has been the seat of the Fitzalan Howards, Dukes of Norfolk. When it was first built, soon after the Conquest, its circular stone keep replaced a timber fort of Alfred the Great's time. The keep still survives, together with the Norman Barbican, several towers and parts of the curtain walls, but much of the castle was destroyed by bombardment and plundering by the Cromwellians after a siege of 17 days.

In the eighteenth and early nineteenth centuries it was rebuilt with rich curvilinear tracery in the romantic fourteenth-century style by Robert Abraham. The magnificent Gothic library in mahogany remains from this period, but at the end of the last century much else was rebuilt by C. A. Buckler in the 'purer' and more severe thirteenth-century style that was then considered more appropriate.

Ten miles to the north-east of Chichester is the great ducal palace and treasure-house of Petworth, built after the 'Glorious Revolution' of 1688 by the insufferably pompous sixth Duke of Somerset. It has a gorgeous triumphal staircase hall with its walls and ceiling painted by Laguerre, who did similar work at Hampton Court, and there is a superb room with carved work of breathtaking loveliness by Grinling Gibbons.

A later owner, Lord Egremont, friend of the Prince Regent and patron of artists, filled two rooms with paintings by Turner, who stayed at the house for long periods. William Blake – then living at Felpham, near Bognor, where he wrote 'Jerusalem' – was also invited to stay, but he left the house-party at Petworth after a day or two because he could not stand the sophisticated company.

Chichester Harbour, with its deep sheltered inlets at Bosham, Itchenor, Emsworth and Hayling, is one of the most attractive yachting centres in England. King Canute may not have ordered the tide to retreat at Bosham, but he probably had a palace here, and his little daughter is buried in the delightful church.

The Romans had a settlement at Bosham, but one of their most important palaces in Britain was built about 70 AD at Fishbourne, at the head of the Chichester Channel. Excavations in the 1960s revealed mosaic pavements and remains of walls. The whole large site is now protected by a modern building, and the many objects found are lavishly displayed in a fine museum.

Further inland from Petworth is Bignor, where the remains of a large Roman villa, discovered in 1811, include several Roman pavements of remarkable beauty, though they are less handsomely housed than at Fishbourne. The mosaic pavement with the dark shadowed face of winter is especially moving.

From Petworth westwards the country becomes richly wooded, unlike East Sussex which lost many of its trees to the Sussex iron industry. About five miles north-east of Chichester are Bow Hill and

Kingley Vale, where there is a remarkable forest of yew trees and a nature reserve sheltering many varieties of wild life. It is a ghostly place, said to be the burial-place of Danish warriors.

A delightful drive from Chichester is northwards by A286 and B2141 through the lovely Chilgrove valley and then into the wooded downland, with the still unspoilt villages of East Marden and North Marden, to Harting Hill on the South Downs Way with a fine view-point looking north. Nearby stands Uppark, a large, handsome William and Mary house of red brick, built in about 1690 by William Talman, the architect of Chatsworth. In the eighteenth century it passed to the Featherstonehaugh family. The magnificent rooms display the successive phases of late seventeenth- and eighteenth-century taste.

Sir Harry Featherstonehaugh kept Emma Hart (later Lady Hamilton) here for a while, and in his old age educated and married his young dairymaid. From her surviving sister the house passed eventually to Admiral Meade-Featherstonehaugh. He and his wife arrived at the house in an immense Metallurgique racing car with a 25-litre Zeppelin engine. Many years later Lady Meade celebrated her departure from Uppark no less sensationally by circling the house in an aeroplane the day before she left.

From Uppark you can drop down to South Harting with its charming cottages and one or two good Georgian houses, and the church with its copper-green spire. Then drive east through little-known villages under the Downs – Elsted, Treyford and Bepton to Cocking and back to Chichester by Singleton and West Dean. The past rural world of West Sussex is preserved in the Weald and Downland Open Air Museum at Singleton. Here various ancient buildings have been preserved from destruction and re-erected.

A centre for more modern arts and crafts has been established a little further on at West Dean College, in a castellated Regency mansion designed by James Wyatt in 1804. There are fine Victorian and Edwardian interiors and furniture. It was the home of Edward James, a famous millionaire collector of surrealist pictures.

From the Chichester ring-road turn north-east for two or three miles off the A285 to Halnaker (half-an-acre), which has some interesting medieval and Tudor remains of a manor house, and a modern one by Lutyens. Above on a hill-top is Halnaker mill, a brick tower-mill recently restored. Nearby is Boxgrove Priory, an enchanting place with some monastic remains and a church of which only the chancel remains.

If you are gregarious, there are splendid sandy beaches at West and East Wittering on the coast, and farther east are the holiday resorts of Bognor and Littlehampton, all noisy and crowded in summer, but quiet and delightful in the off-season, and there are still countless enchanting villages in West Sussex, almost unknown, hidden under the Downs, away from the crowds and busy roads.

CLIFFORD MUSGRAVE

Chichester

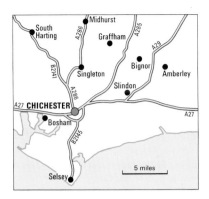

WHERE TO GO

Market Cross: stately compass point for the North, South, East and West central streets.

The Pallants: four charming streets of 18th and 19th c buildings, called North, South, East and West Pallant. Many of the red-brick houses are private homes with exceptionally well-tended gardens, near the town centre but away from the crowds: makes a pleasant walk. At the north-east junction is the Pallant House; in West Pallant the pretty 13th c All Saints' Church.

Chichester District Museum, 29 Little London: situated near the old Roman walls and housed in a former corn store; has a good collection of Chichester relics, from prehistoric to modern times. Also a fine 18th c dolls' house made from old chest of drawers: note the miniature china dishes. Also gallery devoted to collection of Royal Sussex Regiment and varied programme and temporary exhibitions. Museum open April–Sept Tue–Sat 10.00–6.00, Oct–March Tue–Sat 10.00–5.00. Annexe called the Guildhall Museum in Priory Park. Open June–Sept Tue–Sat 1.00–5.00.

Chichester Cathedral: 900 years old with the remains of a Roman floor among all the tombs of marble antiquity. Adjoining the cloisters on the south side is a medieval gatehouse leading to the Bishop's Palace Gardens – formal with flowers and a squat brick tower, then pathways to quiet parkland behind the bustling town. Occasional lunchtime concerts throughout the year. A new exhibition centre with changing shows in one of the arms of the cloisters; nominal admission fee. Brass rubbing during the summer months Mon–Sat 10.00–5.00, and nightly orchestral and choral performances during July festival.

Chichester Festival Theatre: modern building seating 1400 people. High standard of performances and starry casts attract considerable attention. Details from Box Office, Chichester Festival Theatre, Chichester, West Sussex PO19 4AP, tel 781312, telephone bookings accepted. 60 unreserved seats sold on day of performance; plays from May–Sept plus short Christmas season; occasional concerts other months.

Fishbourne Roman Palace: the largest Roman residence yet found in Britain. Ruins spaciously laid out under modern covering with absorbing museum. A visit could take hours: perfect for a rainy day. Open daily March, April and Oct 10.00–5.00, May–Sept 10.00–6.00, Nov 10.00–4.00. Roman herbs and plants for sale in old-palace garden. 1½ miles west of Chichester on A27.

Chichester Harbour: 27 square miles of certified 'outstanding natural beauty'; various sea schools offer sailing courses. For fishermen there's flounder, eel and mullet, for wildlife lovers waders and the occasional porpoise, and miles of coastal paths for enthusiastic walkers. Also, several attractive watering-holes along the way, such as the village of Dell Quay; during the summer months there is an outboard motor ferry connecting Bosham and Itchenor.

Museum of the Corps of Royal Military Police, The Barracks, Broyle Rd:

Cathedral window by Marc Chagall

military memorabilia. Open Mon–Fri 10.30–12.00 and 3.00–6.00, May–Sept also open Sat 2.00–6.00.

EVENTS

Chichester Festivities: special concerts, exhibitions and open-air theatre in and around the Chichester area for a fortnight in July every year.

Tennis: major women's tournament preceding Wimbledon. June. Oakland Park.

Cricket Week: at Priory Park in Aug.

Chichester Cathedral

SHOPPING

Early closing: Thur.
Market day: Wed.
Say Cheese, East St Arcade: over 100 English and Continental cheeses.
Chichester Cathedral Gift Shop: sells unusual items like corn dollies, bottles of English garden scent and scarves with designs from the cathedral. Housed in the ancient bell tower: note seven-foot thick stone walls.
Will Spencer's Cartoon Gallery, 174 Orchard St: former Fleet Street cartoonist now paints his characters on plywood and sells them framed for £4.00 upwards.

FOOD AND DRINK

Egon Ronay's Lucas Guide recommends **Little London**, 38 Little London, tel Chichester 784899, two dining-rooms with imaginative menus, and **Christophers**, 149 St Pancras, tel Chichester 788724, for meals ending with homemade ice cream. In *Just a Bite* Ronay gives star rating to both **Clinch's Salad House**, 14 Southgate, and **St Martin's Tea Rooms**, St Martin's St; also mentions **Alner's**, 14 St Pancras, for meals and snacks. For elegant drinking, **Royal Arms** at Ye Olde Punch House, East St,

aristocratic, wood-panelled, has the feel of a gentlemen's club. **White Horse Inn**, South St, Whitbread pub whose premises in 1416 served as law courts; in 1680 it became a coaching inn. Tunnels lead to the cathedral a few hundred yards away. For serious drinking: the **Eastgate** in Eastgate. Small, unpretentious, with Gales ales and English wines.

WHERE TO STAY

Egon Ronay recommends: **Chichester Lodge**, Westhampnett, tel Chichester 786351, large and excellently equipped bedrooms. **Dolphin & Anchor Hotel**, West St, tel Chichester 785121, once two ancient inns patronized by opposing political factions, now joined by an arch; bedrooms and tiled bathrooms well equipped. Opposite cathedral.
Clinch's Hotel, Guildhall St, tel Chichester 789915: a small family-run hotel, charmingly decorated and serving excellent home-cooked food. In quiet side street near city centre.

TOURIST INFORMATION

In foyer of the lovely Council House, North St. Be sure to visit the mayor's parlour upstairs with its handsome 18th c furniture. Tel Chichester 782226.

Villages and country towns

Amberley

Village built on plateau overlooking the Wild Brooks watermeadows. Castle built as a manor house for the bishops of Chichester, probably in 13th c; little of its history is known. Although privately owned it can be seen from all around the Wild Brooks, the flat flooded land from the river Arun, and is especially striking from Houghton bridge. The church seems part of the castle, but was in fact built the previous century by Bishop de Luffe, who was also responsible for Chichester Cathedral. Blackberries and strawberries grow in the churchyard. In 1877 there were five pubs in the village: now there are two – the friendly Sportsman and the more central Black Horse Inn, which serves bistro meals in charming pocket garden with lily pond and fresh flower baskets.

Amberley has a history of artists – once 15 studios crowded its narrow lanes, and Edward Stott's landscapes and village portraits were often exhibited at the Royal Academy. Now there's the Amberley Fine Arts Centre, housed in an old church. The centre offers courses in painting and photography, with exhibitions throughout the summer. Chalk Pits Museum details local industrial history. Open end May–Oct Wed–Sun 11.00–5.00.

Bignor

Captivating little village near the Roman road – Stane St – which connected London with Chichester. More a hamlet than a village (nearest pub – the White Horse one mile north in Sutton), Bignor's picturesque buildings cluster down steep lanes in an undulating quadrangle. Some houses are thatched, half-timbered; one is medieval with a first-floor overhang. Others look like miniature manor houses with gables and tall mullioned windows. Small 13th c church seems unexpectedly large inside.

Bignor Roman Villa is enclosed in a series of thatched huts. Cows graze almost on top of the Medusa room and baths; the 80ft soft mosaic corridor is particularly impressive. Sit outside with a cream tea and enjoy the spectacular views – heavily wooded downs to one

Bignor's medieval house: note the first-floor overhang

side, rich pasture land to the other. Bignor Park, a 3000-acre private estate with deer, badgers and foxes, is open to the public for select ramblings. Bignor Roman Villa open April–Sept 10.00–6.30, March, Oct 10.00–5.00. Closed Mon except bank hols and during Aug.

Bosham

Pronounced 'Bozzum'. Beauty spot of Chichester Harbour. Closely packed cottages around lovely old quay. A tiny High St with buildings backing on to the harbour and brightly painted sailing boats in front gardens. At the very tip is Quay Meadow, a National Trust grassy field perfect for picnicking and watching the numerous sailing events. It was from this green that King Harold set out on his ill-fated journey to Normandy; a scene from the Bayeux Tapestry shows him praying at Bosham church. The church, built on the site of 7th c monastery, has one of the best Saxon chancel arches in England – simple, graceful with great architectural presence. Beneath it lies the thick coffin of King Canute's daughter; to the right a commemorative tablet with Canute's emblem, the black raven of Denmark. The font is late Norman, with staples inserted by order of the archbishop so witches could not steal the water. On a nearby pillar are ancient graffiti by pilgrims.

Bosham Walk brings together under one roof more than a dozen little shops where craftsmen such as carpenters, weavers and silversmiths can be seen at work. Egon Ronay's *Just a Bite* recommends the Myrtle Tree Coffee Shop for snacks. Drink at the Anchor Bleu public house. Jolly atomosphere, Tamplins bitter. Situated so close to the water as to be precarious as well as picturesque: at high tide the car park is submerged.

Burpham

Village at the end of three-mile cul-de-sac. Lane leading to Burpham now better paved than when Edward Lear called it 'a climax of cart ruts and stones', but this isolated road by the river Arun is still rural and charming. Burpham House is in the soft Sussex colour scheme of red-brick and flint, with manicured gardens and topiary shrubs like chess pieces. Everyone is friendly, helpful, particularly at the Burpham Country Hotel. Angling is the main activity here – permits from the pink George and Dragon.

Its restaurant serves trout, lobster, crab or whatever the local fisherman brings in.

Graffham

Pleasant village on the edge of the South Downs Way. Buchanan of the Black & White whisky family donated the Empire Hall; you can lounge against a grandfather clock and drink his speciality at the 500-year-old Foresters' Arms pub. Also, picturesque White Horse pub.

At the top of the hill lies Graffham church with a commanding view of the valley and smoky-blue hills. Behind the church, road peters out to a dirt track leading to the great hanging woods of the Downs. It is serene and secluded, the only sound that of birds chirping.

Petworth House: has one of England's finest private art collections

Midhurst

Large industrious community but with strong 'village' appeal: a town to picnic in. The Spinning Wheel in North St has good bread and there's a delicatessen practically next door, or try the smaller one in West St for delicious chunks of ham cooked in Chablis. Lots of greengrocers for fruit, off-licences for Chilsdown wine and two picturesque butchers side by side on West St. S. Turner and Sons have china pigs set in the handsome bow windows; Michael Blakiston comes from three generations of butchers and will point out an old family photo not far from the plucked chickens.

Almost all shops 18th c; the intriguingly named Knockhundred Row with antique stores and fresh flowers a very pretty example. *Egon Ronay's Lucas Guide* recommends Knockers bistro for unusual international dishes prepared with skill. Be sure to note the antique toyshop nearby with its enormous working model of a 1928 locomotive.

In South St the Spread Eagle, an old coaching inn, dates back to 1430. The Greyhound Inn, Cocking Causeway, a genuine country pub, with low ceiling and two open log fires, serves Gales beer; so does the Angel, North St.

Cowdray House was begun in the 1490s but caught fire 300 years later, and was reduced to the stately façade which still remains. Skeleton windows frame sky and trees from the other side of the house; some rooms are intact enough to be recognizable and disconcerting, such as the hexagonal kitchen with surviving iron hotplates. A burnt-out altarpiece marks the chapel where an 18th c family scandal occurred: the fifth Viscount Montague shot a priest for beginning mass without him. It's said the Viscount then hid away in a secret chamber, venturing out only at night to be mistaken for a ghost.

Cowdray Park polo matches most weekends from April–Sept; daily during Goodwood Week.

Selsey

Holiday village at the tip of Selsey peninsula. Water on three sides, graced with clean air, high sunshine rate and good beaches. There's hand-baked bread at the Oven Bakery. dressed crab and lobster at the Fisheries; or ask a local fisherman at one of the numerous pubs for some of his daily catch. Best pub is the Lifeboat Inn, standing in the shadow of the real thing – boathouse open every day – with a large garden, Tamplins beer and only 100 yards from the sea. Also on the sea is the Thatched House Hotel Restaurant, recommended for seafood by *Egon Ronay's Lucas Guide.* You can charter a fishing trip at Raycraft's on the High St or take advantage of the nine-hole course at Selsey Golf Club.

Christianity arrived here as early as 681 AD; the site of the old cathedral is two miles north at Church Norton, now covered by Selsey Bill. Legend has it the bells can still be heard ringing under the waters during a sea-storm. Brent geese and ringed plovers inhabit the surrounding mudflats, courtesy of the Pagham Nature Reserve; plants include cord grass and seablite.

Singleton

Tiny, unspoilt village on the hairpin bend of a major road. Downland hills rise behind the mainly Saxon church; in the interior is much Sussex marble, made of periwinkle seashells. Mentioned in Domesday Book, Singleton came into great prominence when Goodwood racecourse was opened in 1801. The Prince of Wales (Edward VII) kept his horses in the village stables (now Pearmans garage); the rector complained bitterly about the shocking behaviour during race week evenings. There's a bowling green at the Horse and Groom; the Fox and Hounds tucked near the church has rustic pegged tables in a pleasant side garden. Buy a glass of local Chilsdown wine here, or a bottle at the 13-acre vineyard overlooking the village. Vineyard's headquarters is an old railway station – winepress in the booking hall. Vineyard open Aug–Sept Sun plus bank hols 2.00–5.00. Parties of 20 can book for a tour.

The Weald and Downland Open Air Museum is on a 40-acre site. Ancient buildings re-erected here include 14th c house; 15th–16th c farmhouse; blacksmith's forge; wheelwright's shop; also, charcoal burners' settlement with turf hut. An old lady who spent her childhood in such a hut advised on the details. Occasional craft demonstrations. Open daily April–Sept 11.00–6.00, except Mon but including bank hols, and Mons in July and Aug; Oct Wed, Sat, Sun, 11.00–5.00; Nov–March Sun only 11.00–4.00.

South Harting

Village at the foot of the Downs – South Downs Way begins just to the west. Large 14th c church is built on a small mound, angled towards the road so that it is in full view of anyone entering or leaving the village. Just outside church walls are ancient stocks and whipping posts; inside under a soaring Elizabethan roof is a glass case containing the pen, letter scales and paperknife of Anthony Trollope, who lived for two years in the white-painted Northend House – on the left-hand side of the road beyond junction. Bertrand Russell ran a progressive coeducational school in the old Telegraph House near Harting Hill. Lots of pubs for such a tiny place: the Coach and Horses has real ales such as Fullers ESB and Badger Best, there is a Watneys pub called the Ship standing at the junction and – halfway between – the sophisticated White Hart Inn, two bars, large fireplace and serving excellent food with great charm.

Slindon

'Horsey' village dramatically sited on a slope of the Downs. Most buildings are 17th and 18th c brick and flint. In the heart of the village is tiny Slindon Pottery, creeper-covered and overlooking a cattle field. Hilaire Belloc lived in Court Hill Farmhouse; another farmhouse called Well House is the oldest building in the village – it was added to in 1654. Somewhere in the depths of the well lie the remains of the last smuggler to be hanged on Slindon Common. At the point the roads converge stands an ancient lime tree, a tree of idleness encircled by a bench. Not far is the Newburgh Arms serving meals and King & Barnes beer. Slindon Church is basically 12th c with a Victorian tower. In the south chapel is a wooden effigy of a remarkably short knight, thought to be Sir Anthony St Leger who died in 1539. Although Mill Lane with its Mill Cottage and Mill House doesn't lead to a mill, there is a pretty pond near The Grange.

A thick stone wall leads to the gates of Slindon House, a stately 16th c mansion with ancient tower, in 3000 acres of National Trust farm and estate land. Once used to store fertilizer from a nearby farm, it is now a boy's public school. Nore Folly, erected at the whim of one of the owners of Slindon House for shooting parties, is half a mile northwest. With splendid views across the Downs to the sea, folly is now a great flint archway beside the crumbling ruins of a summerhouse.

Places to visit

Goodwood House: home of Dukes of Richmond since 1697, originally planned in the shape of an octagon; money ran out before construction could be completed, hence its rather unusual shape. Fine collection of Van Dycks and Canalettos, and a Kneller portrait of Louise de Kerouaille, sent by Louis XIV to spy on King Charles II and ending up the Duchess of Portsmouth. 'Glorious Goodwood' horse races usually held from last Tue in July to following Sat. For a small charge you can watch from the Trundle, a rounded hill and former Iron Age capital city. Goodwood House open May–Oct Sun, Mon 2.00–5.00 (also Tue in Aug) not events days. Tel Chichester 527107. Signposted off A286.

Uppark: red-brick house now owned by National Trust; situated on top of a hill so steep the Duke of Wellington refused its offer because of the constant strain on his horses. Contains red drawing-room with Chippendale furniture and a Queen Anne dolls' house. Open April–Sept Wed, Thur, Sun, Bank Hol Mon 2.00–6.00. $1\frac{1}{2}$ miles south of South Harting on B2146.

Petworth: overlooking beautiful parkland, this late 17th c home contains one of the finest private art collections in England; many Turners – a fine example in the White Library started by Henry, the 'Wizard Earl' of Uppark, named so for his interest in alchemy. The delightfully named 'Pleasure Grounds' where Turner used to paint and fish is lovely cultivated landscape with many fine tree specimens. National Trust. Open April–Oct daily except Mon, Fri, 2.00–

6.00. Open Bank Hol Mon, closed following Tue. On Tue two extra rooms are open. 400 acre deer park always open. Junction of A285 and A272.

Parham: Elizabethan house which once belonged to the Abbey of Westminster. The great hall is flooded with light from tall mullioned windows, displaying to advantage the Tudor portraits and original carved oak screen. The long gallery stretching the length of the house measures 160ft and contains many interesting items such as a Roman lead cistern. Fine examples of needlework and tapestries; upstairs on a four-poster bed there is a monogrammed bedcover thought to have been made for Mary Queen of Scots. Surrounding the house is a huge park of oak trees and grazing deer. Open Easter–Oct Sun, Wed, Thur, and Bank Hol Mon 2.00–5.30. Garden 1.00–6.00. Off A283.

West Dean College and Gardens: gardens have been a part of West Dean since Jacobean times; there are now 30 acres of informal design including massive cedars, ginkgo trees, a gazebo and a 300ft pergola draped with roses and climbing plants. The flint-faced mansion (not open to visitors) operates as an independent adult college for crafts, where courses are available on everything from upholstery to Chinese brush painting. Gardens open April–Sept Mon–Fri 1.00–6.00, Sun 2.00–7.00. Details about craft courses from: West Dean College, West Dean, near Chichester, West Sussex PO18 0QZ, tel Singleton 301. Off A286.

Halnaker Mill: prominent landmark with sails restored, immortalized in a poem by Hilaire Belloc. 1½-mile walk from A285.

Kingley Vale National Nature Reserve: 361-acre site primarily established to maintain what has been described as the finest natural yew forest in Europe, some speciments possibly 500 years old. Over 70 species of birds have been spotted. Foxes and roe deer roam through Bronze Age burial mounds found on the site; weasels and badgers enjoy good hunting grounds. Car park near the village of West Stoke, off B2178.

South Downs Way: this 80-mile trail from Beachy Head to the borders of Hampshire can be traversed only on foot or on horseback. Follows the folds of the Downs, offering stupendous views across rolling countryside all the way to the Isle of Wight. Oak signs point the way, rabbits and foxes are common and most parts of pathway are within easy reach of a quaint hamlet for replenishing picnic supplies. Ordnance Survey maps 197–9 are best. Wear good shoes; sharp flints about. Near the village of Washington, the Way passes Chanctonbury Ring with its view of Cissbury Ring further south. These trees stand distinctively against the skyline and even in daylight are a little spooky; cattle graze around them but few seem to venture into the gnarled, leafy depths.

Arundel: everyone's fairytale town, a castle perched on top of a hill, shops snaking up crooked lanes, cream-tea gardens and Swanbourne Lake. There's a toy museum, a wildfowl refuge and Arundel Festival last week in Aug with Shakespeare in the castle grounds. Details from Tourist Information Office, 61 High St, Arundel, tel Arundel 882268.

Museum of Curiosity, 6 High St, Arundel: this collection of over 2000 stuffed birds and animals is housed in a Victorian building where claustrophobic atmosphere is as important as the animals themselves. Started in 1861 by Walter Potter, a self-taught naturalist and taxidermist. In high glass cases stuffed guinea pigs play cricket, and kittens in costume exchange wedding rings. Opening times vary, tel Arundel 882420.

The National Butterfly Museum, Bramber: a large and unusual private collection, housed in a 15th c building called St Mary's, which has lovely panelled rooms and was once an escape route to Bramber Castle. The Victorian addition contains butterflies from all over the world – some live, some mounted and displayed according to their natural habitat. Open daily (except Christmas and Boxing Day) 10.00–5.00.

ACTIVITIES

Steeplechasing: at Fontwell Racecourse. Arundel–Chichester road A27.
Pick your own fruit: watch for signs on the smaller roads. Hale's Barn Farm near Fontwell allows seasonal picking.

Chanctonbury Ring: near Washington on the South Downs Way

FOOD AND DRINK

Egon Ronay's Lucas Guide recommends **Three Musketeers**, Hayling Island, tel Hayling Island 3226. French dishes. **White Horse Inn**, Chilgrove, tel East Marden 219. Finely balanced cooking and good wine list. **Paddington's Table**, Petworth, tel Petworth 43149. Beautifully cooked international dishes. **Paragon**, Worthing, tel Worthing 33367. Small and intimate, mainly Italian.

TOURIST INFORMATION

Local papers: the *Chichester Observer* and the *Midhurst & Petworth Observer* newspapers both have regular entertainments page. Published weekly on Fri.
Tourist information offices: at Worthing, Arundel, Littlehampton, Bognor Regis, Portsmouth.

Research: Martha Ellen Zenfell.

Rye

'But where is the sea?' could well be the cry of someone visiting Rye, who knows that it was one of the two Ancient Towns, added in the fourteenth century to the Cinque Ports. A full two miles away is the answer: across a flat expanse of shingle and silt which has steadily accumulated over the past 500 or 600 years until it fills what was once a fine natural harbour.

In 1377 the French were able to sail right up to Rye, burn to the ground every timber building and capture its complete peal of church bells. Seventeenth-century illustrations show water close below its cliffs, though shallow by then. As late as 1823 the Town Salts, once used to extract salt from the sea by evaporation, were still sometimes under water. Today they are a children's playground. Past them the river Rother makes its gentle way to a Channel which is often out of sight in the mist.

The winds and tides that have brought such disaster to Rye as a port and spoilt its chance of ever becoming a seaside resort have been the greatest good fortune for today's visitor. Rye has been preserved as little more than a large village, with a population of about 5000. At the same time it has kept that flavour of salty realism which saves it from being a museum – witness the row of 20 to 30 fishing boats tied up on the Rother's bank, in full view of its fortified gateway.

They cast their happy influence over the whole town. The men who walk the streets in Aran sweaters and turned-down wellingtons are not all weekend yachtsmen: many are working fishermen. Shops sell oil-skins, masthead lamps and coils of hawser meant for storms at sea. The fishmongers offer whiting and flounders fresh from the Channel; down by the boats a stall, which specializes in scallops in season, has fish even fresher.

The one surviving medieval gateway, known as the Landgate, is a good place to start to explore Rye. The sharp drop to the left tells vividly of its seaside past. Here a sloping hillside was the site of another defensive gateway and an Augustine friary until the sea washed all away.

A short walk up into the town and you begin to realize that Rye has had a further stroke of luck. Miraculously – no one seems to know how, but perhaps its hilltop position helped – it has been preserved from the developers. Everywhere are complete terraces of houses any one of which would be a landmark in a less fortunate town. The narrowness of its cobbled alleys is even more important in preserving Rye as a strangely wonderful survival from the past. Here the explanation is

Mermaid Street, Rye: on the right is the Mermaid Inn – one time haunt of the Hawkhurst smuggling gang said to have numbered 600

that many a Georgian façade stands above the original medieval foundations.

The Flushing Inn is typical. The elegant dining-room covers a cellar which predates the French destruction. It was once used by Rye's notorious smugglers who hauled their contraband up the sloping cliff from the beach, which at that time lay immediately below.

In a town of Rye's architectural richness, the town hall itself, a respectable brick building with Portland stone dressings, is overshadowed by the much earlier old grammar school. Founded in 1636 by Thomas Peacocke and left to the town when he died, a school until 1908, it now sells dinky china cottages to Rye's swarming summer visitors, but its façade is as fine as ever.

A hundred yards above at the corner of West Street stands the house of Mayor Lamb, much later to be Henry James's residence. This is now the property of the National Trust and contains an elegant panelled room where his library is being re-collected, but sadly the detached garden room where he worked was destroyed by a bomb in 1940.

James could look directly from his front windows up yet another cobbled alley to Rye Church. This impressively large building dominates the town. Broad and solid, with diminutive slate steeple, it crowns the hilltop from whatever direction you look. Below it the houses cluster with the complex haphazardness of a hill-town in Tuscany. Its ancient clock is its showpiece, with 400-year-old mechanism, quarterboys which strike the quarters (but not the hours) and 18ft gilded pendulum swinging above the heads of the congregation in the church below.

Close by the churchyard is a true curiosity: an oval eighteenth-century brick water-cistern, no longer a functioning part of the town's water supply in these days of the water-closet. A little beyond, Ypres Tower (Wipers, to the natives, despite Rye's many families descended from Huguenot refugees) now houses the town's museum. How delightfully manageable are local museums, and Rye's is as good an example as you will find. Here are the uniforms of local regiments, examples of Rye pottery through the ages (it is still a flourishing trade)

Rye: no longer a port, the town is linked to the sea by the river Rother

and the town's old hand-operated fire engine – proof, if any were needed, of the insecurity of life in the nineteenth century.

From the museum's elevated terrace there is one of Rye's finest views. To the east the coast reaches away as far as the cliffs of Dover. To the west stands Winchelsea on its rival hill top. In between, low and squat on the marshes, is Camber Castle, set there by Henry VIII as a defence work, long abandoned by the coast it was meant to guard. Directly ahead the full extent of the filled bay can be seen, and the way sea walls still keep out flood tides. Closer, where Rye's second river, the Brede, joins the Rother, are the yards where Rye's great sailing barges were once built and modern glass fibre designs are now in busy production.

West from the church run the two cobbled streets which above all create Rye's medieval image. Halfway down Mermaid Street stands the famous Mermaid Inn, one-time haunt of the Hawkhurst smuggling gang, said to have numbered 600, where you may drink peacefully today surrounded by an almost overpowering wealth of old oak. It is only one of several dozen buildings of charm and distinction which this street and its neighbour Watchbell Street contain. The old hospital, with high overhanging gables, is especially splendid.

A sharp descent at the end of Mermaid Street leads abruptly to a scene which seems a hundred miles from the medieval alleys and Georgian houses above. Here a cluster of huge warehouses in black weatherboarding and blackened brick stands close to what was once a busy quay. Boats from here came and went not only up the Brede to Broad Oak, and up the Rother to the extensive waterway system above including the Kent Ditch and the Royal Military Canal, but downriver to coastal ports and beyond. One strange cargo was blue flints from the Rother's mouth for Liverpool and the Potteries, where they were ground up for china. Today the warehouses hover between disuse and a new life as garden supply stores and antique emporia.

The charms of Rye are so extensive that the surrounding villages seem almost gratuitous, but Rye itself will not be understood without a visit to Rye Harbour, a little separate village which has grown up beside the Rother halfway to the sea. Inland from Rye, where the country is strangely hilly, divided by deep valleys, the little villages of Brede and Udimore are especially worth a visit, with their white weatherboard cottages, each with a church set almost in a farmyard. So too is Northiam's Great Dixter, a fine example of the use made by local builders of the oak forests which once covered the county. Not far from Northiam, Bodiam Castle rivals for preservation and rustic setting any in the country. In its unspoilt valley it stands with virtually untouched towers and outer walls surrounded by a full moat, while the Kent Ditch passes a field below. It was probably built to prevent an up-river invasion from France and provides impressive evidence of the days when Rye was one of the country's principal ports of entry.

THOMAS HINDE

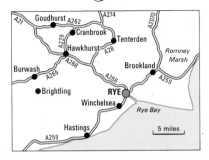

Rye

WHERE TO GO

High St: full of charming buildings. As well as 17th c grammar school, don't miss Georgian Midland Bank, curving window of old apothecary's shop and splendid butchers, Ashbee, which has elaborate wooden canopy in front of the shop with hooks for joints.

Ypres Tower and Museum: oldest structure in town, built 1249 as defence against French, later prison, now town museum. Open Easter–mid-Oct 10.30–1.00 (Sun from 11.30), 2.15–5.30.

Lamb House, West St: Henry James lived here 1899–1914, dictated late novels to secretary in garden room. Garden, hall, two ground-floor rooms with James portraits, books, etc. National Trust. Open April–Oct, Wed and Sat 2.00–6.00.

St Mary's Church: Norman transept, 15th c tower, pretty stained glass (Pevsner says it's sentimental) by Morris and Co.

Rye Pottery: Rye has always been a potting town: this one (est 1850) in Ferry Rd specializes in decorative, commemorative ware. Also makes striped and flowered cups and plates and traditional Sussex pig – head comes off to make cup, body makes jug. See craftsmen as they work. Other potteries include Cinque Ports Pottery, Conduit Hill; David Sharp, Ferry Rd, Iden Pottery and Gopsall – housed in fine windmill in Ferry Rd.

Rye Art Gallery, Ockman's Lane: permanent contemporary collection plus interesting peripatetic shows. Eastern Rooms – linked to main gallery and entrance 107 High St – show and sell enterprising choice of work by young artists, printers, craftsmen.

Model Son et Lumière: eight shows about Rye history, daily in Centre Building, Rye Market. Open spring bank hol–mid-Sept, Mon–Sat.

Rye Festival: early Sept, with special events for children.

SHOPPING

Market day: Thur (cattle market Wed).

Early closing: Tue.

Millers Food Specialists, 92 High St and **The Gate House,** Tower St: both specialize in delicatessen.

Old Tuck Shop, Market St: bread still baked in 1750 brick oven.

Strand Antiques Market, The Strand: excellent hunting ground for modest finds, housed in odd and pretty Georgian building. Also, several good antique shops in centre of town.

Ironmongers Extraordinary, 1 High St: very special kitchen shop, three inter-communicating rooms of an 18th c ironmongers bursting with all sorts of desirable objects – baskets full of clothespegs, wooden spoons, excellent knives, French coffee cups, etc. Everything well designed in mostly traditional shapes and materials. Worth visiting Rye for.

Tower Forge Cottage Industry Centre, by Land Gate: enterprising craft shop – tries hard to sell only original, well-made objects, by craftsmen from all over the country, not just locals. Look for: pretty patchwork bedspreads, bags, cushions etc, and disconcerting dolls, with faces and hands made from cured apples – an American custom.

FOOD AND DRINK

Egon Ronay's *Just a Bite* suggests **Simon the Pieman** and **Fletchers,** both in Lion St, or **Gate House** in Tower St.

Pubs include: **Mermaid Inn,** Mermaid St: American tourists have replaced smugglers, pressgangs and highwaymen here. In spite of oak-panelled quaintness, it has a friendly unforced feeling. Huge fireplace with spits, cauldrons, log fire, plus collection of strange carved chairs. Harveys beer. **Union,** East St: very small cosy pub with shove ha'penny and two football teams. Homemade lunches and Youngs beer. **Ypres Castle,** Gun Garden: tucked away near Ypres Tower. Big garden with views over marshes, children's rooms, darts, serves Whitbread Faversham Trophy.

WHERE TO STAY

Egon Ronay's *Lucas Guide* recommends: **Hope Anchor Hotel,** Watchbell St, tel Rye 2216. Small and cheerful **Mermaid Inn,** Mermaid St, tel Rye 3065, four-poster beds, antiques, friendly atmosphere.

TOURIST INFORMATION

In summer, Regent Cinema, Cinque Port St, tel Rye 2293/4; in winter Council Offices, Ferry Rd, same tel no.

Rye pottery: the traditional Sussex pig

Villages and country towns

Brightling

Was home of a great Regency eccentric, Mad Jack Fuller, who indelibly stamped his personality on landscape. A lovely little village on the top of hill with low golden stone church, tall beech trees, views over rolling valleys; Fuller has given it extra spice of strangeness. In churchyard is his mausoleum: a huge stone pyramid, covered with lichen and grass. Legend has it he is buried inside sitting at a table wearing a top hat and holding a bottle of claret. He decorated his estate with follies, including a sugar loaf at Dallington with conical spire – built to win a wager that Dallington church spire could be seen from his windows – an obelisk 60ft high, a rotunda and a curious observatory designed by Sir Robert Smirke. You can walk across the fields to sugar loaf and peer over gate at observatory, but others now have to be admired from a distance.

In church is a monument to Fuller: its inscription is distinctly cool, but he was a man of many talents, interested in science, music and painting (patron of Turner), obstreperous MP and saviour of Bodiam Castle which he bought to stop it being pulled down. Other good monuments include several baroque ones with skulls, scrolls and weeping putti. Over churchyard wall you can see Fuller's fine late 17th c house, still imposing though much demolished.

Down hill towards Robertsbridge a real discovery of a country pub: the Fuller's Arms. Recently revamped but retaining its intimacy, it is a free house, selling Youngs beer and Bob Luck's vintage cider – 'dark and deadly'; bar billiards and darts. Delicious food – everything home-made: excellent steak and kidney pies, crab tart and luscious puddings. Evening menu grander and more cosmopolitan. Important to telephone the day before to order main course. Brightling 212. (Closed Mon.)

Brookland

Contains one of the most beautiful of famous Romney Marsh churches, lovely Norman and early English buildings silhouetted against the sky in flat landscape, and mostly untouched by Victorian re-

storers. Unusually, belfry detached from the church made entirely of wood and shaped like three candle-snuffers stacked on top of each other – huge timbers are said to come from wrecked ships. Inside wide 13th c church are box pews and a tithe-pen, wooden enclosure where parson weighed out grain, wool, etc, contributed by parishioners. 18th c weights still there. Fascinating Norman lead font decorated with signs of zodiac and labours of months – vine-pruning for March, hawking for May, pig-killing for December. In 1960s a medieval painting of Thomas à Becket's murder was uncovered on wall of south aisle.

Brookland has a pleasant old pub, the Royal Oak.

From here all the other Romney Marsh churches are in easy reach: **Ivychurch** St George, 1360–70, very uniform, has a fortified air, castellated porch and lookout post on the tower against French raiders. Later, smugglers filled vaults below with coffins full of contraband. Inside no pews or chairs – instead a marvellous sense of space and light. **Old Romney** St Clement: big yew stands beside this lonely 13th c church with sturdy tower. Charming interior with a brick floor, pink box pews and minstrels' galley. **New Romney** grand 12th c church with massive tower, outside great variety of Norman decoration, windows and arcading. Locked except 11.00–12.00 and 2.00–3.00. **Lydd** All Saints, 'the cathedral of the marshes'.

Tall, beautiful 15th c tower built by a senior mason of Canterbury Cathedral, beautifully proportioned. Key in nearby shop if locked. **Newchurch, Snargate, Snave** and **Fairfield** churches are worth detours. All have oval text-boards characteristic of the area. The Red Lion in Snargate, which serves Shepherd Neame from the barrel, makes a refreshing stop between churches.

Burwash

Small village not to be missed on your way to Bateman's (see Places to Visit). Built on a ridge, it has long wide High St with pollarded trees. Some particularly lovely houses – with glimpses in between of the deep vale below, site of medieval

Mausoleum of Regency eccentric Mad Jack Fuller at Brightling

iron-smelting. Grandest house is red and grey chequered 17th c 'Rampyndene', high-roofed and tall-chimneyed, a frieze running round above the handsome hooded doorway, carved with birds and a cherub's head.

On the other side of the road, a tempting antique and secondhand bookshop, Lime Tree Antiques, and an impressive little gallery, the Burwash, which shows and sells paintings and prints of real merit, especially wild life and landscapes.

From the churchyard of St Bartholomew's (with Norman tower) another splendid view over the valleys. Nearby, war memorial where a villager lights the lamp on top as a remembrance on the birthday of every Burwash man killed in

First World War. Kipling's son is named on it.

The Bell, charming old-fashioned pub, serves real ale – mulled if it's cold weather. Recommended in *Egon Ronay's Raleigh Pub Guide* for food cooked to order and superb stilton.

Cranbrook

Gentle Kent town on slopes of diminutive river Crane. Two main streets, High St and Stone St, meet in an L-shape by church. Hilly Stone St is the more interesting walk. A few yards down a turning on the right, don't miss seven-sided Providence Chapel (1828), one of England's first prefabricated buildings. You can't miss the 1814 Union Mill, lofty white tower and sails high above the rooftops, fully restored, but electric motors are used to grind corn. Visitors can wander round inside and climb dusty steps to top.

Wealthy medieval centre of the wool trade, Cranbrook has moved quietly on into 20th c without losing charm. Useful centre for everyday shopping, including a secondhand bookshop in Stone St near mill and an excellent stationers. Early closing Wed. Also one of the few cinemas in area, the Regal. Lots of pubs. For real-ale enthusiasts, Duke of York, in High St (Shepherd Neame) and Prince of Wales (free house); the Willesley Hotel, early 'aesthetic' renovation by Norman Shaw, serves lunches and dinners; and Elizabeth I stayed the night at the 16th c timbered George. Local museum in Rectory Cottages tells more of the history. Open Wed, Sat 2.30–4.30.

Lastly, lovely golden St Dunstan's church is called 'the cathedral of the Weald'. Inside, a curious chilly-looking font for total immersion installed by unsuccessful rector who hoped to win back the Baptists to his fold, and four fascinating carved wooden bosses *c* 1300 – 'Green Men' heads entwined with leaves and branches symbolizing man's link with nature. Tourist and Craft Information Office during summer months at Vestry Hall, Stone St.

Goudhurst

Lovely village set on a steep hill with a round pond at the bottom complete with thatched shelter for ducks, geese and swans. Attractive weatherboarded and tile-hung houses on narrow pavements climb stepwise to the top. Then High St twists suddenly out of sight leaving the church, with squat tower and topiary yew arch, looking down over village. Church was scene of last stand by notorious 18th c Hawkhurst smugglers' gang – routed by the Goudhurst militia. Leader Richard Kingsmill was hanged on Horsmonden Heath. 1930s petrol station blends in beautifully instead of being the usual eyesore. Village shop sells delicatessen-type food, basketware and commemorative Goudhurst mugs. A couple of tea-rooms and good supply of pubs: the Eight Bells is the village local; the Vine, a bit grander, also serves food; and the Star & Eagle was once a smuggler's den, joined to the church by a tunnel.

The Union Mill, Cranbrook, built in 1814

Tenterden

Lovely Weald town with long wide High St fringed by trees and grass verges. An air of continuing prosperity: all is beautifully cared for – weatherboarding fresh and white. See how some 18th c houses are hung with mathematical tiles to look like fashionable brick but avoid brick tax. Church of St Mildred has high handsome pinnacled tower: tradition claims a beacon was lit on top during Spanish Armada. Inside, fine Jacobean monument to local gentry, Herbert and Martha Whitfield, kneeling demurely at a prie-dieu.

Excellent shopping centre: the Gourmet's Pantry at 100 High St specializes in the odd combination of locally caught Rye Bay fish and wholesome home-made cakes, pies and jams. Early closing Wed. Good general market on Fri.

Also a small town museum with special section devoted to Col Stephen's collection of early railway relics, open Easter–Oct daily 2.00–5.00, Sat 10.00–5.00. At Town Station enthusiasts have restored first four miles of Kent and East Sussex Railway. Trains run Wittersham and back, Easter–Dec mainly weekends and bank hols, mid-July–end Aug daily. Send sae for details or tel Tenterden 2943.

Plenty of pubs: the Vine, near railway, and White Lion Hotel both serve Shepherd Neame; the oldest-looking, Eight Bells, has an ostler's bell still hanging in the yard; and the Caxton Inn is so called because of Tenterden's doubtful claim that William Caxton was born there. Tourist office in town hall has information on local events and accommodation.

Winchelsea

Laid out in 13th c on a regular chequerboard pattern, it was to be a considerable size. North and south gates still stand nearly a mile apart. Designed as HQ of the thriving wine trade with Gascony, so the buildings had great vaulted wine cellars. Many still exist beneath houses rebuilt in later centuries, and some are under surrounding fields. You can see one at a house called Manna Plat in Mill Rd, also an art gallery and 'refection' – an old word, say the owners, for 'a small repast, food for mind and body'. Splendid cellar, vaulted with stone from Caen in Normandy. Open March–end Oct.

Winchelsea harbour silted up and of 39 blocks planned only 12 were built. Today, though formal plan remains, little external sign of medieval beginnings: exceptions are 14th c Court Hall in High St, Armoury in Castle St and three stone gatehouses. New Gate is now far from the town, alone in a field. But all the houses solidly handsome – look out for a fine 18th c white weatherboarded group in German St. Everything pleasant and prosperous-looking and perhaps a little too neat. Rich and elegant church, St Thomas, has elaborate early 14th c monuments to Alard family, for generations Admirals of the Cinque Ports. Local town museum is in the Court Hall. Open May–Sept 10.30–12.30 and 2.30–5.30, Sun 2.30–5.30.

From Strand Gate you can look out over the marshes and see ruined Camber Castle, built for Henry VIII.

Very few shops; obviously locals stock up in Rye except in emergencies. The New Inn, overlooking churchyard, serves coffee, tea and meals as well as Courage ales. Has an old-fashioned, friendly atmosphere, labradors and log fires.

Places to visit

Bodiam Castle: fairytale castle reflected in a wide moat. Built 1386 to withstand French; towers and drawbridges never put to test, but by 18th c the interior was in ruins. Lord Curzon bought and restored it in 1916. Interesting little museum near the castle with prints and pictures illustrating its history, many relics found during Curzon's excavations and model of the castle in its prime. National Trust. Open April–Oct daily 10.00–7.00, Nov–March Mon–Sat 10.00–sunset. Three miles south of Hawkhurst, one mile east of A229.

Battle Abbey: on site of 1066 and all that. William vowed to build abbey if he won the day. Nothing now remains of original. Mighty castellated gate house *c* 1340 towers over Battle that grew up around it. Beyond it, the abbot's house – now private – and a walk that leads along the twin-turreted upper terrace where Harold's men would have lined up facing Normans in the lush fields below, and through the magnificent ruins of the early 14th c Benedictine abbey. See splendid dorter (monks' dormitory) with lancet windows and elegant vaulted ceilings in the Monks' Common Room. Open all year, May–Sept daily 9.30–7.00, April daily 9.30–5.30, March, Oct weekdays 9.30–5.30 Sun 2.00–5.30, Nov–Feb weekdays 9.30–4.00 Sun 2.00–4.00. Battle High St (A2100).

Sissinghurst Castle Garden: the fame of this lovely garden and of its creators Vita Sackville-West and Harold Nicolson has recently become almost too much for it. Intimate scale, division into small 'outdoor rooms', narrow paths between planting make it unsuitable for crowds who come to admire old roses, white garden, etc. Avoid Sun and bank hol. V. Sackville-West's study in tower of ruined Elizabethan house and long

Bodiam Castle: 14th-century fairytale castle built to withstand the French

library also open. National Trust. Open April–mid Oct, Mon–Fri 12.00–6.30, Sat, Sun, bank hol 10.00–6.30. Two miles north-east of Cranbrook, one mile east of Sissinghurst village.

Bateman's: Kipling's home till his death 1936. Fine stone Jacobean country house – rooms are dotted with mementoes of Kipling's time in the East. Study just as he left it. Beautiful garden, partly designed by Kipling, with elegant square pool, simple lawns and straight yew hedges. At the bottom a little trout stream and Bateman's Park Mill, fully restored and working. National Trust. Open June–Sept Mon–Thur 11.00–6.00, Sat, Sun 2.00–6.00, March, April, May and Oct 2.00–6.00 daily except Fri. Tearoom and gift shop in adjoining oast house. Half a mile south of Burwash on A265.

Smallhythe Place: delightful 15th c timbered museum dedicated to Ellen Terry – for 30 years her home. Five rooms full of theatrical souvenirs and treasures of her career, including jewelled silk and satin costumes. Her bedroom, kept just as she lived in it, the most simple and charming room of all. National Trust. Open March–Oct daily except Tue and Fri 2.00–6.00 or dusk if earlier. One mile south of Tenterden on B2082.

Scotney Castle Garden: one of most romantic man-made landscapes in England. Ruined moated castle is focal point. Fine trees, cedars and cypresses, azaleas and rhododendrons, lily-covered moat, lush waterside vegetation. Early in 19th c Hussey family built house – not open to public – designed by Salvin on summit of ridge overlooking old castle and turned into masterpiece of picturesque. National Trust. Garden open Wed–Sun and Bank Hol Mon May–Sept 2.00–6.00, April and Oct 2.00–5.00. 1½ miles southeast of Lamberhurst on A21.

Great Dixter: 15th c half-timbered manor with great hall enlarged and renovated by Lutyens, who also designed very beautiful gardens. Yew hedges, topiary, lily pond, sunken garden, lots of climbers, unexpected flowers and shrubs – almost overgrown abundance. Planting inspiration for any gardener. In front of house, long grass dotted with wild orchids, fritillaries, daisies – a Botticelli meadow. Nursery specializing in clematis, plus big selection of unusual plants. Open April–mid Oct daily 2.00–5.00 except Mon (open bank hol). Half a mile north of Northiam.

Finchcocks: a gawkily handsome early 18th c country house near Goudhurst where Richard Burnett keeps his huge collection of clavichords, harpsichords, spinets, early pianos etc. Also centre for making, restoring and studying early instruments. Open days are far more than just a chance to look round house and collection – musicians play the instruments, explain their history, dash off musical jokes, answer questions. All very informal and great fun. Also a special exhibition with working models, a shop and tea-room with home-made cakes and licensed restaurant. Open days May–mid-July and Sept Sun, mid-July–Aug Wed–Sun. Parties and groups other days by appointment. Evening concerts, details Goudhurst 211702.

Folk Museum: everything an East Sussex farmer and his wife would have used from 19th c to Second World War in Mrs Townsend's private collection. Complete farm kitchen, dairy, laundry and every sort of agricultural implement. By appointment only. One mile outside Rye at The Cherries, Playden, tel Rye 3224.

Baby Carriage Collection: perambulator enthusiast and authority Jack Hampshire has over 350 baby carriages tucked into every nook and cranny of his home at Bettenham Manor – largest collection in world. Earliest exhibit 1750. Shapes range from homely round and chubby to high-hooded and elegant. By appointment only. Bettenham Manor, Biddenden, Kent TN27 8LT, tel Biddenden 291343.

Bedgebury Pinetum: 100 acres of undulating country where you can see just about every type of pine and conifer. Established 1924, when it was decided that the pines at Kew needed some fresher air. The fir-lined avenues and resin-scented slopes make it a smashing place for a walk or picnic at any time of the year. Rather muddy after a heavy downpour. Part of much larger Forestry-Commission-run Bedgebury Forest. Three miles south of Goudhurst on B2079. Details of other walking and picnic sites in area in *See Your Forests – South England* from Information Branch, Forestry Commission, 231 Corstorphine Rd, Edinburgh EH12 7AT, or visitor centres and forest offices.

Vineyards: Carr Taylor Vineyards – 20 acres producing a white wine with fresh, crisp and full flavour – at Westfield, off A28 five miles north of Hastings. Visitors (by appointment only) can see grapes growing and sample the wine. Tel Hastings 752501. At Biddenden Vine-

Charcoal burners at work in a clearing outside Peasmarsh, near Rye

yards, just outside the village at Little Whatmans, visitors are welcome for guided tours. Book well in advance. About 15 acres producing a medium-dry white wine. Vineyard shop is open daily 10.00–6.00, Sun 12.00–6.00.

Romney, Hythe and Dymchurch Light Railway: miniature steam railway that takes you along 17 miles of coastline from Hythe to Dungeness. Built 1927, perfect and polished replicas of historic locomotives pull trains along 15in gauge track. During Second World War an armoured train patrolled the line. At New Romney, there is a model museum, cafe and railway shop. Frequent service, fare depends on length of journey.

Sussex trugs: at Thomas Smith in Herstmonceux watch these traditional garden baskets being made out of willow and chestnut, 23 different sizes. Workshops open weekdays only 9.00–1.00 and 2.00–4.45. Shop 9.00–4.45.

Characteristic buildings: Martello towers, round two-storey gun turrets built along coast as defence against Napoleon, especially between Dungeness and Lydd (at Dymchurch open to public). Oast houses for drying hops, conical roofs with cowls on top – some converted, some still in use. Windmills – lots of good ones (see Cranbrook and Rye) also Rolvenden, Woodchurch, Ickelsham.

Polishing an engine on the Light Railway

nuclear power station, miles of pebbles dotted with shabby huts and disused railway carriages. The RSPB has a reserve among the shingle and flooded gravel pits for watching great crested grebe, terns, winter wildfowl, migrants, etc. Permits (for which there is a charge) available from Information Centre by car park, one mile down turning off Lydd Rd, Wed, Thur, Sat, Sun. Romney Marsh and Pett Levels also good for watching water birds. Locals swear a pair of flamingoes has been seen at Pett.

Also, look out for the marsh frog from Hungary, at five inches long the biggest frog in Europe. In 1930s a few escaped from a zoologist's garden, and now their persistent croaking can be heard all over Romney Marsh.

FOOD AND DRINK

Egon Ronay's *Lucas Guide* recommends: **Sundial**, Herstmonceux, tel Herstmonceux 2217. Star rating, long menu, French cooking. **Curlew**, Bodiam, nr Robertsbridge, tel Hurst Green 272. Small restaurant, classic French style. **Priory Country House Hotel Restaurant**, Rushlake Green, tel Rushlake Green 553. Charming atmosphere, menu changes daily. **White Friars Hotel**, Boreham St, tel Herstmonceux 2355. Traditional English dishes, Italian specialities.

TOURIST INFORMATION

Publications: *Sussex Express*, every Fri, has regular folk and jazz column with details of pubs and other venues. Also full entertainments guide. *Rye Fixtures*, monthly, gives details of local happenings in and around Rye, free from newsagents.

Tourist information offices: at Battle, Hastings and Tunbridge Wells.

Research:
Pamela Brown and Sarah Howell.

ACTIVITIES

Angling: deep-sea fishing for Rye Bay plaice and sole. Boats for fishing parties can be chartered from: R. Rouse, 49 Ghyllside Ave, Hastings, tel 430047; P. Tapp, Ship Cottage, Rye Harbour, tel Rye 2145; R. Obbard, 4 The Old Schoolhouse, Rye Harbour, tel Rye 2347. Plenty of spots for river fishing – details from Freshwater Society, gen sec J. Fiddimore, Iden Kennels, Coldharbour Lane, Iden, tel Iden 384.

Auctions: look out for billboards with details of country house sales, especially round Battle. Good auctioneer Burstow & Hewett, Battle.

Pick your own fruit: lots of places, eg Norton's Farm, Kent St, Sedlescombe, where there is also a museum of old farming equipment.

Bird-watching: Dungeness can be fascinating if you don't get depressed by bleak and bizarre surroundings – huge

Traditional Sussex trugs: made from willow and chestnut

Devizes

Devizes means 'the boundaries', *les divises* in Old French. Here a Norman bishop of Salisbury, within a few years of the Conquest, built a castle on the boundary between land he was given and land owned by the king. It seems that the bishop was no less than St Osmund, builder of the first Salisbury Cathedral and nephew of the Conqueror.

A smart beginning then for this best of Wiltshire towns, growing up round a castle of the master family of the new masters. And so Devizes continued through time: castle town which became market town, wool town, cloth town, corn town, cheese town. Decidedly a country town, left to its own devices.

Devices, Devizes. The pun came unasked, but it applies. Devizes could develop its own dignity; and here it is: Norman, later-medieval, Tudor, Jacobean, eighteenth-century, Regency, Victorian, and not – yet – too brutally modern. Walk through the wide centre of Devizes and you experience a country town which has changed at a natural rate.

Nowadays you can see Devizes Castle only from the outside, up an alley – or to be exact you see only a parody of the old castle in an over-coat of Victorian masonry. But walk along a handsome street, a hundred yards or so, past bookshop, wine merchant, delicatessen and a classical town hall (whose architect was Baldwin of Bath), and eventually you reach a Norman church of heavy and solemn splendour, St John's; it was probably the chapel of the Norman castle.

A little farther, and there is one of the best of local museums. In this country town liveliness and history combine, as they should do, without a central shabbiness or sloppiness.

The castle was in ruins by Elizabeth I's time, and Devizes continued living for itself and its surroundings. Nothing seemed to happen – though during the Civil War it endured a sharp siege, lifted by a battle on the outskirts (on Roundway Down, in 1643, a field of arms worth inspecting for the steep slopes down which Prince Rupert's cavalry forced the Cromwellians). Devizes, really, was out of the way, and remains out of the way. The Old Bath Road – the older Roman road from Oxford Street to Bath – climbed the downs just to the north, near enough to be civilizing but not destructive. The downland difficulties of that road did eventually popularize a detour through Devizes. So in the eighteenth century the town came by its Bear Hotel where the land-lord would put up his boy to read poetry to the smart guests. The boy, indoctrinated in smoothness, became Sir Thomas Lawrence, President of the Royal Academy.

The Bear and the detour hardly made Devizes the busiest of transit towns. The Kennet and Avon Canal came, hobbling into Devizes up its celebrated ladder of 29 locks. The railway came; and the car came,

Avebury circle: one of Wiltshire's many prehistoric stone sites

and there is no station any more. Abolishing Devizes station may have been stupid. But point it does to that long, long quiescence of a country town. From the town centre you can see a brewery. Once you could see a snuff and tobacco factory, which produced shag in a woodcut wrapping of a negro's head. Most of today's industry hides on the outside of the town, on the way to the downs.

The downs – with the fertile Pewsey Vale – were Devizes' *raison d'être*: they remain Devizes' adjoining delight.

Centuries ago the Danish wife of James I was returning from Bath to London across the downs, across some of that property of the Norman bishop, at Bishops Cannings. For his queen the parson devised (sorry, I can't help it) an entertainment by the village shepherds in which they sang of 'the wide, wild houseless downs'.

So they seem today. The first time I came to the Devizes district, half a century ago, I detrained at another vanished station, Patney and Chirton, and walked over the down to Avebury, hearing sheep bells. The bells have gone (into antique shops), but not the sheep; nor the green sloping and folding of the downs.

The Avebury stones and circles are in easy distance of Devizes, with Silbury, that huge tump which the Roman road had to circumvent. East instead of north-east of Devizes a road skews under the high downs, under Tan Hill (St Anne's Hill), once the site of Wiltshire's major sheep fair, and up the Vale of Pewsey to a neighbourhood supposed to have been of a special Anglo-Saxon sanctitude. Here, above Alton Barnes and Alton Priors and the isolated Barge Inn by the old canal wharves of Honey Street, you have the black long barrow of Adam's Grave, which the Anglo-Saxons a thousand years ago called Woden's Barrow, the burial-place of their ancestors' great god; and beyond Woden's Barrow the running earthwork, ditch and mound of Wansdyke (Woden's Dyke).

Hereabouts is some of the suavest, noblest downlands, some of the airiest walking. Here is the White Horse of Alton Barnes (designed by an itinerant portrait-painter, afterwards hanged for forgery). Here you see the red wings of hang-gliders sailing over the White Horse into the Vale; and on the canal, you can take trips in a motorized barge.

I have thought of Devizes as dividing two downland systems: the Marlborough downland, of which Avebury and Tan Hill are part; and, across the Pewsey Vale, the longer but less exciting scarp of Salisbury Plain. South of Devizes, Potterne is a village to go to, for the black and white house Samuel Palmer discovered on a sketching tour. He persuaded his friend George Richmond RA, who was wealthy from painting the moneyed heads of Europe, to buy it and restore it.

Under the Plain, a few miles away, the church of Edington Priory demands a visit. In its light and space one of the saintliest and most delicious of poets, George Herbert, married a Wiltshire girl, Jane Danvers, on 5 March 1629. Or again across a low green country you find a village cathedral, Steeple Ashton, grandly vaulted with stone at the expense of the wealthy cloth merchants of the village.

I am circling you round Devizes, clockwise. North of Steeple Ashton, still in Vale country, I have to mention Lacock Abbey, home of Fox Talbot, one of the pioneers of what he called the 'pencil of nature', ie photography, and Lacock village, both National Trust (a good restaurant at Lacock as well as a remarkable museum of photography). Then, for another poet and a crystal drawing-room or splendid Perpendicular chapel in the parish church, I cannot omit Bromham. The poet, outside, tamped under a Celtic high cross, is little Tom Moore of the *Irish Melodies*.

Moore's pretty Slopperton Cottage here in Bromham belonged to his patron Lord Lansdowne, at Bowood nearby. Without the Lansdownes, said Tom Moore, Wiltshire would be a 'desert sea'. But he was happy enough there, and one story about him rather epitomizes this lower Wiltshire around Devizes. He and his wife set out for dinner at Bowood. Afraid they would arrive too early, they stopped their coachman and practised country dances in a green lane.

We are nearly in sight again of Devizes, or at least of the fatal slopes of the Roundway battle. Back in the town try Devizes pie (at the Bear), which is, or should be, made of bacon, calf's head, tongue and brains, cold lamb and hard-boiled eggs. Also Devizes fairings, a flat brandy-snap.

And there are inscriptions you ought to read. Was Devizes extra pious or extra sinful? Anyhow, read on the market cross how Ruth Pierce swore she had paid her share of the cost of a sack of corn, and would drop dead if she hadn't. She dropped dead; and there was the unpaid money in her fist. What usually goes unmentioned is that Devizes owes this market cross to that grim fellow Lord Sidmouth, Home Secretary at the time of the Peterloo Massacre.

A more savage memorial outside St John's Church records how a party of five was drowned – justly – when boating on the Sabbath. Moreover, in the church at Bishops Cannings outside the town squats a most odd penitential chair painted with inscriptions about the rewards of sin.

It is an odd place, this beautiful Bishops Cannings, against the slope of the downs, this village in which Devizes had its origin. I haven't tried it, but I am told it is unwise to utter 'Wheel I round' in the pub, on a Saturday night. Why? Because shepherds wheeled the wisest ancient in the village out in a barrow to pronounce on an object they had found near a dewpond. 'Wheel I round,' said the ancient. 'Wheel I round again.' Then he said of the object – a turnip watch – ''Tes dangerous, 'tes a gert tick-toad. 'Eave un in the pond.'

Also in Bishops Cannings they dunged a pinnacle alongside the church steeple – to make un grow – and the carpenter made a big drum for the village band upstairs in his shop, but it was too big to get downstairs or out of the window.

Some people claim the famous story of the Wiltshire Moonrakers – the noodles raking a round North Wiltshire cheese, ie the reflected full moon, out of a pond – for Bishops Cannings, others for Devizes.

But, Devizes being the grown-up child of that village of the bishops of Salisbury, it really makes no difference. Either way, I put these jokes down to an ancient envy – outsiders' envy – of Devizes and all to do with it.

Devizes may doze a little today, but it is one of those rare towns which are managing – somehow – to maintain almost an equilibrium with their past. The modern towniness of Devizes isn't overbearing, that is the point. This favourite town of mine does remain a town for a countryside.

Devizes: St John's churchyard with the castle in the distance: 'a parody of the old castle in an overcoat of Victorian masonry'

GEOFFREY GRIGSON

Devizes

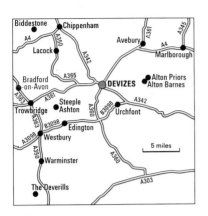

WHERE TO GO

Market Place: Ceres, goddess of plenty, looks down from roof of corn exchange, an ornate stone building still used. North end of Market Place dominated by intrusively large Wadworths brewery, but fine 18th c building which closes off southern end was cheese hall in days when cheese was one of Wiltshire's chief products.
Bear Hotel: famous coaching stop. A bear used to stand on two giant columns opposite the inn – similar columns are let into the back of the building.
St John's: has handsome Norman tower and chancel whose mass contrasts with light ornate Beauchamp chapel. This and other major church, St Mary's, both date from 12th c.
St John's Alley: narrow alley of timber-framed houses opposite elegant town hall.
Long St: the most homogeneous bit of town – a street of fine plain Georgian brick houses lightened by a row of pastel-coloured stucco ones.
Devizes Museum, 41 Long St: run by Wiltshire Archaeological and Natural History Society. Displays of pottery, weapons and ornaments from Neolithic, Bronze and Iron Ages and Roman sites. Open Tue–Sat April–Sept 11.00–1.00 and 2.00–5.00, winter until 4.00.
The Green: surprisingly large open space with pond complete with pair of swans and yew trees of St James's churchyard coming down to its edge. Playground.
Kennet and Avon Canal: sweeps round back of town, with quiet towpath walks. Built 1810, it was soon in competition with Great Western Railway which bought it: then it slowly decayed. Kennet and Avon Canal Trust has reopened most of it and is now working on the magnificent flight of locks up Caen Hill parallel to Bath Rd, to west of town. There are 29 locks in Devizes followed by a 15-mile stretch through the Vale of Pewsey without any. Marvellous walks.
Roundway Down: one mile from town, site of bloody Civil War battle in 1643, when Royalist cavalry charged Waller's forces over edge of escarpment and galloped with such force their front runners went over, too. Now has countryside trail (with leaflet) in covert where Forestry Commission is replacing felled beech wood. Fine views.

SHOPPING

Market day: Thur. Also indoor market on Sat.
Early closing: Wed.
Strongs, 35 Market Place: good old-fashioned bakers with teashop upstairs.
Ronald Lees, 32 St John's St: good bookshop.
Crossed Keys Antiques, Monday Market St: has cheap jewellery, worth a browse.

FOOD AND DRINK

Egon Ronay's *Just a Bite* recommends **Handels Kitchen,** Sheep St, and **Grapevine Winebar,** High St. Most pubs in town supplied by Wadworths brewery which produces four real ales. Pubs seem to divide into two sorts: first, the comfortable carpeted bars, sometimes panelled, such as the **Bear Hotel,** the **White Bear** in Monday Market St, the **Castle** in New Park St, the **White Lion** in Northgate St, and the **Three Crowns** in Maryport St. They all serve food; the last has a tempting menu of home-made pâté, salads and pizzas. The other sort of Devizes pub is also old but to a remarkable extent untouched: the **Pelican** in Market Place, the **Lamb** in St John's St, and the back rooms of the **Elm Tree** in Long St.

TOURIST INFORMATION

Devizes Trust, St John's St, which publishes a town trail leaflet.

Villages and country towns

Alton Barnes and Alton Priors
Two villages which appear to be one – the mixed old and new houses are loosely scattered in a circle around two fields, one either side of willow-lined stream. In middle of one field is a disused church, with a stone path across the grass to it (key available at nearby cottage).

Alton Priors is the only village on the Ridgeway, which descends here to cross the Vale of Pewsey and vanishes. So settlements may go back a very long way. They certainly date from Saxon times.

Alton Barnes has belonged to New College, Oxford, since 14th c. Houses are all raw-boned brick, two with a heavy fringe of thatch. In both villages there are traditional Wiltshire cob and thatch walls.

In St Mary's church monuments tell of William Crowe, poet and divine, who used to walk to Oxford where he was orator. His successor as rector, Augustus Hare, had a most affectionate memorial put up by parishioners whom he tried to help, by giving them allotments on church land, organizing co-operative societies and schooling for the poor.

Adam's Grave and Downs: on Walkers Hill one mile out of villages to north –well worth the walk. A long barrow similar to West Kennet, though not exposed as there. Skeletons and leaf-shaped arrowheads were found there in 19th c excavation. Mentioned in 825 by Saxons who called it Woden's Barrow. Superb site with views across Vale of Pewsey to Salisbury Plain. The other side of Marlborough road is Knap Hill with neolithic causeway camp encircling the top. Milk Hill is a nature reserve with valuable chalk flora, and Tan Hill – the highest point in Wiltshire – is where great August sheep fair used to be held. On Clifford Hill is Rybury Camp where neolithic causeway camp is overlaid with a hill-fort. There are plenty of footpaths across the downs, many of which cross Wansdyke.

Half a mile to south at Honey St is old canal wharf. Nearby is Barge Inn, comfortable Courage pub, with pool table in back bar. On Sun there are hour-and-a-half trips up canal on *Charlotte Dundas*.

Avebury

One of the most famous villages in England – not for itself so much as for the presence of massive prehistoric stone and earth rings and ditches.

The village is a pleasant street of mixed cottages, some of which have the sarsen stones of the circles embedded in their walls. Behind the street lies the church, with the manor house and its farmyard including stables, pond, dovecote and 17th c thatched wood barn. This farmyard is rapidly being developed into a focus for visitors, with basic refreshments, two museums and National Trust shop (but for inexpensive and imaginative gifts try the crafts shop in the main street).

Alexander Keiller Museum, founded by the main excavator of Avebury, is worth spending some time in, as a careful look at exhibits will tell you a lot about famous local sites. Open May–Sept daily 9.30–7.00, March, April, Oct daily 9.30–5.30, Nov–Feb weekdays 9.30–4.00 Sun 2.00–4.00.

Folk Life Museum, in the Great Barn: newly-opened by Wiltshire Folk Life Society, displays include old bits of farm equipment, but most interesting section so far is reprinted photos of now demolished local buildings, and of people who lived in neighbourhood, such as local giant Fred Kempster, who was 8ft 4in, and his friend Brunhilde, who was 4in taller. Open April–Oct every day 10.30–6.00.

Manor House: pleasant unimposing Elizabethan house with some panelled rooms and plasterwork ceilings. Present owners only moved in recently with their good furniture and family portraits. Compartmentalized garden with topiary work. Open daily June, July, Aug, at weekends May, Sept 2.30–5.30, bank hol 10.00–6.00.

St James's church of mixed stone and flint has Norman door and geometrically carved font. Path from churchyard leads across River Kennet with excellent view of Silbury Hill to Avebury Trusloe – a secluded row of handsome houses, Trusloe Manor, a late 17th c stone house, and a thatched farmhouse. Don't miss the avenue of stones leading up to Avebury from Silbury Hill alongside B4003.

Red Lion Hotel in Avebury serves lunches and is usually busy with visitors. If you want something quieter you could try the stone and thatched Waggon and Horses at Beckhampton, a Wadworths pub that also does meals.

Biddestone

The locals think Biddestone beats Castle Combe – the beauty spot up the road – and if it wasn't for the flatness of the site they might be right. Unlike the chalk villages this one is all stone. A handsome series of 17th and 18th c houses stand around a spacious grassy centre, not quite a green, with a duck pond, a cross and the village pump.

On the outskirts of the village to the east is the neatly symmetrical gabled manor house, a 17th c building with clipped hedges and a brick gazebo on garden wall. Small church of St Nicholas at other end of village has endearing domestic atmosphere enhanced by box pews and balcony built to house parishioners of neighbouring Slaughterford whose church was destroyed by Cromwellian troops. They had separate staircases to keep them apart from local people, such was their dislike of each other. Church has no tower, but instead unusual 13th c bell turret with two 700-year-old bells. The font and doorway are Norman, there are a variety of monuments and details of endowments for the poor.

White Horse pub at centre of village is popular, cheerful place, serving Courage beer.

Bradford-on-Avon

A town, not a village. Once one of the most thriving centres of the Wiltshire woollen cloth trade, it went into decline in 19th c.

Centre of town is dominated by Abbey Mill. Built after decline had already set in, it soon became a rubber factory and is now converted to offices. Besides its nationally famous buildings, Bradford has a wealth of other very pleasing ones. The town produces a leaflet if you want help in finding the best walks. The bridge next to Abbey Mill has two medieval arches and a 17th c lock-up on it. Across it, in the flat bottom of the valley, are more fine buildings such as Westbury House, the Liberal Club and some 17th c almshouses.

Tithe Barn is signposted off Frome Rd, stands next to Barton farm, and was built in 14th c to hold the farm's produce. Don't miss a chance to see this almost cathedral-sized barn. The south bank of the river, which also has the Kennet and Avon Canal running through it, has been made into a country park, good for walks.

Saxon church of St Lawrence, next to parish church, was only rediscovered in 19th c as it was being used as cottage. Very small with thick stone walls decorated outside with pilasters. It may be the church referred to as built by St Aldhelm *c* 705 – well worth seeing anyway.

Parish Church of Holy Trinity, next to the river, its churchyard yews go down to water's edge. Typical parish church – bits and pieces from Norman period onwards.

Shops worth investigating include an old watchmakers in the Shambles, the Tudor for home-made cakes, Crops for duck eggs, spices, wholesome bread, dried flowers – lavender, marigolds, rose, camomile and pot-pourri, Terra Cotta for household presents and coffee, and the antique shops in Silver St.

Pubs – plenty of good ones to choose from. In Silver St the Bunch of Grapes, a Bass pub, looks like a shop outside but is remarkably unspoilt; try cosy, gossipy back bar. Kings Arms in Coppice St also welcoming – serves Ushers beer and good food. 18th c Swan has a quiet hotel bar serving Eldridge Pope and Wadworths beer. The popular Canal Tavern is a relaxed Wadworths pub on Frome Rd next to canal. Egon Ronay's *Just a Bite* recommends Georgian Wine Lodge, 25 Bridge St, which has an extensive menu and cold buffet.

The Deverills

A series of hamlets that cluster along the upper waters of the river Wylye. They are the only settlements in this lovely small-scale downland valley. Starting at Maiden Bradley end of valley, houses at Kingston Deverill are scattered loosely round the river which is shallow-bedded and runs over gravel at this point. There are a couple of rows of striped 19th c cottages, built with a decorative mixing of materials characteristic of Wiltshire. The 17th c hall, church and big farmyard complete the group. At Monkton Deverill, the next village, the houses are arranged more formally into a grassy-banked street, away from the river this time, but its presence is marked by a magnificent tall willow tree at the river end of the street. The small church is now hemmed in by a considerable

Lacock's Sign of the Angel restaurant: this unusually attractive village is now owned by the National Trust

amount of new building. The river begins to broaden out at Brixton Deverill, disappearing enticingly as several channels into a thicket of bushes. This, and a copse of trees with a rookery in the top branches, are at centre of village, which otherwise has some archetypal thatched cottages, as well as a neat Victorian villa.

The valley broadens out and rejoins the main road at Hill and Longbridge Deverills where the more serious things of life – work, garage, shop, pub, council houses – are situated. Here the river is used for watercress beds, but it has returned to its willows and poplars by the time it passes Thynne Almshouses, built 1655, and church with monuments to Thynne who built Longleat.

The George is a pleasant Bass pub serving coffee, lunches and suppers – grills, scampi, etc. If you're driving the other way the Somerset Arms at Maiden Bradley is a thriving Wadworths local, also with food.

Edington

A shapeless village that falls down the north edge of Salisbury Plain below the road to Westbury, and so has views looking out across the Avon valley to Steeple Ashton and beyond. Houses are a mixture of new and old, with some brick and thatch and one or two handsome ones like Becket's House and the Priory.

Some scholars think Edington was the site of King Alfred's victory against the Danes in 878. It is mentioned in his will and was later given by King Edgar to Abbess of Romsey, thus beginning its long domination by the church. In 1352 the Bishop of Winchester decided to build a priory and church here. He was William of Edington, who started life in this village before going on to become treasurer and chancellor to Edward III. His combination of temporal and spiritual power is reflected in the magnificent church itself. Pevsner thinks its battlemented exterior 'like a fortified mansion'.

Church also runs highly esteemed music festival in Aug, usually during third week.

Choice of pubs: comfortable Lamb on main road serves food and Ushers beer, as does the George which is in quiet backwater near the village shop.

Lacock

The whole village and the abbey are owned by the National Trust and there are plenty of visitors as a result. With justification, since its architecture is remarkably complete and unadulterated. From the Middle Ages to 19th c villagers lived by weaving in their cottages, but when the industry declined 200 unemployed went into the workhouse or emigrated. Their landlord, the pioneer photographer Fox Talbot, who was also the local MP, petitioned Parliament for help. There is more about local history in a pamphlet of recollections called *A Village in Wiltshire* available from the village's National Trust shop.

Stone and half-timbered houses line the streets, making Lacock look more like a town than a village. The houses date from 15th c onwards, but in spite of variety of period they are all remarkably similar in scale, except for the 18th c Red

Fox Talbot, pioneer of
photography and local MP

Lion which looks exaggeratedly large and red brick by comparison. The church – St Cyriac's – is perpendicular, large and light with an extra window over the chancel arch. Outside, battlements, pinnacles and figures including one smoking a pipe. The Abbey lies on outskirts of village in meadows close to the Avon. The 15th c cloisters, chapter house and range of other rooms survive from the original abbey. The 18th c house has a sequence of pastel-coloured rooms which are pretty and not too grand. Open June–Sept daily 2.00–6.00, April, May, Oct Wed–Sun and Bank Hol Mon 2.00–6.00; closed Nov–March except for groups by appointment.

Fox Talbot Photographic Museum has interesting display of his early photographic equipment and descriptions of techniques leading to his calotype process of 1839. Reprints of his and other early photographs on show, including photogenic drawings made by exposing plants and leaves on light-sensitive paper. Leaflets on sale tell you how to do it. They also sell big collection of photographic books and postcards and prints. Open daily March–Oct 11.00–6.00.

The public bar of Red Lion is welcoming and relaxed with darts for the locals and space to absorb the visitors too. The George is quieter and quainter. For a traditional English meal in a 14th c inn Egon Ronay's *Lucas Guide* recommends Sign of Angel restaurant, tel Lacock 230, which specializes in roasts and delicious vegetables.

Marlborough

A thriving town, which consists primarily of one long curved and widened main street – the market place on Wed and Sat. High St follows line of Kennet which is at bottom of gardens on south side. One, Priory Gardens, is open to public, reached through arch under Jubilee Day Centre.

High St always busy with shoppers and travellers who stop at the many cafes and restaurants. The street is predominantly 18th c, with colonnaded shops including some tactful modern conversions, and a great many tile-hung house fronts whose colour gives a real warmth to the place.

Marlborough College has a dominant presence in the town. Notable old boys include William Morris (expelled), John Meade Falkner, author of *Moonfleet* (also expelled), the poet Louis MacNeice and Sir John Betjeman.

At the College end of town is St Peter's church, an elegant perpendicular building, now run as a very helpful tourist information centre. Behind the church, a row of shops includes an antiquarian bookshop and, at 77 High St, the enticing Kennet Wool Workshop, which sells fleeces and speciality yarns.

Behind other end of High St is the Green, the oldest part of town, now surrounded by handsome series of houses. At the bottom end in Barn St one of the quaint cottages, full of patterns and pottery figures, sells delicious inexpensive home-made sweets, fudge and pep-

permint creams. In New Rd is the splendid saddlers shop belonging to Mr
Chandler the local historian. You can
watch saddles being made. In Oct the
traditional Little and Great Mop Fairs
are held. Savernake Forest about a mile
east of town has Grand Avenue of three
miles of beeches.

Pubs include Ailesbury Arms and
Castle and Ball, both in High St. The
Sun is local for masters from College and
has bells from plague cart on show.

Steeple Ashton

The steeple of the name draws attention
to the church which is splendid though
surprisingly without a spire. It did have
one but in 1670, according to John
Aubrey, it got struck by lightning twice.
The second time it fell through the
church roof, killing two master masons.
Even without a spire, the tower can be
seen from miles around dominating the
plain. Steeple Ashton grew rich from
cloth trade in the Middle Ages, its later
prosperity depended on agriculture and
in 18th c it was renowned for cheese-
making.

The manor farm has a fine range of
farm buildings some contemporary with
the 17th c house, a granary on columns
and an engine shed. The village has a
great variety of domestic buildings ranging from cruck cottages, through brick
and timber-frame houses on stone bases,
to 18th c Ashton House and recent stone
or brick residences with garages.

Post office and general stores really
does seem to have everything. The village pub is the Long Arms, a Watneys
pub serving Ushers beer, ploughman's
lunches, pies and sandwiches.

Urchfont

Urchfont's picture-postcard centre features a duck pond as well as a cedar tree,
three elegant houses and church in the
distance. It has a decorated chancel. In
the garden of Manor Farm is a granary
held up by mushroom-shaped staddle
stones to stop rats getting into corn. A
series of smaller houses and cottages
completes the group around the pond.
Behind the manor farmyard, a lane falls
away into a deep combe with smaller
cottages, gardens and stream well
worth exploring.

Following the road round from the
pond, after a short distance the street
opens out again into the Green with

Steeple Ashton – grandly vaulted with stone at the expense of the wealthy cloth merchants of the village

pleasant rows of houses grouped around
this sloping site.

Turning left from the Green brings
you to the road under the downs with
Urchfont Manor – a 17th c brick house
with stone dressings, now used as an
adult education centre.

The Lamb, a Wadworths pub, welcomes children. Well patronized by
locals, it does a thriving lunchtime trade
in public bar serving sandwiches, pies,
etc. The Nags Head, a free house with
Burtons and Ind Coope beers, has fitted
carpets, huge log fire and regimental
badges.

There are several footpaths up on to
the downs but be careful: there are army
ranges nearby.

Places to visit

Prehistoric sites: at Avebury, Silbury Hill, West Kennet Long Barrow, you can go behind huge standing stones into the reconstructed stone chambers, in which groups of neolithic skeletons were found. Stonehenge is the only site with a closing time – 9.30–7.00 May–Sept and then shorter hours depending on the light. Sadly, the Department of the Environment has now restricted access to the actual stones because of erosion, so you can no longer go inside the circle. There are earth rings of Iron Age hill forts at Scratchbury and Battlesbury and White Sheet Hill, Barbary Castle, Ogbury and Yarnbury, Oliver's Castle and Cley Hill. Since they are all defensive positions they tend to have excellent views and therefore are good places to walk to. Old Sarum has the earth remains of the original town of Salisbury on this site until the present cathedral was built. Wansdyke, thought to be a massive Saxon defence system, stretches for 12 miles across Wiltshire and then, after a gap, on to the Mendips. Wiltshire section has huge bank and ditch to north side and follows ridge of downs from Savernake forest to Morgans Hill north of Devizes.

The Ridgeway is the oldest track in England, and possibly in Europe. It certainly dates from neolithic times when, joining with more recent Icknield Way, it formed route from south-west coast to North Sea. The Countryside Commission has signposted section from Overton Hill near Silbury to the Chilterns at Ivinghoe Beacon. See the book by J. R. L. Anderson and Fay Godwin, *The Oldest Road*, if this long walk tempts you.

Great Chalfield, near Broughton Gifford: this is a magnificent stone, early Tudor manor house with church and outbuildings and a moat encircling the whole complex. Built in 1480 by Thomas Tropnell, it fell into disrepair in 19th c and has been much altered and restored inside, though still features stone masks high up on the walls of hall, through which Tropnell could watch what went on below. Owned by National Trust but only open Wed mid-April–mid-Sept 12.00–1.00 and 2.00–5.00, but church can be visited at any time.

Westwood Manor: in the village of Westwood next to church with splendid Somerset-style perpendicular tower. House is L-shaped, built in several stages from 1400 to Jacobean period. It has a topiary garden adding an extra hedge-room on to house. The hall was divided into two storeys in 17th c, behind it is small King's Room which has wonderful naïve plasterwork of animals, mermaids, etc. Other rooms also have good plasterwork and fine collection of furniture

High-powered horsemanship at Wilton House: one of a set by 18th-century amateur Baron Reis d'Eisenberg

brought together by last owner who gave house to National Trust. Open April–Aug Wed only 2.30–6.00.

Sheldon Manor, outside Chippenham near Biddestone: recently, traces of a deserted medieval village have emerged in nearby fields. 13th c porch but mainly Jacobean with a fine staircase.

Whole house is permeated with charm of its present owners who have collected with a sure eye all sorts of lovely bits and pieces – a series of glass walking sticks, prints, china. More than anywhere else in Wiltshire, there is the sense of a home having been thrown open for you. Have a very pleasant afternoon rounded off by home-made tea on the lawn.

House and garden open Palm Sun–end Sept Thur, Sun and bank hol 2.00–6.00 also Wed 2.00–6.00 in Aug. Parties at other times by appointment, tel Chippenham 3120.

Heale House: the gardens of this house are a lovely place to spend an afternoon – they run down to the Avon at Middle Woodford. The elegant brick and stone-dressed 17th c house hid Charles II for a few days when he was escaping after the battle of Worcester. There is an authentic Japanese tea-house and water-garden in these grounds. Gardens only, open daily Good Friday–autumn 10.00–5.00.

Littlecote Manor, nr Hungerford: long, low, brick Tudor building in meadows by river Kennet. Reputedly haunted since 1578 by cries of William Darell's newborn baby which he threw on the fire and the ghost of mother still looking for it. House has a collection of Cromwellian armour, and site of a Roman villa in park. Open April–Sept Sat, Sun and Bank Hol Mon 2.00–6.00, from July weekdays also 2.00–5.00.

Lydiard Park and Church, Lydiard Tregoze, nr Swindon: until recently it belonged to the St John family. Many of the 17th c members of the family are commemorated in a marvellous collection of monuments in the church. These include an almost life-size gold cavalier – Edward, who was killed at battle of Newbury fighting for Charles I. Covering one wall of the chancel is the St John Triptych – a huge panel painting dated 1615, which has the family tree on the outside and opens to show a group portrait of two generations inside. House elegantly remodelled in mid-18th c, has good collection of family portraits, a charming

17th c painted glass window and imaginative displays of clothes in bedroom and of ephemera. Borough of Thamesdown own house, and grounds are used as park by local people who play cricket on grass at weekends, creating very pleasant atmosphere. Open all year, weekdays 10.00–1.00 and 2.00–5.30, Sun 2.00–5.30.

Longleat: splendid house with four equally important façades, capped by a flamboyant roofline of figures and balustrades. Inside, a high quality line in furniture, paintings, including the definitive portraits of most of the best known Elizabethans. Various side attractions besides safari park include the Victorian kitchens, maze, boats, railway, and pets' corner. Open all the year round, Easter till end of Sept 10.00–6.00, then till 4.00 pm. Safari Park 10.00–6.00 daily March–Oct. There is a well-stocked whole food shop and garden centre.

Wilton House: another fine mansion built on the banks of river Wylye. The Earl of Pembroke was given lands of Wilton Abbey at Dissolution. Sir Philip Sidney wrote his *Arcadia* here. Charles I used to stay frequently with the Pembrokes. Marvellous Double Cube room attributed to Inigo Jones. It and other rooms in the house have excellent collection of paintings – Van Dyck, Rubens, Reynolds, Rembrandt and a charming series of Spanish riding school horses demonstrating their many talents. Fantastic horses are still to be found at Wilton in Arabian Performance show in summer. House open first Tues before Easter–first week Oct Tue–Sat 11.00–6.00, Sun 2.00–6.00, closed Mon, last admission 5.30.

At Wilton you can also take a tour round the carpet factory, weekdays at 10.00 and 11.00 for a small charge. The Weavers Shop in King St has details, tel Wilton 2733.

Corsham Court: a house that has been subject to many face-lifts over the years including one by Nash. It now has a dose of rather heavy Victoriana, mixed in with its overall Elizabethan appearance. Grounds landscaped by Capability Brown. Mainly worth visiting for its fine collection of 16th and 17th c old master paintings, including many big names, and some good furniture. Open all year Sun, Wed and Thur; mid-July–mid-Sept daily except Mon and Fri 11.00–12.30 and 2.00–6.00 or to 4.30 in winter.

Stourhead: the Palladian house was designed by Colen Campbell for the banker Henry Hoare and completed by 1725. His son spent 40 years developing the celebrated landscape garden. National Trust. Stourhead House is open May–Aug every day except Fri 2.00–6.00, April, Sept, Oct open Mon, Wed, Sat and Sun 2.00–6.00 or sunset if earlier. Closed Nov–March. Grounds open daily all year 8.00–7.00 or dusk.

Bowood Park: spacious park laid out by Capability Brown with lake, waterfalls, arboretum with 200 varieties of trees and shrubs, formal terraces near the house and gallery, which is the only bit open to public. The park includes adventure playground with really daring tree-walks, slides, trampolines and swings.

Open daily Good Friday–Sept except Mon 2.00–6.00, Sun and bank hol 12.00–6.00.

Wardour Castle: largest 18th c house in Wiltshire, built in Palladian manner by James Paine. It has a splendid circular staircase and a chapel decorated by Sir John Soane. Used as a school, it is open only during holidays late July–early Sept Mon, Wed, Fri and Sat 2.30–6.00. Nearby is Old Wardour Castle, the ruin of a hexagonal 14th c castle, later made into an Elizabethan house, which belongs to Department of the Environment and is open all year round, May–Sept 9.30–7.00 daily, March, April, Oct 9.30–5.30 Sun from 2.00, Nov–Feb 9.30–4.00 Sun from 2.00.

ACTIVITIES

Bird-Man Flight Training School, Marlborough: If you've ever had the slightest hankering to try hang-gliding, this school offers you the opportunity. Courses range from one to five days. For more information tel Marlborough 52909.

Rode Tropical Bird Garden: remarkable place with about 180 different species of birds including macaws, mynah birds, owls, flamingoes, penguins and ornamental pheasants. It's well worth visiting and is open every day 10.30–7.00 or sunset. Situated near Rode just over the Somerset border, turn off A36 in easterly direction at Red Lion in Wolverton.

Brockerswood Woodland Park and the Phillips Countryside Museum: wood dates back to Norman Conquest.

80 acres open to the public including a large man-made lake with various breeds of ducks and geese.

If you get up a party of about 10 you can arrange to go and have supper at Brockerswood and be shown round by the forester himself. Tel Westbury 822238 for details. Woods open all year round 10.30–sunset. A bit difficult to find but there are signposts, between Beckington and Westbury, a turn off B3099, not far from Rudge and Dilton Marsh.

Angling: day tickets for local stretch of Kennet and Avon canal from Devizes Angling Association, 36A St John's St, Devizes, or from Coles sports shop in Market Place. Canal contains perch, tench, chub, carp, bream, roach, rudd, gudgeon, eels and pike, the latter only to be fished after 1 Sept. For the Pewsey stretch of canal you should write for day tickets to Secretary of Pewsey Angling Association, 11 Chisenbury Court, East Chisenbury, Enford. Day tickets are available from Marlborough Angling Association for stretch up to Great Bedwyn, tel Marlborough 52922, or from Ducks Toy Shop in High St. Day tickets at Bradford-on-Avon can be got from Barton Cottage near the tithe barn, to fish in river. There is also fishing in Avon at Melksham, contact Melksham AA Secretary Mr Abbott, 34 West End, Melksham.

Riding: available at Brympton Riding School, Whiteparish, tel Whiteparish 386; Hampsley Hollow Riding Centre, Heddington Calne, which offers among other things hacking on the downs, tel Bromham 850333; the Old Coaching House Riding Centre at Lacock specializes in children's courses, tel Lacock 338. Not on Sun.

TOURIST INFORMATION

Local papers: the *Wiltshire Gazette and Herald* is published on Thur and *Wiltshire Times and News* on Fri. Kennet and Marlborough councils produce an official guide.

Tourist information offices: the main one for the area is at Endless St, Salisbury, but there are also other centres staffed by volunteers at Marlborough, Amesbury, Mere and Swindon.

Research: Jessica York.

Wells

Cider, snugness, cheese and churches are the best-known attributes of Somerset and even the name, 'land of the summer people' (the Saxons brought their flocks down from the uplands to graze the lush grass of the drying marshes), has a burr of peace and plenty. Somerset is all these things, but even more remarkable than its sleepy charm is the rare variety and contrast of the countryside within 20 miles of Wells.

South of Bath, where the Mendips peter out and the new county of Avon has bitten into the old boundaries, lies a tumble of combes and steep little hamlets with names like Englishcombe and Wellow – everybody's picture-postcard dream of village England, though few of the original village families remain to enjoy it. Farther south is the limestone massif of the Mendips which make a north-east elbow with the Cotswolds and run, never more than 10 miles wide, for 20 miles from Frome to the coast. Beyond and below are the levels where the rivers that splash off the Mendips once lost themselves in a wilderness of mud and water. Drainage ditches called rhines (pronounced 'reens') over the centuries have reclaimed the land: today a silent quarter of black peat, dairy Friesians and pollard willows where some remarkably unflappable herons keep vigil. In the morning, before the sun laps up the mist, the only thing that can be seen is Glastonbury Tor: it looks like the hand of a drowning man.

The Mendips are a bare 1068 feet – at their highest point, Black Down – but hills that rise direct from plains are always more exciting than a gradual swell, and viewing the sudden escarpment from the levels you forget the scale and see only the drama. For bleakness and loneliness this modest plateau can match the wildest parts of Britain: there is a brooding sense of history and prehistory in the hill-forts of Stone Age man and the Beaker Folk, the ancient workings of the Roman lead mines, the vestigial traces of the Fosseway. From the Wiltshire chalklands across to the Severn and the distant hills, High Mendip is a fine eyrie from which to see the coloured counties and feel the past.

Spread out below, almost within mortar range, is the Arthurian legend, and the terrain where the Saxon finally broke the Celt, Glastonbury with its Christian myths and its mysterious Tor where the last abbot was hung, drawn and quartered at the Dissolution. Beyond the Poldens is Alfred's Athelney from where the course of western history was changed, and Sedgemoor, site of the last battle on English soil. Hundreds of Monmouth's defeated rabble were locked overnight in the church of nearby Weston Zoyland on their way to Bridgwater and the tender mercies of Judge Jeffreys. After that, Somerset history mellows, with nothing much angrier than a radical blast from Cobbett as he rejoiced in the plight of the Frome clothing manufacturers.

The Bishop's Palace

And so to Wells, a jewel in its casket of green fields, as they say in the guidebooks, the perfect matrix. England's smallest city has been celebrated in fountains of rapturous prose: suffice to say that it has somehow preserved what Winchester and Salisbury have lost: its complete ecclesiastical identity and a medieval tranquillity that not even the streams of tourists can entirely disrupt. *Horas non numero nisi serenas* (I count only the peaceful hours) is the motto for Wells sun-dials. Or, as Henry James put it, 'It is always Sunday afternoon in Wells.' It is not a museum piece: the houses are lived in (hence the parking space); it has a busy organic life of its own with a thriving market; its administration has always been not by monks but by priests with their feet on the ground. As proof that Wells moves with the times you will find, discreetly measured out on the pavement in a corner of the market place under the shadow of the cathedral's west front, the record Olympic long-jump by Mary Rand of this parish.

The buildings of Wells, including St Cuthbert's, the largest parish church in a county of beautiful churches, rate 54 pages in Pevsner. The cathedral green and the moat, less squalid and scummy than most, make an incomparable setting; the precinct's ancillary buildings, including the consummate chapter house, are the best preserved and finest of their kind; the cathedral itself, twelfth and thirteenth century, is one of the glories of true English Gothic. Small (sometimes 'squat' to its detractors), it has a sturdy harmony, the sculptured figures on the west front depicting the history of Christianity being one of its most remarkable features. The solid inverted arches in the nave inserted in the fourteenth century were not designed to please the eye but to save the tower from collapsing. The famous astronomical clock has four knights jousting on the hour. Unfortunately the famous swans, disturbed by television, departed indignantly a few years ago and their successors have not yet learnt to ring the moat bell at meal-times.

In the town, Vicar's Close, with only a few Georgian alterations, is the oldest inhabited street in Western Europe. Traffic is one-way; the shops in Broad Street have largely resisted knick-knackery: the High Street has a freshet of water down the gutter; almshouses for 'poor Wooll-combers' recall the heyday of the stocking trade; most of the good solid hotels are former coaching inns.

You may prefer to avoid the lions of Longleat and, if you are rotund, the dubious pleasures of pot-holing, but Wookey Hole two miles away must be visited: stalagmites and stalactites, the underground river Axe, a working paper-mill where you can follow the process and buy a sample of the best deckle-edged, Lady Bangor's fairground museum with its carved roundabout animals and swing-boat gondolas, and the 2000-odd moulds in Madame Tussauds's storeroom – all for a very modest inclusive fee. Ebbor Gorge is a miniature Cheddar: sheep-bitten drystone-wall country with fine views over the levels.

Cheddar itself is a bit like the Taj Mahal, in that it is fashionable to deprecate it and there is nothing quite like it. The formidable cleft is best approached from above, if possible on foot and in the early morning before it is clogged by the Carton Folk, latter-day successors of the Beaker Folk. Make for Axbridge under the lee of the hills, with its early anemones and strawberries, the site of a royal hunting lodge under Mendip 'forest' and yet another glorious Perpendicular church.

This is no country for clinical route-planning: obey a grasshopper instinct; submit to the whim of a signpost. Blagdon Lake has romantic seclusion and big trout; Chew Valley Reservoir merely has big trout. The nemesis of the Cotswolds seems to have come to little Wellow with its watersplash: a locked church, the last shop sold for conversion, those dreary painted cartwheels prettifying the pub, a housing estate. Over the brow there is a genuine old-fashioned scrumpy house – and not much else – at Buckland Dinham; cheese-making can be seen every morning at Chewton Mendip; Miss Perkins, the baker's daughter in Holcombe, will produce the key to the tiny church in the fields.

Frome prospers with light industry; recent town planning is a model of discretion; Cheap Street has its own little brook. The old county cricket ground featured one of the best Cinderella stories when the lad Gimblett, up from the farm for a trial, got the thumbs down but was told that if he cared to hang around and make himself useful there might be some pocket-money and a lift home at the weekend. Where-upon several of the county side fell sick, Gimblett had to be picked and, batting as far down the order as they could put him, made a thundering 150-odd – a maiden century and the fastest of the season. The George at Norton St Philip has a monastery foundation, memorable oriels, and some claims to be the oldest hostelry in England. Priddy's gaunt inns are a legacy of Victorian mining.

At Bruton, with its packhorse bridge over the muddy little Brue, the author of *Lorna Doone* went to see the venerable King's School and the discovery of an ancient copy of Magna Carta came at a happy moment for the school's finances. Glastonbury is rather mixed rapture: the peace and grandeur of the abbey ruins, the George and Pilgrim notable for its Late Perpendicular façade, a hospitable place, but a pity they had to call a bottled concoction 'Druids' Piddle'; a pity, too, about the amount of pebbledash and staring brick in a town so near the heartland of graceful and serviceable stone, Doulting, Blue Lias, Ham Hill. 'No Hippies' notices everywhere suggest that Glastonbury has found the pop festival at Shepton Mallet a lasting trauma.

Somerset folk are very much their own people, with a pleasant response to anyone who comes looking for Sleepy Hollow inhabited by chawbacons in smocks. Circling and dipping like a swallow round a pond may not be the best way of conducting a survey but it is the right way of exploring this quiet corner. No planned itinerary is half as re-warding as blundering suddenly on tucked-away villages like Nunney with its Lilliputian castle, Batcombe and South Stoke where church and pub rub shoulders as they should, or Mells, perhaps the jewel of them all, with its Elizabethan manor and great church in a sea of green fields.

CHRISTOPHER WORDSWORTH

Wells

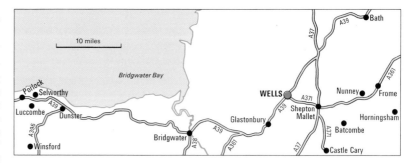

WHERE TO GO

Cathedral: now stands with half west front swathed in scaffolding as masons struggle to save the country's most amazing collection of medieval sculpture – 297 statues and acres of decorative fancies. Pleasing to see 'foliage carvers' credited on list of restoration workers and to know that such people still exist. Inside, superb inverted arches in front of altar were an elegant afterthought, added to brace central tower when it cracked in 1338.

Bishop's Palace: the Bishop still lives here, in house built by predecessors more than 700 years ago. Gatehouse, wall and moat added by Bishop Ralph in 1340 after quarrel with townspeople obviously made him feel insecure. House, grounds and chapel open Sun, Bank Hol Mon Easter–Oct, daily Aug 2.00–6.00. Grounds and chapel only also Thur Easter–Oct 2.00–6.00.

Vicar's Close: built in the middle of the 14th c. No 22 has changed very little since, slit windows, high wall. Street 10ft wider at bottom than top.

The Liberty: passage at top end of Cathedral Close leads out into this street of gorgeous houses, mostly owned by Cathedral School. No 1 is typical amalgam – a fine 18th c house with carved porch hood slammed on to the side of a tall 15th c house. Road curves back round to Cathedral Close passing the Tower House, featured in Elizabeth Goudge's *City of Bells*.

Museum: in Chancellor's House, showing more signs of Georgian alteration than of 15th c origins. Splendid museum, leaping about from prehistoric Wookey Hole finds to Victorian samplers, not forgetting the Mendip miners on the way. Especially rich for natural history and Nailsea glass. Open all year. April–Sept daily except Sun 10.00–6.00, June–Sept also Sun 2.30–5.30, Oct–March daily except Sun 2.00–4.30.

Almshouses: Bubwith Almshouses at bottom of Chamberlain St bequeathed by Bishop Bubwith who died in 1424. Very pretty range of buildings with chapel one end and guildhall the other. Farther up street are Harpers Almshouses dedicated 1713 'for perpetual use and maintenance of 5 poor men, old decayed Wooll-combers of this City'. The building is now converted into flats.

Market Place: Saturday stalls with usual bric-à-brac, clothes, spanners, china, veg and attic hoardings. Pleasing buildings, Georgian bow windows above the shop fronts, covering much earlier work. Penniless Porch squeezed into a corner leads through to Close, and Bishop's Eye nearby is Palace entrance. Inlaid in the pavement near the Porch is memorial of Mary Rand's record-breaking long jump.

The Rib: very pretty house just outside the Chain Gate, in the Bishop's gift. Built in 14th c with magnificently ornate porch and window added later. Rendering has been taken off most walls to reveal fascinating mish-mash of filled-in windows, doors, brick patching and line of 'new' porch.

Tor Hill: on the east edge of the city is a steep wooded climb which gives the best view of cathedral. Access off Tor St, the A371 to Shepton Mallet.

Wells Cathedral – one of the glories of true English Gothic

SHOPPING

Wellspring, by Penniless Porch: excellent bookshop, with full range of guides and maps as well as huge selection of other books.

FOOD AND DRINK

The Anchor, Market Square, does tea, coffee and cakes; also the **Old Priory** in Sadler St. **Talbot's Dining Room,** busy fish and chip establishment, in Broad St, seems to get most of the lunchtime trade. Pubs are strung out in great quantity along Market Place and High St, but CAMRA recommends only one, the **Star,** a great rambling place and once a coaching inn which dispenses Eldridge Pope's Royal Oak brew by hand-pump. The **Crown Hotel** fronting on to Market Place has splendid 17th c façade with three large gables, but round the side a cobbled courtyard shows a much older back, a jumble of roofs, carved windows, leaded panes, all very pretty. Eldridge Pope here too and Bass Charrington's Brew 11, local ciders. The **City Arms,** a Watney's house, used to be the city jail and still has relics to prove it. Pleasant small courtyard with tables and umbrellas, cell doors leading off on the right for instant cooling off.

WHERE TO STAY

The **White Hart Hotel,** recently modernized, and **Ancient Gate House Hotel,** part of Cathedral Close buildings, next to Browne's Gate. Both these in Sadler St.

TOURIST INFORMATION

Office on left of town hall in Market Sq open daily 10.00–5.00, tel Wells 72552.

Villages and country towns

Batcombe
Must be every towndweller's dream of village England: a quiet, civilized gathering of fine stone houses, mullioned windows, pleasing because of sturdiness rather than excessive decoration. A folding of hills all around, mostly green pasture, with a rookery in the valley below. The church, already standing on the highest point, further dominates village with glorious tower: 87ft high, broad and very ornate. A will of 1540 refers to its construction. Stone soars in pinnacles, curls and loops in tracery. Vast yew in churchyard seems as old as church itself.

Pub, the Three Horseshoes (does bed and breakfast), is conveniently next door, a pretty, whitewashed place, selling Courage from the barrel, also Gibbs Mew and Double Diamond. Bar dark and beamy, sole survivor of halcyon days early this century when village had three alehouses. Provis is pretty house on right as one walks down from church, with Victorian conservatory slapped on to much earlier front. Wickham's bull's head crest appears on later extension. Opposite is Rockwells, a fine Georgian house, even finer when seen from the

footpath tunnel, leading to fields beyond. Pleasant walk along footpath to Spargrove (about two miles).

Castle Cary
Castle stormed by King Stephen in 1138 and now only rectangle of keep marks its position on hill north-east of church. Satisfying, busy little town, large church with fine peal of eight bells, and spire, rather unusual in these parts. Victorian restoration made it more florid than it need be.

Peacocks in the garden of South Cottage, South St, and good solid houses in Annandale, up on a raised walkway leading down the hill. In the middle of town is market hall, again part of Victorians' busy refurbishing of the place. It has a clock, bay windows and slightly mothy lions holding up the roof. Half of it is now an agricultural merchant's, the other half a tiny museum with an old fire engine outside. Open daily Easter–Oct 10.00–12.00 and 2.30–4.30. Behind hall in Bailey Hill is circular lock-up built in 1779. There are only four like it in the country. It is seven ft in diameter, and 10ft high with two little iron grilles for ventilation. Post office here is very grand, big five-bay house of 1767. Castle Cary Dairy Products sell cheese, cream and local butter. The Old Bakehouse is a newly opened wholefood coffee and tea

shop, also lunches, with coffee served in summer in courtyard. Cary Antiques in High St has prints and cut glass.

The White Hart is a Courage pub with tables and chairs out on the pavement of Fore St. The Britannia is a central town local, selling real ale, Welsh Worthington, drawn by hand. The George in Market Sq, an old thatched place with a straw swan on the ridge, does good food and home-made teas.

Dunster
Dominated by castle perched high on its wooded mound. There has been a fortress on this site for 1000 years, but highly picturesque appearance of present castle owes more to Victorian alterations of architect Anthony Salvin than to antiquity. Castle held until 1976 by the Luttrell family who had lived here for 600 years. During Civil War, garrison under Colonel Wyndham took over castle for Royalists, but surrendered with honour after five-month siege. Gorgeous plaster ceiling in dining-room and staircase with elaborate bannisters, scrolls and flowers carved in elm. Stables with the original looseboxes, now National Trust shop. Open early April–Sept Sun–Thur 11.00–5.00, Oct Tue, Wed, Sun 2.00–4.00.

Yarn Market in market place is odd octagonal building once used for selling locally woven cloth. Opposite is the Luttrell Arms, an inn for more than 300 years, though originally the abbot's lodgings. Round the corner in Church St is the Nunnery, a fine three-storey house of the 14th c. The top two overhanging storeys are hung with pearly slates.

Footpath leads from Mill Lane down past thatched hen-house to superb old mill, two overshot wheels, now being painstakingly restored. Very old packhorse bridge here. Plenty of places for meals and snacks. Egon Ronay's *Just a Bite* recommends Hathaways, West St, for snacks and meals.

Horningsham
Scattered village with no central core, each cottage safely tucked away into its own garden. It lies sheltered in a bowl, surrounded by wooded hills, at a respectful distance from the landscaped splendours of Longleat's park. The Bath Arms is an elegant stone pub on the west side of the village, serving Wadworths 6X, Ushers pale ale and draught Bass. Good

Vicar's Close, Wells – the oldest inhabited street in Western Europe

food. Pollarded lime trees forming little square outside are known as the 12 Apostles.

Village a mixture of stone, thatch, brick and tile. A pleasant walk from pub up to church leads through avenue of young chestnuts, past long mill pond and village school. Church locked, but good views over the valley and down into surrounding gardens. Some fine 18th c chest-tombs, beautifully lettered. The old meeting house of 1566 in Chapel Lane is now congregational chapel, not locked.

Luccombe

There's a special lushness about this Exmoor village: the houses in a livery of cream wash and glossy brown paint, nearly all thatched. Every conceivable sort of window, gothic pointed, tiny squares, slits, the old glass patched with leading. The only shop is the post office, with stone floor and stable door, rudimentary supplies.

Stoney St leads off by the church, a dead-end for cars, but a pretty walk alongside a stream and waterfalls hung with trees and giant ferns. Hillgate Cottage at the top is the last in the village; after that the street peters out into a track which claws its way back up on to the moor.

Luccombe: the post office is the village's only shop

Very pleasing church, a barrel roof with painted bosses. Some of them are faces squinting down. Pillars decorated with fine carving of grapes and vine leaves. An old market cross stands in the churchyard, three tiers of steps, a shaft but no head.

Unfortunately no pub – the lord of the manor didn't approve – so villagers have to trek to Wootton Courtenay and the Dunkery Hotel, where there are two lively bars, selling Ushers pale ale and Sheppy cider. Pool room, children's room, bar steaks and accommodation. The hotel specializes in riding holidays with horses from Huntscote stables nearby.

Nunney

Best castle in Somerset. It's neither large, nor commanding, but setting and strict symmetry of design are both enormously pleasing. Moat all around and also stream which runs close by. Built in an oblong with a tower at each corner by John de la Mare who received licence to crenellate in 1373. Smashed during Civil War when Parliamentary force, well equipped with artillery, bombarded it into surrender. Roundheads tore out all joists and floorboards so systematically that place was never lived in again. Open weekdays May–Sept 9.30–7.00, March,

April, Oct 9.30–5.30, Nov–Feb 9.30–4.00, Sun from 2.00.

North entrance of castle looks on to jumble of farmyard belonging to Manor Farm, very handsome five-bay house, early 18th c with restrained pediments alternately triangular and rounded along the ground floor windows. Church has some fine monuments, a 14th c knight and a knight and his lady done a hundred years later. Market cross by stream formerly stood in churchyard.

The George is a long, stone-built local looking out over castle, selling draught Bass and Worthington. Real ale up on the main road at Nunney Catch where the Theobald Arms sells Hall & Woodhouse Badger bitter and Taunton cider. Busy pub with friendly atmosphere.

Porlock

The last Saxon king, Harold, landed here when he returned from exile in Ireland, 1052. Straggling main street, not as pretty now as early descriptions suggest, since many old buildings have disappeared. The poet Southey drank at the Ship Inn. Today it sells Perry cider, Ind Coope bitter and draught Bass. Porlock Hill, enormously steep pull out of village on west, is still considered the most engine-testing gradient in the country.

Old church dedicated to St Dubricius, Bishop of Llandaff about 612, is reminder of cross-channel traffic with Wales. At the east end of main street is Dovery Court, remnant of 15th c manor house with surprisingly grand window. Now used as billiard room, information centre and museum.

Very pleasant cafe in High St, the Break, does tea, proper coffee and homemade cakes. *Egon Ronay's Pub Guide* recommends the Ship Inn at Porlock Weir, Porlock's harbour about two miles to the north-west. Good walk from Weir to Culbone, about two miles through woods to church, smallest in England (35ft by 12ft) and pottery, Waistel and Joan Cooper, who are open every day 10.00–7.00 summer. Winter, weekends, or by appointment, Porlock 862539.

Selworthy

Entire picturebook village preserved by National Trust as part of their Holnicote holding. Stunning position on a steep hill looking south over Exmoor, the lane leading to it dark with holly and ivy. Small car park by church, with telescope.

Hillside behind planted by 10th Holnicote baronet who started in 1809 and added a block of trees to celebrate the birth of each of his nine children.

Well-signposted walks throughout these woods. Wide track leads beside churchyard up the combe and bears left on to North Hill. Stone Memorial Hut here commemorates the Sunday walks of the energetic 10th baronet and records some of the quotations from Keble with which he would entertain children and grandchildren on these expeditions. Thatched cottages of Selworthy Green built by baronet as refuge for estate pensioners, grouped round a communal green with interconnecting paths. Periwinkle Cottage serves delicious teas, all home-made, recommended by Egon Ronay's *Just a Bite*.

Remarkably lavish church for such a hidden-away place, with white walls and tower. Lovely south aisle with original wagon roof, richly decorated and windows with finely cut, elegant tracery. Footpath at bottom of hill follows old track to Allerford emerging at packhorse bridge.

Winsford

Small village on south edge of Exmoor, hemmed in by steep wooded hills with the Exe river and the Winn brook pelting through the middle. Pretty little packhorse bridge, cobbled with two arches, now sadly out of scale with surrounding buildings. Plain roughcast cottage with slate roof opposite the post office is birthplace of Ernest Bevin. Immaculate garden, productive rather than aesthetic.

Dominant feature is Royal Oak inn (recommended by *Egon Ronay's Pub Guide*), a long, thatched building curving round a corner, with yard full of dogs, geese and chickens. Owned by large, amiable man called Charley. Bar beamy and dark with great log fire, ancient tankards, horse brasses and hunting pictures. Whitbread draught bitter, drawn the old fashioned way, also Tankard, two different lagers and Taunton cider. Coffee, bar snacks from 10.30 in the morning, also full scale dining-room meals. *Just a Bite* recommends Bridge Cottage for coffee, tea and cake.

Within walking distance up on the moor is odd Caractacus stone, five ft high, probably put up in the 5th c. Writing on stone only discovered 90 years ago, and excavation has shown that it is not a grave. Further to the south-west, crossing the river Barle, are the Tarr Steps, an ancient bridge made of gigantic stone slabs of a sort unknown in this part of the world.

The church at Porlock: King Harold landed here in 1052

—Places to visit—

Bath: crammed with things to see such as Royal Crescent and nearby the elegant Circus built by John Wood, an amateur antiquarian in love with Rome who dreamt of recreating the whole of Bath in its image and from 1724 to 1754 worked on any project he could get his hands on. The Crescent is by Wood's son, who carried on for another 20 years after his father's death. Walking is best in Bath, for pleasure lies not only in grand sweeping conceptions, but in detail of ironwork, cornices, doors and friezes. Pulteney Bridge is Robert Adam's vision, lined with shops in the Venetian manner. Museums for all tastes, 15 of them.

The well-planned American Museum has complete rooms furnished in early settler style. Very pretty stencilled bedroom and outstanding textile collection with quilts of staggering complexity and hooked rugs. Lovely loopy one of a lion hemmed in by prodigious flowers and several odd birds. Open end March–end Oct daily (not Mon) 2.00–5.00, Bank Hol Sun, Mon 11.00–5.00. At Claverton Manor 3¾ miles south-east of Bath via A36.

Glastonbury: very difficult to imagine Arthur and Guinevere here among the red-brick suburban houses and light industry. According to legend, the Holy Grail was buried under a spring on Glastonbury Tor. Abbey is fine complex of buildings, oldest Christian sanctuary in Britain. Near St Mary's Chapel is complete abbot's kitchen from the 14th c: fireplaces in all four corners. Open daily until dusk.

The 14th c Abbey Barn, midway between the town centre and the Tor, now houses the excellent Somerset Rural Life Museum. Fascinating collection of agricultural equipment, carts, tools, with plenty of space devoted to the two great Somerset traditions of cheese and cider making, while an exhibition in the Abbey Farmhouse illustrates the life of a Victorian farmworker, literally from cradle to grave. Open all year Mon–Fri 10.00–5.00, Easter–end Sept Sat 10.00–6.00, Sun 2.00–6.00, Oct–Easter Sat–Sun 10.00–4.00. Chilkwell Street, tel Glastonbury 32903.

Lytes Cary: home of the Lyte family for 500 years until 18th c and rescued from ruin in 1907 by Sir Walter Jenner, son of the Victorian physician, who laid out the present garden. Great parlour had been used as farm store, but early 17th c panelling was undamaged. Path leads through Jenner's currant-bun yew topiary to east front, a jigsaw of different interlocking roof heights, for scarcely a generation went by without some Lyte leaving his mark on the family seat, so that the whole is a Jacob's coat of architectural styles. 15th c great hall with arch-braced roof had new porch and windows added 100 years later. Henry Lyte sat here in 1578 translating his 'Niewe Herbale' from the Dutch and dedicated it to Queen Elizabeth 'from my poore house at Lytes-carie'. National Trust. Open March–end Oct Wed, Sat 2.00–6.00. Three miles north-east of Ilchester.

Barrington Court: Renaissance house, vertical lines of gables and windows, built from honey-coloured Ham stone. Twisted spiral chimney stacks and finials are set along the skyline like monster chessmen. First big country house bought by National Trust and only one with garden designed by Gertrude Jekyll. Owned originally by Henry Daubeney who financed an extravagant existence at Henry VIII's court by gradually selling off all his country estates. Fine furnishings purloined, rather than original: staircase roof from Hereford, dining-room screen from King's Lynn. National Trust. Open Wed 10.15–12.15 and 2.00–6.00, Oct–Easter 2.00–4.00. Three miles north-east of Ilminster.

Brympton House: drive ends up at Tudor west front of house with stables and clock tower on left, priest house and church on right. Used until recently as school, but present young owner regained possession of house, his family's property since 1731, and has done most of restoration work together with his wife. Collections of gloves, wedding dresses, cricket memorabilia and country-life museum. Wine sold from Brympton vineyard. Teas in stables. Open Easter, May–Sept Sat–Wed 2.00–6.00. Two miles west of Yeovil.

Coleridge Cottage: much changed since Coleridge lived here for three years. *The Ancient Mariner* took shape during a walk with Wordsworth – who lived three miles away at Alfoxden – and contains many references to this area. National Trust. Open (parlour only) April–Sept Sun–Thur 2.00–5.00. At Nether Stowey, eight miles west of Bridgwater.

Montacute: glows like a rich honey confection in its Ham stone. Curiously reflects many present architectural obsessions: great expanses of glass, for which Elizabethans had a passion, and built to demonstrate the wealth and importance of its owner, Edward Phelips, an ambitious and successful lawyer. If possible, sneak round and see it first from the east side, the original entrance, where the builder crammed in every eye-catching novelty he knew, bays, columns, gables, statues, framed by the original garden gazebos and balustrades. Gallery at top of house is now hung with impressive exhibition from National Portrait Gallery. Occasional summertime concerts. National Trust. Open daily (except Tue) April–Oct 12.30–6.00. Teas at the house. Four miles west of Yeovil.

Tintinhull: small enough to covet, a gentle, balanced house showing all the virtues which Sir Henry Wotton, writing in the 16th c, advocated in good building, 'commoditie, firmness and delight'. It started off as a plain Somerset farmhouse, hauled out of the mud by the addition in 1700 of a fine façade on the west. Garden is a delight made up of a series of separately hedged rooms, a

Glastonbury Tor – burial place of the Holy Grail

formal layout planted with anarchic informality. Most borders are mixes, small trees, shrubs, ornamental gasses and bulbs jostling with the flowers. Great spillings of roses, dahlias and broom in the borders by the formal pool, restrained behind by bulwarks of yew. In high summer, huge tubs of waxy Regale lilies stand all along the terrace. National Trust. Open April–Sept Wed, Thur, Sat and bank hol 2.00–6.00. Five miles north-west of Yeovil, half a mile south of A303.

Sheepskin factory: John Wood, Old Cleeve, Minehead. Tanning, dyeing, cutting, free guided tour of whole process Mon–Fri at 11.00, also Thur at 3.00. Factory seconds shop open Mon–Fri 9.00–4.30, March–Dec also Sat 10.00–4.00.

Cider farm: R. J. Sheppy, Three Bridges, Bradford-on-Tone, Taunton (A38). Until last war most farms of any size made their own brews. Sheppy still does. Orchards, cider-making plant and museum open to anyone interested. Shop sells the cider and traditional mugs

to drink it from. Open Mon–Sat 8.30–dusk. Easter–Christmas Sun 12.00–2.00.

Craft Centre: Newhouse Farm, Moor Lane, Clevedon. Housed in former farm with outbuildings now turned into studios. Photographs, landscape paintings, silverware, wax flowers, tiled tables. Carving and wood-turning demonstrations Sun afternoons. One barn a country-life museum, another a restaurant. Open daily but museum and restaurant closed Mon (open bank hol).

Costume dolls: Peggy Nisbet, Oldmixon Crescent, Oldmixon Industrial Estate, Weston-super-Mare. Tour includes art room, cutting dept, etc. Best to tel first: Weston 21141. Open Mon–Fri 8.30–4.30.

Telecommunications Museum, 38 North St, Taunton: highly technical collection showing telephone, telegraph and other transmission equipment, including an old manual telephone exchange of 1900. Biggest collection of its kind, but strictly for communication freaks. Open Sat 1.30–5.00.

Shoe Museum, Street: PR exercise

for Clarks, whose factory is here. Collection of slippers, boots and shoes from Roman times to our own. Open May–Oct Mon–Fri 10.00–1.00 and 2.00–4.45, Sat 10.00–1.00.

Fleet Air Arm Museum, Yeovilton off A303: development of Navy's air service from early beginnings in 1903. More than 40 planes, some still being restored. Special exhibitions include five *Ark Royals* and 'Warneford VC', first man to bring down a Zeppelin in 1915. Concorde 002, first British prototype, also on view. Open Mon–Sat 10.00–5.30, Sun 12.30–5.30 or dusk if earlier.

Wookey Hole: whole complex now owned by Madame Tussauds who have blasted a tunnel through to the seventh and eighth chambers of the cave complex. Odd stalagmite in first chamber known as Witch of Wookey, turned to stone by Glastonbury monk. Also, Tussauds' store room, rusticated heads no longer important enough for London. Open daily April–Sept 10.00–6.00, Oct–March 10.00–4.30. Excellent walk near here leads up through mysterious Ebbor

Gorge under ceiling of branches to lonely Mendip plateau above. Two Nature Conservancy trails.

Cheddar: Cox's cave discovered in 1837 – Cox was hacking away at rock face to make room for new cart shed. More spectacular Gough's cave opened up 40 years later. Open daily from 10.00–6.00 or dusk if earlier with separate charges for each section. Walk for free at Black Rock Nature Reserve nearby with pleasant circular route through wood and downland (about $1\frac{1}{2}$ miles).

Steam Railways: East Somerset Railway, Cranmore Station, Shepton Mallet. Brainchild of wildlife artist David Shepherd. He has biggest steam loco in Britain here: Black Prince plus seven other locos, six passenger coaches and 17 wagons. Open April–Oct daily 9.00–5.30, steaming along $\frac{3}{4}$ mile track Sun and Bank Hol Mon, Nov–March Sat, Sun only 9.00–4.00. West Somerset Railway, Minehead. Steam trains run from this station to Williton and Bishops Lydeard (Taunton). Write to station for timetable or tel Minehead 4996.

Wildlife Park, Cricket St Thomas: not a safari park, the more fearsome beasts are behind bars, but deer roam in paddocks along the river and birds fly in tropical walk-through aviary. Home of the National Heavy Horse Centre. Penguin enclosure. Open daily 10.00–6.00.

Wellington Monument: (two miles south of Wellington) started 20 Oct 1817 after local gentry decided they ought to do something to mark the achievements of His Grace (though he never lived there). 175ft of sleek ashlar stone, the obelisk stands high on the Blackdown Hills, visible across half Somerset. Staircase of 235 steps leads to the top.

High Ham Windmill, two miles north of Langport: last survivor of several that once stood round here. Substantial stone-built tower with sail blocks, but most of milling machinery gone.

FOOD AND DRINK

Egon Ronay's *Lucas Guide* recommends **Old Parsonage Restaurant**, Farrington Gurney, tel Temple Cloud 52211. Hot, home-made rolls, cooking by proprietor. **No 3**, Magdalene St, Glastonbury, tel Glastonbury 32129. Inventive menu. **Milk House Restaurant**, Montacute, tel Martock 3823. Unusual wine list. **Oak House Restaurant**, The Square, Axbridge, tel Axbridge 732444. Robust food in rustic surroundings. **Well House**, Poundisford, tel Blagdon Hill 566. Interesting dishes from fresh local produce are most satisfying. **Hunstrete House**, Hunstrete, Chelwood, tel Compton Dando 578. Georgian country-house hotel serving imaginative dishes.

TOURIST INFORMATION

Local papers: *West Somerset Free Press*, published every Fri. *Wells Journal*, every Thur.

Exmoor National Park Information Centre, Exmoor House, Dulverton, Somerset, TA22 9HL, tel Dulverton 23665.

City of Bath Information Centre, Abbey Churchyard, Bath, tel Bath 62831.

Tourist information centres: also at Chard, Cheddar, Glastonbury, Minehead, Taunton, Wellington, Wincanton.

Research: Anna Pavord.

Cirencester

There is a little formula that goes something like this:

'You live in the country, don't you?'

'Yes.'

'Whereabouts?'

'Gloucestershire.'

'Oh, *lovely*!' Said vaguely, sometimes accompanied by a sigh.

This is soul-damping because I always want to say: so is London lovely. What about the river in certain lights? What about the way spring can suddenly invade a street, making you want to run? Or summer blackbirds bouncing their voices off courtyard walls like bathroom baritones? Sometimes I think the Great God Pan has fled to the town, driven from the countryside by the bulldozers and aeroplanes of our industrious farmers. It's like a war here. If I were a fox I'd move to Wandsworth.

To me that 'Oh, *lovely*!' sounds like a dream of 'peace' and 'nature' that does not exist and would probably be insupportable if it did. Gloucestershire is covered with old cottages 'done up' in the country-boom of the 1960s with patio and picture-window, now deserted by the original dreamers because they could not stand the loneliness – or the inconvenience.

I live in the country because I can't concentrate in the town: there are so many better things to do there. But the country is inconvenient.

In our village there used to be a shop run by a very old lady who had been born in it. When she died the shop died with her. Villages die almost by government decree: cottages are condemned, or two are turned into one to bring them up to an urban standard; so, fewer people live in the village and first the school goes, then the shop, then the buses.

Without a shop, or a bus service to speak of – the village never had a pub – you take to the road for contact. And this is the first important difference between country and town life: the significance, glamour, necessity of *roads*.

Our town is Cirencester and, by way of lanes, there are two roads into it, the top and the bottom road. If we lived a few yards to the north it would be balmy Cheltenham, in the vale, that drew us; a few yards to the west it would be Stroud of the steep streets. But for us it is Cirencester and the bottom road is a new one by local standards. It twists along the watermeadows of the little river Churn – from the top of a double-decker bus you see what an exquisite valley they wrecked last century.

The top one is a different matter: Roman, stern and straight as

The Thames near Lechlade at dawn: the town gets its name from the river Leach which enters the Thames here a ruler. It is the old Ermin Street that joined Roman Gloucester with Roman Cirencester and the limestone tower of the parish church is centred on it: you see it across the flat tops of the hills from miles away. The Cotswolds are like a crusty cake risen from the plain, with nooks and valleys the cracks in the crust. We live on the flat uncracked bit and you can see for miles, when the wind doesn't make your eyes water.

The story of this road is the story of pubs, which are just about the only buildings for the 10-mile stretch. Not long after the steep climb from the Severn plain is the Golden Heart – and that was Roman too: wine jars have been discovered in its cellars. It is the place on the march when the legion would begin to grumble, and the centurion would fancy a breather himself. A few miles farther on, at the old turnpike (with another road behind it, overgrown, once used by prudent sheep-drovers to avoid the toll), is the Highwayman, done-up with horse-brasses and warming pans; but its antiquity is vouched for by its depth from the road: the traffic goes by at eye-level.

At the Golden Heart, so often has the Roman road been mended that wheels go by above your head, and at the Five Mile, 'my' pub, the hubcaps of the juggernauts are on a level with the low ceiling. Almost alone in the neighbourhood the Five Mile has hardly been touched since Oliver Cromwell was supposed to have stayed there. But many are the hands I have seen rubbed at the thought of the goldmine that could be made of it, refurbished.

Gloucestershire is full of such 'goldmines', whose owners become sadder and poorer by the day among their slowly cracking plastic tables in the open-space bar – the snugs and divisions swept away in the 1960s. Snugs where the cider-junkies sat, grunting eloquently, like Thomas Hardy characters, while the squatters – drop-outs before the phrase was even coined – crept down from their beautiful derelict cottages in the hills to join them. These cottages are now let for high rents or, more likely, levelled to the ground . . . I tell you, if you want to see change, come to the country.

Off the road are the villages: Brimpsfield, with its castle mound, whose lord owned lands far into Wales; the Duntisbournes, with their Saxon-Norman churches, burial mounds, ancient tracks and sudden nooks of cottages with real cottagers residing. None of these has a pub; then, as now, everyone was linked, for public life, to the road. But they do have smooth, sculptured fields that catch every change of light, and drystone walls that grow mosses green as cress and lichens that go from bright rust to black, from yellow-green to an intricately textured white.

If you don't turn off, to be lost in sunken lanes, soused in sudden unexpected fords, you keep the tower in front of you and reach Ciren-cester, briefly diverted by a bypass that cost a magnificent line of trees. The first things you see are the shining agricultural machines lined up for sale by the river Churn: green, red, yellow, blue; tempting as boiled sweets, making you wish you had a need for a postbox-red muckspreader, or a daffodil combine-harvester.

After that you are in Dollar Street and are affected by a sense of modest but solid importance. Cirencester is at the joining of several ancient roads; it was the second-largest Roman city, and still seems quietly conscious of it. This first street is a good amalgam of every century from the seventeenth to the present: butchers, who make their own sausages; a grocers, run by an old lady who appears when the doorbell tinkles; booksellers; antique shops as old as the objects they sell. At the end is the dark-green cedar tree in the yellow embrasure of the church tower and after that you are in the open Market Place, a street as pleasing and elegant, in its small way, as the High in Oxford.

On the draughty corner of it is Charlie Barnett's fish and game shop, where that legendary opening batsman, of Gloucestershire and England, shows the world his boundary-hitting forearms mottled with cold after a spell of filleting or of drawing the insides out of pheasants. People stand on the pavements in the Market Place and talk to each other. If you visit a shop anywhere more than twice you are likely to be known by name – but tentatively, unintrusively. Country people know they may spend a lifetime greeting each other so they go slowly. But in the town, on neutral ground, some of the careful privacy of the village is relaxed.

The town is neither 'timeless' nor 'leisured': it bustles, but calmly. Everything is on the human scale. The stone buildings are seldom more than three storeys high; there is plenty of sky. If you stand at the bottom of the Market Place, opposite the Fleece, and watch the curve of the Georgian shop fronts – painted grey or blue or brown, matching the sky-tones – as it reaches up to the carved decorations on the church porch, you see how good it is: neither over-preserved nor ruined, and the right size.

Of course, Cirencester is a country town – standing opposite the Fleece, your back is to Hayes the saddlers (a friend noticed its labels on saddles in the Argentine) – but, if you feared such a thing, there is no daunting sense of tweeds and sheepskin, no confidential shouting over the roofs of Range Rovers.

Even the great house (Earl Bathurst's) is discreet, behind a yew hedge so high that the gardener must use a fireman's ladder to clip it. Most of its park, beloved of Alexander Pope, is open to everyone; in the summer, balloon races start from there and the wide sky is filled with coloured exclamation marks, panting hot air into themselves with bright gusts. They do not spoil the sky: they enhance it.

Sky is what you notice, in the town and out of it. Leaving, sitting in your car on the top road is like being in a box at a theatre of constantly changing light-effects. Turning off into the lanes there is little sense of a change of scale: the sky-parish still carries on, and on. You vie with the occasional car you meet, which of you shall most politely give way, both of you humbled by the sky.

Sky, a sense of width, spoils you: after a few years you find it difficult to breathe properly without it.

P. J. KAVANAGH

Cirencester

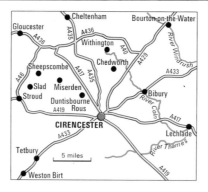

WHERE TO GO

Market Place: most prominent feature is the church, and St John the Baptist Porch, built in 1500. The outside of the church shows the last stage of the true gothic style, with soaring windows, huge arches and plenty of perpendicular panelling. The 15th c tower contains the oldest ring of 12 bells in the country; interior is rich and sumptuous, dating from 1515, made possible by the prosperity of the wool trade. Note the seven-light window above chancel arch, an architectural feature mainly confined to the Cotswolds.

Corinium Museum, Park St: spacious museum housing one of the country's finest collections of Roman antiquities. Includes full-scale reconstructions of mosaic craftsman's workshop and a kitchen with menu for a Roman dinner party – stuffed dormice a speciality. There are fine floor mosaics and an intriguing word-square puzzle, called the Acrostic, reading the same across and down. Museum takes its name from Corinium, the Roman name for Cirencester, which was the second largest town in Roman Britain. Open May–Sept Mon–Sat and bank hol 10.00–6.00 Sun 2.00–6.00, Oct–April Tue–Sat 10.00–5.00 Sun 2.00–5.00. Closed Christmas.

Corn Hall: Victorian building with unusual details, such as carved masks on the key-stones. Houses information centre and the occasional indoor market.

Cirencester Park: mansion (not open to public), built in 1714–18, is the home of Lord Bathurst. With only an enormous 36ft semi-circular yew hedge, mentioned in the *Guinness Book of Records*, separating it from the town, estate's 3000 public acres make a perfect town park. Wooded landscape was designed by the first Earl Bathurst and Alexander Pope. Beech trees, sycamores and ash trees mingle with 18th c follies and picturesque outer buildings, one called Pope's seat. Also, nature walks, a model farm and polo some summer Sun afternoons.

The Delahaye Gallery, 24 Castle St: exhibitions of work by various artists. Open 9.00–5.30 Mon–Sat, closed Thur pm and Sun.

Cirencester Workshops, Cricklade St: the Old Brewery buildings, turned into bright crafts complex, now houses two potters, a clock-face painter, saddlers and leatherworkers, a cane-and-rush seating worker, knitter, weaver, etc. Each craftsman works at least eight hours a week in view of the public. Gallery with changing exhibitions. Excellent coffee house. Restaurant, workshops, shop and gallery open Mon–Sat 10.00–5.30.

Abbey Grounds: attractive parkland with lake, trees and shrubs, swans and wildfowl on the river Churn. Remnants of the old Roman walls nearby.

EVENTS

Mop Fairs: each Oct.

Cirencester Park with its famous yew hedge – the gardener uses a fireman's ladder to clip it

SHOPPING

Market Day: Mon, Fri (cattle market, Tetbury Rd, Tue. Cirencester sheep fair held every Sept).

Early closing day: Thur.

Great Western Foodstore, Cricklade St: pretty green-trimmed shop selling 25 types of cheese, 10 of home-made ice cream, cider and whole-wheat bread.

Abbey Butterflies Ltd, Silver St: individually framed butterflies, also luminous jewellery made from butterfly wings. Back part of shop devoted to live specimens of tarantulas, South American spiders and all things creepy.

FOOD AND DRINK

Egon Ronay's Lucas Guide recommends the **King's Head Hotel Restaurant**, Market Place: extensive menu of international dishes. Egon Ronay's *Just a Bite* recommends **Ann's Pantry**, 25 Market Place: coffees and teas, while *Egon Ronay's Pub Guide* commends the **Plough Inn**, Gloucester Rd, Stratton: a good cold table offering salads, surrounded by beef and other meats. Pubs include: **The Black Horse**, Castle St. This 1470 building used to be a wool merchant's house; bedrooms have exposed beams where wool is calcified into the wood. Occasionally visited by a lady ghost in a brown dress. Extended licence on Tue; Courage. **Bear Inn**, Dyer St: thought to have been an old coaching inn. Cobblestones outside. Courage. **Courtyard Bar**, Market Place: free house attached to the **King's Head Hotel**. Sparse and functional. **Drillman Arms** and the **Corinium Court Hotel** serve real ale.

WHERE TO STAY

Egon Ronay's Lucas Guide recommends: **Stratton House Hotel**, Gloucester Rd, tel Cirencester 61761. Handsome old Cotswold stone house with comfortable and modern bedrooms in the new wing. **King's Head Hotel**, Market Place, tel Cirencester 3321. Friendly coaching inn with old beams and well-equipped bedrooms.

TOURIST INFORMATION

Corn Hall Building, Market Place, tel Cirencester 4180.

Villages and country towns

Bibury

William Morris declared it to be the most beautiful village in England. Certainly Bibury is a delight – even the modern buildings seem well integrated. Unfortunately, in the high season, tour buses crowd its narrow streets and hordes of motorists, pausing to inspect huge trout hovering just below the water's surface, create massive congestion.

Nucleus of village is the Old Mill, now a museum, and the Swan Hotel, its circular flower beds mingling with the pools of Bibury Trout Farm. Even more pleasant is Bibury Court Hotel, a 17th c manor house standing in lavish grounds with a free house pub in what used to be the grain store. Catherine Wheel free house up the road has Courage Directors bitter straight from the barrel.

Cotswold stone abounds in Bibury – best seen in the medieval cottages of Arlington Row, a weaving factory in 17th c but now private residences owned by National Trust. Between mill and almshouses lies the swampiest village green ever – Rack Isle, a wildfowl reserve where geese and ducks roam freely. Arlington Mill is a 300-year-old corn mill now put to use as a country museum. Under the auspices of the Cotswolds scholar, David Verey, museum houses an excellent collection, including agricultural implements, old photographs, a very early refrigerator and a handsome Victorian printing press.

Bibury Trout Farm open every day April–Oct 2.00–6.00. Trout recipes on sale. Arlington Mill open daily, March–Oct 10.30–7.00 or dusk. Nov–Feb weekends only.

Bourton-on-the-Water

With its 17th c cottages and low bridges arched over shimmering water, Bourton is a popular beauty spot. Amenities abound – from a motor museum in the old mill to a bird zoo, gardens for cream teas, restaurants, and the pleasant green along the banks of the river Windrush. The exceptionally beautiful 19th c church has a 14th c chancel and a Georgian tower, offering sanctuary even in the desperately overcrowded high season. The Cotswold Perfumery with its

oak beams and open fireplace sells perfumes, aftershaves and colognes made on the premises.

The Old New Inn, built in the early 18th c, has a sundial inscribed 'Silas Wells 1718'. In the back garden lies the interesting model village, an exact replica of Bourton, with buildings as high as a child. Recorded music from the village church comes from the model version, and there are miniature trees and running water.

The model village at the back of the Old New Inn, Bourton-on-the-Water

Chedworth

Village built on hilly ledges with distinctive stone cottages – one with a stone arch, some vine-covered and tiny, all with bright flowers in front. Village sprawls for more than a mile, with views of superb countryside. Opposite a tiny waterfall, the elegant Seven Tuns Courage pub has two bars, tree-stump tables outside for picnicking.

Norman windows light the Norman church tower which has a 13th c belfry. Nave and windows paid for by Henry VII. Be sure to see all the pock-marked gargoyles on the church's outer walls.

Denfurlong Farm is a private, working farm open to the public. Two trails pass through the fields of the farm. Watch cows being milked, and harvest during July and Aug. Good for urban children. Booklet describes particular points of interest.

Chedworth Roman Villa lies down narrow single-track roads where rabbits and clear country views provide distraction. You almost pass it before you see it, tucked down a side-road overlooking the valley. Excavated 1864–6, site includes several open-air rooms of mosaics. The figure of winter is especially pleasing, with hare in one hand and tree branch in the other. Be sure to see the suite of baths; also the heating system with its stone hypocaust pillars looking like tombstones. National Trust. Open March–Oct Tue–Sun and Bank Hol Mon 11.00–6.00 (closed Good Friday), Nov–mid Dec, Feb Wed–Sat 11.00–4.00.

Duntisbourne Rous

One of three Duntisbourne villages: the others are Duntisbourne Leer, a collection of high barns and gold-stone cottages with a ford, and Duntisbourne Abbots, which has a grave known as Jack Barrow where an earthen vessel, a stone chest and a huge sword were found, a glamorous youth hostel, plus an even longer ford. (Near all three villages is the hamlet of Middle Duntisbourne.)

Duntisbourne Rous is a cluster of cottages and a farm in a deep hollow, with a tiny church perched on a steep bank overlooking the valley and a stream. Church is believed to be Saxon, because of the herring-bone work on the north wall, although fairly recent studies say it could not be earlier than the 12th c. A rare possession for a village church is the crypt, with its small Norman east window. Rustic and unspoilt, church also has a Norman chancel arch of unusual design with mouldings which are continued around the underside of the arch. Guide to Duntisbourne Rous parish on sale in the rectory next door.

Lechlade

Market town taking its name from the river Leach flowing into the Thames a few fields away. Once famous for its barge traffic, now has only bright holiday boats. Centre of town is the Market Place, with the great 'wool' church of St Lawrence. Shelley wrote his 'Stanzas in Lechlade Churchyard' here in 1815, and with its dark trees, eerie elevated tombs nearby dovecotes, it is certainly an impressive place. Note the weatherbeaten gargoyles high on the front walls, with contemporary drainpipes coming out of their mouths.

Lechlade: this Old Father Thames was once at the river's source

Next to the church stands the old vicarage, now a creeper-covered antique store. Other attractive shops nearby are F. Brooks for home-made bread and pâté, local honey, and the 300-year-old bookshop, cosy and low-beamed.

Eat pheasant pie at the Swan pub, fresh fruit from the farm by St John's bridge – look for signs – or trust *Egon Ronay's Lucas Guide* which recommends the 13th c Trout Inn. This attractive inn, with flagstone floors and stream at the side, was probably frequented by William Morris when he lived down the road. Or buy your dinner from the Little Farringdon Mill Trout Farm. A mill on this site dates from the Domesday Book; current one stopped working only 15 years ago.

Miserden

Immaculate village clustered around a tree of idleness, a giant sycamore surrounded by a bench. Most of village owned by Misarden Park estate, responsible for much of the uniformity and tidiness about the place. All new building material comes from the local quarry which supplied the stone for the older houses – built in the 17th and 18th c. Carpenters Arms pub has mullioned windows and serves evening meals. also Whitbread. Late Saxon church has a nave with a wagon roof; more visible Anglo-Saxon remains are the heads in the north and south doorways. The rectory is 14th c.

In Anvil Barn, Michael E. Roberts does forged work in iron, bronze, aluminium and copper; also fire canopies. Open daily but call first, tel Miserden 244.

Misarden Park is a 13½-acre estate with lovely gardens and an Elizabethan manor house. House not open to the public, but grounds open occasionally. There are colourful herbaceous borders, a rockery, roses, cedar trees and a magnificent sculptured yew hedge.

Sheepscombe

Friendly, unpretentious village lying on both sides of a valley. Flowers are wild and the golden-stone buildings bereft of ornamentation. Most cottages cling to the slopes, either uphill or downhill as that's the only way to go. Gleaming like a beacon at the top of one of the hills is the Butchers Arms, with an elevated grassy garden overlooking church and village.

Slad

Certain things in Slad have changed since Laurie Lee wrote about his life here in *Cider With Rosie*, but then again certain things haven't. The school in which the small boy was content 'to slop around and whine and idle' is a school no longer, and the old winding road through the village has been usurped by a modern one which bypasses it completely. The golden-stone houses still perch on steep slopes – sturdy, utilitarian cottages built for harsh winters and hard work. The little church still stands, as does Laurie Lee's house, down over the bank with a billy-goat in front. Spend an evening in the Woolpack pub and you may get to know Slad a little.

Weston Birt

Trim village lying on the Wiltshire border, one long row of pretty cottages overlooking a golf course. At the end of the village stands 19th c Weston Birt House, designed by Lewis Vulliamy. Its façade is 120yd long with towers and octagonal chimneys puncturing the skyline. Now a girls' school and closed to the public, its splendid exterior and Italian gardens can be seen from the churchyard. The serene, secluded St Catherine's church, nestling to one side, contains the recumbent figure of Robert Staymer Holford, who commissioned Weston Birt House; he has two marble angels supporting his head and a greyhound lying at his feet.

The well-known Weston Birt Arboretum, covering some 250 acres, is run by the Forestry Commission. Main attractions are spring flowering shrubs and trees, and the heady blaze of autumn colours, but it is worth visiting at any time. Visitors are encouraged to stray from the footpaths, so boots are a good idea. Ornamental trees and shrubs in the ancient woodland known as the Silk Wood. Open to the public every day 10.00–sunset.

Further along the road is Hooks House Pottery, where Christopher White makes stoneware in an old pheasant roost: note nesting boxes in wall. Using glaze made from the ashes of local trees, Chris hopes to utilize the arboretum's close proximity to come up with even more exotic glazes.

The Hare and Hounds Hotel has three bars serving real ale, with an attractive restaurant.

Withington

Pretty village along the banks of the river Coln. Within parish has been found a burial barrow, probably Bronze Age, and a Roman villa. Since the excavation in 1811, the 4th c mosaic and other findings have been moved to the British Museum. Withington church has a Norman doorway and fragments of medieval glass.

One way to learn about Withington is to frequent the Mill Inn and buy its illustrated guide. The Mill is said to date back to the Domesday Book. In summer there's the riverside garden looking on to parkland; in winter, log fires in huge open fireplaces. The Mill House, of Cotswold stone, was opened as a restaurant in 1964. Near where the water-wheel once stood, the chef prepares grills and roasts turned on a spit by a miniature replica of the original water-wheel. Hotel gazebo with its circular walls is an incongruous but pleasant modern addition. During warm weather eat outside by the river. Popular for Sun lunches.

Places to visit

Halles Abbey: one of the last Cistercian houses to be founded in England, built in 1246 by Richard, Earl of Cornwall, fulfilling a vow made on escaping shipwreck. Now a splendid ruin with 17 cloister arches. Museum which adjoins it gives idea of how abbey must have looked during late Middle Ages. Open March, April, Oct Mon–Sat 9.30–5.30, Sun 2.00–5.30, May–Sept 9.30–7.00, Sun 2.00–7.00, Nov–Feb 9.30–4.00, Sun 2.00–4.00. One mile east of A46 nr Winchcombe.

Horton Court: typical Cotswold manor house. North wing *c* 1140, rest built in 1521 for William Knight, later Bishop of Bath and Wells. The front doorway shows Knight's coat of arms. Some 20yds away is a detached ambulatory, 50ft long with a vaguely Italian flavour about it. Only Norman hall and ambulatory open, April–Oct Wed, Sat 2.00–6.00 or sunset if earlier. National Trust. ¾ mile north of Horton village, off A46.

Snowshill Manor: Tudor house which once belonged to Catherine Parr. Bought in 1919 by scholar and rich eccentric, Charles Wade, who lived in spartan conditions, devoting his time to various collections. One room is given over to old compasses, ship models and nautical artefacts, another to lacemaking and weaving tools, while The Room of a Hundred Wheels houses relics of simple locomotion from boneshaker bicycles to hobby horses. National Trust. Open April (or Easter Sat if earlier), Oct Sat, Sun, Bank Hol Mon (closed Good Fri), May–Sept Wed–Sat and Bank Hol Mon 11.00–1.00 and 2.00–6.00 or sunset if earlier. Four miles west of junction of A44 and A424.

Buscot: 18th c house in the Adam style with interior sympathetically restored to display fine furniture and the Faringdon collection of paintings. Some Rembrandts, a Gainsborough landscape and works by Rossetti, Madox Brown and Burne-Jones. 55-acre park includes beautiful water-gardens. Open April–Sept Wed–Fri, also 2nd and 4th Sat and Sun of each month 2.00–6.00. National Trust. On A417.

Badminton House: fine example of the Palladian style, Badminton has been the home of the Duke of Beaufort since 17th c. Good collection of Italian, Dutch and English paintings. Entrance hall with its carved inner portals is where family invented the game of badminton; all original playing courts had dimensions of this hall. Lovely Grinling Gibbons carving of the chimney-piece in dining-room. Badminton is also famous for its three-day horse trials in April. Buffet teas available in the orangery – stables, hunt kennels and church open to public. Open each Wed from early June–early Sept 2.30–5.00. Off B4040.

Kelmscott: delightful summer home of William Morris and family from 1871 to his death in 1896. This simple low-beamed farmhouse contains most of Morris's possessions and many of the products of his talent. Evidences of Rossetti's joint tenancy can be seen from the fine drawings of Morris's wife Janey and daughters Jenny and May. Pleasing green-painted furniture (the only survivors of their kind) designed by Madox Brown, and everywhere the soft muted patterns of Morris's tapestries and fabrics – some rescued out of dog baskets by present owner A. R. Dufty. Very much a home rather than a museum. Open 1st Wed of each month, April–Sept 11.00–1.00 and 2.00–5.00. Off B4449 east of Lechlade.

Sudeley Castle: King Ethelred the Unready held the estate as a royal deer park in the 10th c. Castle retains buildings dating back to 12th c. 300 years later it was rebuilt by Baron Sudeley with the spoils of the French wars. Catherine Parr lived at Sudeley after King Henry VIII's death, and now lies entombed in white marble in the 14th c St Mary's chapel. Her prayerbook is on public display, as are paintings by Turner, Reynolds, Rubens and Constable. Castle open daily 12.00–5.30 (grounds open from 11.00) March–end Oct. Off A46 near Winchcombe.

Prinknash Abbey and Pottery: standing in the grounds of an ancient abbey *c* 1300 – once the home of the abbots of Gloucester – is a new Benedictine monastery, started in 1939 and completed in 1972. Streamlined, functional, abbey is nevertheless imposing. Here the monks train potters; visitors can watch them work and purchase earthenware and stoneware. Candles and incense also made on premises. Pottery factory open Mon–Sat 10.00–5.00, closed 12.30–1.30 for lunch. Excellent bird park in grounds.

Choral services in abbey church most weekdays and Sun. Off A46 near Painswick.

Great Coxwell Tithe Barn: built in the 13th c with Cotswold stone walls and

Local farmer carries a lamb across the ford at Duntisbourne Leer

a roof of stone tiles, it measures 152ft long. Barn's 'nave' is supported by two rows of slender oak posts successfully resisting dislodgement for 700 years, resting on stone bases seven ft high, an indication of barn's impressive size. National Trust. Open daily at reasonable hours. South-west of Faringdon between A420 and B4019.

Cotswold Wildlife Park: zebras, rhinos, leopards, crocodiles and other wildlife in landscaped gardens designed to blend with the animals and birds. Spacious lawns for picnicking, adventure playground for children. Open 10.00–6.00 daily, 10.00–dusk in winter. Off A361 nr Burford.

Cotswold Farm Park: contains the most comprehensive collection of rare breeds of British farm animals on display in the country. See bristly prehistoric breeds of pig, beautiful rare poultry, and the white-tailed Old Gloucester cattle without whom there would be no Double Gloucester cheese. Fresh farm produce on sale at weekends during May, June, Sept and daily during July, Aug. Open May–Sept 1.30–6.00. Off A436 on minor road nr village of Guiting Power.

Smerrill Farm Museum: 2000 farm items housed in a Cotswold barn. On Sun at 3.00 a shire horse is hitched to traditional farm cart for rides (weather and demand permitting). Open every day except 24–26 Dec, 10.30–6.00. Between Cirencester and Kemble on the A429.

Winchcombe Railway Museum: items of railway interest including signals, tickets, etc, but excluding locomotives. Laid out in pleasant garden surroundings. Easter Sun–Mon, May, spring, summer bank hol Sun and Mon, first full week Aug daily 2.30–6.00. On A46.

Witcombe Roman Villa: a large courtyard Roman villa in which a hypocaust (underground heating area) and mosaic pavements are preserved. Open any reasonable hour, keys at farm house next door. Free. Off A417.

Cheltenham Spa: elegant Regency town. Take the waters at the Pittville Pump Rooms, visit the Gustav Holst museum or the Cheltenham art gallery

Cottages at Upper Slaughter near Bourton-on-the-Water: in the foreground is the river Eye, a tributary of the Windrush

and museum, walk along the Promenade with its fine ironwork balconies or go to the Everyman Theatre. Box office tel Cheltenham 25544. Enjoy the Cheltenham Festival of Music (July) or Festival of Literature (Nov), go to the races (Gold Cup, March) or watch cricket (County Cricket Week, Aug).

ACTIVITIES

Guided walks in the Cotswolds: the Cotswold Warden Service, created to assist farmers, landowners, residents and visitors to continue farming the land efficiently while enjoying the amenities, conducts a series of free guided walks through beautiful countryside. Programme from libraries and information centres.

FOOD AND DRINK

Egon Ronay's Lucas Guide recommends: **Old Woolhouse,** Northleach, tel Northleach 366. Star-rating; delicious speciality dishes. **Country Elephant,** Painswick, tel Painswick 813564. Two picturesque dining-rooms, appetizing home cooking. **Mr Baillie's,** Stroud, tel Stroud 5331. Set menus with intriguingly different dishes, very good wine list. **Springfield House Restaurant,** Chalford, tel Brimscombe 3555. Regency-style dining-room, good country cooking with fresh ingredients. **The Close Restaurant,** Tetbury, tel Tetbury 52272. Elegant dining-room and international dishes. **Whatley Manor Restaurant,** Easton Grey, tel Malmesbury 2888 – mainly French dishes. **Crown of Crucis,** Ampney Crucis, tel Poulton 403. Traditional Cotswold inn with appealing specialities. **Pinks,** Fairford, tel Fairford 712355. Inventive dishes, friendly and informal.

TOURIST INFORMATION

Local papers: *Gloucestershire Echo,* published daily and *Wilts and Gloucestershire Standard* and *Gloucestershire Chronicle* published Fri.

Tip: compared with some parts of England, the Cotswolds can be expensive. **Tourist information centres:** at Cheltenham, Gloucester, Stroud, Burford, Tetbury and Swindon.

Research: Martha Ellen Zenfell.

Chipping Norton

It is the approaches to the villages and small market towns of the Oxfordshire Cotswolds that delight me first of all, the views of them from far away – and that usually means from high above. The journey along these bleak, exposed roads, running in all directions across the top of the county, matters just as much as the slow descent, the arrival among the huddled houses. Drive, ride or stride along any one of them. Stop and look. It is like being on a camel's back. There is so much sky all around you, you feel you could reach up and touch it.

Especially on clear days of winter and early spring, you really can see for miles; hills recede one behind another into the far distance, mauve or grey-blue. There is no shelter from the sun in high summer, or winds that whip across the open land; and snow is driven hard against the occasional birch or fir screen and those long walls of grey local stone, intricately made, the fingerprint of the area. A kestrel usually hovers on the spot above verge and ditch; rooks and crows beat upwards on great ragged wings and wheel down on to treetops; the bleating of the foursquare, sturdy Cotswold sheep carries a long way.

Time and again through the long, bitter spring of 1979, we went on to these uplands, longing to look down into the valleys of the Windrush or the Evenlode, and across to the opposite slopes, to see the first, soft flush of green spreading out, to soften and blur the view, enfold the grey rooftops of the villages. March went out, then April; May came in with raw winds and stinging sleet; the leaves seemed frozen; blossom was beaten off the branches before it was ever full. Yet it seemed somehow right and satisfying to be up here on such harsh days, for this is a beautiful part of England in a quite unexpected way. The popular image of the Cotswolds is different: all honey-coloured stone, chintzy gardens and calendar cottages in the sunshine, sparkling streams and mossy churchyards. You do find something of that, but it is not the best or most typical aspect.

I live in Oxford now, a fine city; but we escape from it most weekends into this Cotswold countryside, for the architecture and landscape and views, animals and birds, history and atmosphere, food and drink, and shops, rivers, streams, trees and gravestones.

The A40 going west is one of those high, broad roads with fine prospects on every side, but we wind off it and down towards Old Minster Lovell. I am haunted by the ruins of the manor house there, standing, roofless, full of ghosts and echoes, in the watermeadows

Old Minster Lovell – 'standing roofless, full of ghosts and echoes, beside a curve of the lovely river Windrush'

beside a curve of the lovely river Windrush. Behind its crumbling walls, tower, two wells, is the village church in a garden-like graveyard. This is a fine place for birds, because of the combination of water, stone walls and seclusion.

About a mile along the valley, tucked into itself, is Asthall, a perfect village. A small bridge straddles the river, whose banks are evocatively willowed, and St Nicholas is one of the loveliest of all the Cotswold churches, because it is modest, small, plain and utterly typical. There are higgledy-piggledy gravestones, including several with the curious, rolled tops. Inside it is cool, smells musty. Eighteenth-century memorial tablets, austerely lettered, are set into the floor; a stone arch is carved with birds' beaks.

There is something all of a piece and harmonious about the villages of this valley, and often a stream or brook runs through them, like a lively spirit. Swinbrook has one, and a shallow, splashy ford, too. I was first brought here by Nancy Mitford's sublimely funny, utterly English novel, *The Pursuit of Love*. Swinbrook was her home, the book is set here. 'Uncle Matthew' is buried here, and so is Nancy, under an elegant, simple stone and next to one with a fitting epitaph for her sister, Unity Valkyrie Mitford – 'Say not the struggle nought availeth.' The church is spacious, imposing, high-standing, in great contrast to the homelier ones of less grand villages around. Inside, the stone effigies of the Fettiplace family lie in tiered shelves, reclining stylishly on their elbows.

Swinbrook seems to keep you at arm's length, as Uncle Matthew would have done, and I prefer to do that myself to Burford. Seen from the top of the hill, it unrolls like a dove-grey braid down to the river-bridge, quite unchanged for 500 years. But it *is* changed, and spoilt quite, by traffic and proliferating gift shops.

Never mind. Another haunted place is nearby. Little Barrington is set around a peculiar green, like a bowl – a turfed-over quarry. I always imagine people, houses, a whole secret past, buried there. It is a very silent place, the houses seem closed. There is nowhere quite like it.

Chipping Norton is a big market town with an everyday, workaday air that I like, as well as a magnificent setting and some handsome buildings. You feel that its lifeblood flows as healthily as it did in the past; even the numerous antique shops seem to concentrate on the useful – good old tables, chairs and dressers – rather than on the fanciful-decorative. This is the highest town in the county and the views are breathtaking, surprising you as you glimpse them at the end of the steeply sloping side streets off the market square. But we really come here for my husband to indulge in 'the most delicious doughnuts in the world', feather-light and crisp and home-made at the 17th Century Pantry.

We've discovered other sources of good food in the area but, after doughnuts and before lunch, we need exercise. Because Oxford is so low, damp and enervating it's marvellous to take in lungfuls of fresh air, walking up to the Rollright Stones. And what ghosts are here, too!

Broughton Castle: built in 1306, it passed to the Saye and Sele family in 1451

What visions from the remote past you might see, dancing in and out of the great stone circle. There is always a faintly keening wind, even on blazing hot days when the sun casts sinister shadows from the tall Whispering Knights. How amazing to think that these monoliths were here before any of the rest – the church, barns, stone walls, villagers' houses.

I lean against them, my small daughter runs in and out playing hide-and-seek, other children climb and clamber familiarly over these ritual objects of the Bronze Age. Across the road, the solitary King Stone, handsome as a Henry Moore, dominates the skyline. You feel you could take off and fly from here. Larks do, straight up and up and out of sight, only their song trailing back like a kite-tail. Far below is Long Compton, honey- and butter-coloured, in the fold of the hills, looking like every wayfarer's dream of shelter and rest.

I love this spot, so eerie and isolated and forlorn, and yet one in which you also feel surrounded and companioned, and not far from safety. So much of the pleasure of this whole landscape lies in the contrasts – within minutes, you go from the open heights, down into the valleys which embrace you in foliage, the villages within old walls.

So, after the elements and prehistoric evocations of the Rollrights, we lunch in Shipton-under-Wychwood, with its gentle village green and welcoming inn, the Shaven Crown, which is all old courtyards and archways, stone steps into secluded gardens, heavy oak doors. Their home-made soup is creamy, pâté gamy and orangey, sausages gigantic and chips satisfactorily uneven.

In May, when it is all freshly, sappily green, or October, when the leaves are on the turn from gold to russet and nut-brown, the road leading on to Charlbury is a joy, because the village is partly surrounded by woods, lying like animal pelts over the backs of the hills, the remains of the ancient Wychwood forest. Sometimes we lunch here, at the Bell Hotel, because of the fresh grilled sardines with lemon and herbs and baked eggs in cream, and because the dining-room, all pine, with botanical prints, is so pretty.

We drive towards home on the minor roads which wind up and down delightfully, stopping at Woodstock – especially in winter, because the shops are so good for Christmas shopping, particularly for children's clothes, toys and books. Around the town hall and museum, I am always reminded of some French market-place – all it needs are café tables on the cobbles. Alas, in summer the town is choked to death by tourist coaches and it is because of Blenheim, the making and marring of Woodstock.

We often go there, not into the house itself – I like to look at that magnificent pile from the end of one of the long, long avenues. No, we leave the car where we can, and pay a modest 10p to walk for as long as we like in the grounds, to enjoy English landscape gardening at its finest, look at ducks, moorhens and swans on the great lake and squirrels and tree-creepers in the woodland, admire the Duke of Marlborough on his plinth in the meadow. In winter, the slopes and paths are full of happy families with gnome-like children on toboggans, the lake freezes and the sun sets early like a fireball behind black trees. We came on Boxing Day and it was like a friendly local park – even in high season, only a few of the visitors to the palace explore the grounds.

My roots and memories are not in this part of England, yet I feel a great affection for it: the villages seem to encourage a sense of belonging, a warmth and closeness, and the Cotswold uplands are glorious, airy, open and free. It's an overcrowded, over-visited area, and yet for much of the year the minor roads are empty, the villages peopled by residents. As always, the majority stick to the main guidebook sites, the major roads. Even in high summer, you can go for a walk and have a corner to yourself with no trouble at all.

SUSAN HILL

Chipping Norton

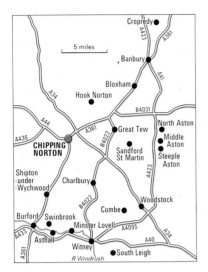

WHERE TO GO

High St, Market Place, Middle Row: wide and straggly centre. At one end, neo-classical town hall, 1842, portrait-hung council chamber used for club meetings, dances, dog shows and so on; at other end 16th c Guildhall. Numerous 18th c frontages, notably Barclays Bank, White Hart Hotel and Westminster Bank. Shop at 20 High St (The Playpen) has 14th c vaulted basement. Occasional visits, by appointment only, on Thur afternoons.

Almshouses, Church St: picturesque row of gabled cottages, the gift of Henry Cornish, in 1640, the inmates to be eight poor widows of the town 'of honest and Godly life and conversation'. Still in use.

Church of St Mary the Virgin: one of the finest in Oxfordshire and a reminder of 15th c wool-trade wealth based on sheep called 'Cotswold Lions'. Graceful nave rebuilt around 1485, traces back to 12th c. Lovely east window reputedly from pre-Reformation Bruern Abbey. Intriguing monuments, collection of brasses set along wall (no rubbings). Vicar condemned to death by hanging from tower after 1549 rising against Edward VI's new prayerbook.

Chipping Norton Theatre, Spring St: professional theatre established four years ago in ex-Salvation Army Citadel. Attractive 180-seat auditorium. Policy is to book live professional shows from panto to opera; cinema three nights weekly; gallery stages exhibitions, jazz on Sun lunchtimes, roomy bar with Hook Norton ales from barrels on counter. Closed July (touring local villages with children's play scheme) Aug children's films. Tel Chipping Norton 2350.

Pool Meadow: pleasant walk through churchyard (look for tombstone of Phillis, wife of John Humphreys, itinerant rat catcher, 'struck down to her last lodging 1763') leads down to splendidly scruffy stream-side fields, sometimes verging on semi-bog, just right for older children's adventures. Probably once the fish ponds for nearby medieval castle of which only grassy mounds remain. Continue on to cemetery to find, tucked among the standard urns and angels, 'Davey's Grave', an exuberant memorial featuring full-size five-bar gate in black marble.

Bliss Tweed Mill: William Bliss founded woollen-cloth business 1746. Present mill built 1872 after previous buildings burnt down. Architect George Woodhouse, from Lancashire, designed factory to look like majestic country house, but dominated by central high chimney set on domed tower. Achieved reputation for excellent products – a Bliss cloth coat would last a lifetime. Bitter strike of 1912 still talked about. Shop open Mon–Fri 9.00–12.00 and 1.00–3.00, not Tue afternoons. Tue afternoon tours of mill booked up months ahead.

Mop Fair: Sept. Town centre closed off by amusements. Survival of annual hiring fair when indoor and outdoor servants displayed the implements of their trade. (Old joke: 'I've made inquiries about your character and I'll take you on.' 'And I of yours, sir, and I'll not come.')

SHOPPING

Market day: Wed (name Chipping means market, dates from 13th c). Also, try Women's Institute market in basement of Methodist Chapel, West St, for vegetables and home-made cakes and jams, Fri 9.30–11.30.

Early closing: Thur.

Antiques: a dozen shops in all with five clustered in Horsefair. Roy Walker, at 21 Horsefair, typical of 'serious' shops, offers mainly Cotswold country furniture in oak and elm. For a completely different experience, at the other end of town, T. Aldridge, College Place, has amazing pile of metal junk.

Auctions: sales announced in local papers. John Hunt of estate agents and auctioneers James Styles and Whitlock, 9 Market Place, tel Chipping Norton 2539, says items often lotted up without catalogue, inspection on morning of auction.

'The most delicious doughnuts in the world' – at the 17th Century Pantry in Chipping Norton

ACTIVITIES

Sport: swimming pool, outdoor but heated; golf club, nine-hole course welcomes visitors on weekdays (tel Chipping Norton 2383); tennis club holds sessions at grammar school Tue, Thur, Sun; centre of Heythrop Hunt which has its kennels a short distance out of town; cricket, interesting team to watch, playing good club standard.

FOOD AND DRINK

17th Century Pantry, Market St: morning coffees, afternoon teas, self-selection salad bar. Everything made on premises, including home-baked bread, cakes, fudge, doughnuts. **Una's Fish Bar**, New St: fish and chips from 17th c building. Pubs include: **Bunch of Grapes**, Middle Row. Dates from 17th c with original windows in back room. Hook Norton ales. The **Blue Boar**, Goddards Lane. Reputedly haunted by nun. Pool table, two dartboards, fruit machine, jukebox (loud). Charrington I P A.

WHERE TO STAY

Crown and Cushion Hotel, High St (tel Chipping Norton 2533). AA two star. Old coaching inn. 16th c bar features beer of the month. Barbecues steaks and lamb cutlets) in beer garden in summer. **White Hart Hotel** (Trust House Forte), High St (tel Chipping Norton 2572). AA two star. Old coaching inn, may date back to 14th c, one bedroom has four-poster. **Fox Hotel**, Market Place (tel Chipping Norton 2658). AA recognized. Friendly hotel. Originally 16th c coaching inn, still has 16th c fireplace in cosy bar with high-backed corner settle. Issues fishing permits. **King's Arms Hotel**, West St (tel Chipping Norton 2668).

TOURIST INFORMATION

Free town guide from Guildhall. *Chipping Norton News* from Co-op (itself a force in Chipping Norton affairs) and other shops.

St Mary's, North Aston: below this window are decorative tiles

Villages and country towns

The Astons: Steeple, Middle and North

Intriguing example of social history: Steeple Aston, set out along north and south sides of small valley with modern estates tending to fill the gaps, is by far the largest because, as an 'open' village, it took in population forced to move from 'closed' villages such as Middle Aston where single proprietors would not allow new housing. Steeple Aston ratepayers complained of supporting other people's poor.

Steeple Aston South St has 17th c farm house, 19th c cottages and the Red Lion, comfortable free house serving Wadworths, good restaurant, and useful collection of encyclopedias for sorting out arguments. North St has the older houses, the church of St Peter, thatched cottages dating back to 17th c and The Grange, a large house rebuilt in 19th c as an odd-looking castle.

North Aston, a small village straggling along the edge of a large green, has a real surprise, an unmade track that curves around the front of North Aston Hall ('Jacobethan' according to Jennifer Sherwood in *The Buildings of England*) to St Mary's church, virtually hidden behind. Building dates from around 14th c but interior has all the dark romance of a Victorian restoration: note decorative tiles on chancel floor.

Bloxham

Large village with grandly imposing church at one end and All Saints School at the other. St Mary's has 14th c tower and spire (198ft), an abundance of spectacular carving, wall paintings, monuments, windows by Morris and Burne-Jones etc.

For an interesting walk head from St Mary's across the main road (rammed through in 1870) into Church Passage, beside the Hawk and Partridge, which leads into a winding network of streets preserving the old village layout. King's Road has some of the earliest cottages (back to 16th c); Little Green has Sycamore Terrace, five golden 17th c cottages under one thatched roof; Unicorn St, with vehicle width limit of 6ft, was once the main road; Frog Lane, the narrowest

of alleys, leads down to a stream where children fish for minnows.

Back across main road to the Joiners Arms, 16th c house and oldest pub in village, and on to Elephant and Castle, 17th c coaching inn with massive archway. Publican Charles Finch has found out about the history while uncovering fireplaces and restoring oven in bakehouse, now being turned into restaurant ('three fires meant a man working full-time cutting wood all year round'). Darts, shove ha'penny on hundred-year-old board, hot meals, no piped music or jukebox, serves Hook Norton ales.

Good cricket team playing out of a shed but in Premier Division of Oxfordshire League.

Burford

Proud of being a town rather than just a village. Wide and handsome High St runs up hill from bridge over river Windrush. One-time coaching centre (note several inns with archways leading to courtyards) but has retained pre-18th c layout because east-west turnpike road (now the A40) took route along valley ridge, although numerous heavy lorries now rumble through north-south.

Large and attractive church of St John Baptist, beside river, dates from Norman times although mainly remodelled in 15th c. Packed with monuments reflecting wool-trade wealth. Look for tomb of Edmund Harman, barber-surgeon to Henry VIII (licensed to run a razor over the king's throat), with its carved rows of children and, for some reason, playful American Indians; also tables of benefactors. Spacious tombs in churchyard, the rounded tops represent wool bales, reputedly used by poachers to store catch.

Remarkable number of 14th–16th c merchants' houses although often with 18th c frontages; look for touches such as fine doorways to side passages. The Tolsey, 16th c pillared building in High St, was where market tolls taken and courts held – the lavatories behind were once the town jail. The Tolsey now houses a museum displaying the town mace, local documents and so on. Open Easter–Oct, daily 2.30–5.30. Hour-long tours of the town start from The Tolsey, May–Oct Sun, also July–Aug Wed at 3.00. For tourist information and accommodation service call at the Welsh Shop a few yards further up The Hill where

St Mary's, North Aston – the church dates from around 14th century

Tom Litt, owner of the Mason Arms at South Leigh, is one of the few publicans in Britain who brews his own beer

Patrick Wise and relatives happily share knowledge of area.

Proliferation of antique shops attracts dealers and collectors. Try Jonathan Fyson, next to the Cotswold Arms; Lloyd and Greenwood, next to the imposing Methodist chapel; and Roger Warner, in an interesting 16th c house with 18th c frontage next to the Highway Hotel. Patrick Walker in Falkland Hall (oldest entirely stone-built house, 1558) sells definitive selection of wood-burning stoves.

Egon Ronay's Lucas Guide recommends the Winter's Tale Restaurant, Oxford Rd, tel Burford 3176. The 17th c Bay Tree Hotel in Sheep St has a marvellously convoluted series of small public rooms with high-set fires, large flagstoned restaurant and delightful garden; owned and staffed entirely by women. Huffkins, The Hill, has delectable home-baked fruit tarts, quiches, cakes, etc.

Pubs include the Lamb Inn, Sheep St, dating from 15th c, serving Wadworths against a background of cream and brown, wooden chairs and flagstones; the Masons Arms, Witney St, has filling home-made snacks; the Royal Oak, a bit farther along Witney St, issues fishing permits, has a pool table and serves Wadworths.

Charlbury

Large village or small town with a station putting it within commuting distance of London. A stroll along Church Lane, through pleasant churchyard of St Mary's with its large trees, up Church St and back along Market St gives the flavour of the older parts of town.

Museum, an extension next to public library in Corner House, Market St, has graceful Oxfordshire hay wagon and small collection of photographs and domestic articles. Open Mon–Sat, shop hours, ask for key in chemists across the road.

Cornbury Park, just across the railway and River Evenlode, contains the last remnants of Wychwood Forest which once covered much of the area. The view from a minor road to Leafield running along the back of the estate gives some idea of how wild it must have been. Park not open to public.

The Bell Hotel, Church St, tel Charlbury 810278, has dining-room, good snacks and Wadworths. Pubs include the 17th c Bull in Market St. A jolly place with darts, dominoes and so on. Beams come from dismantled ships built from local trees.

Combe

Small village, high on ridge with views all round, set on two sides of large triangular green, houses arranged along walks rather than roads. Part of Green Close Cottage dates from Stuart times but most cottages early 18th c. Beautiful church of St Lawrence built all of a piece in 1395 after village moved to present situation from site in valley: look for medieval glass paintings of company of angels in tracery lights. Scene of riot in 1822 when Rector of Lincoln College, Oxford, fell out with curate he had appointed to living.

Worth visiting post office in thatched cottage tucked away in dead-end beside church. Picturesque cricket ground by church with one of better-known village teams, plays in Premier Division of

Oxfordshire League. Pub: the Cock Inn. Darts, fruit machine, collection of match boxes, seats outside and swings, serves Morrells.

Cropredy

Scene of minor battle in 1644, midway through Civil War, when Charles I, commanding the Royalists, showed tactical skill in winning the race for Cropredy bridge across the river Cherwell. Spacious 14th c church of St Mary the Virgin features some of the left-overs: armour, cannonballs; also a glittering brass lectern shaped like an eagle, a rare pre-Reformation example dating from 15th c. According to tradition, the villagers saved it from the ravages of Civil War by sinking it in river bed. Listen to the two-second tick of clock pendulum swinging in tower.

The church, churchyard and row of cottages together with the thatched fifteenth century inn, the Red Lion (Watneys), form a tight centre to the village set beside the Oxford Canal which runs for boats alongside the un-navigable Cherwell.

The great dovecote at Rousham House, near Steeple Aston, set in William Kent's superb gardens

Great Tew

Particularly picturesque village: curving rows of 17th and 18th c thatched cottages built of gold-coloured ironstone, set on side of valley amid gardens and clumps of great parkland trees; a village green with stocks and village school. The overall effect results from early 19th c landscaping of the estate, part of it to a design by Humphrey Repton.

The 19th c manor house hides among the many splendid trees.

Sadly, everything was allowed to run down into dilapidation and, in some cases, ruinous dereliction, but now the post office has new thatch, several of the cottages are being restored and the village is coming back to life. The Falkland Arms pub which reopened last year has stone floors, open fires, darts, shove ha'penny and bar-skittles. Hook Norton and Donnington ales.

St Michael and All Angels is a tonic, a Norman church rebuilt in 13th and 14th c, approached down long avenue of lush laurels. Look for monument to Mary Anne Boulton reclining gracefully in literary contemplation.

Hook Norton

A solid little township called 'Hooky' by its inhabitants. Long main street winds its way from brewery (Hook Norton ales) at Scotland End to Railway Hotel beyond East End. Look for semi-circular bulges on older houses where staircases have been added on. Early 20th c prosperity based on ironstone workings providing golden building stone and iron ore, but steel company and quarries closed down after Second World War. New housing estates sit in the old quarries. Railway closed 1951 although viaduct piers still march across the fields to South Hill where Berkshire, Buckinghamshire and Oxfordshire Naturalist Trust keeps a section of the route as a nature reserve.

Impressive church of St Peter has Norman font with jolly sculptures of Adam and Eve and some of the signs of the zodiac, also a 19th c manual-pumped fire engine. At East End Farm, potter Russell Collins has installed two kilns, exports domestic stoneware to Europe as well as selling to Heal's, Liberty's, and direct to visitors.

Pubs include the Gate Hangs High, out of town on road to Sibford, characterful, serves Hook Norton ales. The

Bell, a Mitchell and Butlers house in the main street, provides an amiable meeting place. The Red Lion (Watneys) and The Sun (Hook Norton) stand side by side opposite church.

Sandford St Martin

One of the trimmest villages of all, reflecting 19th c limitation on growth imposed by two main estates. Worth seeing for the green, a triangle of grass with magnificent evergreen trees, the high wall of Sandford Park to one side, the darkly mysterious plantation of trees round the manor house to another, and an impressive farmhouse entry through double-doored archway into courtyard to the third. Follow the three roads out of the village. One goes from large house, to detached cottage to terrace. One twists down towards the mill and a combination of controlled stream and manicured lawns. One leads past the church of St Martin, with more evergreens in the churchyard, and the elegant 17th c Sandford Park. Visit the cricket ground for view across park of artificial lake with imposing 18th c bridge.

Shipton-under-Wychwood

Huge green provides focus at one end of spread-out village: drinking fountain commemorates disaster of 1874 when 17 men, women and children from village, emigrating to New Zealand, were among passengers of ship that caught fire and sank off Tristan da Cunha.

Church of St Mary, dating from 13th c, is a fine place to search for details and oddities. Look for double-sided brass (no rubbings) and contemplate Elizabeth Tame lying naked in her open shroud.

Shipton Court, now split into flats, presents an impressive Jacobean front, early 17th c, to a quick view from the road. 19th c scandal involved last baronet, Sir John Chandos Reade, a large amount of drink and a dead butler.

Places to eat and drink: the Shaven Crown Hotel, High St, by green (tel Shipton-under-Wychwood 830330) dates back to 15th c and traditionally functioned as hostelry for Bruern Abbey. Tudor archway entrance, courtyard garden and two-storey-high central hall. The Lamb Inn, High St, tel Shipton-under-Wychwood 830465, has restaurant (dinner only, Mon–Sat; lunch only, Sun) which serves snails reared by the proprietor, and pub which spreads an extensive and tempting lunchtime buffet along one end of the counter and serves Hook Norton ales.

South Leigh
Two-part village worth visiting for church at top of hill and pub at bottom. St James, mainly 15th c, displays an expanse of wall paintings which provided instruction in the days when congregations could not read: the mouth of hell, seven deadly sins, Last Judgment, St Michael weighing souls, devils at their unhappy work. Later on John Wesley, still High Church at the time, preached here.

The Mason Arms (closed Mon) is one of the few home-brew pubs of Britain. Every week Tom Litt, proprietor and brewer, produces up to a hundred gallons of malty Sowlye Ale from the brewhouse behind the pub. Add to that a thatched roof, wide lawn with handsome box tree, public bar open in evenings with darts and bar billiards, plus a good restaurant (tel Witney 2485).

Windrush Villages: Swinbrook, Asthall, Minster Lovell
Follow the Windrush from Burford for this pleasant series of riverside hamlets. Swinbrook church, St Mary's, is so small that six reclining statues of members of the Fettiplace family, trying to lie at ease in full armour, are piled up bunk fashion. Churchyard has graves of Nancy and Unity Mitford whose family home had been in Swinbrook. The Swan, near the river, is a pleasant old country pub serving Courage.

Asthall, with its twisty streets, has the grandeur of the 17th c manor house, St Nicholas's church dating back to 12th c and the Maytime Inn, bar snacks, a restaurant specializing in country cooking and Morrells Varsity from the wood.

Minster Lovell, with long, cottage-lined main street, has picturesque ruins of 15th c church, St Kenelm's. Between them these two produce a fair number of gruesome tales: man perished in hidden room (the only servant with access died); girl trapped in heavy chest (hide-and-seek); woman had eyes put out (blood-stained bible in evidence). Egon Ronay's *Lucas Guide* recommends the Old Swan for restaurant and bar.

Woodstock
Charming, busy place beside Blenheim Park, full of teashops, pubs, hotels. Has had royal connections since before the Norman Conquest as a base for hunting in the once extensive Wychwood Forest. The High St and Market Place, leading to the main entrance to Blenheim, provide a pleasant prospect of Georgian buildings. Oxfordshire County Museum, in handsome Fletcher's House, Park St, is clearly set out. Bookshop, coffee-bar and garden to picnic in. Open May–Sept Mon–Fri 10.00–5.00, Sat 10.00–6.00, Sun 2.00–6.00, Oct–April Tue–Fri 10.00–4.00, Sat 10.00–5.00, Sun 2.00–5.00. Woodstock Leathercraft, Harrison's Lane, is last factory remaining from once thriving glove industry. Open Mon–Sat 9.00–6.00.

Places to eat and drink: Egon Ronay's *Just a Bite* recommends Mawney's Kitchen, 52 Oxford St, open Wed-Sun 10.00–5.30, for home baking. At the other end of the scale, the Bear Hotel Restaurant, Park St, tel Woodstock 811511. Pubs include; the King's Head, Park Lane, a cosy yet lively place which specializes in hot jacket potatoes with fillings such as chicken and curry sauce. The Queen's Own, Oxford St, still has some of that chest-high dark brown wainscoting, plus jukebox, darts and other games, serves Hook Norton ales.

Places to visit

Blenheim Palace, Woodstock: birthplace of Sir Winston Churchill, buried in nearby Bladon churchyard. Sir John Vanbrugh's early 18th c Italian-styled masterpiece surrounded by park designed by Capability Brown. Blenheim also features Churchill exhibition, 15in gauge steam railway, garden centre and walled garden, gift centre and restaurant. Palace open daily mid-March–Oct 11.30–5.00. Park open daily all year 9.00–5.00.
Broughton Castle, south-west of Banbury: fairytale moated castle set in parkland, built 1306 and passed by marriage, in 1451, to second Lord Saye and Sele whose family still owns it. Puritan stronghold during Civil War, many relics on show. Open June–mid-Sept Wed, Sun 2.00–5.00, July–Aug also Thur, and Bank Hol Mon and Sun. Parties at other times by appointment. Tel Banbury 2624.
Chastleton House, West of Chipping Norton: fine Jacobean building built 1603 on land bought from Robert Catesby, a Gunpowder Plot conspirator. House remains virtually unaltered with great hall, long gallery and great chamber notable. Topiary garden, try to guess what clipped box bushes represent (camel? tea-pot?). Open all year Mon, Tue, Thur, Fri 10.30–1.00 and 2.00–5.30, Sat, Sun 2.00–5.00.
Compton Wynyates, north-west into Warwickshire: hidden in a secluded valley, one of the most beautiful of all Tudor houses, built between 1480 and 1520. Interesting garden of clipped evergreens. Great hall, Henry VIII's bedroom and 48 tall, red-brick chimneys in different designs. Open Aug 11.00–6.00 daily.
Rousham House, Steeple Aston: built around 1635 and immediately became Royalist stronghold in Civil War. William Kent remodelled the house about 1738 and laid out the superb gardens, the only surviving example of his work. Wooded slopes, terraces, cascades and sham ruins combine to achieve 'an effect crystallising Nature'. Open April–Sept Wed, Sun, bank hol 2.00–5.30; gardens daily 10.00–6.00.
Combe Mill Steam Beam Engine, near Combe: sawmill for Blenheim estate on banks of river Evenlode houses 1852 steam beam engine with original Cornish boiler, water-wheel, workshop machinery and blacksmith working at forge. Open Spring and Aug Bank Hol Sun and Mon, and Sun in mid-Oct, 10.00–6.00. Tel Witney 881206.
Cotswold Folk and Agricultural Museum, Asthall Barrow Farm, Asthall, nr Burford: collection of locally used items in background settings. Open May–Oct first and third Sun in month 2:30–5.30.
Potteries: Russell Collins in Hook Norton; Deddington Pottery, The Tchure, Market Place, Deddington; Reg Mills and Dave Sutcliffe, Boot Barn Pottery, Stonesfield.
Prescote Manor, Cropredy, across canal from village: houses Prescote Gallery, selling items by British craftsmen, licensed buttery. Open Easter–Christmas Wed–Sun, bank hol 10.00–5.00.
Rollright Stones, north of Chipping Norton beside road but on private land: hilltop Bronze Age circle of standing stones, maybe 3500 years old, known as the King's Men, with single outlying marker stone, the King's Stone, and

The Rollright Stones – the 'King's Men' may be 3500 years old

300yds off another group, the Whispering Knights, remnants of a megalithic tomb.

ACTIVITIES

Adderbury Morris Men: may turn up anywhere in area during April–Aug, as their programme is 'very fluid'. Traditionally tour the Cotswold towns on Aug Bank Hol Mon.
Angling: rivers Evenlode and Windrush provide fine sport with wild brown trout and good coarse fish, pike and chub. Nortonian Angling Society arranges permits, available from the Fox Hotel, Chipping Norton.

Auctions: Buckell and Ballard, Banbury, auction antiques, furniture, silver, etc, at their Parson's St premises, 'normally on a Tuesday about twice a month', tel Banbury 53197.
Aunt Sally: look out for the Aunt Sally pub leagues around the area. Played in summer by teams of eight, throwing sticks like rounders bats down 28ft pitch to knock doll off iron post, two umpires shout 'doll' for clean hit. Start with Waggon and Horses, on the London Road, Chipping Norton. Morrells and draught cider.
Spiceball Park Sports Centre: swimming pool, squash court, indoor bowls rink. Tel Banbury 57522.

TOURIST INFORMATION

Local papers: *Banbury Guardian, Evesham Journal* and *Witney and West Oxfordshire Gazette*, published on Thur, *Oxford Times* and *West Oxfordshire Standard*, on Fri.
Tourist information centres: Abingdon and Burford.
Guidebooks: *Gardens of Oxfordshire*, booklet describing gardens opened under the National Gardens Scheme, with dates. From Mrs David Hodges, Brook Cottage, Alkerton, nr Banbury, Oxfordshire.

Research: Humphrey Evans.

Hereford

Herefordshire is shaped roughly like a wheel, each spoke bearing its load of delight. The hub is Hereford, with its castle grounds, ringed by earthworks and the remnant of a moat, and medieval buildings, especially in our black-and-white, and red-and-white, local half-timbered tradition. The city is bounded on three sides by pink sandstone walls and on the fourth by the river Wye.

The principal monument is the cathedral of St Mary and St Ethelbert, with its early English lady chapel, bishop's chantry and library with 1444 chained books. One of its greatest treasures is the *Mappa Mundi*, depicting the world as our ancestors saw it in the year 1300, round and flat. Here, every third year since 1727, music lovers have come to enjoy the Three Choirs Festival.

From Aylston Hill or from the castle grounds you can look across the Wye to near hills and the far mountains of Wales. This, to my mind, is Herefordshire's especial charm: from every hilltop there are distant views. You can set out with a picnic lunch to visit ancient British earthworks, Roman fortified towns, Danish hill-camps above the Wye, or Norman castles built to discourage the Welsh.

In all parts of the county are Norman and early English churches built in sandstone or limestone, sometimes with half-timbered belfries and decorated with quaint sculptures (of which Kilpeck has the most famous examples). Shobdon, a church restyled in the eighteenth century in 'Georgian Gothick', with painted woodwork and plaster mouldings, is as pretty as a wedding cake. Farms and barns follow with, since the late seventeenth century, the addition of a pleasing russet brick.

When I first came here, after some years in London, I wondered how to tolerate my neighbours' leisurely ways. The shopkeeper would finish a conversation with a friend before attending to you. And now that I belong here it is sometimes embarrassing to be held in conversation while other shoppers are awaiting their turn.

The people have a musical, lilting speech ending on a high note, derived from preponderantly Welsh ancestry. For centuries it has been the ambition of the small Welsh farmers to accumulate sufficient means to move from their infertile mountain holdings into the verdant valleys of Herefordshire, from which their ancestors were ousted by the Saxons long ago. The proof of their success is that most of the people you will meet here have Welsh surnames such as Probert (Ap Robert), Evans (Efan's son), Price (Ap Rhys) and so on.

Unlike much of England, Herefordshire has escaped exploitation of its countryside for industrial and urban development. It has a host of

Eardisland and the river Arrow

Ewyas Harold, between Abbey Dore and Pontrilas, a Norman frontier post

historical monuments, going back to Stone Age man. For example, we have 12,000-year-old bones from the Old Stone Age, of men and mammoths, woolly rhinos and cave bears, found in the once-inhabited 'Arthur's Cave' above the river Wye. And on the crest of a hill at this side of the Golden Valley, looking westward to the Black Mountains of Wales, is 'Arthur's Stone', a 5000-year-old burial chamber, roofed by one huge, flat, rectangular stone which was formerly covered by a mound of earth to form a typical long barrow of the New Stone Age.

And the county also includes Offa's Dyke, built by the Saxon King of Mercia, from Chepstow in the south to Prestatyn in the north as a territorial boundary between 'England' and 'Wales' (a splendid long-distance footpath for hikers now runs the full length of the Dyke).

From the mid-eighteenth century, Hereford became the cradle of several notable stage careers. Roger Kemble – himself a distinguished actor-manager – fathered John, Charles and Stephen Kemble and that much-admired tragic actress, Sarah (Siddons). Hereford's brand new theatre is called the Nell Gwynn, because we cherish the tradition that she was born in Hereford within a stone's throw of the Bishop's Palace. Her grandson, who became Bishop of Hereford, may well have inherited his grandma's histrionic magic and preached from our cathedral pulpit persuasive sermons in praise of divine love.

On the practical side for visitors, Herefordshire has splendid hotels, large and small, plenty of 'bed and breakfasts' and caravan sites by lake or river.

CHRISTOPHER SANDFORD

Hereford

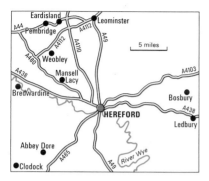

WHERE TO GO

Cathedral: dedicated to St Mary and St Ethelbert, a king of East Anglia who visited Hereford in 793 with a view to marrying Offa's daughter. Mercian king unkindly murdered Ethelbert, who was later canonized as martyr. Cathedral, red sandstone, grew up round his shrine. Rather homely compared with Salisbury or Wells, and much restored after collapse of West Tower in 1786, but interesting inside. *Mappa Mundi* is enchanting world map made by Richard of Haldingham, Prebend of Hereford Cathedral in 1290. Fine marble monument of Alexander Denton and his young wife, Anne, who died in childbirth at the age of 17. Still with original colours. She has rich robe of red and blue, with gilt trimmings. Chained library is largest collection in world, housed in splendid panelled room at the top of stone spiral staircase. Wycliffe's Bible of 1420 here, Caxton's *Golden Legend*, and earlier hand-lettered manuscripts of extraordinary beauty. Open daily 10.30–12.30 and 2.00–4.00. Occasional concerts.

High Town: a central pedestrian complex. Good place to loiter and listen in, especially on market day. Not a lot of original building left, though at west end in High St, a lovely little timbered house, carved and balconied, is squashed between Marks and Spencer and Littlewoods. Butter market in Market Hall, myriad little stalls, duck eggs, vast speckled turkey eggs, posies of flowers and home-made preserves, brought in by farmers' wives.

Church St: prettiest street in town, leading from cathedral close and coming out in High Town, lined all the way with Hereford's most pleasant shops – no traffic. Hereford Book Shop in mayor's house of 1627. Kemble Galleries are run by Society of Craftsmen. Tiny doll's house miniatures in cherrywood, pottery, hand-knitted jerseys and jewellery.

Old House: black and white Jacobean house, once part of a row, now a museum, stranded alone in High Town, richly carved and decorated. Wonderfully hefty oak furniture, cupboards, chairs, panelling with some early wall paintings. Four-poster beds upstairs. Open Mon–Fri 10.00–1.00 and 2.00–5.00, Sat 10.00–1.00.

Coningsby Hospital Museum: fine group of buildings, including original hospice and chapel of Knights Hospitaller of St John of Jerusalem. Now sadly enmeshed in schools, garages and light industry. Quiet serene quadrangle of almshouses, still lived in. Chapel now museum with armour, emblazons and heraldic devices of crusaders. Open Easter–Sept Tue–Thur Sat–Sun 3.00–5.00. Behind courtyard is ruined blackfriars monastery and 14th c stone cross used by Dominicans for open air preaching, only surviving example in England.

Widemarsh St: slightly shabby, with much nice detail. Gunsmith and general ironmonger, P. Morris & Son, has pretty, shallow bow front and old hooks for hanging goods outside. Former doorway to 17th c timber-framed house now blocked up, has thickly carved Jacobean brackets. One shows a leering satyr with odd cylindrical breasts.

Museum: in the library building, Broad St. Good local collection: costumes, military relics and agricultural machinery. Weapons from the Battle of Mortimer's Cross in 1461. Display of local traditions and superstitions, including tale of Black Vaughan, a man so feared that 12 parsons read his spirit into a silver snuff box which was buried in Hergest Pond. Open weekdays 10.00–6.00 all year, Thur and Sat 10.00–5.00 May–Sept, winter 10.00–4.00.

Churchill Gardens Museum: Regency house at 3 Venn's Lane with Victoriana, costumes and gallery devoted to local Edwardian artist Brian Hatton. Open 2.00–5.00 daily.

SHOPPING

Market day: Wed (butter market daily except Sun, farm produce Wed, Fri).
Early closing: Thur.
Pierpoint Gallery, Church St: good secondhand books and prints.
The Pine Centre, Widemarsh St: cheap baskets, bags, picnic hampers, toys and anything made from cane.

Mansell Lacey post office: a 17th-century cottage with dovecote

FOOD AND DRINK

Egon Ronay's Lucas Guide recommends **Green Dragon Hotel Restaurant**, Broad St. For snacks, lunches, toasted sandwiches, coffee, **Patties Coffee House**, St Peter's Close, is excellent, also **Cathedral Restaurant** in Church St. Pubs include: **Grapes Tavern**, Church St: Whitbread house, ancient beamed building which still has original oak-panelled room where 'London Letter', delivered by stagecoach, was read aloud weekly by chairman. **Queen's Arms**, Broad St: appealing small pub. Very pretty carved frieze outside and warm welcome inside. **Bowling Green**, Bewell St: Whitbread Best Bitter from Tiverton and pale ale from Cheltenham.

WHERE TO STAY

Egon Ronay's Lucas Guide recommends **Green Dragon Hotel**, tel Hereford 2506.

TOURIST INFORMATION

Shire Hall, St Owen's St, Hereford, tel Hereford 68430.

River Wye

Villages and country towns

Abbey Dore

Village at the head of the Golden Valley, a remote, placid place which follows the wanderings of the Dore river. The Normans supposed that the Welsh *dwr* 'water' was really French *d'or* 'golden'. Not always so peaceful, as string of motte and bailey castles, posted only a mile apart along the valley, testifies.

Great parish church is remnant of Cistercian Dore Abbey, founded in 1120. Huge nave, once 250ft long, disappeared after suppression in 1535 and whole place degenerated into barn until the Scudamore family took it over. Church is now an odd composition of transept and chancel with tower added later.

Inside, oak screen, pillars and some splendid early murals. Behind the altar on the floor is a collection of stone bits and pieces which must have been part of the original abbey. In a south window, medallions of very early glass, gorgeous colours.

Luckily, church has got grant to rescue wall paintings before they flake away. Poor-box, dated 1639, stands by the door, and wild bees have nests either side of the porch.

Neville Arms is rather plain pub, stamped with the crest of the Marquis of Abergavenny, which sells Whitbreads.

Just on the edge of the village on Wormbridge Road is Abbey Dore Court which has splendid walled kitchen garden with espaliers and model veg, young orchard, herbaceous borders, and a river walk with hostas and herb garden recently added. Specializes in ferns. Open daily 10.30–6.30 or dusk if earlier.

Bosbury

Sits quietly among the hop fields, the kilns peering up over the landscape like witches in pointed dark hats. Church tower here is quite separate from church, a monstrously thick 29ft square, meanly lit by narrow lancet windows. Built in the 13th c and probably intended as a refuge in those warring times.

In churchyard are ashes of Edna Lyall, Victorian novelist, who wrote a string of best-sellers in her time. Even Gladstone praised them and John Ruskin had *In the Golden Days* read to him as he lay dying.

Bosbury is the setting for *In Spite of All*.

Pretty row of black and white cottages opposite the church and a pub, the Bell, which sells Whitbreads beer and draught Guinness. Track leads off by Bridge House and continues as footpath along the little river Leadon with tiny sandy beaches and the pungent smell of wild mint.

Bredwardine

Ideal for a Kilvert pilgrimage as he spent his last two years here as vicar and is buried in a disappointing grave of white marble in the churchyard. Marvellous position above the Wye and Kilvert's rectory right next door. 'Showed my father round the garden,' he wrote in 1878. 'He was much pleased with everything. The house and garden were much larger and more beautiful than he had supposed.' Rectory now private house. Track leads round to right of church into meadow, site of old castle and fish ponds, still recognizable.

Magnificent 17th c inn, the Red Lion, stands in commanding position at the little crossroads, soft red brick with the old slightly greeny glass still in the windows. The place is run like a country house, so that everyone sits down at eight o'clock and eats what is put in front of them. Good food and old oak furniture. Mr Stockwell, the owner, organizes the estate's salmon fishing on the Wye.

Clodock

A Welsh bit of England this, hanging on to the foothills of the Black Mountains. Churchyard, full of names like Price, Watkins, Parry and Prosser, bounded by river Monnow which falls over weir and flat stone slabs to reach the bridge and large water-mill below. Superb churchyard – not a stone has ever been moved.

Church itself is Norman mostly but with 17th c woodwork. A three-decker pulpit dominates the little building.

The river runs one side of the churchyard, the lane another and Mrs Prosser's alehouse, the Cornewall Arms, takes up the third, a low whitewashed place. You walk into a dark stone-floored room, with huge wooden settle by the fire, a table and some Victorian engravings. No bar. Mrs Prosser draws the beer in the kitchen and brings it through.

Eardisland

Uncommonly pretty village, half strung out along the road, half grouped round the river Arrow, surrounded by old cider orchards and hop fields. Even the garage is ancient black and white. Very fine trees all around, so that the whole effect is of being in some splendid park. Just by the bridge is Staick House, an L-shaped building, with one wing a 14th c hall of great magnificence, massive stone roof and carving. Topiary peacocks in front garden.

Unusual dovecote near the old whipping post belongs to the manor, itself an uneasy amalgamation of timber frame and Queen Anne. Manor is now the Arrow Furniture Mart.

Nearby a bric-a-brac shop, selling fenders, fire irons, old flagons in a little shed. Open Sat–Sun, bank hol 10.00–4.00.

Place of pilgrimage for C A M R A enthusiasts, since the Cross Inn sells Penrhos ales from the county's newest brewery, based at Lyonshall. Penrhos use their own spring water, local hops and mill their own malt. Output is necessarily limited, so are outlets. Close by is another good pub, the White Swan, which does bar lunches and dining-room dinners and dispenses Marstons.

Ledbury

Busy little place, just west of the Malvern hills, market day Tue. Needs its bypass; far too much traffic perilously close to overhanging buildings.

Centre dominated by market house, built up on 16 piers of Spanish chestnut. Connecting this with the church is a pretty cobbled street, no traffic, called Church Lane, marvellous black and white buildings packed cheek by jowl, with the elegant spire of St Katherine's, 203ft high, soaring up at the end. Old grammar school on left has been restored and turned into a Heritage Centre – horrible term but good idea – showing development of town from Anglo-Saxon days when it was Liedberghe. Open daily Spring Bank Hol–Aug Bank Hol 11.00–5.00. Next door is Prince of Wales, 15th c inn selling Whitbreads. Talbot Inn, New St, has bullet holes from Civil War in dining-room, fired in 1645 when the dashing Prince Rupert surprised Roundheads in dawn raid and drove them out of town.

Edward Barrett buried in church. Brewers pub here sells Marston bitter, Whitbreads pale ale and Westons cider, in a front-parlour setting.

Some pretty 18th c houses in The Homend, especially No 36, with a splendid great shell hood, carved with an anxious face peering out from the boss.

Leominster

For 500 years one of the great wool markets in England. Local wool, 'Demster ore' was renowned for its quality, mentioned by Skelton and Ben Jonson. The minster that gave town its name is there no longer, destroyed in the Dissolution, but priory church remains. One of the few surviving ducking stools in the country housed here, last used in 1809, when one Jenny Pipes was paraded round town and then ducked.

Grange Court, the old town hall, now stands overlooking priory grounds. Built in 1633 by John Abel, King's carpenter, he smothered it with every kind of decorative device, caryatids, Amazons, Ionic columns, lions, monsters, fleurs-de-lis. Pulled down in 1853 from its central site because it was a hindrance to traffic, it was put up again on its present site and nearly sold to an American in the 1930s. Now home of Leominster council's technical dept.

Drapers Lane is pleasant small passage lined with shops, no traffic, with even smaller alleys snaking off on either side under overhangs of timbered buildings.

In Etnam St is good folk museum, specializing in local lore, costumes, uniforms, farm implements. Open Mon–Sat 10.00–1.00 and 2.00–5.00, Sun 2.00–5.00. This street also has good pubs. Chequers Inn, about 400 years old, is a comfortable, gabled place with steak bar and Ansells beer. Royal Oak is solid market pub, open until 5 pm on Fri (market day). They sell Penrhos, Courage and Theakstons. *Egon Ronay's Pub Guide* recommends the bar snacks – especially the superb granary bread – at the Talbot Hotel, West St.

Mansell Lacy

Pretty village which straggles along a loop of lane leading off the Kington road. Post office must be most quixotic in England, a timber-framed 17th c cottage, with dovecote.

Yazor brook wanders through this sheltered valley, past early 16th c cottages with apple orchards behind.

Church much altered in the last century, but hayrakes hang in the porch and the grass grows lushly all around.

Pembridge

Once a busy market town, with a Royal Charter granted way back in 1240. Now that Hereford has taken over, market hall stands slightly forlorn in little central square, completely dominated by New Inn (actually early 17th c). Very pretty timbered Whitbread pub with gabled wings, smothered in wisteria. The Greyhound, also selling Whitbread, is even older, with wonderfully intricate timbering. Its buildings bulge and lean in all directions: a surveyor's nightmare, a tourist's paradise.

Church is rather hidden away, approach up a flight of steps by Church Cottage in the square. Most unusual 14th c bell house, detached from the church. Probably a refuge for the village, as stone walls are immensely thick, with loop holes.

At the east end of the village is a little row of almshouses with an inscription at either end. The first gives details of the benefactor, the second proudly records: 'This hospitall was bielded by me Thomas Powle Carpeinter according to the Doners will in 1686.'

Weobley

Stunning geometry of black and white, a well-served village with good shops, good pubs and interesting things to see.

Church tower is massively embattled and, once again, built quite separately from the church. A place of safety when the marauding Welsh came curdling over the border. Fine marble monument to Colonel Birch, a Parliamentarian who captured Hereford and became Governor. Later quarrelled with Cromwell, changed his colours and helped put Stuarts back on the throne. He bought an estate here and spent a fortune refurbishing the church.

Willow Gallery sells spinning gear, local crafts, plants and herbs, Spinning demonstrations every Sat and Sun afternoon. Weekend courses on vegetable dyeing, spinning, weaving. Tea and coffee also served. Open daily 10.30–6.00. The Crafts Shop, Bell Square, sells pottery, needlework, fudge. Open Mon–Sat 9.00–1.00 and 2.00–5.30. Teas also served at the post office in the Tudor Tea Room. Open 3.00–5.30.

Local tug-of-war team trains on Whitbread Tankard in Ye Olde Salutation. Other pubs include the Unicorn and the Red Lion, a splendid inn with seven bedrooms and excellent food. Bar is comforting, lots of dark beams, sofas, settles and engravings. Strongbow keg cider and Whitbread Trophy.

Weobley village – 'stunning geometry of black and white'

—Places to visit—

Bradnor Hill: Welsh marches, constantly fought over in Middle Ages, have now sunk into well-earned tranquillity. Best view of all here, in a county famous for them. To east stretch woods, meadows and winding streams of England, to west is Radnor Forest and dark mountains of Wales, far to south is Hereford and the great plain that was once the kingdom of Mercia. National Trust. Half a mile north-west of Kington.

Offa's Dyke: great earthwork which stretches the length of the Welsh border, from the Dee to the Severn. Made about 785 by King Offa to keep marauding Welsh out of Mercia. Large rampart, also ditch, usually on Welsh side, with the best preserved stretch around Knighton. Long distance footpath runs whole 168 miles. Information Centre at The Old Primary School, West St, Knighton, produces excellent guidebook.

Symonds Yat: Yat Rock probably best of viewpoints on River Wye. Very awe-inspiring to stand on this rocky crag, 400ft high, with steep cliffs falling away on either side to rapidly flowing river, especially as Wye makes great sweep of four miles before passing from one side of this narrow neck of land to the other.

Berrington Hall: elegant house built in 1778 for Thomas Harley, a rich banker from an old Herefordshire family. Capability Brown chose the site for the house and landscaped the park, including huge artificial lake. Brown's son-in-law Henry Holland built the house, which is restrained, almost severe outside, but elaborately decorated inside with stucco, painted panels and a splendid staircase. National Trust. Open April–Sept Wed, Thur, Sat, Sun, bank hol 2.00–6.00, Oct Sat–Sun 2.00–6.00. Three miles north of Leominster.

Croft Castle: embattled towers still stand at each corner, probably 14th c, but front softened by Gothic bays and parapets along the roof line. Gothic staircase inside and splendid collection of Gothic furniture. Grounds here escaped axe of 18th c landscape brigade, so there are flourishing formal avenues, oaks 40ft round and sweet chestnuts stretching for half a mile, said to have been grown from Spanish chestnuts cast up from an Armada ship wrecked on the Welsh

Kilpeck Church

coast. National Trust. Open April–Sept Wed, Thur, Sat, Sun, bank hol 2.15–6.00. 5 miles NW of Leominster.

Lower Brockhampton: surrounded by a deep moat, the house has elaborately carved bargeboards and an op-art exterior of black and white, part of the framing close-set uprights, the rest in more regular squares. Improbable gatehouse built later at the edge of the moat, also timbered, the top storey overhanging all round, defying gravity. Again, beautifully carved boards along the roofline, decorated with running design of foliage. Much the best of the black and white manors of this border country. National Trust. Medieval hall only open Feb–Dec Mon, Wed, Fri, Sat 10.00–1.00 and 2.00–6.00, Sun 10.00–1.00. Two miles east of Bromyard.

Eastnor Castle: splendidly medieval in appearance with its turrets and towers, but actually built in 1814 for the first Earl Somers, who fancied himself as a Norman baron. Fine state rooms, one designed and furnished by Pugin, and a big collection of armour, paintings and tapestries. BBC filmed both *The Pal-lisers* and *Little Lord Fauntleroy* here. Open Sun, Bank Hol Mon mid-May–Sept, also July–Aug Wed, Thur 2.15–6.00. 2 miles E of Ledbury on A438.

Goodrich Castle: mountain of stone, set in green fields above the Wye, commanding crossing made by old Roman road from Gloucester–Monmouth. Oldest part is keep, square Norman tower of three storeys, standing out prominently in courtyard. Whole thing surrounded by exceptionally deep ditch hacked out of solid rock, crossed by a drawbridge. Last fortress in country to hold out for Charles, under command of Sir Harry Lingen, but after long siege, walls were breached and castle slighted. Here Wordsworth met 'little cottage girl' who later inspired 'We Are Seven'. Open May–Sept 9.30–7.00 daily, March, April 9.30–5.30 daily, Oct weekdays 9.30–5.30 Sun 2.00–5.30, Nov–Feb weekdays 9.30–4.30 Sun 2.00–4.30.

Kilpeck Church: tiny Norman church tucked away in south of county, must be one of the most perfect in England, lavishly decorated inside and out with serpents, birds, dragons, fish and angels.

Eye Manor: home of Christopher Sandford. Exhibition of period costume, needlework, paper sculpture, Beck Collection of costume dolls, and Mrs Sandford's corn dollies. Books produced by Mr Sandford's Golden Cockerel Press also on view. Open Good Fri, Easter Sun, Mon, Tues, then Wed, Thur, Sat, Sun till end June, Wed–Sun July–end Sept daily 2.30–5.30. Four miles north of Leominster.

Tintern Abbey: best seen by climbing up one of the many paths through the woods and looking down on soaring arches and elegant tracery.

Burton Court: early 14th c hall, open to the roof, swallowed up in later Georgian enlargements, with front redone in 1912 by Sir Clough Williams-Ellis (of Portmeirion) in a style which Pevsner describes as 'free Tudor'. Good exhibition of European and Oriental costumes and curios. Open Spring Bank Hol–mid-Sept Wed, Thur, Sat, Sun, bank hol 2.30–6.00. 5 miles W of Leominster.

Arthur's Stone, Dorstone: uncovered chamber tomb of the third millenium BC. Series of side slabs make entrance passage which bends sharply before entering chamber. Massive capstone is more than 20ft long. Three leylines centre on this point.

Marcher Castles: after the Conquest, William parcelled out border land territory to followers who might get in the way and let them grab what they could the other side of Offa's Dyke. First Norman assault led by William Fitz-Osbern in 1067. Series of frontier posts secured by motte and bailey castles at Raglan, Wigmore, Ewyas Harold and Clifford. Afterwards came massive fortresses of Chepstow, Monmouth, Abergavenny and Goodrich. Consolidation of holdings followed, with more castles at Caldicot, Longtown and St Briavels, and second line of defence running between Skenfrith, Grosmont and White Castle.

Cider makers: small independent cider firms still survive, where cider can be bought from the makers. H. Weston & Sons are at Much Marcle; R. & F. H. Fleming at Auberrow House, Wellington and Symonds Cider and English Wine Co at Stoke Lacy, nr Bromyard. Symonds also produce pear, apricot, blackcurrant and cherry wine. Cider making can be seen Sept–Dec after apple crop is gathered.

ACTIVITIES

Fishing: permits and information from Hatton's, 73 St Owen St, Hereford, or Dean's, 31 Broad St, Ross.

Boats: for hire from Old Ferry Inn, Symonds Yat West, or Saracen's Head, Symonds Yat East.

Bicycles: for hire from Little & Hall, 48 Broad St, Ross, tel Ross 2639.

FOOD AND DRINK

Egon Ronay's Lucas Guide recommends: **Angel Inn,** Kingsland, tel Kingsland 355. Popular traditional pub that serves good grills daily and more elaborate dishes Thur–Sat. **Penrhos Court,** Lyonshall, tel Kington 230720. 18th c barn with short table d'hôte menu changing daily.

TOURIST INFORMATION

Local papers: *Hereford Evening News,* daily, *Hereford Times,* Fri, and *Leominster News,* published on Wed.

Tourist information centres: at Bromyard, Kington, Ledbury, Leominster and Ross.

Research: Anna Pavord.

Ludlow

In the days when we could indulge our fancies in a lordlier way, one recipe for the perfect lifestyle was a Japanese wife, a French mistress, a Chinese cook, in an English country house. Personally I would gladly leave the other ingredients to chance and settle for a house in Broad Street, Ludlow, or in a village like Upton Cresset or Bitterley, and some trout-fishing in A. E. Housman's 'valleys of springs of rivers by Onny and Teme and Clun' – not to mention Corve, Rea, Kemp, Cound, Lugg, Unk and all the other little streams with earthy monosyllables that lace South Shropshire and the Welsh Border in a wide loop of the Severn.

If you need confirmation that there is plenty of the green and pleasant land still left, this is the region where you will find it: rich hanging woods, red loam, red Hereford cattle and the white-faced Friesian cross, three local breeds of sheep, a maze of lanes so deep that you sometimes have to steer by the stars, really thick-set hedges, broad and narrow valleys between rugged hills, and, at the heart of it, Ludlow with its church and castle, a crown on green velvet.

The nearest towns of any threatening size are Telford and Wolverhampton 50 miles away, and as the mass of the Clees thrusts out towards the Midlands like a breakwater and Clun and Radnor Forest and the Montgomeryshire hills stand sentinel in the west, it is difficult to realize that over the horizon in Coalbrookdale was the cradle of the Industrial Revolution.

The big angling clubs have been steadily infiltrating (the water holds grayling which means round-the-year fishing); the Forestry Commission has ruined some vistas with well-meaning conifers; the landlord of the pub at Culmington has recently shot three of the latest foreigners, mink. But away from the A49 little changes: people are few; the hamlets are often no more than a church and a couple of farms; time sleeps on undisturbed by the hum of a distant tractor; and life keeps to a rhythm that was old when the men of Clun, out of patience with the disruptions of the Civil War, banded together as Clubmen to fight both factions in defence of the harvest.

Castle ruins recall the feuds and forays of Norman and Welsh; but, as to village England, to feel its thinning pulse one needs to be somewhere like the church at Leebotwood where generations of Corbetts of Longnor Hall are buried and the list of King's Shropshire Light Infantry names on the roll of honour is unbearably long for a tiny community. Snailbeach below the Stiperstones (a prospect of 10 counties from the gaunt ridge) breathes a different kind of desolation from the spoil and shafts of long-abandoned lead mines and the ghosts of the miners who were left there to grub for survival.

Because this is working country, not tourist country, the villages are

The Feathers Hotel, Ludlow – 'a flourish in half-timber and moulding'

not self-consciously quaint: black and white Tudor, mellow thatch or sandstone, brick and stucco (but hardly any bed and breakfast signs) – every twisty lane is a lottery. Some villages are built in the form of a laager, reflecting an ancient self-containment and an eye for defence; old manors are often working farms; old churches built in troubled times are squat and strong, while many later ones tend to be plain and dowdy. Notable spires are few; after Housman had written, 'The vane on Hughley steeple veers bright, a far-known sign,' he discovered to his embarrassment that no steeple existed; but this Wenlock Edge village is worth a pause. Much pride and care goes into the cottage gardens and the climate has encouraged a remarkable amount of modest topiary.

Signposts are eccentric if not wilfully misleading, as though to baffle the Germans still – or perhaps Norman men-at-arms? The area does justice to real ale but judging by the distance between hostelries those Shropshire lads must have brewed their own. Being remote from the tourist conveyor-belt has certain disadvantages: a decent meal is hard to come by, with two creditable exceptions in Ludlow.

The harsh-looking slopes that would only be sheep-walks in Wales are often dairy and arable right to the tops, so one stumbles on farms and villages at unexpected heights. Contrast and diversity meet the eye at every turn, from the orchards and hopfields of Tenbury Wells, just across the Teme in Worcestershire, and once on the main coaching road to North Wales (admire the Royal Oak and King's Head), to grey moor-land villages like Cardington (the oldest pub licence in the county), under the lee of Caer Caradoc (one of a dozen places claimed as the site of Caractacus's last stand); from cosy Bromfield at the confluence of Teme and Onny, with its churchyard herb garden and 'superbly vulgar' chancel ceiling, or Church Stretton with the worn dignity of a pensioned-off Victorian spa, to the sterner landscape and Noncon-formist rigours on the Western approaches of the March; from steep Bishop's Castle (the Three Tuns brews its own beer, and note the splendid Midland bank) and even steeper Knighton (the staircase in the Norton Arms) to Aston-on-Clun in its watermeadows – and why is the inn called the Kangaroo?

Welsh drovers kept to the top of Clun Forest to avoid paying toll; from here to the Long Mynd in the Mary Webb country and the southern spine above the Teme where Offa's Dyke crosses the valley and the view is breathtaking. Stokesay Castle in a sylvan setting by the Ludlow road is the best preserved example of a fortified manor house (thanks largely to the unseemly haste of its Royalist garrison to sur-render). Shipton Hall in Corvedale is an Elizabethan gem. Onibury church engagingly has a photograph gallery of dead vicars on the walls, Leintwardine, among lapwing fields, boasts a Roman history and the handsome White Lion beside a likely-looking pool where the Clun joins the Teme. From Wigmore to the south-east in Herefordshire, Edward Mortimer set out for the Crown of England. Munslow up a narrow lane is like a fragment out of T. F. Powys: Georgian rectory, dishevelled churchyard dark with yew, church rich with the odour of decay, shady pond, derelict farmyard deep in stale manure. Knucklas has the romantic ruins of a Mortimer keep and the legend of King Arthur's marriage there to Guinevere, daughter of a local giant.

All roads still lead to Ludlow, chief citadel of the Marcher Lords and in quieter times the place where sensible men of means repaired to for the winter. A city that is set on a hill cannot be hid, and although Ludlow ranks as only a small town, with a quarter of Shrewsbury's population, it commands the surrounding countryside from its own knoll with complete authority. There is a dreamlike quality about it seen from the east into a setting sun, but it is even better first viewed from the rolling ground to the west and approached across the beautiful medieval Ludford bridge below the town, the Teme having grown to man's estate by now. Looking up at the beetling cliff of the castle from the river, the prospect is almost as thrilling as Anselm's Durham from the Wear: strength, composure, and history printed on every well-preserved stone. Stephen failed to take it from Matilda; Edward V was proclaimed King, and Prince Arthur, elder son of Henry VII, died here; it was the last Royalist stronghold to fall; Milton's *Comus* was first performed in the Great Hall. Equally commanding is St Laurence Church where Housman is buried, the largest parish church in Shropshire.

Wide and cobbled Broad Street is one of the pleasantest streets in any English town, climbing up to the eighteenth-century Buttercross with Georgian houses merging gracefully with half-timbered shops – and never a 'shoppe' in sight. Like the countryside around it is not a museum for tourists, although it can't help attracting them. Planned on the grid system in the Conqueror's time Ludlow has looked after itself, but to demonstrate that practical considerations take precedence over antiquity there is the ghastly brick excrescence of the town hall. The Feathers Hotel (1603), a lovely flourish in half-timber and moulding, makes some concessions to the spirit of tourism with its mob-capped waitresses but nothing has yet eroded the friendliness and comfort, and in the little slypes and alleys that give a charming twist to the general symmetry there are several inns of venerable pedigree. Long may it all stand!

CHRISTOPHER WORDSWORTH

Ludlow

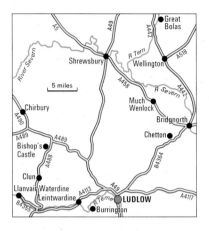

WHERE TO GO

Castle: the reason for the town, which was laid out on a strict grid system under the castle's protection. Inner bailey built about 1085 by Roger de Montgomery, but much bigger outer bailey added in 12th c. Deep ditch separates the two, overlooked by massive keep expanded from gatehouse tower of original castle. Splendid view from the top over the Marches. Little princes, Edward and Richard Plantagenet, later murdered in London, lived here for nearly 10 years in Pendower Tower. Pretty walks round outside of castle laid out by Countess of Powys in 1771. Open daily May–Sept 9.30–6.00, winter 10.30–4.00.

Museum: squashed into top floor of Buttercross, robustly classical building in the middle of town. Exhibits excellently displayed in period groups, a 9th c Viking sword, some enchanting 14th c tiles from priory of Austin Friars, decorated with animals, chilling collection of torture weapons excavated from castle dungeons, together with a scold's bridle and old whipping post, well-worn. Wide-ranging selection of fossils from surrounding limestone. Open Easter–end Sept Mon–Sat 10.30–12.30 and 2.00–5.00. Also Sun 10.00–1.00 and 2.00–5.00 in June, July, Aug.

Broad St: wide and satisfying with an interesting mixture of rooftops and frontages. Ancient black and white at the top, overhanging the pavement on pillars with a covered walkway underneath. Angel Hotel on the site since 1555, old entrance still survives. Local preservationists fought hard for cobbles which slope from pavement to road. Broad Gate which closes off street at bottom is last remaining town gate.

St Laurence: biggest parish church in Shropshire, light pink sandstone tucked away in College St on the highest point in town. Musical box carillon plays tunes at 8.00, noon, 4.00 and 8.00, but there is also a proper peal of eight fine bells. Gorgeous glass, especially window of St Catherine, and entertaining misericords in the chancel.

Town walls: were built, a mile of them, between 1233 and 1304, breached by seven gateways, but only Broad Gate survives. You can see part of the town wall running along by St John's Lane. The ditch that ran outside has been filled in and grassed over. Mill Gate stood just below the junction of Mill St and Camp Lane and the wall survives here both to east and west. Small 18th c houses in Upper Linney butt right on to it.

The Tolsey: odd building marooned in the Bull Ring. Court of Pye Powder (from the French *pieds poudres*) was once held here, in which disputes concerning markets and fairs were heard and settled before the dust was shaken from the feet.

Feathers Hotel: an exuberant showpiece of carpentry devices – with lozenges, cusps, scrolls, faces. Fine plaster ceiling in the first-floor dining-room, which includes vine, oak, rose and thistle panels.

SHOPPING

Market days: Mon, Fri, Sat in Market Hall (cattle market Mon).
Early closing: Thur.
Dinham House, Dinham: lovely red-brick Georgian place where Lucien Bonaparte once lived. Now Ludlow Craft Studios for pottery, jewellery, toys.
Castle Bookshop, 5 Castle St: excellent local collection.

FOOD AND DRINK

Egon Ronay's *Just a Bite* recommends the **Feathers Hotel,** also **Penny Anthony's Restaurant,** 5 Church St, for bumper butties and seafood pancakes. Pubs include: **Blue Boar,** Mill St: bar food and Ansells Bitter. **Wheatsheaf,** Broad St: shelters beside the town gate. Pleasant pub, serving Robinsons; also steaks, trout, omelettes and sandwiches. **Rose and Crown,** Church St: pretty timbered pub, with tiny courtyard in front. Grills and snacks, Greenall Whitley beers.

WHERE TO STAY

Egon Ronay's Lucas Guide recommends the **Feathers Hotel**.

TOURIST INFORMATION

The Information Centre, Castle St, tel Ludlow 3857.

Stokesay Castle – **'the best preserved example of a fortified manor house'**

Villages and country towns

Bishop's Castle

Small market town which climbs up the hill in an assortment of styles. Town hall at the top is very superior, about 1785, round windows gazing down the thoroughfare. Basement was a prison cell, the windows still heavily barred.

Kings Head in High St is a Whitbread pub, but round the corner in Salop St is the Three Tuns where the landlord, Peter Milner, brews his own beer. He will supply casks to order. Gaynor Pottery in Salop St does tea, coffee and freshly prepared sandwiches. Also sells bric-à-brac. Pine Apple Shop has small hand-made wooden toys and candles. Maker sits painting toys in the front of the shop. Castle Hotel on site of Norman castle is fine seven-bay stone house.

Market day fixed in 1292 as Fri.

Bridgnorth

Built against the cliffs of the Severn Gorge the pink rock bulges through brick facings, and flights of steps twist and snake down the steep escarpment. A cliff railway connects High Town with Low Town down by the river. Open weekdays 8.00 am–9.00 pm Sun 12.00–9.00. Pleasant walk along the river, lined with lime trees, caves hollowed out from the rock. One iron sign says: 'This cave was occupied as a dwelling until the year 1856.'

Cartway leading up from the river has pretty little houses and, on the right, an intricate timbered building, Bishop Percy's House (1580), now a boys' club. It is open only by appointment (tel Bridgnorth 3298).

At the top of Cartway, a ghostly faded hand points the way to High Town. Bridgnorth is keen on signs, many of them marvellous great cast-iron ones. Unfortunately some of the prettiest shops are now empty, but Waterloo House with cast-iron colonnàde of 1802 has recently reopened as an antique bottle shop. Castle is worth a visit if only because the keep leans at an angle far greater than the tower of Pisa – 17° out of true. Castle Walk is old-fashioned promenade, good views.

Home-made pies and thickly sliced home-cured bacon at Ye Olde Pie Shoppe

Shire horses are a feature of the Acton Scott Working Farm Museum at Church Stretton

in High St. Any number of excellent pubs in High St selling Banks mild and bitter, the Railwaymen's Arms at the Severn Valley Railway Station, for Simpkiss bitter, Banks mild, Ansells mild and bitter. Free admission to platform if you show your CAMRA card. Bambers in St Mary's St is a restaurant specializing in grills and casseroles. Open 7.00–9.30 pm. Recommended in *Egon Ronay's Lucas Guide*.

Burrington

Tiny, quiet hamlet at the bottom of heavily wooded hills. Irish yews line the path to the church, a pretty little building with timber belfry, but falling to bits inside. Superb set of cast-iron grave slabs lined up outside against the east wall, the earliest 1619, the last 1754. Strong lettering in relief, beautifully designed with coats of arms below. On one an A slipped in the casting and is now in perpetuity trapped askew.

Splendid stone and timbered farmhouse with a two-storey gable, an old orchard at the back with tree house. Just below is an L-shaped range of cottages, crumbling, but very pretty, lath and plaster on top of original timber construction. Even the post box is a VR one. At the back of one cottage is complete cider press, a huge stone trough that must once have pressed enough juice to send the whole valley into a coma.

Chetton

High and remote village eight miles east of Wenlock Edge and up a dead-end off the Bridgnorth–Ludlow road. The church has been 'restored' several times and only the doorway and the chancel are medieval. The chancel arch rests on two odd heads, male and female, very large and simply carved. Quaint framed notices at the back of the church recall more feudal times. One, advertising a memorial service for King Edward VII on Friday, 20 May 1910, asks householders 'to make such arrangements as they conveniently can in their households to ensure the attendance of themselves, their families and servants on this solemn occasion'.

Path leads round the outside of the churchyard (medieval masonry built into the retaining walls) to Ye Olde Inne, a pretty stone pub with garden and gorgeous views out over this gentle country. Cosy bar with settles and beaten copper tables and steaks, gammon or trout in dining-room.

Chirbury

Six roads meet here close to the Montgomeryshire border, suggesting that the village was once far more important than it is now. View west to Berwyn mountains, behind is Corndon and Stapley Hill. The Herbert Arms stands in a dominant position, a tall Georgian place, white painted brick and symmetrical sash windows. Fine coat of arms on the board. Meals in dining-room or bar, and six bedrooms for visitors.

A unique bronze matrix of the Blessed Mary of the Well was dug up in the churchyard last century. It had been used in the early Middle Ages for casting tokens to sell to pilgrims who came to the Holy Well at Rorrington. Earthenware replicas of it can be bought in the church.

Very pretty village school, black and white timbered, built in 1675 by the autocratic Parson Lewis, who defied villagers and tradition by using part of the graveyard for the purpose. The Glory Hole, next to the Village Hall, is a bright jumble of whole foods, furniture, crafts and toys. It is open 10.00–1.00 and 2.00–4.30, closed all day Thur.

Small but interesting Bronze Age circle near here, Mitchelsford: 37 little stones buried deep in the gorse and long grass of Stapley Hill.

Clun

A very Welsh bit of Shropshire, the name itself a corruption of the Welsh 'Llan'. The approach to this quiet little place is a roller-coaster ride. Gaunt remains of a castle standing high to the west. Footpath leads off to the left from Buffalo Lane and emerges at the earthworks, all that now remains of the castle's outer baileys. Brilliant defensive position with River Clun bounding it on west and north. Good place for picnics, sharing the meadow with dark-faced Clun sheep.

Little square dominated by court house, now town hall, late 18th c with an arched ground floor which was once open on all sides. Little cupola and lantern perch on top. Museum here has good collection of flint arrowheads, knives and scrapers gathered from surrounding hills. Open Tue and Sat 2.30–5.00 Easter–Nov, or by request to Florida Villa nearby, tel Clun 247.

Pretty humpback bridge over river, five arches with triangular breakwaters. Bridge House does tea, coffee and homemade cakes. Further up in High St is the Sun, long, old inn selling draught Bass, Ansells mild and M&B Springfield bitter. Old Bakehouse restaurant in the same building; interesting food, including local lamb cutlets in cucumber, ham and mint sauce. Sir Walter Scott stayed at the other inn, the Buffalo, while absorbing local colour for *The Betrothed* in which Clun Castle appears as Garde Doloreuse.

Great Bolas

Peaceful little village set among great flat meadows bordering the River Teme. The church is the main thing to see, mostly red brick of 1729, and beautiful inside; simple box pews, white painted walls with a most unusual round-headed window behind the altar.

Great scandal here in late 18th c when Earl of Burleigh, disconsolate after his wife's elopement with a curate, came to live here under the unimaginative name of John Jones. He then married bigamously a local beauty, Sarah Hoggins, the miller's daughter, but got into a terrible tangle when he inherited the family estates on the death of the 9th Earl of Exeter.

The house he built, Burleigh Villa, is a

Leintwardine – 'among lapwing fields boasts a Roman history'

large red-brick place, now marooned in a
sea of corn. It is not open to the public,
but you can see the front by walking out

and make for the side aisle where the
gothic lettering proclaims 'free seats'.
Organ still has original hand bellows,
stool for unfortunate bellow-slave.
the organist gets stuck, a built-in
organ will play 10 different tunes.
es are written up in copperplate on
or of the barrel device.

Red Lion Restaurant is a long,
whitewashed, stone pub recom-
d by *Egon Ronay's Lucas Guide*.
m brick-floored with wood-burn-
e, the other bar dark and beamy.
dining-room looking over the
meals by arrangement only.

Wenlock

riory with a little town clustering
inge. Now a little town decorated
ruins of a priory. William Gilpin,
n 1809, found the ruins not up
h: 'If they had been connected
ther by fragments of old walls
ected with the ground by a few
rubbish, and a little adorned
d, we should have considered
higher style and looked at them
esque.' Peevish remarks, for

of Bridgnorth Castle: it
n angle of 17°

painted in gold gothic script on the ends,
Menachty, Skyborrah. Informative
churchwarden says locals get upset if
strangers sit in their pews, so be warned

they are lovely. Topiary puppies leap
in golden yew around the cloisters.
Open weekdays May–Sept 9.30–7.00
Sun 2.00–7.00, March, April, Oct 9.30–
5.30 Sun 2.00–5.30, Nov–Feb 9.30–4.00
Sun 2.00–4.00.

Most pleasant town to explore, good
coffee shops, one at the Malthouse,
another at Scotts in the High St. Small
museum on corner by guildhall with
excellent local collection and information on the area. Open April–Sept
Mon–Sat 10.30–1.00 and 2.00–5.00 Sun
2.30–5.30. Wonderful range of textures,
Georgian brick, limestone, timbering
and no difficult intrusion of modern
building. Pigs and chickens at a farm in
the middle of town.

Gaskell Arms Hotel is pretty creeper-
covered Regency hotel selling M&B ales.
George and Dragon is pleasant pub in
High St; Banks bitter and Simpkiss
bitter served here. James II stayed at
the Talbot in 1687 and touched for the
king's evil. No record of whether he
cured anybody.

—Places to visit—

Attingham Park: fine porticoed
house with broad expanse of parkland.
Best view of the whole is from the Tern
bridge on the Shrewsbury road. Good
plaster ceilings, painted boudoir and
John Nash picture gallery with iron-
framed roof cast at Coalbrookdale.
National Trust. Open Easter–end Sept
Tue–Thur, Sat, Sun, bank hol 2.00–
5.30. Teas at the house four miles south-
east of Shrewsbury.

Benthall Hall: Benthall family left
Hall in mid 18th c, tried to buy it back in
1844, managed to rent it for a few years
early this century and at last, in 1934,
obtained possession again. Present occupant Sir Paul Benthall, is 12th in line of
descent from original 16th c builder.
South front unaltered since then with
gabled roof line, moulded brick chimney
stacks and mullioned windows. Entrance
porch has hiding place like many houses
in this Catholic part of the country. Five
stone tablets form quincunx above door,
probably a secret sign for Catholic
sympathizers. National Trust. Open
Easter Sat–Sept Tues, Wed, Sat 2.00–
6.00, Bank Hol Mon ground floor only
2.00–6.00. 4 miles north east of Much
Wenlock.

Wilderhope Manor: now a youth hostel, lying east of Wenlock Edge looking over wide, mild Shropshire landscape that seems unaltered from the day the house was built in late Elizabethan times. Rugged solid stone building with stone roof, towering chimney shafts. Plaster ceilings are special attraction, with all the symbolism that the Elizabethans delighted in. National Trust. Open April–Sept Wed, Sat 2.00–4.30, Oct–March Sat 2.00–4.30. 7 miles south west of Much Wenlock.

Acton Burnell Castle: in bosky valley, castle (actually a fortified manor) was started in 1284 by Bishop of Bath and Wells after he had got a licence to crenellate and permission to use timber from the king's forests for the building. Open any reasonable time. 7 miles west of Much Wenlock.

Boscobel House: Pevsner is dismissive: 'Panelling and a little plaster of the early 17th c is all there is, unless one considers hiding-holes architecture.' Rich in marvellous associations though, from its beginnings about 1600 when it was built by John Giffard, a Catholic, as a place of concealment. Charles II stayed here after the miserable Battle of Worcester in 1651. Harrison Ainsworth's *Boscobel* gives highly romantic account of the King's adventures. Open weekdays May–Sept 9.30–7.00 Sun 2.00–7.00, March, April, Oct 9.30–5.30 Sun 2.00–5.30, Nov–Feb 9.30–4.00 Sun 2.00–4.00. Closed 1.00–2.00. Four miles east of Tong, 4½ miles north of Albrighton off A41.

Hodnet Hall Gardens: 60 acres of landscaped gardens, filling the valley below the house and divided up so that there is always some patch in full bloom. Daisy-chain of lakes and pools that extends along the cultivated garden to the wilder natural part where there are lots of wildfowl. Collection of big-game trophies in 17th c tearoom. Open April–mid-Sept weekdays 2.00–5.00 Sun, bank hol 12.00–6.00. 5½ miles south-west of Market Drayton.

Stokesay Castle: approached through a gatehouse which comes straight from a picture-book. Charming timber framing, narrowly placed posts below and lozenges above. Some lovely carvings. Beyond are medieval stone buildings of fortified manor, surrounded by a moat. It surrendered during Civil War and so escaped any damage. Sumptuous Elizabethan panelling and fireplace. Open daily except Tue summer 10.00–6.00 winter 10.00–4.30. Closed Nov–Feb,

Mitchelsford Bronze Age circle on Stapley Hill near Chirbury

three quarters of a mile south of Craven Arms.

Ironbridge Gorge Museum: In 1709 Abraham Darby first smelted iron here using coke, a technical breakthrough. Museum is a complex of unique monuments to industrial past, including first iron bridge ever built. Severn Warehouse Visitor Centre has slide and tape show explaining background. Coalbrookdale Museum of Iron tells story of iron making in Britain from iron age to present day. Blists Hill Open Air Museum pounds with the noises of working sawmill and whines of 19th c pit winding engine. Coalport China Works Museum has magnificent display of porcelain and explains history of works and its people. Open daily April–Oct 10.00–6.00, Nov–March 10.00–5.00. (Telford.)

Oak Cottage Herb Farm, Nesscliffe, nr Shrewsbury: ornamental herb garden, including cottage garden plants and container plants for sale. Open all year at any reasonable time, but best to telephone first (Nesscliffe 262).

Burford House: home of John Treasure and of famous clematis nursery, Treasures of Tenbury. Garden with collection of rare plants. Ground floor of house also open with flower arrangements from the gardens. Open early April–mid-Oct daily 2.00–5.00.

Country Life Museum, White House, Aston Munslow, nr Craven Arms: buildings include Norman dovecote, cruck hall, 17th c cider house and other buildings of many different styles and periods. Furnished with wonderfully arcane domestic implements. Open Easter–Oct, times under review, tel Munslow 661.

Weston Park: Restoration house with herds of deer and rare breeds of sheep, woodland adventure playground, aquarium, architectural and nature trails, pony rides, lunches and teas. Open Aug daily, May–July daily except Mon and Fri, April and Sept weekend and bank hol only. Grounds open 11.00, house 2.00–5.30.

Long Mynd: whaleback hill marvellous for walking or riding. Crossed by medieval track, the Portway. In mist and drizzle a stark and intimidating prospect, in sunshine – superb. Carding Mill Valley, signposted from Church Stretton, is one of many pretty ravines at foot of Long Mynd. Good walk up to Light Spout waterfall.

Acton Scott Working Farm Museum, nr Church Stretton: demonstrates life on an upland farm before petrol engine. Work with shire horses shows 19th c arable techniques. Traditional crafts such as quilting, spinning, lace-making, wood-turning, bee-keeping demonstrated weekends. Corn harvesting also in Aug with stubbles cleared and gleaned by sheep and poultry. Open June, July, Aug 10.00–6.00 daily. April, May, Sept, Oct weekdays 1.00–5.30, Sun and bank hol 10.00–6.00.

FOOD AND DRINK

Egon Ronay's Lucas Guide recommends: **Old Hall Restaurant**, Cressage, nr Shrewsbury, tel Cressage 298. Timber-framed inn with simple menu featuring well-prepared traditional English and French dishes. **Howard Arms Hotel Restaurant**, Ditton Priors, nr Bridgnorth, tel Ditton Priors 200. Cottagey, candelit place with interesting meat and game dishes. **Albright Hussey**, nr Shrewsbury, tel Bomere Heath 290523. Historic moated manor house complete with peacocks. Cooking by proprietor. **Penny Farthing**, 23 Abbey Foregate, Shrewsbury, tel Shrewsbury 56119. High standard of cooking – guinea fowl in cream and port.

TOURIST INFORMATION

Tourist information offices: Bridgnorth, Church Stretton, Ironbridge, Much Wenlock, Oswestry and Shrewsbury.

Research: Anna Pavord.

Uppingham

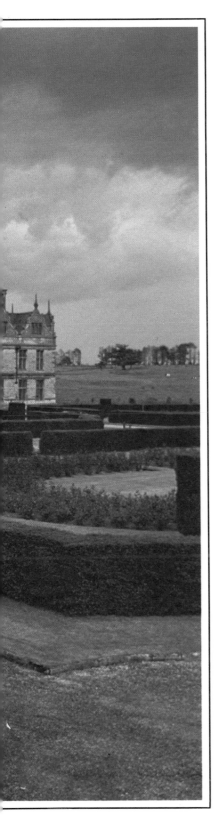

Many of us can remember Hilaire Belloc's casual description of the Midlands 'which are sodden and unkind', and so they can be, those leagues of heavy claylands. On the other hand, one can think of the miles of hawthorn hedges in full summer flower. That beautiful writer and naturalist W. H. Hudson knew this and marked 18 May as the very crown of the summer in the Midlands. When I read this many years ago I adopted it into my calendar and could calculate how early or late (usually late) the spring was, to within a matter of days.

This is, in winter, the landscape of the great hunts – the Quorn in Leicestershire, the Cottesmore centred upon Oakham in Rutland, and the Pytchley to the south in Northamptonshire. The details of the meets and the days are set out in the bible of hunters, *Bayley's Hunting Directory*. No matter what you may feel in theory about hunting the fox, the blood stirs when you see the pink-coated hunt in full cry across the green Midland pastures: very like deploring militarism and yet being elated by a fine military band in action.

The East Midlands begin a few miles to the east of Leicester, where the uplands rise to 600 or 700 feet and roll away eastwards to the sudden edge of the Fens just beyond Stamford. They are by no means all heavy clayland; two belts of good building stone cross the land diagonally, parallel with each other: the sheep-grey oolitic limestone loosely called 'Cotswold stone', and the marlstone or ironstone, which ranges in colour from a dark soft velvety brown to a bright orange, depending on the amount of iron ore in the stone. However, the workings are nearly up to the medieval gateway of Rockingham Castle, and to the very edge of the most haunting of Elizabethan country houses, Kirby Hall, built of the oolitic limestone between 1570 and 1575 and 'modernized' by Inigo Jones in 1638–40. This house was begun by Christopher Hatton, one of Elizabeth's great officers of state, rivalling Lord Burghley's great palace at Burghley just outside Stamford; Kirby is smaller in comparison and infinitely more lovely to look at.

The stone belts have produced some extremely attractive small towns. Forget the red brick of the boot and shoe towns of Northamptonshire, but make pilgrimages to such lovely places as Oundle and Stamford, Uppingham and Oakham.

The town is dominated, but not too obtrusively, by the grand buildings of the school (another Elizabethan foundation), and puts one in mind of a former age when a rich abbey dominated some little town at its gate and gave it most of its trade and *raison d'être*. Because the main street has escaped butchery, by an accident of topography, it retains scores of small specialist shops and shows very little of the chain-store

Kirby Hall – **'the most haunting of Elizabethan country houses'** aspect of main streets elsewhere; and, thanks to the school, it has a splendid bookshop. Uppingham market is a delightful miniature in keeping with the size of the market place, a tiny bit of an older and more peaceful England.

Oakham is mainly built of the limestone, with a grand church, and a school founded at the same time as Uppingham (1584) by the same Leicester archdeacon. Uppingham owes its greater fame as a public school to one man, Edward Thring, who became a headmaster in 1853 and transformed the ancient grammar school into one of the leading public schools of England. Oakham had no such man as Thring but thrives quietly. Like Uppingham, it still retains the original school building of 1584. Oakham's market is a larger affair than Uppingham's, full of colour and varied local speech. But the best in this region is the Tuesday market at Melton Mowbray, which is mentioned in a record of 1077 as a going concern. The market held just before Christmas is a covered one and a grand sight for gluttons with its multitude of doomed turkeys, all alive, often carried by the buyer under his arm while he goes on to other things. Nor must one forget Melton pork-pies and Stilton cheese.

Stamford, too, has a lively market, but here the grand feature is the mid-Lent fair, once one of the four international fairs of England based on cloth, and now a pleasure fair. Fair-people would converge on Stamford for days beforehand – all the main roads into the town were lined with the waiting fairmen – but no move was allowed until the clock of St Mary's, the lovely medieval church, struck noon on the Sunday morning. Then the procession started to roll in from all sides.

The East Midlands were near enough to London for many of the great officers of state of Elizabethan and Jacobean England to build country houses there. Besides Kirby and Burghley there is Holdenby (another Hatton house), half ruined and half restored; the spectacular Burley-on-the-Hill, built by Daniel Finch, Earl of Winchelsea and Nottingham; the ruined Exton and its parish church with beautiful tombs and monuments, particularly the Elizabethan ones.

Wandering around Rutland and the neighbouring parts of Northamptonshire and East Leicestershire is one of the purest pleasures of life: so many splendid parish churches large and small, so many grand houses (not forgetting ruined Fotheringhay where Mary Queen of Scots was beheaded on a February morning in 1587, within sight of the truly magnificent parish church).

The East Midlands are dull only to those speeding along the motorways. Beyond the speed and the noise of the juggernauts there lie some of the loveliest landscapes and architecture that England can show. Originally, they lacked only stretches of water to complete the scene, the rivers being small and slow, but the Eye Brook reservoir, opened in 1940, and now the huge Rutland Water, recently opened, add the last touch of shimmering beauty to the green countryside.

W. G. HOSKINS

Uppingham

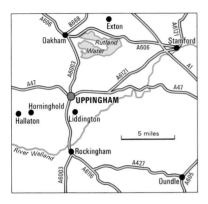

WHERE TO GO

Market Square: the centre of this small country town – greengrocer, seedsman, pub and Georgian post office neatly arranged around it, church tucked attractively in the corner. Church of St Peter and St Paul: on one side hustle and bustle of market-place, on the other, leafy countryside and bright green hills. In between, sadly, the gloominess of drastic Victorian restoration. Elizabethan pulpit survived and some interesting Norman figures – Christ, bearded saint and two angels.
Uppingham School: at 8.45 and 3.30, pavements crowded with school boys. School buildings dominate south-west corner of the town, most of them dating from 1860 onwards, light gold and buff stone. Around the quadrangle Victorian Gothic; along the High Street, Jacobean style with asymmetrical turret and statue.
Uppingham Theatre, Stockerston Rd: enterprising programmes from jazz musicals to Shakespeare. Based on term-times. Box office tel Uppingham 3955.

SHOPPING

Market day: Fri.
Early closing: Thur.
Baines, High St West: old-fashioned confectioners selling tea and honey. Warm currant loaves and chocolate cakes that come in yard lengths chopped off to the amount you require. Next door, their own tea-room. Good range of snacks and cakes.
Old Constable's Bookshop, High St West: secondhand books from floor to ceiling, ranging from academic to light-hearted novels.
Nelson's, High St: traditional crusty pork-pies, sausages and potted meats.

FOOD AND DRINK

Pubs include: the **Vaults,** Market Square: friendly little pub. Free house with food at lunchtimes, tables and chairs outside on the square for a fine summer's day. The **Crown,** High St: busy pub on market days. Everards ale and generous portions of well-cooked food at lunchtime. **Exeter Arms,** Leicester St: little low-fronted high-gabled pub with coat of arms carved in the stone by customer to pay off his drinking-debts. Everards ale, bar snacks, pool and darts.

WHERE TO STAY

Egon Ronay's Lucas Guide recommends: **Falcon Hotel,** High St, tel Uppingham 3535, old stone coaching inn, traditional furnishings and two bars.

The Fox and Hounds at Exton: owned by Melbourns, a brewery which has stopped brewing but supplies Sam Smiths

Villages and country towns

Exton

A delightful village. Modern buildings on the edge if you approach it from A1, but in the middle a huge green, circled with trees. Thatched cottages and graceful stone houses all around it. The hunt meets outside the Fox and Hounds, large and pleasant pub serving Sam Smiths ales, bar snacks and restaurant newly opened. Tables and chairs in the garden and trout stream running past at the bottom. But village's real treasure is the church and even if you're not a great enthusiast this one shouldn't be missed. It stands in Exton Park. You can drive right up to it but short walk through the parkland gives glimpses between the trees of romantic ruins of old hall, burnt down in 1810, and new hall, a school, Jacobean style with gables and turrets. Nine monuments altogether, dating from 1379 to 1771, including medieval tomb-chests, magnificent Elizabethan carving and a host of great baroque pieces, especially that by Grinling Gibbons.

Hallaton

Large and attractive village with a mixture of brick and stone houses and cottages, some thatched, around a small green with strange conical Buttercross. Down turning off High St, tiny museum has local farming implements, open Sat–Sun 10.00–6.00. Curator Mrs Whigham takes visitors on a guided tour of the village if given a few days' notice, tel Hallaton 295. At far end of the village, the broach spire of St Michael's and its beautiful decorated turret; inside porch, dramatic Norman tympanum of St George slaying the dragon. Churchyard looks out over rolling Leicestershire hills.

Some good pubs. The Royal Oak, part Elizabethan building, is a free house serving Marstons ale and very much a darts pub. The Bewicke Arms, another free house, has Ruddles and Marstons ales, plus good food. In the field behind it, high spot of Hallaton's year – the bottle-kicking match on Easter Monday against neighbouring Medbourne: first team to get the bottle – a small wooden cask – three times over the stream on its side of Hare Pie Hill wins. All tactics allowed! Then giant hare pie is distributed to the players and the evening ends in the pub.

Horninghold

Just down the road from Hallaton, an estate village – no pubs or shops – but golden stone houses spaced out at angles around a curve in the road. Stream trickles by at one end. Prosperous-looking with trim and tidy lawns, some handsome houses, and cottages that were built around the turn of the century. St Peter's church is well worth a special visit: simple and atmospheric – white walls, clear windows and some poppy-head bench ends.

Liddington

Two miles south of Uppingham, one long main street with golden ironstone houses. Triangular village green with ancient stumpy cross and watch tower with conical roof that leads to the church, mainly 15th c, light and airy with high arcades. Look for rare clay acoustic jars high up in the chancel. Next to church is the Bede House, a 15th c palace built for Bishops of Lincoln and converted after Reformation into a hospital. Maze of empty galleries and rooms conjure up mitred bishop and medieval bonnetted clergy. Upstairs, audience chamber with fine panelled ceiling, delicately carved oak cornice and arms of Bishop Smith (1496–1514) over fireplace. On ground floor, timbered gallery which linked the bedesmen's rooms. Open weekdays May–Sept 9.30–7.00 Sun 2.00–7.00, March, April, Oct 9.30–5.30 Sun 2.00–5.30, Nov–Feb 9.30–4.00 Sun 2.00–4.00.

Two old stone pubs both serving real ale: Marquess of Exeter, comfortable and roomy with Ruddles and Marstons ales, good snacks and a restaurant. Old White Hart, quaint country inn, Greene King ale among others, snacks, darts and a garden.

Oakham

Once Rutland's county town, it lies in Vale of Catmose. Long history: it belonged to Anglo-Saxon queens from 10th c until reign of Henry I.

Leading off High St, large market square with polygonal Buttercross and stocks. Just behind it, Oakham Castle, built c 1180 for mighty De Ferrers family (perhaps by same builder as Canterbury Cathedral). Walls are crammed with strange array of horseshoes – dues extracted from every peer passing through the town. The type of coronet on the top denotes the rank. Open daily except Mon 10.00–5.30 Sun 2.00–5.30.

Plenty of pleasant shops and places to eat. Good mixed market – clothes, veg, cheese, etc, Wed and Sat, Fri – cattle. Early closing Thur. Two busy market town hotels, the George and the Crown, both serving local Ruddles ale, bar snacks and meals. Tourist information

Hallaton village green with its 15th-century conical Buttercross

office in the library gives details of local events. The County Museum in Catmose St displays ancient Rutland documents, fossils, Bronze Age, Roman and Saxon finds and interesting local bygones. Open all year Tue–Sat 10.00–1.00 and 2.00–5.00 also Sun 2.00–5.00 April–Oct.

Oundle

Small country town, its handsome stone houses almost blackened by traffic passing through from Peterborough to Northampton. Oundle School and the church, with handsome crocketed spire, form the hub of the town. The school occupies several honey-coloured stone buildings, Georgian to Jacobean style, linked together by lanes and alleys.

Rare type of jeweller – E. Skiba, 51 West St – with excellent range of old timepieces, from station clocks to art deco. The Pudding Bowl, North St, is a jumbly antique shop with plenty of secondhand books to browse through. Early closing Wed. General market Thur.

Talbot Hotel is one of the handsomest buildings – old coaching inn rebuilt 1626 with stones from Fotheringhay Castle. Bar snacks, restaurant and pleasant walled garden.

Just off A605 in opposite direction, a curious little place – Ashton. A model village, a bit contrived but very picturesque. Built around turn of century, matching thatched cottages around enormous green, at one end wooden

tables and chairs outside the Butterfly pub. Inside walls are crowded with butterflies – Mrs Lane, the lady of the manor, is a keen lepidopterist. Some of the cottages now being let as holiday homes (Inquiries: Estate Office, Ashton, nr Oundle).

Rockingham

Pretty cinnamon stone village clinging to side of hill that leads up to castle. 17th and 18th c ironstone houses and cottages, their Collyweston slates all furry with lichen. Quite unspoilt, the last rural outpost before chimneys and furnaces of Corby steelworks, just three miles away. Halfway up, village store cum post office and friendly inn, the Sondes Arms, a Whitbread pub – snacks, restaurant and darts.

Stamford

Ancient market town of Georgian squares and church spires, dipping down to river Welland and its green meadows. In 15th c rich wool merchant William Browne built the cloistered hospital in Broad St; in Elizabeth's reign Lord Burghley built several houses dotted throughout the town. In Georgian times it was the centre of social life in the area and the town hall, assembly rooms and theatre were built. The latter two now used as an arts centre with exhibitions, concerts and children's shows.

Lively town with lots of shops. Try to visit markets on Fri or Sat. Cattle market on Mon. Early closing Thur. Good fish and chips at the Model Fish Bar in Broad St and home-made cream cakes, teas and snacks at the Central Café, Red Lion Square.

All Saints Brewery has been turned into a fascinating little museum that will explain the mysteries of real ale to the uninitiated. Open April–Sept, days and times not yet decided. Tel Stamford 52186. Pubs – lots: the George, 1728, at the bottom of St Martins Hill boasts of having put up 'at least three kings and many famous travellers'; restaurant recommended by *Egon Ronay's Lucas Guide*. The Bull and Swan, a little farther up the hill, a Melbourns house, with Sam Smiths bitter, is cosy and friendly.

—*Places to visit*—

Belvoir Castle: pronounced 'beaver'. Home of the Dukes of Rutland, overlooking Vale of Belvoir. Several castles have risen and fallen here, this one dates mainly from early 19th c. Military regalia – fascinating prints showing battle strategies and spears used by the dervishes at Omdurman. Attractive Chinese rooms with hand-painted wallpapers, but in others, decor sometimes lavish in the extreme. Family portraits and famous paintings, including Holbein's Henry VIII. Delightful steeply terraced gardens with Carolean statues and peacock. Open Easter–Sept Wed,

Thur, Sat 12.00–6.00 Sun 2.00–7.00 Bank Hol Mon 11.00–7.00, Oct Sun only. Seven miles west-south-west of Grantham.

Burghley House: magnificent Elizabethan palace built by Elizabeth I's Lord High Treasurer, William Cecil. Roofscape a fantastic jumble of cupolas, chimneys, steeples and balustrades. Inside, a daunting array of works of art – silver fireplaces, great canopied fourposters with exquisite embroidery, Chippendale commodes, impressive painted ceilings by Verrio – his masterpiece, the Heaven Room, is said to be the finest painted room in England. Paintings by Veronese, Rembrandt, Brueghel and so on. Old kitchen is part of the monastery that originally stood on the site. Still visited by Royal Family. Burghley Horse Trials, Sept. Open April–1st Sun in Oct Tue, Wed, Thur, Sat, bank hol 11.00–5.00, Sun and Good Fri 2.00–5.00. One mile south-east of Stamford.

Deene Park: lovely stone house dating from 16th c built around a courtyard. Great hall has splendid hammer-beam roof and heraldic glass. Home of Brudenells for over 450 years, and still very much lived in today, handsome rooms are hung with some fine paintings. Several mementos of Lord Cardigan, the most illustrious Brudenell, including head and tail of his horse Ronald who led and survived the disastrous charge of the Light Brigade. Surrounded by park-

land, lake and delightful gardens with old-fashioned roses, rare shrubs and trees. Open bank hol Sun and Mon and Sun June–July 2.00–6.00. Parties at other times by special arrangement. Off A43 six miles north-east of Corby.

Quenby Hall: fine Jacobean country house *c* 1620. Exterior has hardly changed – flat-roofed, symmetrical and uncluttered, with red and grey diamond-chequered brickwork and corners picked out in cream stone. Inside, extensively restored but it has some impressive stone fireplaces, delicately carved pomegranate frieze, ceilings and wooden panelling. The first Stilton cheese is said to have been made here by housekeeper Mrs Orton. She passed the secret on to her daughter who in turn sold the cheese to her brother-in-law, landlord of the Bell Inn, Stilton, and so it got its name. Open June–Sept Sun only and bank hol Sun and Mon, 2.00–6.00. Nr Hungarton seven miles north-east of Leicester.

Rockingham Castle: dramatic setting perched on steep hill above Welland valley. Norman castle used as royal residence by early English kings, particularly King John who left an iron chest here on his way to the Wash, unfortunately without the treasure. In 1530 lease granted to Edward Watson whose decendants have lived here ever since. Extensions gradually added from then on – keep and curtain walls destroyed by Roundheads during Civil War. The castle was used by Dickens as a model for Chesney Wold in *Bleak House*. A great friend of the family and regular guest, he produced special plays for them in the long gallery. In the grounds, a walk of blurry elephant-shaped yews, once used for making bows. Vast lawn is called the Tilting Ground. Open Easter–Sept Sun, Thur, Bank Hol Mon and Tue following them, 2.00–6.00. A6003 two miles north of Corby.

Stapleford Park: charming old house with some 20th c amusements. Early 16th c wing with statues in niches; date on it, 1633, refers to its 'repayr'. Inside delightful rooms with some curious features to look out for – fireplace with grate coming right out into room, pierced so that it doesn't smoke; carving by Grinling Gibbons or his craftsmen with distinctive pea-pod and, when carver got bored with flowers and leaves, a bunch of carrots. Park has plenty to keep the children busy: small zoo, crazy golf,

Oakham market – 'full of colour and varied local speech'; an excellent place to buy Stilton and local pork pies

astraglide, trampolines, etc, plus miniature railway ride to house – Lord Gretton is a great railway enthusiast – and model steamers on the lake. Also in grounds, Georgian church. Pews face inwards – until 1880 women on one side and men on the other – and at the back a gallery with fireplace installed by 4th Earl of Harborough, a clergyman, so that he could keep his back warm while preaching the sermon. Open Easter Sun–Thur, April–May Sun only, June–Aug Sun, Tue, Wed, Thur, Sept Sun, Wed, Thur to last Sun, Bank Hol Mon and Tue. Grounds 1.30, house 2.00–6.00. Animal Land and other amusements from 10.30. Admission charge includes miniature railway and boats, rest extra. Five miles E of Melton Mowbray off B676.

Woolsthorpe Manor: childhood home of Sir Isaac Newton and now a small museum dedicated to him. Modest but charming farmhouse contains room where he was born, his study and in the garden an apple tree thought to be graft of famous original. National Trust. Open April–Oct Mon, Wed, Fri, Sun 11.00–12.30 and 2.00–6.00. Seven miles south of Grantham, half a mile west of A1.

Kirby Hall: Elizabethan house started in 1570 and given the Renaissance touch by Inigo Jones *c* 1640. Last half of 17th c was golden age of Kirby. Sir Christopher Hatton brought back 'birds or beasts or pretty things from foreign voyages' and the gardens were famed for their exotic plants. Sadly, it gradually fell into decay and crumbled away. Now preserved in state of semi-ruin: you can wander through long echoing galleries and deserted rooms. Gardens gradually being restored to original plan. Open weekdays May–Sept 9.30–7.00 Sun 2.00–7.00, March, April, Oct 9.30–5.30 Sun 2.00–5.30, Nov–Feb 9.30–4.00 Sun 2.00–4.00. Off A427 two miles south-east of Gretton.

Lyveden New Bield: built by Elizabethan eccentric and Catholic recusant Sir Thomas Tresham in the shape of a cross symbolizing the Passion, it now stands in the middle of a Northamptonshire field, strange and compelling. Planned to have elaborate lantern roof but Sir Thomas died before it was finished. National Trust. Open any reasonable time. Off A427 four miles south-west of Oundle.

Another of his enigmatic buildings is

Kirby Hall – 'long echoing galleries and deserted rooms'

Triangular Lodge symbolizing the Trinity. Everything is constructed round the number three – three sides, three storeys, trefoil windows, three gables on each side, etc. It's even a pun on his own name. Open all year, times as for Kirby Hall. At Rushton between A6 and A6003.

Fotheringhay: just a steep grassy mound with grazing sheep left of castle where Mary Queen of Scots was beheaded. River Nene meanders lazily around it and in the distance, lofty church with flying buttresses and tiers of turrets and pinnacles – a reminder of more ancient splendours.

Naseby: defeat by the Roundheads here led Charles I to the scaffold. Now the spot is marked by museum with model layout of the battle and relics from the field. Open Easter–Sept Sat, Sun, Bank Hol Mon 2.00–6.00. Purlieu Farm, off B4036 between Market Harborough and Daventry.

Losecoat Field: battle in Wars of the Roses where Edward IV routed the Lancastrians, 12 March 1470. Exact site thought to be marked by wood called Bloody Oaks. 2½ miles north-east of Empingham, by deserted village of Hardwick – just one farm there now.

Deserted villages: remains of villages that were flourishing during early Middle Ages but were struck by the Black Death and left empty and deserted, sometimes the final blow coming with enclosure. Many in this area but you need to know what to look for. Good example is at Pickworth. Easy to make out amongst the hummocks and hollows where the old medieval cottages stood. A few remnants of crumbling chimney stacks and stone walls sprouting trees, and in the middle of a field, the solitary remains of the church arch.

Wing Maze: medieval gravel and turf maze. Tiny and a bit disappointing at first sight but its purpose gives it a gruesome fascination. Thought to have been brought over from France by Benedictine monks as a form of penance whereby wrongdoer crawled on hands and knees to the centre to the jeers of watching villagers.

The Avenue, Clipsham: for topiary addicts – avenue to Clipsham Hall lined with yews clipped in animal shapes – elephant, deer, hounds. Look for initials of Amos Alexander who first shaped the trees in 1880.

ACTIVITIES

Rutland Water: centre of most activities in the area. Huge reservoir created 1970 to supply expanding Northampton and Peterborough. Prettily landscaped with wooded slopes and waterside rambles, village of Hambleton jutting out into the middle on long peninsula and lovely Georgian Normanton church, half-preserved so that upper storey and tower stand up above waterline. Stocked with half a million brown and rainbow trout – fishing from shore, boat and coaching for beginners. Permits from Whitwell Lodge open 7.30–7.30. Sailing – Olympic-standard course with sailing club on south shore, members only, but bring your own boat and sail north shore, weekends and bank hols only. Plenty of wildlife in the area with 350-acre nature reserve at the western end. Butterflies, including meadow brown and orangetip, all sorts of waterfowl and animals – badgers, foxes, roe deer. Reserve split into different parts – Lyndon Hill open to the public weekends and bank hols 12.00–6.00; Egleton, with special facilities for bird-watching and nature study, permits needed. Further details on this and all other amenities from Whitwell Lodge (both well signposted) or Recreation Officer, tel Empingham 321.

Riding: with three famous hunts meeting in the area – Quorn, Cottesmore and Pytcheley – plenty of riding schools. Approved by British Horse Society: Belvoir Vale Riding Centre, Stathern, nr Melton Mowbray, tel Harby 60637; Centaur School of Equitation, Cold Newton, Billesdon, tel Billesdon 443.

FOOD AND DRINK

Egon Ronay's Lucas Guide recommends: **Noel Arms,** Langham, tel Oakham 2931. Pub restaurant with mixture of English and foreign dishes – steak and kidney pie, Stilton cheese fritters. **Candlesticks,** 1 Church Lane, Stamford, tel Stamford 4033. Mediterranean-looking restaurant with creative French-based menu. **George of Stamford Restaurant,** St Martins High St, tel Stamford 2101. International and traditional English cuisine. **Royal Restaurant,** St Paul's St, Stamford, tel Stamford 52505. Tasty, well-prepared Italian dishes. **Haycock Inn Restaurant,** Wansford, tel Stamford 782223. 17th c coaching inn with varied menu.

TOURIST INFORMATION

Publications: *Rutland & Stamford Mercury* (Britain's oldest newspaper) for entertainments and events. Every Fri. **Tourist information offices:** Melton Mowbray, in the Carnegie Museum; Stamford, in Council Offices, St Mary's Hill.

Research: Pamela Brown.

The horseshoes of Oakham Castle: dues collected from peers

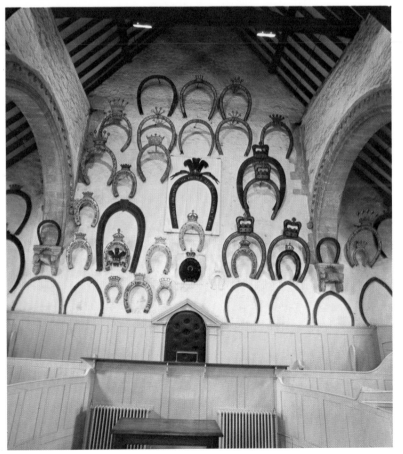

—Framlingham—

There are several Suffolks. Framlingham is embedded in the most distinctive, the one I think of as the real Suffolk. So are Laxfield and Cratfield, Fressingfield and Wingfield, Debenham and Eye. Georgian and Victorian writers called it the Woodland, or High Suffolk.

The Woodland is still a usefully descriptive term. Some very old woods, copses and hedged fields, with tall oaks reinforcing the hedges, have somehow managed to survive the emptying of the landscape by the remorseless New Agricultures of the past 130 years and by the elm disease. The height of High Suffolk is another matter: always only a relative term, but worth getting the sense of if you think of visiting these ancient farmlands.

Height is certainly a consideration in siting a castle. Yet Framlingham Castle (in this, indeed, like Wingfield Castle) beautifully illustrates the surprises and pleasures of looking at High Suffolk. Approach from the north-east, from Badingham and beyond, and you arrive disconcerted, suddenly within easy arrow-shot of all those inscrutable slits in the broad stone walls and flanking towers. The moat, a small canyon, is concealed from view, as the castle has been. The lane from Badingham runs on the same level as – sometimes higher than – the ground floor of the castle, which may never have sported a high-rise keep; and the way from Badingham still winds through screens of trees and hedges, relics of the Woodland.

Climbing the little valley from the south, from Wickham Market, you do see the walls at a distance, but deceptively 'hull-down', merging innocently into the landscape of the large skylit horizon. Only from the west and north-west, advancing from the line of a cross-country road constructed by Romans and faithfully maintained by their successors for 2000 years, are you confronted by the full strategic splendour falling from those castle walls, as they rise 40ft above another 40 foot drop into the valley. Here you see why this site was chosen. Here you begin to understand High Suffolk.

Now that most of the trees and tall hedgerows have vanished, this Suffolk is made up of increasingly long views across the invisibly stream-carved plateaux of heavy clays left here by the last of the glaciers. This scenery's chief pleasures lie perhaps in detecting and following the winding brooks that run out from the ditches and drains of the higher levels – a dizzy 100, or 150, or even 200 foot – gradually broadening down towards the sea into the valleys of the Blythburgh river, the Minsmere river, the Aldeburgh river and its tributaries including this one at Framlingham, the Deben (pronounced Deeb'n)

Woodbridge tide-mill: the last of its kind in England

flowing from Debenham (pronounced Dibbn'm) to the estuary near Woodbridge and, finally, the Gipping.

To get the setting clearer before we see Framlingham itself, here are jaunts out to the coastal heaths, marshes and beaches, visiting some of Suffolk's greatest treasures. First, three neighbours: the sparkling flint-and-glass mid-fifteenth-century churches of Blythburgh and Southwold, and the churchtower and ruins of Walberswick, once their great contemporary, built out of fortunes they made only after the roaring North Sea had devoured Dunwich. The fate of that early-medieval port, which had eight or nine parishes in King John's day and competed with Ipswich, is vividly illustrated there in a small museum.

All but about three of Suffolk's 500 medieval churches are rewarding. Three not to miss near Blythburgh are Westhall, for setting and architectural details; Wenhaston, for its affecting painted *Doom* or *Last Judgment*; and Bramfield for its medieval screen, its seventeenth-century marble of Mrs Coke by Nicholas Stone, and, among early Georgian floor-slabs, the tragi-comic account of Bridgett Applewhaite's unhappy marriage.

A detour back to Framlingham takes in Walpole (its simple seventeenth-century Congregational chapel, a great rarity, recalls Suffolk's stern independence in those times), and Heveningham, a supremely dignified example of the way a London-made fortune can enrich a pastoral/arable landscape. Gainsborough would have laughed at it, but the very slightly ponderous Palladian house by an established 'City' architect was transformed within by James Wyatt, and shows his decorative virtuosity at its best. Its park-setting by Capability Brown fits so naturally into the surrounding country that you take its pleasures for granted.

Returning to Framlingham over level clays, you may be lured off course by the pinnacles of Laxfield's churchtower – almost in the best Somerset class – to examine its brilliant flint-and-limestone panelling ('flushwork') and the contents of another good small museum opposite. Eye, farther west, is proclaimed by another of the half-dozen very noblest towers in Suffolk, and another Norman castle-site, its bailey shaping this small islanded inland town. South over the watershed from Eye, try Debenham (pleasant ancient street starting beside the infant Deben and rising to square churchtower founded on Anglo-Saxon stonework), Helmingham (quadrangular moated hall, romantic like a Loire château, with park of oak and deer), Woodbridge (fantastically dutch-gabled shire hall-cum-market cross beside yet another good Perpendicular church with massive tower on Market Hill perched above Deben estuary, moorings and tide-mill).

Next, Orford (yet another castle, this one royal, with church to match), and Iken, Snape and Aldeburgh. Aldeburgh's estuary gliding down from Snape is associated with Crabbe and with Britten and the festival. Also with Lord Clark's irresistible autobiography. Alongside its incomparable concert-hall, Snape Maltings now houses the Britten-Pears School of Advanced Musical Studies. Sometimes, during courses, the musicians take a breather and follow the river up to Framlingham. With them we will look at the town.

First the castle, the town's *raison d'être*. A sensible pre-Civil War lawyer ordered its emasculation, yet its formidable outward appearance survives perfectly, no longer draped by dark swags of ivy, backcloth to many Victorian picnics. It was the baronial answer to Orford, but fell to King John in a mere couple of days. The last baronial, or rather ducal, inmates, the Howards, softened its grim appearance by sticking red-brick barleysugar chimneys (mostly dummies) round the walls. Houses along Castle Street have their back gardens in the ditch of the outer bailey. There the town starts, with its own defensive ditch presumably marked by the ring of Fore Street. Within that ring, Double Street performs its own beautiful curve.

Leave the castle at main crossing of outer bailey: the parish church is then on your right, and then the Market Hill, triangular, sloping steeply to Bridge Street, with Unitarian chapel (1717) on the right and two rows of almshouses at the bottom: one founded by Hitcham, the disarmer of the castle, the other by Mills, a seventeenth-century wheelwright and Baptist, entombed in his front garden farther along Station Road.

The tower and whole church are generously proportioned, the interior effect stunning. The hammer-beam roof is one of the most beautiful even in Suffolk; the Thamar organ aloft under the tower for a moment recalls King's, Cambridge; the Howard tombs in the chancel are princely. For contents this church is as exciting as neighbouring Dennington's.

Reeling out into the market place, one notes unfavourably Eastern Electricity's showroom-fascia, and remembers two visitors here from Aldeburgh some 80 years ago: Flinders Petrie, the Egyptologist, and Thomas Hardy. Opposite the Crown, a large shop bore three times across its front in big letters: GEORGE JUDE. Petrie to Hardy: 'You wouldn't call that Jude the Obscure!'

John Cordy Jeaffreson, a lesser novelist, was brought up beside this market place. His *Book of Recollections* (1894) is not only pleasant in itself, but contains one of the best descriptions of the Woodland and its transformation over the Victorian years.

Already Jeaffreson was writing: 'On discovering they were hurtful to the crops, by guarding them from breeze and sunshine, the New Agriculture lowered the height of the hedges and had recourse to other measures for making the Woodland less woody.' He was spared the spectacle of modern Tannington, a large arable parish three or four miles away, with hardly a tree or a hedgethorn in sight, and the unnatural baldness spreading into Saxtead.

NORMAN SCARFE

Framlingham

WHERE TO GO

Market Square: triangle where twisting streets meet. Delightfully compact centre best seen on foot. Mellow old buildings in narrow streets, especially Castle St and Church St; lovely sequence of Georgian cottages in Double St; 17th, 18th and 19th c fronts on Market Hill.

Lanman Museum: local history. Open April–Sept Tue–Sat 10.00–12.30 and 2.00–4.30, Sun 2.00–4.30.

Castle: first glimpse of hilltop castle very impressive – especially when approached from the Dennington road. Earliest record of castle from about 1100, when Henry I granted it to Roger Bigod. No stone buildings until tenure of son Hugh, 1st Earl of Norfolk, c 1150. Henry II dismantled it in 1175 but it was rebuilt by Roger Bigod II, about 1200, who put up existing walls and towers, still in almost perfect condition. It then took on present shape, characterized by great curtain wall and 13 towers – an innovation in Europe at the time. Remains of great hall, c 1200, now form part of Poor House. Many alterations made in Tudor times by the Howards, Dukes of Norfolk. Open May–Sept daily 9.30–7.00, April daily 9.30–5.30, March, Oct weekdays 9.30–5.30 Sun 2.00–5.30, Nov–Feb weekdays 9.30–4.00 Sun 2.00–4.00.

St Michael's Church: stately, perpendicular throughout, built mid-15th–mid-16th c, apart from chancel arch believed to date back to 12th c. Hammerbeam roof – with hammer-beams concealed under fan vaulting – considered one of most beautiful in Suffolk. Chancel has one of the finest sets of early Renaissance monuments in England – six tombs in north and south chapels of the Howards and Mowbrays. Note organ and organ case, by Thamar, Peterborough, 1674, and the Flodden helmet, funeral armour of Thomas Howard, Earl of Surrey, who led English rearguard at Flodden.

SHOPPING

Market day: Sat.
Early closing: Wed.
Castle Bookshop, Castle St: unusually well-stocked and well-tended.
Regency House Antiques, Market Hill: good for browsing, lots of brass and bric-à-brac.
Carley & Webb, Market Hill: pâtés, jams, honey, candies, chocolates. At back of shop, entrance in Fore St, discover the Grape Vine winebar and licensed coffee room offering delicious cold buffet selection, plus wines. Open lunchtimes and some evenings.
Amadeus House, Church St: fascinating shop with large selection of woodwind instruments.
Framlingham Craft Shop, 24 Bridge St: good for gifts, tea-cosies, corn dollies, butchers' aprons and attractive stationery.

FOOD AND DRINK

Pubs include: **Castle Inn,** near castle gates: sit outside on fine days. Serves soups, sandwiches, basket meals, steak and kidney pie. Pool room. Landlord has collection of ancient musical instruments. **The Railway Inn,** Station Rd. Landlord Charlie has been there for nearly 50 years. Music and pub games. Serves Adnams ales.

WHERE TO STAY

Egon Ronay's Lucas Guide recommends: **Crown Hotel,** Market Hill, tel Framlingham 723521. Half-timbered 16th c coaching inn. Real ale served in bar.

Framlingham Castle – these walls were built about 1200

Crow's Hall, Debenham: picturesque remains of fine Suffolk private house

Villages and country towns

Aldeburgh

More a thriving seaside town than a village but fame of festival hasn't spoilt its delightful 'fishing village' character. At Market Cross Place stands charming timber-framed Tudor moot hall, once the town's centre. It now stands only yards from the sea, which over centuries has whittled away shoreline, and is a museum containing items of local interest. Open daily mid-July–mid-Sept, 10.30–12.30 and 2.30–5.00. Also certain times Easter–early Oct, but times can vary.

Lots of fishing boats drawn up on shingle, fresh fish for sale. Local fish and chip shop does brisk trade, its speciality: Aldeburgh smoked salmon. High St has some good shops and pretty Georgian doorways. Church of St Peter and St Paul stands on hill outside old town. In north aisle is bust of George Crabbe, poet and one-time curate, born here 1754. His poem *The Borough* was inspiration for Benjamin Britten's opera *Peter Grimes*, set in village. Local residents Britten and Peter Pears founded the Aldeburgh Festival in June 1948.

Many lively pubs including the Cross Keys on Crabbe Street, a 16th c pub, overlooking sea; the Mill Inn at Market Cross Place, opposite moot hall, serves food; the White Hart in High St has an outside grape vine which invades bar. All these pubs serve Adnams. *Egon Ronay's Lucas Guide* recommends Uplands Hotel Restaurant, Victoria Rd, tel Aldeburgh 2420.

Six miles from Aldeburgh is Snape, centre for much of Aldeburgh Festival. Here Maltings beautifully converted into awe-inspiring concert hall. Character of original buildings retained. Programme details: Aldeburgh Festival Office, High St, Aldeburgh. Tours of concert hall, Wed afternoons during summer. Egon Ronay's *Just a Bite* recommends Granary Tea Shop at Snape Maltings. Some excellent pubs nearby include 15th c Crown Inn; Golden Key; Plough and Sail.

Blythburgh

Holy Trinity Church is one of the grandest of all Suffolk's churches. An impressive, large building – 128ft long, with 83ft tower. Its size in proportion to present tiny village indicates one-time importance of Blythburgh as a port. Body of church dates from mid-15th c, tower *c* 1330, remains from earlier building.

Inside striking whiteness, lightness and emptiness. Rare combination of grand proportions and bare simplicity. Notice beautiful painted roof, and carved bench ends representing the Seven Deadly Sins and scenes from farming year. Jack o' the Clock, in shape of knight in armour, dating from 1682, used to announce entry of clergy at start of service. When rope is pulled, head turns and hatchet strikes bell. 15th c Seven Sacraments font damaged when spire crashed through roof of west end in great storm of 1577. Aldeburgh Festival concerts sometimes held in the church. The Priory, north-east of church, has remains of Augustinian priory in garden.

Westwood Lodge, once a manor house, has ancient red-brick step-gables, plain white-brick front and superb views.

The White Hart Inn is a historic, gabled building thought to have been ancient ecclesiastical courthouse.

The Blyth estuary is an excellent spot

The 'crinkle-crankle' wall in Heveningham Hall gardens

for bird-watching. Footpath starts near White Hart Inn.

Dunwich

Almost all of this once thriving cathedral city has been swallowed up by sea. Of its former splendour there remains walled clifftop quadrangle – once a priory wall – now surrounding a smallholding.

In its heyday, at time of King John, Dunwich had nine churches and several religious houses. Daily markets were held in several market-places. Then Dunwich was important port, owning 80 'great ships'. King John granted charter giving all rights over wrecks on its shores, for annual payment of 5000 eels. The sea's advance was recorded even at time of Domesday Book, but worst on-slaught occurred in 14 c. Last of the nine churches, All Saints, began to disappear down cliff in 1904. Tower went over in 1919. In 1968–9 site of town's western gate, Middle Gate, disappeared down edge of cliff. Present church of St James, built in classical style in 1830 by Robert Appleton and rebuilt in the Gothic style in 1881. In churchyard, see Norman apse of Lazar Hospital Chapel.

Visit tiny museum chronicling

The Otter Trust at Earsham

town's strange past. Among relics are photographs recording 'the passing of All Saints' and King John's charter of 1215. Open Easter Sat, Sun, Mon, then Spring Bank Hol Mon–Oct Sat, Sun, Tue, Thur 2.00–4.30, Aug daily 2.00–4.30.

Village pub is the Ship, dimly lit and full of nautical atmosphere. Walls of Fo'cs'le Bar draped with fishing nets. Adnams ales and gravity beer from the wood. Also live music and pub games.

Laxfield

Many of the thatched and timbered houses in this delightful village are of great historic or architectural interest. The half-timbered guildhall, built 1461, is now restored to house a museum and community centre. Open end May–mid-Oct Sat, Sun 3.00–5.30, Aug Wed 3.00–5.30. The church, at end of main street, is built around handsome 100ft tower decorated with flint panels. Inside, memorial to William 'Smasher' Dowsing, Puritan destroyer of church ornaments, who did so much damage to many of the loveliest Suffolk churches. His diaries gave detailed accounts of his works of vandalism. Also look at font

Debenham: traditional craft of rush weaving

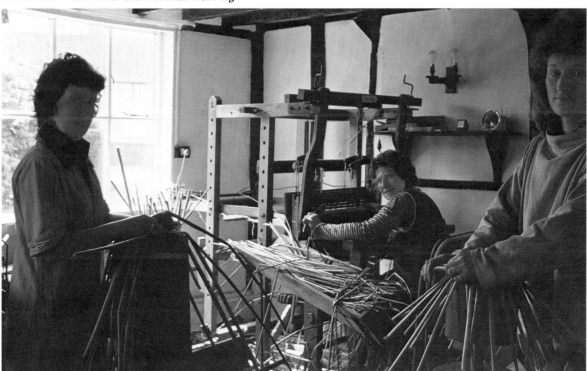

with Seven Sacraments and Baptism of Christ.

There's an antique shop in The Street, specializing in brass beds and a bit further down is the 'Mid Suffolk Gun Store', which not only sells guns but buys old ones, and collections.

The Kings Head (known as the Low House) is a unique country pub virtually unchanged this century. It has no bar at all, just high-backed church pews. Local men gather here to drink real ale, play crib and dominoes and eat kippers, served on Friday nights. The Royal Oak is a comfortable, welcoming pub, where food is eaten at rough-hewn wooden tables. Until as late as 1855 neighbouring farmers would meet buyers every week at the Royal Oak to sell corn by sample. Adnams ales served.

Within easy reach of Laxfield are two villages whose churches should not be missed. Dennington has one of the finest churches in Suffolk, containing a wealth of medieval treasures and superb furnishings. Most memorable are the parclose screens at east end of each nave-aisle. Also, carved benches, poppy-heads and armrests depicting animals, birds and creatures from mythology.

St Mary's at Cratfield has very beautiful Seven Sacraments font.

Southwold

Old-fashioned graciousness and windy charm. Set on cliff-top, its long seashore lined with jolly bathing huts and its many Georgian buildings grouped around delightful wide greens, it is a resort with lots of character. Most famous landmark is white lighthouse, put up on North Green in 1899.

The church, St Edmund's, is one of the most impressive in Suffolk. Pevsner calls it 'the epitome of Suffolk flush-work'. Has fine 100ft perpendicular tower. Present building dates from 1430 and has a late 15th c Southwold Jack (similar to the Blythburgh Jack o' the Clock).

Facing church is little Dutch-gabled museum on Bartholomew's Green. Open June–Sept Tue, Wed, Fri 2.30–4.30. Sun during Aug.

Out on grass-clad Gun Hill stand cannon said to have been sent to Southwold in 1746 by the Duke of Cumberland after Culloden.

In Sailors' Reading Room on sea front you can steep yourself in town's nautical

history. Built in 1869, it contains sea-faring relics and models of ships, including the famous yawl *Bittern*. The walls are crammed with prints and old photographs.

Market Place forms a triangle. In centre stands town pump of 1873. On north side, where ivy-clad Swan Hotel adjoins Town Hall, stands stone marking tercentenary of Great Fire of Southwold, 1659, when most of original town was destroyed. There's also a clock showing high tides.

Sutherland House, in High St, now a restaurant, dates from 15th c. Once residence of Duke of York, High Admiral of Fleet, later James II.

A shop in High St sells glorious amber and other semi-precious stones. At tiny Sole Bay Bookshop, built 1662, sign over shop reads, 'Thomas Pierson Prestwidge, Lapidary, established business here 1853.' Another indication of wealth of semi-precious stones to be found on these shores. George Orwell ran a shop here for a time.

There are also some good antique shops and art galleries. Repertory theatre at St Edmund's Hall during summer, end July–early Sept. Egon Ronay's *Just a Bite* recommends Squier in High St. Cosy tea-room behind bakery serves delicious home-baked cakes and goodies and hot lunchtime savouries. *Egon Ronay's Lucas Guide* recommends Dutch Barn restaurant, telephone Southwold 723172.

Southwold is the home of Adnams Ales. Present brewery stands near lighthouse. Parts of the cellars date back 300 years. Beers are brewed solely from malted barley, hops, water and sugar. Thus Southwold boasts some good pubs serving real ale: King's Head, High St, lively meeting place with display of local art; Southwold Arms, pub games; Lord Nelson, East St, good hearty pub with live music, and Sole Bay Inn next to lighthouse, friendly, one-bar pub, which serves good ploughman's lunches and sandwiches. Live music and pub games.

There is a tourist information centre in the town hall, Market Place.

Walberswick

Once a prosperous port, this tranquil seaside village has remained relatively unspoilt, in spite of recent influx of 'arty' inhabitants. Off beaten track, set be-

tween river Blyth and large expanse of reed-filled marshes, it offers idyllic views across heath, marsh, and sea. Colours are beautifully soft and muted. Many painters have tried to capture essence of place.

Beach offers extensive sand dunes, planted with marram grass and superb views across to Southwold. If boatman is in the mood, he will ferry you across the Blyth from quay. More regular service operates during the summer months. Also on the quay, freshly caught fish for sale.

Church, now lying outside village, stands within impressive ruins of its larger medieval predecessor, of which only tower, 1426, south aisle and porch remain. Church lost tithes at Dissolution. Great bell was sold in 1585 and in 1643 'Smasher' Dowsing (see Laxfield entry) destroyed 40 windows and defaced 8 tombstones.

The long main street has some lovely big old houses. Halfway down, you will find Mary's, where on fine days you can eat in pretty garden. Egon Ronay's *Just a Bite* recommends lunches of locally caught fish, home-cooked gammon, omelettes and home-baked cakes. Children's portions served. Often exhibitions of paintings held here. Closed Mon, except bank hol. In 18th c building near village green, with swings and slides for children, is one of finest pottery shops in country, with work by over 20 craftsmen potters. Called The Potter's Wheel, it has now spilled over into three adjoining buildings which house artists' gallery, print room and garden room. Here teas are served in delightful surroundings amid plant containers and garden ornaments (10.30–12.00 and 3.00–5.30, closed Tue).

Walberswick is popular with golfers, birdwatchers and walkers. On outskirts of village is National Nature Reserve, established to safeguard this outstanding area of heathland, woods, marshes and mudflats. Rich variety of birds and other wildlife to be seen. Written permit needed for certain parts. Apply Nature Conservancy Council, 60 Bracondale, Norwich, tel Norwich 20558/9. This whole coastline, between Kessingland and Felixstowe (named the Suffolk Heritage Coast), has been designated an 'area of outstanding natural beauty'.

Anchor Hotel and Bell Hotel, 600-year-old pub near beach, serve Adnams.

James Fisk's clematis nursery at Westleton

Westleton

Village where much local skill is in evidence. The large, barn-like thatched church is one example, part of which dates back to *c* 1300. Another is the flint school-house, built in 1842 by local man, 'Bobbler' Brown. More local skill can be seen just outside village on Darsham Rd at Fisk's Clematis – the only nursery in the country devoted entirely to this climbing plant. Lovingly grown by James Fisk, a 'local boy', they are now exported all over the world. Many varieties in flower from May–Oct. Nurseries open weekdays 9.00–5.00 Sun 10.00–5.00 during summer.

Near priest's door of church, witch's stone is to be found. Legend has it that if you put your handkerchief in grating of church wall and run eastwards, northwards and back again by west end of church, you will hear the devil clanking his chains below the grating.

The Crown Inn, facing church, serves Adnams and has a stable buttery. The White Horse Inn also serves Adnams and has a fine set of hand pumps.

Caroline's Country Collection exhibits old domestic and agricultural implements, toys, dolls, bygones and a replica of an old Suffolk cottage. Open Mon, Tue, Thur, Fri, Sat 10.00–1.00 and 2.00–5.00, Sun 2.00–5.00.

Another good reason for stopping in Westleton is the delightful tea-shop. At Central House you help yourself to mouth-watering cakes displayed temptingly on hall table: iced coffee cake, chocolate gâteau, meringues, simnel cake. Or stop by for the Westleton Festival in Aug.

Wickham Market

The lead spire of All Saints is landmark for many miles around. From the tower 30 other churches are said to be visible. This ancient little town is set around Market Square and parish pump. Church, which is slightly tucked away on The Hill to south of square, dates from 1299, though north chapel is 15th c and spire rebuilt in 1790s. Alas, Wickham Market no longer has a market (square now used as car park) but markets are held at nearby village of Campsea Ash on Mon.

White Hart Hotel, late Georgian with nine-bay front, faces square. Adnams served. Alongside is tiny Barclays Bank housed in pretty yellow-brick Georgian building. Taylor's Wine Cellar, recommended in Egon Ronay's *Just a Bite*, is in timber-framed building originally thought to have been old Anglo-Saxon manor house. Excellent cold food, also home-made soups, fresh fruit pies.

From Market Square, road descends down to river Deben, where there is a pretty bridge, fine water-mill and water-wheel, still working.

Woodbridge

A delightful old-world market town on River Deben, with narrow streets of historic houses rising gently up hill from bustling boat-flanked quay. Centre of town and tide-mill have been designated outstanding conservation areas. At one time an important trading centre with thriving shipbuilding industry, now a favourite haunt of yachtsmen and shopping centre for many of the surrounding villages. Boats can be hired from the Quay.

Walking through winding streets you find a combination of 16th c dwellings and Georgian shop and house fronts. Town owes much to Thomas Seckford, 16th c benefactor who built splendid Shire Hall. Now used as magistrates' court, it dominates Market Hill in centre of town. Also see Market Hill Pump, dating from 1876. Seckford also endowed the grand Seckford Hospital and Almshouses in Seckford St and his ghost is said to roam Seckford Hall, an ancient house with Tudor chimneys and gables just outside the town.

See also timber-framed Angel Inn in Theatre St, and remains of Georgian theatre. The Abbey, Church St, once manor house and seat of Thomas Seckford, stands on part of site of Augustinian Priory, founded 1190. Note charming entrance to Glover's Yard (off Market Hill), with 16th c black and white cottages, scene of former glove-making industry. The tide-mill, now beautifully restored, is open to the public Easter, bank hol weekends, June–mid-July Sat and Sun, mid-July–mid-Sept daily, mid-Sept–mid-Oct Sat and Sun 11.00–1.00 and 2.30–5.00. First built in 12th c, present building dates from 18th c and is in working order. Also there's Buttrum's Mill – along Burkitt Rd. Fine example of tower windmill. Now carefully repaired and restored.

Egon Ronay's Pub Guide recommends the Mariners Arms where the American landlady brings an American influence to bear on the bar snacks. In *Just a Bite* is Sherlock's Wine Bar, owned by actor Douglas Wilmer, full of Holmesian memorabilia. Home-made soups, pâté, quiche, smoked ham, mackerel, chicken. In Church St, the Ancient House is a good cake shop which serves teas.

Places to visit

Heveningham Hall: fine Georgian mansion in Palladian style. Interior decoration by James Wyatt; beautiful park (sheep grazing, river) and gardens by Capability Brown include orangery by Wyatt, now being restored. See typical Suffolk 'crinkle-crankle' wall used to shelter tender plants. Inside, note superb entrance hall. House and gardens open April–Oct Wed, Thur, Sat, Sun, Bank Hol Mon 2.00–6.00, also Tue May–Sept Sun, Bank Hol Mon gardens open 12 noon. Fishing from 16 June. Five miles shouth-west of Halesworth.

Glemham Hall: red-brick Elizabethan house with later façade, walled rose garden with fine trees. Queen Anne furniture. Open Easter Mon, then Wed, Sun, Bank Hol Mon until end Sept 2.00–5.30. An A12 between Wickham Market and Saxmundham.

Helmingham Hall Gardens: ornamental wildfowl, black swans on moat, native cattle and safari rides in deer park. Fresh produce and bedding plants for sale. Open end May–Sept Sun 2.00–6.00. On B1077 nr Ipswich.

Leiston Abbey: remains of 14th c abbey including transepts of church and range of cloisters. Open May–Sept weekdays 9.30–7.00, March, April, Oct 9.30–5.30, Nov–Feb 9.30–4.00. Sun from 2.00.

Orford Castle: Henry Plantagenet's revolutionary castle with multi-faceted keep and chapel set in walls. Opening times same as for Leiston Abbey but every day.

Bungay Castle ruins: twin towers and massive flint walls are all that remain of original Norman castle. Saxon mounds. Open daily.

Thorpeness: eccentric early 20th c showpiece, built as holiday village, laid out by dramatist and author Glencairn Stuart Ogilvie. Fantasies such as water tower disguised as house and called 'House in the Clouds'. Artificial lake, the 'Meare', only 3ft deep, so safe bathing for children. Post-mill brought from Aldringham. Two miles from Aldeburgh.

Saxtead Green Post-mill: shining white post-mill in full working order, stands in middle of village green. Now listed as ancient monument. Some parts are 18th c, though superstructure dates from 1854. Open daily except Sun. Nr Framlingham.

Letheringham Water-mill: a watermill has stood on this site since before Norman Conquest. Partly Tudor millhouse looks out over beautiful lawns and

Helmingham Hall – 'romantic like a Loire château, with park of oak and deer'

Easton Farm Park: the Victorian dairy

herbaceous borders, with pea-fowl, pheasants and ornamental ducks all around. Present mill built 250 years ago and was working until 60 years ago, when machinery dismantled. Open April– mid-May Sun only, mid-May–Sept Wed, Sun, bank hol 12.30–6.30. Close to village of Easton (nr Wickham Market).

Dunwich Heath and Beach, National Trust: one mile of glorious sandy beach and gravel cliff with 214 acres of heathland. Access all year round. From Dunwich to Westleton stretch the 'wild walks' – an extraordinary expanse of dark heathland that borders Minsmere Nature Reserve. This area designated nature reserve in 1956. Inquiries to Nature Conservancy Council, 60 Bracondale, Norwich.

Minsmere Nature Reserve (RSPB): 1500 acres of marsh, lagoon, reed, heath and woodland. Large and varied terrain supporting immense variety of birds. Permits needed from Warden. Or contact RSPB, The Lodge, Sandy, Beds, tel Sandy 80551. Day permits to fish obtainable from warden.

Easton Farm Park, Easton: Victorian farm buildings, built by Duke of Hamilton as model dairy farm on his Easton Estate, house James Kerr's collection of early agricultural implements, farm machinery and country bygones. There is a detailed reconstruction of Victorian

dairy in the original octagonal building. Watch the cows being milked each afternoon (2.30–4.00), and see collection of farm livestock including many rare breeds. Also pets' paddock; adventure playpit; machinery and craft demonstrations; fishing in the Deben (from 16 June). Nature trail, designed by Nature Conservancy Council, laid out around lovely riverside meadows and woodland. Open April–Oct daily 10.30–6.00. About 2½ miles from Wickham Market.

Suffolk Wild Life Park: Kessingland, nr Lowestoft: grassland, with lake and wildfowl, pets' corner and play area.

Otter Trust, Earsham, nr Bungay: four species of otter in semi-natural enclosures; three lakes, waterfowl, Muntjac deer, riverside walks. Open March– Nov daily 10.30–6.00 or dusk if that is earlier.

Rendlesham Forest, nr Woodbridge: about six miles in area. Mostly Scots and Corsican pines, with scattering of oak, birch and poplar. Stronghold of fast-disappearing red squirrel, and refuge for fallow deer. Picnic site.

Aldewood Forest, nr Aldeburgh: Scots and Corsican pines established on former sandy wastes. Excellent views and picnic areas.

Anglia Vineyards: 10-acre vineyard and winery producing and bottling Broadwater wine. Vineyard viewing:

Aug and Sept (conducted tours for groups by appointment). Broadwater House, Bruisyard, just north-east of Framlingham.

Aspall Cyder House: family concern since 18th c making organic cider, apple juice, vinegar. 18th c equipment on view in shop. Aspall Hall, half a mile north of Debenham.

Lonely Farm Leisure Park, nr Saxmundham: woodland and grassland with caravan park; trout and coarse lake fishing. Also pub.

ACTIVITIES

Beachcombing, fossil-hunting: 11-mile stretch of shingle beach from Aldeburgh to Orford Ness is beachcombers' paradise. Lucky finds might include amber, cornelian and good specimens of banded agates. Also excellent for fossil-hunting, as is Easton Cliffs, north of Southwold.

Walking, picnicking: lots of good walks and plenty of designated picnic areas.

Bird-watching: especially good on the marshes near Walberswick and round Minsmere.

FOOD AND DRINK

Egon Ronay's Lucas Guide recommends **Fox and Goose**, Fressingfield, tel Fressingfield 247. Superb restaurant in old guildhall, timber-framed front. No menu as such – you arrange your meal in advance and food is ordered and cooked to individual requirements. Main dishes can include fresh trout, lobster, venison, pheasant. **Bassett's**, London Rd, Halesworth, tel Halesworth 3154. Cosy former bakery with red brick, beams and old agricultural implements. French country-style cooking.

TOURIST INFORMATION

Publications: *East Anglian Daily Times, Framlingham and Eye Mercury*, weekly; *What's On in East Anglia, East Anglian Magazine*, from newsagents; *East Anglia Guide*, from East Anglia Tourist Board, 14 Museum Street, Ipswich.

Tourist information centre: Ipswich.

Research: Sandra Newman.

Norwich

When Daniel Defoe, in 1723, crossed the bridge over the Waveney and passed from Suffolk into Norfolk, he saw 'a face of diligence spread over the whole country . . . throng'd with great and spacious market-towns, more and larger than any other part of England so far from London . . . exceeding full of inhabitants'. At that time, half a century before the beginning of the Industrial Revolution, Defoe was told that 'there was not in all the eastern and middle part of Norfolk any hand unemploy'd if they would work'. The looms and combing-shops and twisting-mills of Norwich – all busy with wool – made it a prosperous place, one of the great cities of England. And because of this the market towns that lay between Suffolk and the city prospered, too – Thetford, Diss, Attleborough, Wymondham, and many, such as the Buckenhams and Hingham, that are no more than villages today.

Going through these places now, and the spacious acres of emptiness that surround them, Defoe's sense of business and peopled 'diligence' is hard to imagine. No motorway thrusts into Norfolk. Indeed, it seems to lie out on the edge of everything, at the end of the line: large-skied, open but apart, not obviously winsome and charming, a place to be defined in negatives. The old Noël Coward jest – 'Very flat, Norfolk' – settles the matter for those who aren't intimate with it.

But, for a start, it *isn't* flat – not for the walker or cyclist anyway. Stand on Mousehold Heath north of Norwich and you can see the whole city below you, encircled with green, as contained as Florence surveyed from Fiesole. Only far beyond the city, in the mysterious green mazes of the Broads, do you find real flatness – and there it is flatness relieved by the mirror images of water and meadow, meadow and water. To the south, lanes twist along shallow valleys and up winding declivities, between broad ridges. Cylindrical flint church towers, Saxon and Norman, define the rising and falling fields, emphasizing their solitariness but rejecting anything that could be called monotony.

Draw a compass pencil 20 or 25 miles round Norwich and see what varied landscapes you've enclosed: heath, marshland, Breckland, well-wooded parkland, pasture, as well as the Broads. But, more impressively, see how many great churches, halls and fine houses are set in those landscapes – the solid surviving evidence of the prosperity Defoe noticed. Norwich is probably the finest medieval city in England: cathedral, castle, the 'thrice 12 churches' George Borrow wrote of, twisting streets and alleys within its walls, and a market in the middle that itself feels like a living transplant from the Middle Ages.

It is a handsome city, and it knows it, and it is known; and it is still prosperous. Less well known is the effect of the old wealth on the whole

Sutton Mill, near Hickling, is the tallest in England. It still has all its machinery, and is open to the public

area round about, from the magnificent wool churches of Cawston and Salle to the warring towers of Wymondham Abbey, product of long squabbling between monks and townspeople; and the splendid houses of landowners, merchants, bankers and noblemen – Blickling, Holkham, Felbrigg, Earlham, Ditchingham, Rainthorpe, Houghton.

Norfolk even exults in its isolation, its separateness, in being independent and unruly: 'Norfolk do different' is the pawky local phrase. It has bred rebels, from Boadicea onwards. In the year 60 AD, this Queen of the small tribe of the Iceni swept out of the region at the head of a people who managed to burn down the Roman cities of Colchester, St Albans and London, before they were defeated and she took poison. The ghostly remains of the administrative capital the Romans imposed on the subjugated Iceni can still be seen a few miles south of Norwich: a broad field surrounded by earth and flint ramparts, now Caistor St Edmund. Centuries later, the carts of the masons who built Norwich's cathedral and churches trundled off with ready-made building material – so, as the old Norfolk rhyme has it,

> Caistor was a city when Norwich was none,
> And Norwich was built with Caistor stone.

And there were the brothers Kett, Robert and William, yeomen farmers who in the summer of 1549 led a rebellion against the new land enclosures because 'the pride of great men is now intolerable'. Twenty thousand rallied and took on an army of German mercenary artillery commanded by the Earl of Warwick. Like Boadicea, the rebels were defeated: William was hanged alive in chains from one of the towers of Wymondham Abbey, Robert from the walls of Norwich Castle. And from such independent stock came many of Cromwell's followers in the next century – only that time, of course, they won.

But Norfolk has nurtured painters and poets too, artists of all kinds. The very earliest English composer came from one of the two tiny villages of Forncett, in a tangle of lanes south-west of Norwich: John of Forncett, the monk who wrote the air for 'Sumer is icumen in' some time in the early thirteenth century, and left it at Reading Abbey. Strangely, this most un-Cumbrian landscape attracted the young William Wordsworth: his sister Dorothy for seven years in the 1780s and early 1790s kept house for her uncle when he was rector of Forncett St Peter (the rectory is still almost exactly as it was), and there was talk of building a cottage for William in the rectory grounds.

A bit farther south, near the Waveney, Diss has the odd distinction of having harboured two very different poets – John Skelton, that marvellous early Renaissance satirist in exile from Wolsey's London; and the infant Mary Wilson. More importantly, the painters Crome and Cotman in the late eighteenth and early nineteenth centuries led a school of painters – the Norwich School – which coherently memorialized the region itself. Their panoramic cloudy skies, subdued and subtle contours, wind-braced distances, pastoral but not domesticated, are still there.

The agricultural changes established by the time of Crome and

Cotman have themselves changed: the turnips of 'Turnip' Townshend and the potatoes of Coke of Norfolk have to a great extent been replaced by sugar beet. But dairy cows are as important as they were in Defoe's time. The white clapboard water-mills which used to be powered by such tributary rivers as the Tas have mainly stopped work. Most – such as the one next door to our own Mill House in Tharston – have been converted into houses themselves. Some are empty, or derelict.

Indeed, the newcomer to these parts should prepare himself for some dereliction, apparent ruthlessness, and even plain ugliness. This is the very landscape of Wesker's *Roots*. The farms are often neither tidy nor picturesque. Many hedges have been completely levelled, or have been savaged and reduced by mechanical grabs. The villages lack Devonian prettiness, and tend to go in for new brick bungalows carrying such rueful names as 'Kostalot' (though some of the small towns, such as Wymondham and Diss, have escaped such insults and have distinct personalities). Much has been lost, and is still going: empty and ruinous churches, cottages and village houses which – having survived 200 or 300 years – no longer seem worth the upkeep, farm outbuildings which it's cheaper to replace with utilitarian dutch barns.

But the destruction or neglect have sometimes been compensated for in other directions. When property prices elsewhere were soaring, Norfolk stayed relatively cheap, and drew in from London and other parts people who weren't doers-up of cottages for rural weekends but who wanted to make it their home. Potters, painters, weavers, makers of musical instruments, craftsmen who make bow-topped waggons (and live in them) have settled in and have often become a real part of the community: village schools, churches, WIs – as well as pubs and shops and summer fairs– have benefited. Norfolk village life may not be what it was a hundred years ago; for one thing the population has often shrunk – our own village was bigger in the nineteenth century than it is today. But the newcomers have adapted rather than colonized.

What brought me to live here began as mere chance. I had no connections with the place until I was invited to spend a term at the University of East Anglia, near Norwich, as Henfield Writing Fellow in the summer of 1972. What was meant to be a sabbatical from the *New Statesman* turned into a sabbatical lifetime. The old mill house we'd bought with notions of holiday retreat became home.

I've never regretted it, even when in the winter of 1978–9 the snow drifted deep in every road round about and cut us off for three days. And even if I can't sentimentally convince myself that I 'belong' here, my thoughtful Viking ancestors gave me some cause to feel I do: both north and south of our house, within 20 miles, there are three villages called Thwaite – place-names redolent of ancient forebears who may have come here, as the old history books put it, to rape, pillage and burn, but who stayed and settled. They had the right idea.

ANTHONY THWAITE

Norwich

WHERE TO GO

Cathedral and Close: built around 1100, the Cathedral Church of the Most Holy and Undivided Trinity is one of the most complete Norman works in Britain. Don't miss wood-carving in choir, depicting Tudor life, or the Norman bishop's throne in the apse behind the high altar. The cloister, biggest in England, is splendid place for shady meditational walks. Outside in close is Norwich School with fine doorways and staircase. Stroll on past handsome greens, fine houses and pretty gardens to the watergate, Pull's Ferry, at far end of close. Once a canal ran from here to the cathedral; now Broads cruisers tie up outside on the river Yare.

Castle: Norman keep, second biggest in England after White Tower in Tower of London, now looks very spruce after Victorian refacing. Inside is gallery with large collection of paintings, including fine assortment of Norwich School works. Also collections of porcelain, silver, plus exhibitions on natural history and local archaeology. Open Mon–Sat 10.00–5.00, Sun 2.00–5.00.

Other museums: Stranger's Hall, in medieval town house, is museum of domestic life with furnished rooms illustrative of different periods between 16th

Norwich cathedral, one of the most complete Norman works in Britain

and 19th c. Mon–Sat 10.00–5.00. Bridewell, local industry museum in magnificently forbidding black flint former prison. Mon–Sat 10.00–5.00. St Peter Hungate, church museum in one of Norwich's medieval churches, fine collection of church art, vestments and medieval carved alabaster. Mon–Sat 10.00–5.00. Royal Norfolk Regimental Museum, Britannia Barracks, military history 1685–1959. Mon–Fri 9.00–12.30 and 2.00–4.30.

City Walls: of the original $2\frac{1}{4}$ miles of medieval wall only bits and pieces survive. Walls at Carrow Hill and Bracondale still show battlements, and Cow Tower, at other end, is brick-built, 50ft high and 36ft in diameter.

Churches: Norwich has 36 medieval parish churches within walls. Don't attempt the lot unless immune to architectural indigestion. Here's a selection: St Peter Mancroft – magnificent, wealthy, built 1430. Contains tomb of Sir Thomas Browne, author of *Religio Medici* and *Urn Burial* and a local doctor. Mysticism buffs should not miss little Church of St Julian off King St, where St Julian received vision that led to her *Revelations of Divine Love*. Her little whitewashed cell not original, having been bombed in war. St Gregory's, Pottergate, has medieval painting of St George in armour. St John, Timberhill, displays arms of Sir Thomas Erpingham, who appears in Shakespeare's *Henry V* and is buried in cathedral. St Peter Permountergate has fine wooden stalls. St Michael-at-Coslany, Colegate, worth seeing for fine flintwork on walls.

If you can face more ecclesiastical architecture after that, see Octagonal Chapel off Colegate St, built 1756, and called by detractors 'a cucumber house for the forcing of Nonconformists'. Old Meeting House, round corner, is even earlier, being one of the first Nonconformist chapels in England. Finally, there's the imposing Catholic cathedral of St John the Baptist, Unthank Rd – Victorian Gothic at its grandest.

Guildhall: together with St Peter Mancroft and 1930s City Hall, forms a frame to market-place. Built of flint in early 15th c, with neat 1850s turret.

Sainsbury Centre, University Plain: princely collection of modern and ethnic art donated by supermarket supremo and housed in award-winning modern building like posh aircraft hangar. Tue–Sun 12.00–5.00.

Assembly Rooms, Theatre St: very handsome 1754 building, now incorporating a cinema and good lunchtime restaurant.

Theatres: Theatre Royal, Theatre St, is an unusually successful regional theatre, receiving major national and international productions (tel 28025); Maddermarket, St John Maddermarket, is 18th c chapel adapted 1921 to form Elizabethan-style theatre staging Shakespeare, classics (tel 20917).

Rivers: Yare and Wensum pursue meandering courses through Norwich and surrounding villages. Many fine industrial buildings and old warehouses line banks in city centre, and the Wensum flows past cathedral close.

St Andrew's Hall, St Andrew's: best surviving friar's church in England, says Pevsner, now used for concerts, shows and events of all kinds.

SHOPPING

Market: daily, except Sun.
Early closing: Thur.
Black Horse Bookshop, Wensum St: practically everthing in print on East Anglia, plus excellent selection of other books.
Crofts Perfume Shop, Pottergate: heady scent assails you as you enter. Knowledgeable staff will supply nearly all makes of scent as well as Crofts' own brand. Also sachets, perfume bottles and other aids to elegant odour.

Culpeper the Herbalist, Bridewell Alley: fresh and dried herbs, herb plants for garden, herb pillows and cushions, soaps, cosmetics, pot-pourris.
Hovells Basket Shop, Bedford St: everything from a plant pot to a rickshaw, all made of cane. Also new pine furniture.
London St: a pedestrian precinct that really works. Lots of good shops in relaxed, traffic-free environment.
Mustard Shop, Bridewell Alley: huge range of mustards, pots, tea-towels, etc, in old-world atmosphere (actually opened 1973) created by local mustard magnates Colmans. Includes little Mustard Museum for those who like their history spicy.

FOOD AND DRINK

Winkles seafood bar, Old Post Office Yard, Bedford St, serves excellent seafood and salads. Above is **Parson Woodforde** restaurant, also good. *Egon Ronay's Lucas Guide* recommends: **Marco's Restaurant,** Pottergate; **Hobbs Restaurant,** Fye Bridge Rd. Egon Ronay's *Just a Bite* recommends: **Briton's Arms Coffee House,** Elm Hill; **Café la Tienda,** St Gregory's Alley; **Just John's Delaticatique,** White Lion St; **Pizza Place,** Pottergate; **Waffle House,** St Giles St; **Wine Press,** Guildhall Hill. Pubs include: **Adam and Eve,** Bishopgate: 'Circa 1249', says sign, 'oldest pub in Norwich'.

One of the angels on the fine hammerbeam roof of Cawston church

Tucked into a side street by cathedral close, this charming little pub serves excellent food, Norwich bitter and morning coffee. **Bell Hotel,** Orford Hill: Adnams, Greene King and Ruddles in handsome, popular coaching inn with lots of bars. **Ferry Boat Inn,** King St: 17th c free house with jolly vibes and log fires. Greene King, Wethered, Abbot ale and Whitbread, plus good food. Heavily beamed, medieval cellars, air ripe with rich Norfolk vowels. **Maid's Head,** Tombland: lovely bar in ancient hotel. Abbot ale. **Norfolk Wherry,** Castle Meadow: modern; the only Norwich pub run by Ind Coope.

WHERE TO STAY

Egon Ronay's Lucas Guide recommends: **Castle Hotel,** Castle Meadow, tel 611511; **Maid's Head Hotel,** Tombland, tel 28821; **Hotel Nelson,** Prince of Wales Rd, tel 28612; **Hotel Norwich,** Boundary Rd, tel 410431; **Post House,** Ipswich Rd, tel 56431.

TOURIST INFORMATION

Bureau in 16th c Augustine Steward House, Tombland, home of the Lord Mayor who tackled Kett's Rebellion. Tel Norwich 20679 or 23445.

East Anglian hand-carved sign

Villages and country towns

Coltishall

This Broadland village graces the banks of the River Bure with an elegance that makes light of the summer hordes. It's an ancient and handsome place, particularly good for the inspection of reed thatches. These reeds, cut on the Broads, make a roof which stays snug for upwards of 60 years – three times as long as straw. Coltishall church is thatched. Its north wall has two round Saxon windows and a spattering of Roman tiles.

This is a good shopping village, having plenty of places to get everything from antiques to ice cream. The Red Lion has Adnams on draught as well as Whitbread, and the Rising Sun, next to the river and patronized by the boats which berth alongside, is a pleasant place from which to contemplate grazing sheep.

Hingham

In 1637 an apprentice weaver from Hingham, one Samuel Lincoln, took ship for the New World and religious freedom. He did nothing himself to grace the history books, but his great-great-great-great grandson, Abraham Lincoln, *did* make history. There's a bust of Abe in the church, presented by people in the States, and an ancient baulk of timber by south door comes from the Old Meeting House at Hingham, Massachusetts, the oldest church in continuous use in the USA. While in the church – a handsome decorated building and for that reason unusual in perpendicular Norfolk – don't miss the monument to Lord Morley, who died in 1434. It's said to be among the best in England.

Hingham is most elegant with lovely Georgian and Queen Anne houses clustered round two fine greens. There are the usual village shops; the White Hart is as friendly a pub inside as it is distinguished outside, and serves Norwich bitter from the handpump and Trumans. Transatlantic links continue almost everywhere; for instance, a block of granite embedded in the wall of the Post Office was given by Hingham, Mass, which itself apparently exhibits another boulder from Hingham, Norfolk, which the great Abraham's ancestors used as a mounting block outside the church.

New Buckenham

History here began with the Normans. Shortly after the Conquest, William's butler built a keep two miles away at Old Buckenham, but 80 years later his son started a new moated stronghold at what is now New Buckenham. The village grew up in its shadow. His castle is a ruin now – not a manicured, turnstiled one, but rough, shaggy, and deliciously overgrown. Get the key from Castle Hill garage (small fee charged), walk up a grassy lane, turn over the placid, willow-hung moat and let yourself in through rusty iron gates. Odds are you won't be disturbed, but the owners don't take kindly to abuse of the privilege by digging or the use of metal detectors.

The village clusters prettily round a trim green with, in the centre, a 17th c market-house complete with whipping post. The church, 15th c and rather grand, stands in an immaculate churchyard.

At Banham, three miles south-west, is a concentration of attractions: International Motor Museum has lots of shiny old cars (open daily in summer 11.30–5.00). Zoo and Monkey Sanctuary has acres of primates and other beasts and boasts much success in breeding (open 10.30–6.30 or dusk if earlier). Don't let these delights seduce the gaze from Banham village, which is charming, and has the distinction of a pub a little way out, the Garden House, serving only cider and British wines, Real ale drinkers can get Wethered in the King's Head in New Buckenham.

Reedham

Once a Roman station, later HQ of King Edmund martyred by Danes 1000 years ago, Reedham is now a stopping place for Broads cruisers which line the riverfront in summer, disgorging sunburnt sailors under the tolerant eyes of a colony of swans among the reeds on the far bank of the Yare.

Although several miles from the sea there's a salty tang in the air from the miles of marshes to south. Two shops on the riverfront sell postcards and tourist knick-knackery, and there's also a couple of general stores. Two pubs, Lord Nelson and Ship, serve hot meals and snacks, as does Ferry Inn (free house with Adnams and Tolly Cobbold) at Reedham Ferry. Don't miss the ferry itself, a curious, clanking, chain-powered affair which provides the only vehicular crossing of the Yare between Norwich and Yarmouth. Three miles north-east is handsome Berney Arms Mill, over 70ft high, built 1870 and now restored to perfect order. Inside is an exhibition of windmilling photographs and information. You can't reach it by road: take the footpath along the river, use a boat or go by rail (there's a halt by the mill).

Reedham church stands in fields north of village, next to 18th c hall and an unusual craft workshop, Pettit's, specializing in making things from feathers. Reedham is a good spot for birdwatchers, with solemn herons flapping over the river and other marsh and river birds.

Reepham

A charming and dignified little town with a cluster of well-proportioned 18th c houses round a handsome market square. Don't let the quietness here deceive you into thinking there's nothing to see. Four miles south-east at Great Witchingham is naturalist Philip Wayre's Norfolk Wildlife Park, where lynxes, bison, bears and 1400 other unconventional beasts roam the Norfolk pastures. Open daily 10.30–6.00 or sunset, whichever is sooner.

Three miles east of Reepham, at Cawston, is one of the great parish churches of England. Built in 15th c, it is grand and richly appointed, and Sir Gilbert Scott thought the hammer-beam roof the best in the country. Other treasures of this lovely building include the plough gallery in west arch, and a 14th c leather chalice case, very fine, and still in excellent condition.

Cawston church, magnificent as it is, is not the last word in Norfolk parish churches. A mile or two away, at Salle (pronounced Saul), is another, if anything even finer. As large and rich as many cathedrals, Salle church stands in breathtaking loneliness in the midst of silent fields, and serves the spiritual needs of fewer than 200 parishioners. Both these great monuments were built from Norfolk sheep profits in the 15th c.

Reepham itself has the curious distinction of two churches in one churchyard, plus ruins of a third. St Mary's has a beautiful 14th c tomb inside, on which the effigy of the occupant, Roger de Kerdiston, reclines on lumpy pebbles. Reepham, Cawston and Salle churches all have fine brasses.

Crossing the Yare: ferryman at Reedham ferry

After so much architecture, have a glass of Norwich bitter at the King's Arms in the Market Place, a no-nonsense country hostelry, or at the convivial Sun Inn 100 yards down the road. Or try Greene King with your meal at the Old Brewery House, now a hotel and restaurant.

Sheringham

Until the 1890s Sheringham was a flinty fishing village. Now also a miniature seaside resort, it manages the difficult feat of combining the best of both. Fishermen still put out in their beamy crab boats to tend lines of pots, and grateful holidaymakers eat their catches at a dozen stalls and cafes. Pinball machines and kiss-me-quick hats among savoury old pubs that still belong to the fishermen, not the visitors. The two Lifeboats (Tolly Cobbold and Greene King) and the Lobster (Norwich) are salty through to the woodwork.

Shopping's no problem here. All the usual beach and picnic impedimenta are available, of course; Bertram A. Watts of Church St would be a splendid bookseller in a town five times as big; and Dorothy's Antiques, Waterbank Rd, is friendly and knowledgeable about cranberry glass, commemorative china, clocks. (Early closing, Wed.)

Shingle beaches and beetling cliffs stretch for miles: stroll east to Beeston for a ruined priory, or west to Weybourne for another. Weybourne has a little steam railway that chugs there from Sheringham, with the sea popping up between the hills all the way. These beaches and cliffs, part glacial moraine from the last Ice Age, and part washed down from coasts further north, make good rock- and fossil-hunting. Agate, cornelian, jet and amber turn up, as well as fossil sea urchins and belemnites.

Worstead

The last Worstead weaver died in 1882, but for hundreds of years before the clatter of industry echoed from the fine houses round the square, still with their lofty ceilings to take the 12ft-high looms and great cellars for storing wool at an even coolness. And the great church, built on the backs of Norfolk sheep, still bears mute testimony to the ancient prosperity of Worstead. From the outside it is a noble building of flint and freestone, with a tower 109ft high. Inside is the other side of Worstead's history. As weaving moved to Norwich (and finally to the Pennines to take advantage of water and coal) the village declined until quite unable to maintain such a vast and splendid fabric.

There is still some magnificence to note – the ringers' gallery, font, and chancel screen, for instance – but decayed glory permeates the atmosphere despite a costly modern restoration programme. The southernmost figure on the screen depicts the virgin Uncumber, who was threatened with an unwelcome marriage by her dastardly father and grew a miraculous beard in self-defence. He crucified her out of pique, as she is represented here, but Uncumber still lives on as the patron saint of beards.

Next door to the church is the New Inn, an inviting local festooned with gins, harness, shears and other curiosa of rustic ironmongery, and possessing a pretty garden where you may drink Norwich beer and savour the latter-day tranquility of this cradle of industry.

Wymondham

Pronounce it Windham. Epitome of the Norfolk market town. Hardly an undistinguished building in the place, from half-timbered octagonal market cross of 1618, to great abbey church whose two towers dominate the countryside.

Abbey, surrounded by monastic ruins, was founded in 1107. Its towers are relic of a centuries-old feud between townspeople and monks for control of the church. In 1249 the Pope arbitrated and gave the east end to the monks, the west

to the town. The monks then churlishly ran a wall across, blocking their end off. West tower, 143ft high, was built by the townspeople, east by the monks. But Henry VIII settled things once and for all by dissolving monastery and pulling down the east end – sparing the tower, however.

The fitting end of any walk round Wymondham is the ancient and dignified Green Dragon Inn. Built in 14th c and awash with curious carving inside and out (Norwich bitter). The Cock, Cock St, is friendly local that serves a cold buffet lunch. Real ale buffs can get Greene King and Adnams at Feather, Town Green.

Three miles toward Norwich on A11 is Kett's Oak, an ancient tree under which Wymondham rebel Robert Kett gathered forces in 1549 for rising against land enclosure. Another venerable tree, four miles west, is Hethel Old Thorn, at least 700 years old, still flowering, and protected by the smallest nature reserve in England. Next to Hethel church, which is not easy to find.

Wymondham has usual shops for small town. Rose and Crown Antiques, Damgate St, specialize in dolls.

—Places to visit—

Churches: Apart from those already mentioned, a further selection might include: Attleborough (unique rood loft), East Harling (15th c monuments and good glass), Happisburgh (sailors' graveyard), Ranworth (splendid screen), North Tuddenham (good glass), Shipdham (Tudor lectern), South Lopham (Norman and very butch), Elsing (superlative brass monument), round towers at Aylmerton, Gresham, Matlaske and Bessingham, Cromer (150ft tower), East Dereham (grave of Cowper the poet), Trunch (medieval font cover), Knapton (outstanding double hammer-beam roof).

Windmills: Sutton Mill nr Hickling has complete machinery and is tallest mill in England, Horsey Wind-pump north of Yarmouth open at irregular times; Berney Arms nr Reedham and Stracey Arms nr Acle both open to public.

Ruins: ecclesiastical ones at Bacton, North Elmham (Saxon cathedral), Hickling and Horning on Broads, plus those already mentioned. Ruined castles

Restoring the medieval rood screen at Worstead church

also at Baconsthorpe and Caister nr Yarmouth (the latter with motor museum). Roman ruins at Caistor St Edmund nr Norwich, and Burgh Castle nr Yarmouth.

Museums include: Bressingham Live Steam Museum and Gardens, with road, rail and stationary engines, narrow-gauge railways and footplate rides; also six acres gardens. Open Sun, Thur mid-May–end Sept 1.30–6.00, also Bank Hol Mon and Wed in Aug 1.30–6.00. Cromer Museum has geology and natural history Mon–Sat 10.00–5.00, Sun 2.00–5.00. Also Lifeboat Museum at Cromer. Glandford Shell Museum, nr Cley, has world-wide collection of shells. May–Sept Mon–Fri 9.00–1.00 and 2.00–5.00, Sat–Sun 2.00–5.00, Oct–April Mon–Fri 9.00–1.00 and 2.00–4.00, Sat 2.00–4.00. Norfolk Rural Life Museum, Gressenhall, nr East Dereham, has exhibits covering 200 years of rural Norfolk. Open mid-May–Sept Tue–Sat 10.00–5.00, Sun 2.00–5.30.

Thursford Collection, Thursford Green, north-east of Fakenham: steam railway, engines, fairground equipment, mighty Wurlitzer organ and other fairground and street organs. Easter–31 Oct daily 2.00–5.30; Nov–Easter Sundays only 2.00–5.30.

Stately homes: Blickling Hall, Aylsham, is vast and magnificent Jacobean house in noble gardens. National Trust. Open daily except Mon and Fri, April–mid-May and first two weeks Oct 2.00–6.00, mid-May–Sept 11.00–6.00.

Gardens: Fairhaven Garden Trust,

Bromholm Priory, Bacton, was one of the great pilgrimage centres of England until the Dissolution

South Walsham, private woodland and water-garden by Broad. Open Easter–end Sept Thur, Sat, Sun, bank hol 2.00–6.00. Sheringham Hall, rhododendron gardens. Open every day 3.00–5.00.

ACTIVITIES

Boat hire: motor-boats available by the hour almost anywhere on Broads and rivers between Wroxham and Yarmouth. Rates vary. Difficult to get sailing boats by the hour or day.

Broads boat tours: from Wroxham. Nature tours from Pleasure Boat Inn, Hickling.

Fishing: sea fishing abundant from boats or beaches. Inland, good coarse fishing at Blickling Hall Lake, Costessey Pits, five miles north-west of Norwich, River Bure between Aylsham and Burgh (permits from Anglian Water Authority, 62–4 Thorpe Rd, Norwich). Coarse fishing without permit from boats on Hickling Broad, but not in bird sanctuary. Other Broads, mostly fishing from boats. Trout fishing in Bure between Aylsham and Cromer (permit from Anglian Water Authority).

Nature trails (open all year round unless indicated): Bacton Wood, 1½ miles; Felbrigg Hall, Cromer, 1½ miles, April–Oct; Bure Marshes, ½ mile, accessible only by boat; Hickling Broad, 2hr water trail, June–Sept; Hoveton Great Broad, ½ mile, May–mid-Sept except Sat and Sun am; Lion Wood, Norwich, ¾ mile; Mousehold Heath, Norwich, 1½ miles; Ranworth, ¼ mile, April–Oct except Sat am; Wensum Forest Trail, North Walsham, 1½ mile.

FOOD AND DRINK

Egon Ronay's Lucas Guide recommends: **Buckinghamshire Arms Hotel Restaurant,** Blickling, tel Blickling 2133; **Phoenix Hotel Restaurant,** Dereham, tel Dereham 2276.

TOURIST INFORMATION

Publications: *Eastern Daily Press* covers everything in Norfolk, especially good for local auctions.

See also Information under Framlingham.

Research: Michael Osborne.

King's Lynn

King's Lynn sits at the foot of the Wash, that large bite out of the east coast of England where King John is supposed to have lost all his treasure in 1215. He had been feasted by the burghers of Lynn, then as now a thriving port, but was caught by a nasty October high tide as he made his way west towards Newark. Not long afterwards he died.

Today Lynn is a natural centre, the railway terminus of the London–Cambridge–Ely main line, the funnel for trade between the Midlands and the eastern counties, and the bridge that links 'high' Norfolk, stretching towards Norwich in the east, and 'low' Norfolk, the flat marsh and fen lands south of the Wash.

Lynn's royal connections are stronger than in the days of King John. A few miles away to the north-east is Sandringham, one of the Queen's private estates and a major tourist attraction.

Lynn itself is set mainly on the east bank of the estuary of the wide and muddy River Great Ouse. Many of the streets near the river, particularly those close to the twin-towered St Margaret's Church, are very much as they were a couple of centuries ago.

If the town has a focal point it is Tuesday Market Place into which King Street leads. Almost all the buildings here are Victorian or earlier. Indeed, viewed on a Tuesday morning from an upper window of the most impressive of them all, the Duke's Head Hotel, it is a scene of bustle with stalls packing the square on an east–west axis – everything, in fact, that a country market should be. Here too is unrivalled free entertainment as the hucksters bid for attention – and custom. The king of Tuesday Market is John, who with his sidekick Malve runs a bargain-basement linen and household goods stall in the south-west corner. The saucy patter is aimed at the predominantly female audience.

The new shopping centre is to the south-east and partly on the site of the old cattle market which has now been moved to one of the industrial estates. Although less pleasing architecturally than the old streets, it was sensibly planned as a pedestrian precinct and it is only on market day that finding a free car-park space can be a problem. Those travelling from the west can choose a neat dodge by driving to West Lynn on the other bank of the Ouse, and then reaching the centre by means of the pedestrian ferry which sets them down less than a hundred yards from Tuesday Market.

The ferry passes in the shadow of just one of the many canning factories that reflect much of the area's prosperity – the land. The rich silt fields of Marshland and the black peat of the Fens mean agriculture at its most prosperous. 'Wheat, beet and 'taters', as the saying went,

Burnham Overy Staithe: the nearest harbour to Nelson's birthplace, Burnham Thorpe

used to be the staple rotation, but now one is just as likely to see fields of beans, carrots, rhubarb, and even courgettes. Immediately to the south of the town, acres of apple orchards and fields of strawberries abound. Meanwhile, as farming becomes more mechanized, so Lynn is increasingly industrialized with factories for such household names as Campbells (soups), Jaeger (clothes) and Wedgwood (glass).

Travel west and the roads tend to take geometric shapes following the dykes that are known locally as 'drains'. Wisbech, 'the capital of the Fens', looks Dutch, with the River Nene dominating the centre. The windswept area to the south of the Wash is very much the country of Dorothy L. Sayers's *The Nine Tailors*, best sampled by driving north along one of the many cul-de-sacs ending in vast flood banks. The banks themselves, and the salt marshes beyond, are marvellous vantage spots for birdwatchers as well as being the ideal habitat for samphire, a wild asparagus that flourishes between late July and early September and is widely served as a local delicacy.

To the east of Lynn we are in the highlands of Norfolk, relatively speaking. Once again we can talk of land- as opposed to sky-scapes. But the north coast is also often flat, sometimes marshy and given over to long stretches of sandy, if windy, beaches (although Hunstanton at the north-east corner of the Wash is the only resort until you reach Sheringham and Cromer 35 miles farther east). Nature reserves (such as Thornham and Scolt Head) abound with plenty of inlets where sailing thrives (Brancaster and Overy Staithe). The villages look and are prosperous; weekend cottages are common. It is in these parts that the roads criss-cross more disused railway lines than anywhere else in Britain, with the closure of the multi-branched Midland and Great Northern Joint line pre-empting Beeching by four years. But one stretch, from Sheringham to Weybourne, has been preserved and offers trips in old coaches hauled by restored steam locomotives.

Nor can one go far without passing a church. There are so many that Pevsner's *Buildings of England* series (Penguin) has to be divided into two volumes for Norfolk. My favourites among those in Lynn's orbit are at Walpole St Peter (to the west), which has a public right of way running *under* the chancel, and at two of the Wiggenhalls (to the south) – at St Germans and St Mary Magdalen, which have medieval churches varying in scale but both intriguing in content (St Germans, remarkable bench ends).

One may, of course, go searching for King John's lost treasure. But where? The Wash has receded since the 13th century, thanks to successive attentions of drainage engineers, as can be seen by the position of the lighthouses near a most unusual swing bridge over the River Nene at Sutton Bridge. Once the lights indicated the mouth of the river, now they are several hundred yards short of where it issues into the Wash. Meanwhile somewhere in this area, buried who knows where under centuries of silt deposits, lies King John's treasure, lost that nasty autumn night more than 600 years ago.

ION TREWIN

King's Lynn

WHERE TO GO

Fermoy Centre, King St: lively arts centre housed in fascinating group of old buildings. Films, concerts, plays put on in early 15th c Guildhall of St George. Its impressive beamed interior quite unspoilt by recent conversion. National Trust. Mon–Fri 9.00–1.00 and 2.00–5.00, Sat 10.00–12.30 when not in use. Also Fermoy Art Gallery for exhibitions and Red Barn which has space for big paintings and demonstrations of craftsmen at work. Centre headquarters of festival in July, but closed Aug, tel King's Lynn 3578. Next door is Museum of Social History with toys, costumes, furniture, also brass-rubbing centre. Open Tue–Sat 10.00–5.00. Many fine Georgian houses in King St itself.

Custom House, Purfleet Place: graceful, classical building stands overlooking river, sailing boats, swans and bright green mud, designed in 1680s by local architect, Henry Bell, twice mayor of Lynn.

Clifton House, Queen St: through Bell's handsome archway with barley-sugar columns are courtyard and tall Elizabethan lookout tower. Climb to top for views of town and Wash. Inside house, now offices, are rare 14th c tiled floors and brick vaulted undercroft. Open Mon–Thur 8.45–1.00 and 2.00–5.15 (shuts 4.45 Fri).

St Margaret's church: imposing exterior with two 12th c west towers, looks especially good on Sat when busy market, as old as the church itself, is held in its shadow. In churchyard, pleasing headstones decorated with doll-like angels – characteristic of area. Interior rather bleak, but two splendid elaborate 14th c brasses – one has border showing peacock feast held for Edward III.

Trinity Guildhall: striking, chequerboard-patterned 15th c building in flint and stone with matching Georgian and Victorian additions. Regalia Room contains many treasures including beautiful 'King John's Cup' – earliest surviving piece of English secular plate, but still not old enough to have really been part of John's lost hoard. Open Mon–Sat 10.00–4.00.

Lynn Museum, Market St: everything from flint arrow-heads to stuffed birds to Victorian flowery lavatories. Open Mon–Sat 10.00–5.00, closed bank hols.

Wedgwood Glass, Oldmeadow Road, Hardwick Estate: watch glass-blowing and hand-cutting in traditional manner. Mon–Fri 9.00–3.00. Two types of tour: a) conducted tours for groups, book in advance, last tour 1.25; b) less comprehensive, no guide.

SHOPPING

Market days: Tue, Sat, cattle market, Tue.

Early closing: Wed.

Scupham's, 103 Norfolk St: traditional pork butchers selling home-made meat pies and all sorts of savouries such as pork haslet and boiled pigs' feet.

Taylor's Celebrated Seeds, 142 Norfolk St: have been packaging their own seeds for over 200 years.

Donaldson's, 126 Norfolk St: old-fashioned fishmongers.

Prime's, 22 Broad St: good new bookshop. Surprisingly there is now no secondhand bookshop in the town.

Castle Acre's ruined castle

FOOD AND DRINK

Best place for a summer drink – terrace of newly opened **Riverside Restaurant** behind Fermoy Centre. They serve Greene King beer and also have a garden bar and barbecue. Bar snacks very good value, also restaurant, a converted 15th c warehouse. **Crown and Mitre**, Ferry St, is an old local with pool table, down-to-earth atmosphere and Norwich bitter. **London Porter House**, London Rd, a tiny unspoilt Victorian pub, serves Greene King beer. *Egon Ronay's Lucas Guide* recommends **Duke's Head Hotel Restaurant**, Tuesday Market Place, for sound cooking, above average wine list. *Just a Bite*, recommends **Antonio's Wine Bar**, Baxter Plain, for pizzas and pasta.

WHERE TO STAY

Egon Ronay's Lucas Guide recommends **Duke's Head Hotel**, Tuesday Market Place, tel King's Lynn 4996.

TOURIST INFORMATION

Town Hall, Saturday Market Place, tel King's Lynn 61241. *Around Lynn* is a well-illustrated booklet about the historic parts of the town published by King's Lynn Preservation Trust.

Walsingham's old pump is still in working order

Villages and country towns

Binham

Compact flint village surrounded by miles of empty countryside, with beautiful ruins of an 11th c Benedictine priory. The nave and most of the west front – used as parish church after the Dissolution – are almost intact and the great west window, bricked up in 19th c, has fine tracery. There is a battered octagonal font and 15th c benches with grapes and flowers. Open May–Sep 9.30–7.00, Sun 2.00–7.00, winter daylight hours.

The village itself is a cluster of pretty old cottages – some made from bits of demolished priory – round a green on which stands the shaft of the old cross. There is an important-looking white house, Manor Farmhouse, with impressive porch. Nowadays about 300 people live in Binham: a century ago there were more than 500 inhabitants, and it does have a rather sad air of reduced circumstances. Only one of Binham's original three inns survives, the Chequers, a free house which serves morning coffee, bar snacks and grills.

The Abbey House Hotel Restaurant looks comfortable and chintzy; menu features vegetables from garden, home-made soups and pâtés.

Blakeney

Typical of the villages along this coast, where the sea is separated from dry land by wide expanses of drying sands and the quay flanked by miles of salt marshes. At Blakeney the superb natural harbour, now crowded with yachts, is protected from the sea by Blakeney Point – a spit of land which is continually being pushed further west by the tides.

Blakeney Point is a National Trust Nature Reserve, 1100 acres of sand and dunes, home of innumerable birds, the occasional seal and many rare plants. From the quay take a boat trip to Blakeney Point Nature Reserve and Bird Sanctuary.

Facing the quay, and tucked into the hillside, are the remains of the old, stone-built guildhall, dating from 15th c. The large, somewhat forbidding church of St Nicholas stands up on a hill, away from the main village. Its slender north-east tower contains a beacon light which used to guide ships in to the harbour. Two narrow streets of shops wind down to the quayside. Hampers, in the High St, is a delightful little shop with sunshine-yellow striped blinds, selling home-made flans, pâtés, pies, and all sorts of picnic food.

The liveliest pub in Blakeney is the King's Arms, which serves Norwich beers. The Blakeney Bar across from the Blakeney Hotel is also popular and serves reasonably priced buffet lunches.

The Burnhams

A cluster of villages centering round Burnham Market, with elegant wide main street and Georgian houses, now mostly shops, around its long green. See pink-washed bank, old-fashioned post office and pharmacy, and tiny yellow-fronted bakers. The Hoste Arms pub stands next to rather grand Burnham House. Bowers, 'high-class' provision merchants, stocks home-made pâtés, many cheeses, and doubles as off-licence. There's a delightful seafood restaurant called Fishes, specializing in Brancaster oysters.

Burnham Thorpe, Nelson's birthplace, with many signs of 'the hero', notably in the pub the Lord Nelson – full of prints and memorabilia. There is no bar, just a room full of high-backed pews – the landlord, Les Winter, hands the drinks round. Legend has it that Nelson was born in the huge flint barn next to the pub. His father was rector of the church; his brother and sister are buried by its porch and his father lies in the chancel. Church and Nelson Hall, a nearby house, contain many relics, including his medicine chest, his silver goblet, some of his letters.

Burnham Deepdale's proudest possession is an ancient Norman font, depicting months of the year, to be found in the church of St Mary.

Burnham Norton has an Anglo-Saxon church tower and Norman font and here ($\frac{1}{4}$ mile east, by road) are to be found the remains of a Carmelite friary, founded 1200.

Burnham Overy is a very pretty village with the River Burn running through it. Here the grouping of water-mill, maltings, Georgian brick mill house and a row of cottages makes a picture-postcard scene. This section now belongs to National Trust. Near church can be seen remains of medieval cross.

As sea receded, Overy Staithe was built, also very picturesque. West Harbour Way has fine range of granaries and maltings, some now turned into smart holiday homes. Modern pub, the Hero, has cosy bar and serves coffee, bar snacks.

Castle Acre

Tiny, unspoilt village lying within outer bailey of 11th c castle, built by William the Conqueror's son-in-law. Approached through impressive Bailey Gate – together with vast earthworks, all that remain of castle. Beautiful village sign is the work of Harry Carter of Swaffham, who has designed and carved many of the best signs in East Anglia.

In lush meadows west of village past large parish church of St James, part 13th, part 15th c, are the ruins of 11th c Cluniac Priory. Full of atmosphere. Open May–Sept daily 9.30–7.00, April daily 9.30–5.30, March, Oct weekdays 9.30–5.30 Sun 2.00–5.30, Nov–Feb weekdays 9.30–4.00 Sun 2.00–4.00.

Old-fashioned village shop doubles as tea-room. The Ostrich, a Greene King house, with big open fireplace and beer garden, faces village green.

Cley-next-the-Sea

Cley – rhymes with sky – is no longer next-the-sea. It is more than a mile away but, like Blakeney, it was once a wool port. The 18th c custom house shows that there must have then been a flourishing wool trade with the Continent. The curving beach lies beyond expanse of salt marshes. Norfolk Naturalists' Trust acquired marshlands in 1926 and established a Nature Reserve, the very first in Great Britain.

Windmill on old quay, now restored as private house, is favourite subject of artists. In winding main street is Whalebone Books (specialists in books and clothes for birdwatchers) decorated with cattle and sheep's bones; and the Cley Forge Gallery, an old blacksmith's shop, sells toys, crafts and pottery. Fishing is much in evidence here. You can buy fresh sea bait daily outside The Long House in main street; also tiny shop selling freshly caught fish, crabs, shrimps and cockles.

About a mile inland is residential part of village, with green bordered by pretty cottages. Nearby stands noble 14th c church of St Margaret. South transept is roofless – never finished owing to Black

Lavender fields, with poppies behind, at Choseley near Thornham

Death. Nearby Three Swallows serves Norwich beers and prints on wall depict local bird-life.

Little Walsingham

Famous for its priory and shrine and a place of pilgrimage since medieval times. Ruins of 12th c Augustinian priory can be seen standing in the beautiful abbey gardens. All that remains of the great church is the 15th c east window and part of the east wall which has been incorporated into the big 18th c Abbey House. On south side are remains of refectory. Abbey Grounds are open July–Sept Wed, Sat, Sun 2.00–5.00; also in Aug on Mon and Wed.

Near the shrine is the parish church of St Mary. The 14th c building was gutted by fire in 1961 and has since been largely rebuilt. About 100 yards west of church, where Fakenham Rd leaves High St, are the extensive ruins of 14th c friary, in the grounds of private house.

The whole village is full of fascinating old buildings, many dating back to Elizabethan times, and the best way to appreciate them is on foot – there are lots of archways and alleyways to be investigated. In the Common Place, a lovely little cobbled square, at the end of the High St, is the old octagonal pump that still works. The flint-faced Shire Hall has been turned into a museum. Open daily May–Sept, including Sun, 10.00–12.00 and 2.00–4.00, Oct Sat and Sun only. Inside, the old courtroom is being restored to 18th c authenticity. Interesting shops include an old-fashioned drug store and Shrine Shop, full of religious books, cards and souvenirs, in Common Place, and The Secret Garden (Susan Riley Ceramics), in High St, where beautiful pottery is

hand-made on premises.

The Black Lion pub behind High St has garden, serves Norwich beers, lunches and bar snacks; near Anglican shrine is the Knight's Gate, originally row of 16th c flint cottages, good for home-made game pies, fresh local trout. In High St, Friar Tuck's, decorated in bright green, does teas, coffees and snacks. The Old Bakehouse, a medieval building with Georgian additions, serves teas, coffees and meals, and has old wall ovens, beam for sack-hoist and magnificent open fireplace.

Stiffkey

Straggling little village in very picturesque setting – it's in the valley of the River Stiffkey, little more than a stream, with cows grazing on rolling pastures behind.

It achieved notoriety in the 1930s when its rector, the Rev Harold Davidson, self-styled 'prostitutes' padre', was unfrocked for associating with 'loose women' and ended up being mauled to death by a lion in Skegness. He is buried in the churchyard. Stiffkey's other claim to fame is its 'Stewky Blues' – fine cockles which are harvested locally.

Stiffkey Hall is a Tudor house, flint with brick dressings. To the east of house lie gardens with walled terrace and circular towers. There were once two churches standing in the churchyard, but now only St John's remains – a mound is all that is left of St Mary's.

Thornham

Quite different in character from flint villages near Blakeney. Here, most of the old houses are built of chalk, both red and white (known as 'clunch' in Norfolk). The church, inn and 17th c manor house form charming group. Beautiful 13th c church doorway with traceried 15th c door. At its top is a fox preaching to congregation of geese.

If you take Staithe Road down towards sea, now almost a mile away, separated by marshes, you'll find Life Boat Inn facing green. Originally built as farmhouse 400 years ago. In evenings, lit only by gas and oil lamps, with coal fires on chilly nights, it is full of atmosphere. Real ale served. At lunchtimes, try french bread with delicious fillings of turkey, crab or prawns and salad.

Wells-next-the-Sea

Sadly, the picturesque quayside has been very nearly ruined by candyfloss/burger/bingo invasion. Market day is Wed, when town becomes very lively. Wandering round narrow streets, you'll find many interesting old buildings – shops include an art gallery, the Wells Bookshop and several antique dealers.

St Nicholas's church in Church Plain was struck by lightning in 1879 and rebuilt, faithfully copying earlier church. Luckily original doorway with carving of birds pecking grapes, and traceried door to priest's vestry in north chancel wall, escaped damage.

Centre of town is The Buttlands, with big green surrounded by well-proportioned Georgian houses. Facing green, the Globe Inn, a Greene King pub serving bar snacks. Other pubs serving real ale include the Crown Hotel, the Buttlands, and the Edinburgh in Station Rd.

Wisbech

The capital of the Fens is a cross between a market town and a port with many fine 18th c buildings. The River Nene, its banks so shored up that it seems more like a canal, runs right through the town. Facing each other across the water are two rows of big brick houses, all different, but completely harmonious. The North Brink is the grander; its most imposing building is Peckover House, built in 1722 for a rich Quaker. It has a suitably restrained exterior, but inside the decoration becomes surprisingly elaborate, with some beautiful rococo plasterwork. Lovely garden with rare old maidenhair tree, unchanged Victorian layout and planting. National Trust, open April –14 Oct, Tue, Wed, Thur, Sat, Sun and bank hol 2.00–6.00.

Wisbech worthies include Thomas Clarkson, the anti-slavery campaigner, who has a Gothic monument near the bridge. Clarkson's collection of African artefacts is on show at the Wisbech and Fenland Museum, Museum Square. It also has local archaeology and natural history sections and some good pottery and porcelain, including the Sèvres breakfast set from which Napoleon drank his coffee on the morning of Waterloo. Open Tue–Sat 10.00–1.00 and 2.00–5.00 (closes at 4.00 Oct–March).

Near the Museum are two charming 18th c crescents that fit together to make a circus with an eccentric Regency villa in the middle, built on the site of a Norman castle. Markets on Thur and Sat – stalls piled with excellent local fruit and veg. Lots of pubs to choose from including the Rose and Crown, an old coaching inn in High St with wisteria-covered inner courtyard, and Red Lion, North Brink, which serves Elgood beer brewed just down the road.

Places to visit

Baconsthorpe Castle: ruined 15th c manor house stands desolate in middle of farmlands. Consists of outer gatehouse, later converted into dwelling, a moat, massive inner gatehouse and parts of great hall and curtain wall. Open May–Sept weekdays 9.30–7.00 Sun 2.00–7.00, March, April, Oct weekdays 9.30–5.30 Sun 2.00–5.30, Nov–Feb weekdays 9.30–4.00 Sun 2.00–4.00. Three miles east of Holt.

Castle Rising: Shell of Norman castle and nine Jacobean almshouses, with chapel, court and treasury. Entrance to keep is by lovely flight of steps with three round archways. At top, see delightful room, all Norman except for 14th c stone vaulted roof. Set in pretty village on road from King's Lynn to Sandringham. Open daily May–Sept 9.30–7.00, Sun 2.00–7.00, winter daylight hours.

Creake Abbey: 13th c remains including presbytery and north transept with chapels. Open Wed, Thur, Sat May–Sept 9.30–7.00, March, April, Oct 9.30–5.30, Nov–Feb 9.30–4.00. Nr Burnham Market.

Felbrigg Hall: Motto 'Gloria Deo in Excelsis' in giant stone letters runs along balustrade on roof of early 17th c house. Inside, the great hall, dining-room and

library, together with splendid furnishings, date from 18th c. Now owned by National Trust, hall stands in fine park – many of the trees were planted in 1680s. Parish church also in park. Traditional walled garden and woodland walk. Teas and picnic area. Open April–Oct Tue, Wed, Thur, Sat, Sun, Bank Hol Mon 2.00–6.00. Nr Cromer on B1436.

Holkham Hall: vast, severe Palladian mansion made of white brick. Built by William Kent for Thomas Coke, Earl of Leicester, mid-18th c – still owned by family. Inside, lavish pink marble hall, dramatic staircase, decorated ceilings to state rooms. Sumptuous furnishings; paintings include works by Gainsborough and Rubens. Beautiful grounds with lake and wildfowl. Garden centre and pottery shop, bygones collection, tea-rooms, open seven days a week, 10.00–5.00. House open every Thur from last Thur May–last Thur Sept; July and Aug, Mon, Wed and Thur; Spring and Summer Bank Hol Mon

Sandringham – one of the Queen's private estates, open during the summer

11.30–5.00. Just outside Wells-next-the-sea, on A149.

Houghton Hall: largest country house in Norfolk, built in beautiful Yorkshire stone for Sir Robert Walpole, first Prime Minister of England. Magnificent interior designed mainly by Kent. Set in great deer park. Walpole thought cottages which stood in park spoilt the view so he had them rebuilt outside gates, giving Goldsmith his theme for *The Deserted Village*. Tea-room and picnic area. Open April–Oct Thur and bank hol, grounds 10.30–5.30, house 11.00–5.30; Sun, grounds 12.00–5.30, house 1.30–5.30. One mile off A148 between King's Lynn and Fakenham.

Sandringham House and Grounds: Norfolk Jacobean style, bought in 1862 by Queen Victoria for Prince of Wales. Set in magnificent grounds. Flower garden across road from east entrance. Just inside west entrance is church of St Mary Magdalene, full of royal memories. Also in grounds: nature trail, picnic areas, shop, cafe, motor car museum. Open Easter–Sept, times vary; for details tel King's Lynn 2675 Mon–Fri office hours. House and grounds closed 21 July–9 Aug.

Marshland churches: as well as the wonderful 15th c church at Walpole St Peter, there are others well worth seeking out, most set in sprawling, undistinguished villages, especially Tilney All Saints – lovely hammer-beam roof; Terrington St Clement – pinnacles, flying buttresses, a separate tower and painted font-cover; Walsoken – Norman with fine arcade and chancel arch; West Walton – 13th c with detached tower; Walpole St Andrew – curious little room on the roof for a priest.

Nature reserves: coastline between Hunstanton and Sheringham designated 'area of outstanding natural beauty'. Still largely unspoilt, with extensive shingle ridges, salt marshes, sand dunes and cliffs, rich in animal and plant life.

Holme: foreshore and sand dunes, fresh marsh and salt marsh which provide variety of habitats. Access from either Thornham or Holme village (by car). Visitors should contact warden, The Firs, Broadwater Lane, Holme, tel Holme 240. Also Holme Bird Observatory. Contact warden.

Tichwell Marsh Bird Reserve: public footpath leads to shore, from where reserve can be viewed. Off A149 Thornham–Brancaster road. Warden, 3 Horseshoe Cottage, Tichwell.

Brancaster Manor: mainly foreshore, sand dunes, reclaimed marshland and salt marshes. Unrestricted access from Brancaster village.

Scolt Head Island: separated from mainland by creek with extensive salt marshes and sand dunes. Access by prior arrangement. Local boatmen at Brancaster Staithe will ferry visitors to island in summer. Contact warden, Dial House, Brancaster Staithe, tel Brancaster 330.

Holkham: largest coastal reserve in England, extending from Burnham Overy to Stiffkey. Access from Holkham village, along private road to beach; by foot along sea wall from Overy Staithe; or along beach from Wells. Part east of Wells can be reached on foot from Stiffkey. Certain areas of restricted access. Contact warden, The Hips, Station Rd, Burnham Market, tel Burnham Market 341.

Morston Marshes: salt marsh, dissected by many creeks. Access via track from Morston Quay. Also by public footpaths along landward edge of marsh from Blakeney and Stiffkey.

Blakeney Point: National Trust reserve, three-and-a-half-mile shingle spit running west from Cley. Breeding and migrant birds, and interesting flora. Access by foot from Cley, or by boat from Morston and Blakeney, two hours before and after high tide. Check with local boatmen in advance. Or contact warden, Point House, Morston, tel Cley 740220.

Cley Marshes: large numbers of migrant birds. Restricted access, but public footpath along east bank provides good views over marshland. Contact warden, Watchers Cottage, Cley, tel Cley 740380.

Snettisham Pits: reserve borders the Wash, with gravel pits. Three miles west of Dersingham. Access by road. Warden, School House, Wolferton, King's Lynn.

ACTIVITIES

Angling: plenty of sea, coarse and trout fishing. Sea fishing – Mr Robin Bishop of 32 Langham Rd, Blakeney, tel Cley 740200, takes fishing parties out to sea from Morston Quay. Boats can also be hired and fishing parties catered for at Blakeney Quay. Other good spots at Sheringham, Cromer, Weybourne.

Coarse fishing – Bayfield Lake, roach. Permits required. Holkham Estate: permits from Holkham Estate Office. Letheringsett, 1½ miles west of Holt: permits from Mr Leveridge, The Watering, Cley Rd, Holt. Trout fishing – River Glaven, one mile south of Blakeney: fishing permitted along 1½ miles of right bank and access via Wiveton Bridge. Contact Anglian Water Authority, 62/64 Thorpe Rd, Norwich, for permits, rod licence. Guides available.

Horse riding: Weybourne Riding Centre, Cherry Trees Farm, Weybourne, tel Weybourne 268; Greens Riding Stables, Spearman's Yard, Wells, tel Fakenham 710609.

Boat trips: from Blakeney to the Point: contact G. Bean, The Quay, Blakeney. April–Oct only. Also motor-boat trips from Morston Quay and Brancaster Quay. Richard Searle, 3 South Beach Rd, tel Hunstanton 2342, does trips to Seal Island, also half-hour trips to new lighthouse and cliffs. June–Sept daily. You can hire canoes, sailing and rowing-boats from Burnham Overy Boat House Co, Burnham Overy Staithe.

Nature trails: Holme, Hunstanton – two miles April–Sept. Sandringham – one and two miles April–Sept. Scolt Head Island – three-quarters of a mile May–Aug.

FOOD AND DRINK

Egon Ronay's Lucas Guide recommends: **Gasché's Swiss Restaurant**, Weybourne, nr Holt, tel Weybourne 220 – unusual Swiss and French dishes; **Mirabelle**, Station Rd, West Runton, nr Cromer, tel West Runton 396; **Black Horse Inn**, Castle Rising, nr King's Lynn, tel Castle Rising 225 – pub restaurant. Mainly grills and roasts.

TOURIST INFORMATION

Publications: *Lynn News and Advertiser* and *Eastern Daily Press*. Also *What's On in East Anglia*, monthly. *East Anglia Guide* from East Anglia Tourist Board, 14 Museum Street, Ipswich, who also have map and gazetteer, and *Camping and Touring Caravan Sites in East Anglia*.

Tourist information office: at Walsingham.

Research: Sandra Newman.

Lincoln

Lincolnshire is the second-largest county for area, but the twentieth for population: this means wide open spaces. Despite the industrial spread of Scunthorpe and Flixborough, the maritime growth of Grimsby and Immingham, and the fun fringe that spreads along and behind the coast from Cleethorpes to Skegness, Lincolnshire has changed little in the past century. It is a secret and unknown county, partly because it is not on the road to anywhere, and partly because of the myth that it is all flat fenland. But those who bother to penetrate the beautiful Wolds return spellbound.

The defensive outworks of the Wolds would be the market towns of Spilsby, Horncastle, Wragby, Market Rasen, Caistor and Brigg. These towns are a Lincolnshire speciality, like spicy sausages and haslet. They are brick-built, pleasant and unassuming, bustling with farming affairs, and with few high-flying architectural monuments.

Real architecture belongs to the Fenland where the churches are magnificent and the Boston Stump the wonder of the Gothic world. En route to Lincoln, Boston and Spalding are towns that should not be missed for anything; Spalding with its tulip festival is a little Dutch town in England.

Lincoln dominates the western approaches to the county. From Retford and Newark across the Trent, the cathedral draws the traveller like a magnet. The Romans called their town Lindum Colonia and carefully planned its strategic situation. They set it on a high limestone ridge that runs north-south across the county, and along it laid out their Ermine Street practically all the way from Stamford in the south to Winteringham in the north, near where Ouse and Trent meet to make Humber. Roman Lincoln in 300 AD was a huge and massive walled city pierced by four gates. The Newport Arch, or north gate, is still there, and the west gate is miraculously buried in the castle earthworks. South and south-east the Cliff, as it is called, drops steeply down to where the Romans laid out another square city whose south gate was on the site of the present Stonebow. Here was trade and commerce on the banks of the River Witham, and to Brayford Pool, now with its pleasure boats, the Romans brought their Foss Dyke canal from the River Trent.

There are still two Lincolns: the one below, busy and brash; the other, touristy and polite, centred on the cathedral and castle. Steep Hill and the Strait are the connecting artery. Up the Cliff wind narrow streets and passages, some like Greestone Stairs tortuous, and even today evoking a feeling of surreptitiously entering the embattled city above. Inside the late fifteenth-century Stonebow is the Guildhall,

Louth – 'on market days it is friendly and bustling'

which contains one of the finest collections of maces, swords and other civic insignia in the country. Before it the Norman high bridge crosses the Witham, and still has its row of sixteenth-century timber-framed houses and shops, an epitome of old London Bridge. Scattered down here are four important medieval churches, including St Mary Le Wigford, St Benedict and St Peter at Gowts with Anglo-Saxon towers.

From the Stonebow the aspirant for the upper city might first call at the Greyfriars, a late twelfth-century undercroft of the Franciscan church, now housing a city museum. This is on Saltergate, and from here an interesting approach to the cathedral could be via the Usher Art Gallery, well set by Sir Reginald Blomfield in 1927 on Temple Gardens, so called from the exquisite half-hidden neo-Greek temple nearby. The Usher is a must for aficionados of Peter de Wint and English coins and medals. By Temple Gardens, Greestone Stairs will introduce the visitor, puffing, to the cathedral close, and the wonderful palimpsest of ruined Bishop's Palace, Vicar's Court, and other medieval houses clustered here on the Cliff's edge.

Alternatively, the pedestrian can take the Strait due north of Stonebow and mount Steep Hill, for Lincoln's speciality of two Norman houses: first the Jew's House; then, farther up, Aaron the Jew's House, very picturesque. Steep Hill debouches on to Castle Hill, really a wide confluence of streets, with the castle on the left and Exchequer Gate on the right.

The castle is now a huge walled enclosure of trees and lawn containing Sir Robert Smirke's Tudor-style Assize Courts of 1823 and John Carr's brick classical jail of 1787, its chapel a choking space in which felons were ingeniously self-locked into tall cubicles. You leave it shuddering, relieved to be out in the wooded part, as pleasant to dally in as the arboretum off Lindum Terrace, presided over by a tame stone lion.

There can be few more thrilling experiences than passing through Exchequer Gate to be confronted by the rearing cathedral's west front. The cathedral was built in the south-eastern corner of the Roman city on the very edge of the Cliff, as if deliberately flaunting by its upward display the inner containment that had prevailed before.

For sheer bravado of building to the glory of God so as to be seen from a maximum distance, nothing excites me as much as Lincoln Cathedral. It is a building which enlivens the mind because of its variety and innovation.

Sunk into the west front is the Norman cathedral, consecrated in 1092; behind it extend successive building operations, which can be identified by the ingenuity of their vaulting: the crazy vaulting of St Hugh's Choir; the richer, more ornamental system of the wondrous Angel Choir. Everywhere the eye can exult in something ingenious, such as the syncopated rhythm of the blank arcading of the south wall of the south transept. And don't forget the chapter house, because in the adjacent cloisters is the added bonus of a south range by Sir

Christopher Wren. With box trees in tubs between its classical arcades, and a little added sun, this might be some cloister in Perugia.

Afield from Lincoln there are the market towns to enjoy. Take the A46 to Market Rasen and make a diversion to the remote church at Snarford, where the romantic St Pol tombs bring one as close to the magic of the Elizabethan age as perhaps anything else in England. From Market Rasen take preferably the Wold road to Caistor, the one via Walesby, and then make for Louth via Croxby and Swinhope.

Louth, the Queen of the Wolds, is unspoilt, perfect, with a majestic parish church. On market days it is friendly and bustling, and it has splendid old pubs in which solicitors and farmers eat with rural enjoyment. Everyone loves Louth and there is nothing in England to compare with it.

There is marvellous Wold country to explore, within the triangle formed by Louth, Horncastle and Spilsby. Here churches and hamlets such as Oxcombe or Farforth, Ruckland or Biscathorpe seem to be in a timeless sleep. This is, of course, Tennyson's country: he was born at Somersby in 1809 and went to school in Louth. Little has really changed since his day.

There are other possibilities: leave Lincoln or approach it by the Cliff road, the A607 from Grantham; take in Belton House and have a look at R A F Waddington, a reminder that this is still a county of air-fields; or deviate to Woodhall Spa via Bardney, where bumps in the field mark one of the greatest of Benedictine abbeys in Europe. Woodhall has a fine golf course, its Unique Kinema in the Woods and the glorious thirteenth-century church at Kirkstead. Beyond Woodhall stands Tattershall, one of the finest sixteenth-century brick castles in England.

Lincolnshire has never been a county of great touristy houses. One day Grimsthorpe will be open, and then that will be among the dozen musts in the country. But near Spilsby there is Gunby Hall of 1700, plain and appealing, and between the Trent and Lincoln there are two Elizabethan experiences: the spectacular ruin of Torksey Castle, and the urbane Doddington Hall, a major late Elizabethan house designed by Robert Smythson and set in lovely gardens.

Lincolnshire is too big to capture in one visit. It is too varied, for the Fen, the Marsh, and the Wolds have almost three identities, and then there is nothing in this country like the long coast, where south of Skegness birds are your only companion. It can absorb and reject and will always be a place of mystery. That is its magic.

JOHN HARRIS

Lincoln

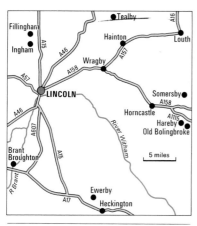

WHERE TO GO

Downhill Lincoln: market area south of River Witham joins pedestrian precinct section of High St, including row of 16th c timber-framed buildings on bridge across river, to provide bustling shopping centre. South of the river for railway stations, bus stations and vast engineering works that underpin the city's prosperity: past products include traction engines and First World War tank. North for museums, library, theatre, Guildhall. Look for bold 19th c red-brick extravaganzas: castellated drill hall, Constitutional Club, corn exchange.

Uphill Lincoln: the cathedral, with the castle beside, sits high on edge of limestone ridge sweeping in from north. Uphill Lincoln has own pleasant shopping street, Bailgate, the relaxed splendour of Minster Yard, the medieval jumble of Steep Hill and the Strait. The Lincoln of tourists passing quickly through, the professional classes, the church people: curiously little toing and froing goes on between Uphill and Downhill.

Castle: originally built by William the Conqueror in 1068 to consolidate his control of the English. Later users added the 18th–19th c red-brick jail, which now holds Lincolnshire archives, and 19th c turreted Assize Courts. Entry from Castle Hill, open space opposite cathedral: walkway on top of castle wall gives impressive view of cathedral west front. Open weekdays Oct–March 10.00–4.00, April–Sept 10.00–6.00, Sun Oct–April 2.00–5.00, May–Sept 2.00–7.30.

Cathedral: look for diagram explain-

Lincoln Cathedral – 'draws the traveller like a magnet'

ing lovely east window with scenes from life of Christ and Old Testament: Jonah's whale appears particularly toothy. Cathedral is focus for poetry readings, concerts, drama and so on. Opens 7.15, closes Sun 6.00, weekdays May–Aug 8.00, Sept 7.00, Oct–April 6.00. Library, with copy of Magna Carta, open weekdays 10.30–6.30. Brass-rubbing centre open weekdays 10.00–5.00, Sun 12.00–6.00.

Museums: City and County Museum, in former church of Greyfriars, Broadgate. Archaeology, history and natural history: stone axes, Viking weaponry, Lincolnshire wildlife. Open weekdays 10.00–5.30, Sun 2.00–5.00. Guildhall, above the Stonebow. Fine collection of civic insignia. Open first Sat in month 10.00–12.00 and 2.00–4.30. Museum of Lincolnshire Life in romantically castellated 19th c barracks, Burton Rd. Domestic life, work and industry: maze of galleries interestingly crammed with pieces from houses and workshops. Also Transport and Industry Gallery with traction engines and agricultural machinery. Open weekdays 10.00–5.15 Sun 2.00–4.30, Sat, Sun June–Aug late opening until 6.00. Closed Dec, Jan.

Usher Gallery in Temple Gardens, Lindum Rd. Based on collection of James Ward Usher, 19th c jeweller who made fortune selling replicas of 'Lincoln Imp'. Sculpture; paintings from 16th c Italian school to 20th c works; ceramics; coins; Alfred Lord Tennyson memorabilia. Look for gallery devoted to Peter de Wint, 19th c artist living in Lincoln, with many paintings of Lincolnshire scenes. Open weekdays 10.00–5.30, Sun 2.30–5.00.

SHOPPING

Markets: general, Thur, Fri, Sat; fruit and veg, daily.
Early closing: Wed.
Steep Hill: is the place for antique shops and the like:
Anthony Cotton at 26/27: sells silver.
Tony and Anna Cockram at 46: specialize in clothes and paraphernalia.
Richard West-Skinn at 22: has maps, prints and secondhand books.
Richard Pullen, silversmith, at 64: will make individual jewellery and has rings and other small pieces of silverware in stock.
The **Crafts Centre**, Jews Court: run by Lincolnshire and Humberside Arts, displays and sells work by local potters, artists, embroiderers.

ACTIVITIES

Sport: tennis on West Common; golf at Carholme Club or municipal course on South Common; fishing, mainly for roach, bream, pike, permits from tackle shops; swimming pools at two sports centres, also squash courts.
Theatre Royal, Clasketgate: a well-preserved Victorian theatre seating 500, features pre-West End shows and touring productions, tel Lincoln 25555.
Pleasure Fair: on South Common, April, Sept.

FOOD AND DRINK

For a special meal try recently opened **White's Restaurant** in 12th c Jew's House, 15 the Strait, (tel Lincoln 24851). Closed Mon lunchtime, Sun. Menu changes weekly with such variations on French/English themes as halibut with green butter sauce. Evenings, in airy room seating 25, can be pleasantly jolly. Pubs include: **Cornhill Vaults**, Exchange Arcade, Cornhill: extensive and atmospheric cellar bar noted for its food. New Orleans jazz some evenings. Serves Ruddles, Sam Smiths. **Straits**, the Strait: wine bar with room to sit and talk. **The Strugglers**, Westgate: lively local pub under castle walls. Note Lincolnshire dartboard, all black, no outer bull or treble ring. Serves draught Bass. **The Witch and the Wardrobe**, Waterside North: pleasant riverside pub that attracts a young clientèle.

Egon Ronay's *Lucas Guide* recommends **Eastgate Hotel Restaurant**, Eastgate, for capable cooking, and **Mitchels**, 94 Newland, a warm friendly bistro. Egon Ronay's *Just a Bite* recommends **Spinning Wheel**, 39 Steep Hill, for coffee, omelettes, home-made chocolate cakes, and the **Wig and Mitre**, Steep Hill, which serves Ruddles, Sam Smiths, good snacks including home-made pâté.

WHERE TO STAY

Egon Ronay's *Lucas Guide* recommends the **White Hart Hotel**, Bailgate (tel Lincoln 26222), a famous old hostelry tucked in beside cathedral; **Eastgate Hotel**, Eastgate (tel Lincoln 20341), a modern hotel near cathedral.

TOURIST INFORMATION

90 Bailgate (tel Lincoln 29828). City Information Centre, City Hall, Beaumont Fee (tel Lincoln 32151) provides usefully detailed list of 'What's On in Lincoln'.

The wide open spaces of Lincolnshire – at Hareby near Spilsby

Villages and country towns

Brant Broughton

Long, lazy, wide main street; manor house at north end; many pleasant houses in village in stone, red-brick and white paint. Beautiful 14th c church of St Helen at south end with elegant steeple and inspired 19th c restoration by Canon Frederick Sutton. He made much of the stained glass himself, baking the colour on in an oven set up in the Old Rectory (now an educational training centre), and went on to do windows at Lincoln Cathedral. All the ironwork, gates, candlesticks, candelabra, came from the village forge of Frederick Coldron. His grandson, Bob, still runs the forge. In a ramshackle pantiled shed opposite Church Lane, blacksmith Jim Fahey shoes up to four horses a day.

The Generous Briton, a Courage pub, has darts and dominoes.

Ewerby

Like many of these flat-land villages, appears from a distance as a church steeple rising from a clump of trees. Set along one road it has a bit of everything: a fine church; large red-brick Dower House; new bungalows; dwellings in red and yellow brick: a couple of houses in striking early-Victorian Tudor; the smallest of thatched cottages; and even an old advert ('Franklyn's Fine Shagg. Always good to the end').

The Finch Hatton Arms is a popular pub and restaurant.

Fillingham

In Fillingham, a track beside church puts you bang in middle of a vista with lake behind, church to one side, long, low, thatched farmhouse to the other, and a vast grassy field sweeping up the escarpment of the Lincolnshire Cliff to a gap in the trees and a view of restrained 18th c Gothic castle. For a few years in 14th c, Fillingham's priest was John Wycliffe who translated the Bible into English and branded the Pope as Antichrist; he died of a stroke but Pope Martin V had his remains dug up and burnt.

From Fillingham, slip over to Ingham for the Black Horse, a friendly and attractive village local with bar snacks, darts, juke box. Serves Sam Smiths.

Jim Fahey, the Brant Broughton blacksmith, shoes up to four horses a day

Hainton

A little place, yet somehow straggly, memorable for monuments in Heneage chapel of St Mary's church. (The Heneages, who have been here 700 years, still live in Hainton Hall.) Peer through an iron gateway at memorials ablaze with heraldic colour. Even the figures are painted: Sir George Heneage, died 1595, lies black-bearded and full-armoured on top of his alabaster tomb.

The Heneage Arms does bed and breakfast and serves Ind Coope.

Heckington

Large village with one of the grandest churches in Lincolnshire. Take a look at the late 19th c stained glass above the altar: nine orders of angels, saints and prophets, whales, polar bears, pelicans and even a Red Indian. Wander round beside the church to find a mix of basic red-brick cottages and large houses such as St Andrew's Villa.

A detour down to the railway station turns up Heckington's landmark, an eight-sailed windmill with its gear intact; originally built as a five-sailer in 1830, its sails and cap blew away in a storm around 1890. John Pocklington bought the mill, shifted working parts from dismantled eight-armer at Boston and had local carpenter John Hodgson make sails. Open during office hours, since the Pocklingtons still run a coal merchants on the site.

Pubs include the White Horse, Church Street, serving Watneys and

Youngers, and The Royal Oak, Boston Rd, serving Sam Smiths.

Louth

Pleasantly confident country town, tucked under seaward side of Wolds. Past prosperity, based on agriculture, shows in vast cattle market and large hotels once packed with market-going farmers. The market has shrunk because many animals are sold direct to food processors, but it still works wonders on the afternoon licensing hours.

Prodigious church with spire soaring over 250ft; sparsely decorated, perhaps because Henry VIII took all its treasures after Louth figured prominently in the Lincolnshire Rising of 1536, protesting against plans to suppress the monasteries. Many lovely buildings, particularly in Westgate. Alfred Lord Tennyson

went to school in Louth and C. Parker and Co (Parkers the newsagents are still in the same shop in the Market Place) published his first book of poems: he and brother Charles took a day-trip to Mablethorpe on the proceeds.

Louth Naturalists, Antiquarian and Literary Society Museum in Broadbank displays butterflies, local sketches and bygones. Open Wed 1.45–4.00, Sat, Sun 2.15–4.30, Thur in Aug only 2.30–4.30.

Pubs include Boar's Head, Newmarket, a pleasant place serving Batemans; the Wheatsheaf, Westgate, 17th c inn serving Bass; the Turk's Head, Aswell St, a town-centre pub serving Wards.

Early closing Thur; general market on Wed, Fri, Sat; cattle market, Fri.

Old Bolingbroke

Largish village set in hollow of low hills below Wolds; size perhaps reflects long-forgotten position as centre of thriving estate, birthplace of Henry IV, son of John of Gaunt. A pleasant place, although the outskirts straggle off into factory farms.

Most obvious sign of past status is the moated castle, first built by Earl of Lincoln in 11th c, strengthened later, then pulled down by Parliamentarians during Civil War: much of the stone went to build village houses. The church is another relic of the past: attractive, a reasonable size, yet only a part of what was here in 14th c. The mill pond, where a stream runs through some scrubby land beside the castle, has silted up but look over the wall beside house on other side of road to see water still falling through the race where wheel once was.

The Black Horse has been knocking its bars into one, with pool table, darts, fruit machine; serves snacks and Batemans.

Aficionados of the picturesque may like to climb the hill to Hareby, little more than a T-junction, but with Hareby House looking out over the southward slope to Kirkby Mill on its ridge, a large white thatched house, and a duck pond beside a red-brick cottage with trees set about.

Somersby

Birthplace of Alfred Lord Tennyson, whose father was rector here. One of the smallest villages of all with just the church, an embattlemented red-brick manor house and the old rectory, now a

private house. The small church has a few Tennyson relics, including a Valentine he sent.

Tealby

Large village with attractive centre, some striking houses spreading along outer roads. The village runs down the hill in a series of terraces from the church of All Saints to the tiny River Rase. To the south-west, road to Thealby Thorpe runs past the King's Head, a thatched, white-painted Courage pub, and the late 18th c Watermill House which has water pouring over the sluice.

At the other end of the village, a lesser road drops down to a ford and some tidy cottage gardens beside the stream. Although access is forbidden, this track leads on to what was the site of Bayons Manor, which villagers called 'the Folly', demolished in 1964. Bayons had once been a reasonably ordinary Regency house lived in by the Tennysons. Charles Tennyson, MP for Lambeth and uncle of Alfred Lord Tennyson, conspired with his father to change the family name to the more aristocratic Tennyson d'Eyncourt, then, around 1835, set out to make Bayons something more in keeping with this new status. He ended with one of the most impressively romantic 'medieval' castles ever built, complete with drawbridge. Lincoln's Usher Art Gallery displays a drawing of the vanished fantasy-made-stone.

Ramblers are featured in the stained glass windows of Walesby Old Church

—Places to visit—

Doddington Hall, west of Lincoln: late Elizabethan manor house built by Robert Smythson. The interior is Georgian, with excellent joinery, furniture, pictures, porcelain and textiles. Cream teas. Open Wed and Sun May–Sept, Bank Hol Mon incl Easter 2.00–6.00.

Old Hall, Gainsborough: 15th and 16th c black and white manor house, with collection of bygones, furniture, paintings, china, dolls and period dresses. Open weekdays all year round, also Sun Easter–Oct 2.00–5.00. Closed Christmas, Boxing and New Year's Days.

St Germain's Church, Thurlby, southwest of Lincoln: follow a grassy track off the tree-lined road to this tiny and ancient-looking church notable for its woodwork, from the early 19th c oak door to the jolly pew ends with their trefoils, crowns and crosses. Various inscriptions show the close connection with the Bromheads of Thurlby Hall next door: the stained glass windows above the altar commemorates Gonville Bromhead, awarded the V C after the Battle of Rorke's Drift in 1879, and his elder brother Edward.

St Mary's Church, Stow, north-west of Lincoln: dates back to Anglo-Saxon times, an enormous building to find in a small village, although Stow does lie on what may have been a significant crossroads. Forbidding without, the church is both austere and magnificent within: wonder at the decoration of the restored Norman chancel.

Tattershall Castle, south-east of Lincoln: massive brick-built keep survives from fortified and moated castle raised by Ralph, the third Lord Cromwell, who fought with Henry V at Agincourt and later became Lord High Treasurer of England. Museum contains local archaeological finds, collection of postmedieval pottery, model of castle as it was. National Trust. Open weekdays 11.00–6.30 or sunset, Sun 1.00–6.30 or sunset. Closed Oct–end March 1.00–2.00 and Christmas and Boxing Days.

Dogdyke Pumping Station, near Tattershall: 1855 Steam Beam Engine and Scoop Wheel. Open (and in steam) May–Oct first Sun in month and Easter Sun 2.00–5.00. Access from A153.

Old Church, Walesby, north-east of Market Rasen: set high and lonely on a

Walesby Old Church with a view across the Wolds

hilltop above village, with views across Wolds. Can be bleak and slightly spooky in the wind. Restored, but roughly furnished. Adopted by Lincolnshire Ramblers Association who hold annual service there: stained glass window shows bare-kneed ramblers. Friends of Old Church, Hon Sec Mr R. S. Mason, Greensleeves, Walesby.

Tattershall Coningsby village conurbation: overflown by R A F jets but look for Mr R. P. Bedford's house in Lodge Road, Tattershall, with his collection of more than 80 horse-drawn ploughs outside and horse brasses in the living room. ('Three weeks and three tins of Brasso to clean them.') Coningsby Church has brightly painted clock, the largest in the world with only a single hand.

ACTIVITIES

Angling: for Anglian Water Authority Licence contact Fisheries Officer, Anglian Water Authority, 50 Widebar Gate, Boston, Lincs, tel Boston 65661.

Walking: the Viking Way now runs north-south through the Wolds, from the Humber Bridge to Oakham, way-marked and described in six sections in leaflets published by Lincolnshire County Council, on sale at tourist information centres and elsewhere. For a particularly pleasant ramble, try the five miles of grassy Roman chariot-way above Great Sturton on the western

edge of the Wolds. For an afternoon stroll, Hartsholme Country Park nr Lincoln, with lake and wood.

FOOD AND DRINK

Egon Ronay's Lucas Guide recommends **Magpies**, East St, Horncastle, tel Horncastle 7004, for enjoyable home cooking, and **Dower House Hotel Restaurant**, Spa Grounds, Woodhall Spa, tel Woodhall Spa 52588. Serves good local produce.

TOURIST INFORMATION

Tourist information centres: Louth; Woodhall Spa, summers only. **Publications** *Lincolnshire Echo* (evenings), *Lincolnshire Chronicle* (weekly).

Research: Humphrey Evans.

Tomb of Sir George Heneage at Hainton church

Dogdyke Pumping Station near Tattershall: it works by steam

Bakewell

Snobs have a phrase for it: day-trippers' paradise. And so it is. Praise the Lord, and pass the Thermos.

The Peak District is like some gigantic version in natural, rural form of that most urban of English creations, the garden rockery. It is roughly 40 miles long, north to south, and at its widest the best part of 20. The top end, geographically, is also the higher, just clearing 2000 feet. Some rockery! But its position supports the analogy. It is encircled by the back doors of Manchester, Oldham, Sheffield, Barnsley, Derby and Stoke, to name but the largest of the industrial communities which dearly need the garden of the Peak. Given a sunny weekend or bank holiday they claim it by the drove, producing a confluence of dialects that puts the foraying visitor from distant parts – say, Birmingham – properly in his place as an outsider, however amiably received.

Close proximity to so many densely populated towns has had important effects on the Peak District. The crucial battles for the right of public access to open country (nationally) were fought here, sometimes physically: rambler versus gamekeeper, occasioning actual bodily harm. There was need for spectacular mass trespass, back in the days of hobnails, before legislation freed the splendidly wild tracts of Kinder Scout and Bleaklow to coming generations who now tread as they wish – or as the maze-like topography of these strange plateaux dictates.

These northern heights of the area are the most dramatic features of what is called the Dark Peak: not by reason of some mysterious truncating of the hours of daylight as against those enjoyed by the southern section, known as the White Peak, but because of the characterizing gritstone rock. Gritstone is a severely clerical grey in the kindest weather. In the grimmer sort it can look sooty black, so that you navigate from one weirdly rearing landmark to another, plunging in and out of deep peat-ditches, utterly black, like the wandering hero from some early moon-shot serial of tuppenny-rush times.

There are rocks like huge black mushrooms, cotton reels, egg-timers, capstans, thumbs, boots, anvils. One set is called Boxing Glove Stones, and the name is aptly descriptive. These oddities are peculiar to the place, just as the words for certain other natural aspects of the landscape are. A 'clough' is a valley. Those peat ditches are 'groughs'.

The guidebooks, quite sensibly, emphasize that the Kinder and Bleaklow plateaux can be dangerous spots in bad weather, even though their altitude and their shape seem hardly to justify reference to them as 'mountains'. The point is that they often demand the use of map and

Well-dressing at Youlgreave, a village 3 miles south of Bakewell

compass even from devotees who walk them obsessively. Kinder has the bigger following, with the exquisite cul-de-sac village of Edale at its foot and the choice of numerous walks which can begin and end there without retracing of footsteps.

The village is a cosy huddle in a broad green vale, worth a visit merely to look at: something indefinable in the scale and arrangement of buildings against setting. True, there is now a sizeable car park, plus public lavatories; but this was a necessary piece of tidying-up, rather than 'development', and it left the village itself unmolested.

Edale is the southern starting point of the Pennine Way. A little purpose-built bridge across the gurgling Grindsbrook stream replaces the felled tree that used to set walkers off on the 250 miles to the Scottish border. Crossing Grindsbrook at this point does not, of course, render an obligation to keep going for the two weeks that the Pennine Way commonly requires. Countless carloads of the elderly frail, the infantile and the perfectly hale and lazy simply wander on a couple of hundred yards to find a picnic spot and perhaps dip their toes in some chilling little ring of bright water. You can day-trip to Edale very pleasantly. You can ski there, too.

The title 'cradle of English rock-climbing' is generally attributed to the Lake District, and more particularly to Wasdale Head, from where debonair Victorian gentlemen – they had to be gentlemen, otherwise they would not have had the leisure to make the journey or the money to afford it – discovered exhilarating sport on Great Gable and Pillar. But it is a fair argument that the Peak District provided the nursery for modern English climbing. The reason, again, is the simple fact of the Peak's accessibility to places where a lot of people live. Two of the legendary figures in post-war mountaineering, Joe Brown and Don Whillans, took their first steps towards extraordinary activities in the Alps and Himalayas by grappling inquisitively with the odd 40 or 50 feet of upright Peak gritstone.

Brown went looking for light and air not available to him in one of the gloomier bits of Manchester. Whillans found it equally necessary to break out of Salford. They have reason to be specially grateful for the Peak; but in this they are merely the most famous in a multitude who hold a lifelong attachment to the district and the airy adventure it so readily offers.

Peak District rock-climbing gives plenty of scope to the novice, but it also provides some alarming challenges to the most expert. The extra merit of the latter category, as far as the non-climber is concerned, is that you may just chance to get a close-up view of one such brute being tackled as you pause in a stroll from your parked car. There is a considerable thrill in this, it may not need to be said – except that the excitement is heightened by a sense of privilege. The climber is not putting on a show: he is practising his special skills for the personal satisfaction of it.

On a brilliant May Sunday I turned about 20 yards off a popular footpath, hoping to find climbers in action on the crags overlooking a valley road with its straggle of houses and muffled traffic, nose-to-tail. Sure enough there were the expected little groups of serious faces, much red rope, crash helmets and some cautious work to give relaxed entertainment. Then quite casually a lone youth appeared at the foot of something no one else was attempting, and began moving upwards. He was dressed in denim shorts and a singlet, with no rope, no helmet. Clearly he was merely trying out a couple of moves, and would drop back to earth again in a moment or two. He did not. He went up and up. A little bag of chalk dangled from his belt at the small of his back, and between moves he dipped his fingers into it. That was his only aid to security as he progressed from one scratch on the rock to another, until ending the climb with a couple of little diagonal hops.

It was a piece of private athleticism of dazzling ease. I suggested to the other climbers that what I had just watched may have impressed them, as well. They agreed. They checked with the guidebook and said the climb was graded 'exceptionally severe', beyond which difficulty of ascent a man needs wings. This sort of climbing also happens elsewhere, of course, but it is particular to the Peak District that it can be happened upon quite so effortlessly.

Men with wings were, in fact, hovering in the sky not far away at the time: hang-gliding is the newest of Peak sports. On the same afternoon a village cricket match close to the hotel I stayed at in Baslow featured the ghost of W. G. Grace, bearded and vast-bellied and showing signs of grumpiness in the heat. Had I wished, I could have gone underground to admire electrically floodlit caverns. Instead I took a walk along a lane running beside the River Derwent, where the noise from the main roads was abruptly gone: small enterprise hugely rewarded.

It is roughly around Baslow where the gritstone begins to give way to the limestone that provides the southern part of the district with its name of the White Peak. In strong sunlight the drystone walls have the gleam almost of snow. This is pastoral, wooded country, very gentle on the eye. It contains villages and hamlets which make a virtue of aimless meandering: usually a no-nonsense pub, probably a photogenic hump-backed bridge over a glinting stream with a 'private fishing' sign, and a tranquillity to play tricks with your sense of time. Arguably, the definitive White Peak meander is to drift southwards from Hartington into Dovedale, through Beresford Dale, Alstonefield and Milldale, and then north again via Tissington. The old railway lines hereabouts have been turned into grassy tracks – the ironware removed – so that one may now walk along winding, gentle gradients, springy under foot and often banked around head height on both sides. The effect of these sunken green trails is both eerie and soporific.

A good base from which to 'do' the Peak? Bakewell is an exceptionally attractive small town, with a resplendent Gothic-arched bridge over the River Wye. And it has a notably good bookshop – thereby satisfying my personal test of small towns worth a linger.

ARTHUR HOPCRAFT

Bakewell

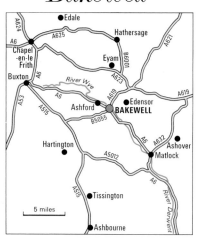

WHERE TO GO

Old Market Hall: early 17th c building with low mullioned windows. Now houses Peak National Park Information Centre. Information on all aspects of Peak Park – walking, wildlife, events, etc, with occasional illustrated talks upstairs. Displays show history of Bakewell.
All Saints: high on hill overlooking town, a typical Derbyshire church, mainly 13th–14th c, low and embattled with tower and spire. Built on Saxon site, 9th c cross in churchyard and mass of fragments of ornamented Saxon masonry inside south porch and at back of church. Chapel has monuments to Vernon family of Haddon Hall.
Old House Museum, Cunningham Place: beyond church at top of hill, museum of local bygones in one of Bakewell's oldest buildings, dating from 1534. Open daily Easter–end Oct 2.30–5.00.
Old Town Hall, King St: built 1602 with town hall and courthouse at top and St John's Hospital on ground floor but altered 1709 when almshouses were built just behind. In 350 years an astonishing variety of occupants including school, working-men's club, fire-engine house, butter market and fish shop. Restored and now used by local antique dealer.
River Wye: winds round Bakewell with 14th c bridge the favourite postcard scene. From here, a short walk through sheep-filled Scots Gardens leads to Holme Hall, a fine old country house of 1626; Lumford Cottages, built originally by Arkwright; and narrow 17th c packhorse bridge that takes you back over river to Victoria Mill (with gigantic water-wheel) and to Bakewell again.

SHOPPING

General and cattle market: Mon.
Early closing: Thur.
The Bookshop, corner King St/Matlock St: Derbyshire must be one of most documented areas – excellent selection of guides stocked here, plus a few secondhand editions. Open Mon–Sat and Sun afternoons 1.30–5.30.
Antiques Coffee House, Buxton Rd: rambling shop, rooms piled high with china, bric-à-brac, old clothes and 19th and early 20th c country-made furniture.
Butchers' shops: try their oatcakes to take home and fry with eggs and bacon, and, from Nelsons, Buxton Rd, warm crusty pork pies.

FOOD AND DRINK

Pubs include: **Peacock Hotel,** comfortable local near Market Place serving Wards beer – jolly atmosphere and jukebox; **Red Lion,** The Square, a free house pleasantly done up with restaurant and steak bar; the roomy **Wheatsheaf,** nearly opposite, serving Mansfield beer, bar meals, cobs and sandwiches. Egon Ronay's *Just a Bite* recommends **Old Original Bakewell Pudding Shop,** The Square, for famous pudding of almondy custard in light fluffy pastry, also wide variety of snacks, breakfasts and lunches; and **Country Kitchen,** 5 King St (behind craft shop), for tasty home-made soups, pizzas, cakes and 'things on toast'.

WHERE TO STAY

Egon Ronay's Lucas Guide recommends **Rutland Arms Hotel,** The Square, tel Bakewell 2812. If you're having a drink in the bar, try local sparkling Ashbourne water instead of soda with your whisky.

TOURIST INFORMATION

National Park Information Centre, Old Market Hall: Open April–Oct daily 10.00–6.00, Nov–March daily 10.00–6.00 except Wed, Thur. Closed for lunch 1.00–2.00. Telephone Bakewell 3227.

The Gothic-arched bridge in Bakewell

Villages and country towns

Ashbourne

Delightful town with friendly people and splendid architecture. Two main streets, Church St and St John St, full of fine Georgian buildings and interesting little backwaters. St Oswald's at end of Church St is one of Derbyshire's grandest churches, dating from 13th c. Nearby, pink-grey 17th c almshouses with tiny mullioned windows and angled chimney stacks. Near town centre in St John St, ancient sign of the Green Man and Black's Head Hotel spans the road – grinning one side, glum the other. At Hamilton House, Church St, recently opened toy museum with Georgian board games, 1930s train sets, giant Meccano model, among other things. Also operates a dolls' hospital. Opening times April–Oct weekdays 11.00–5.30, Sun 2.00–5.30, Nov–March Sat 11.00–5.30, Sun and Bank Hol Mon 2.00–5.30. Nearly opposite, at 30b, Kenneth Upchurch's antique shop specializes in the bright lustres of studio pottery of 1920s

Eyam's international sundial

and 1930s, particularly William Moorcroft.

Good place for take-away food: in Victoria Square, Pizzeria da Sandro for lasagne, cannelloni, pizza, etc; fish and chip shop in the market place; and celebrated Ashbourne gingerbread from the Gingerbread Shop in St John St (also teas) and the Green Dragon Bakery. Market Thur and Sat, early closing Wed. An abundance of pubs: George and Dragon in Market Square has Home beer and toasted sandwiches plus darts and dominoes, the favourites around here. The White Hart, Church St, with piano, Marstons beer, snacks, darts and dominoes.

Pubs stay open all day, with windows boarded, for the famous Shrove Tuesday football match when town divides into 'up'ards' and 'down'ards' – those who live above or below Henmore Brook. Any method of passing the ball allowed, except by car, and goals are scored by touching walls of two old mills three miles apart. Of the 300 players a side, some wind up in the river and some with broken limbs, but it's talked about for the rest of the year.

Ashford in the Water

Pretty village just outside Bakewell that grew up round ancient ford over River Wye. Sheepwash Bridge has stone pen at side where sheep were rounded up and pushed in the water to swim downstream to rejoin their lambs. Church, mostly Victorian, has 18th c maidens' funeral garlands hanging in the aisle – curious lampshade shapes trimmed with ribbons and rosettes, sometimes with a glove hanging from the centre, carried in funeral processions of girls who died before their wedding day. Until 1905 Ashford was centre of the black marble industry, a dark limestone quarried on edge of village, polished jet black and used for inlay – good examples at Chatsworth and Buxton Museum. Quarries now lie under A6.

Two pubs, both with real ale – the Bull's Head has Robinsons beer and snacks; the Devonshire Arms, large pub with garden where children are welcome, has Stones best bitter, meals, pool, darts and dominoes.

For scenic route home take road to Monsal Dale where railway viaduct, which enraged Victorian conservationists, cuts through rocky valley (but car

park at top gets crowded in high season). Farther on in valley, least Satanic of mills, Georgian Cressbrook Mill with cupola that housed bell to summon the workers.

Ashover

Sleepy village on side of Amber valley, surrounded by green meadows and wooded hills. Favourite centre for geology students because of strange rock formation here. Many attractive Georgian houses, some three-storeyed like town houses, and exceptionally pretty school with shaped gables and dainty criss-cross leaded windows. Now used as Sunday school only. Church with soaring spire is set amid grand old limes. Its lead font, decorated with figures of the Apostles, is one of about 30 in the country, and dates from 12th c when Ashover was great lead-mining centre. Pubs have character: Crispin Inn is said to date from 1416 when men of Ashover returned from battle of Agincourt fought on St Crispin's Day, Home beer, sandwiches, dominoes and darts; Red Lion Inn, an enormous pub with mock Tudor exterior and Mansfield beer, snacks, pool, darts and dominoes.

Edale

According to the locals not a village but a 'booth', a scattering of houses like its neighbours Nether and Barber Booth. Set deep in a dale and surrounded by giant hills, Mam Tor, the 'shivering mountain', and Kinder Scout, it's become the walking centre of the Dark Peak. Unceremoniously announced, the Pennine Way starts here, now trekked every year by thousands. Peak National Park Centre has excellent range of guides to walking, wildlife, geology, history of the moors, and operates a camping site – very popular so book early. Details from National Park Centre, Aldern House, Baslow Rd, Bakewell, DE14 1AE, enclosing sae.

Little Victorian church – the drystone walls around it were pulled down by the massive snow drifts in 1979. A couple of general stores selling hikers' and campers' provisions, and craft-cum-gift shop also has 'walkers' extras'. Good cheery pub, the Old Nag's Head, has Theakstons beer and bumper-sized Cornish pasties. For accommodation, Landmark Trust's skilfully converted 19th c Edale Mill has been described by one visitor as having 'the right combination of luxury and puritanism'. Details from Landmark Trust, Shottesbrooke, Maidenhead, Berks, tel Littlewick Green 3431.

Edensor

Pronounced Ensor. Interesting estate village rebuilt 1838–42 on edge of park by sixth Duke of Devonshire who wanted it out of sight of Chatsworth. Designed by Paxton and his assistant John Robertson, using an extraordinary mixture of styles – Swiss chalet roofs, Italianate windows, bargeboarding and Elizabethan sugar-twist chimneys. Church built later (1867) by Sir George Gilbert Scott, with Paxton buried in huge tomb chest in centre of churchyard. Combined post office, village store and Stables Tea Rooms with first-rate cream teas and iced cakes.

For those who want to find out more about history of estate villages (of which there are many in Derbyshire), Gillian Darley's fascinating **Villages of Vision** is a Paladin paperback.

Eyam

Pronounced Eem. Famous 'plague village' that tried to contain the disease by shutting itself off from rest of country under leadership of Rector William Mompesson. Germs arrived in box of cloth sent from London to village tailor in 1665. By 1666 about 250 of the 350 villagers had died. Many cottages marked with names and dates of victims who died in them. Private museum has more relics – admission by appointment, tel Hope Valley 31010.

In front of Eyam Hall, three-tiered Jacobean manor house with plain gables and mullioned windows, is a dell called Cucklet Church where Mompesson preached in the open air, thinking it less infectious. Commemorative service held here on last Sun in Aug. Well-dressing takes place in last week of Aug. St Lawrence's church has Mompesson's chair (found in Liverpool junk shop) and, in churchyard, Saxon cross carved with mixture of pagan and Christian symbols. On wall, remarkable Georgian sundial from which you can work out time in such faraway places as Isfahan, Mexico and Calcutta. Two tiny antique shops with pretty china, small fish and chip shop, and several pubs, including Bull's Head serving John Smiths beer and excellent toasted sandwiches, and

Almshouses in Ashbourne, a town with some splendid architecture

Miners Arms with Stones beer, hot food, ploughman's lunches.

Hartington

Open village with large market square and duck and goose pond. Pink and grey stone church stands high above, with battlements, pinnacles and gargoyles. Good place for exploring Beresford Dale and Upper Dove, less crowded than further down the valley. Favourite haunt of local 17th c hero Charles Cotton who helped his great friend Izaak Walton write the chapter on fly fishing in *The Compleat Angler*, 1653. Their famous fishing temple still stands above Pike Pool, not easy to find or accessible to public, but it's enough for most anglers to fish in the same waters. Just outside Hartington, walkers and cyclists can join the Tissington Trail – 11½ miles of converted Ashbourne–Buxton railway track through superb countryside. Two or three general stores, gift shops and tearooms, while the Charles Cotton Hotel – his poems on the wall – is a pleasant friendly pub with Bass Worthington beer, meals and snacks.

Hathersage

Hillside village used by Charlotte Brontë as Morton in *Jane Eyre*. Again, church stands high up on hill, castellated and pinnacled with gargoyles of tiger's head and muzzled bear. Robin Hood's Little John is said to be buried in outsize grave in churchyard. Inside, brasses commemorate the Eyres, old Catholic family.

Good open-air swimming pool. Delicious ice creams from Bannermans, and plenty of pubs and places to eat to choose from. The Little John is a Whitbread pub, the Hathersage Inn has Sherwood Forest restaurant, and Scotchman's Pack Inn, at top of hill near church, has Little John's chair, home-made steak and kidney pie with mushy peas, Stones bitter and draught Bass.

Close by is Stanage Edge, where pioneer rock-climbers such as J. W. Puttrell originated the sport in 1890s. At the bottom are scores of abandoned millstones, cut from the rock but for some reason never taken away.

Tissington

Old estate village down long, gated avenue of limes, hard to match for its restrained beauty. Large pond and green at one end with little Norman church, raised up on a grassy slope. Jacobean Tissington Hall, built 1609, is home of the FitzHerberts, lords of the manor since 15th c. In the Old School Tea Rooms tempting home-made cakes are served with a good pot of tea and fine china. Also morning coffee and light lunches.

Much visited, especially around welldressing time (Ascension Day), Tissington is said to be the village where it all started. Two traditions: one that the purity of the springs kept Tissington free of disease during the Black Death; the other that in great drought of 1615 Tissington's wells never ran dry. Five wells altogether are dressed with intricate and colourful pictures made up of petals, seeds, berries and lichens pressed into clay.

Places to visit

Bolsover Castle: dramatic ruins of Jacobean castle perched on hill-brow overlooking smoky collieries and railway sidings. Built 1612 on site of Norman castle by Bess of Hardwick's son Sir Charles Cavendish – Hardwick Hall on the horizon. Magical atmosphere with medieval-style keep (closed at present for repair) and great baroque riding school, long gallery and terrace. On outside wall of gallery, unique architectural feature – banded shafts, like cannons, between the windows. Charles I and Queen were stupendously entertained here on 30 July 1634 at cost of £15,000. Destroyed, not surprisingly, a few years later by Parliamentarians in Civil War. Open May–Sept daily 9.30–7.00, April daily 9.30–5.30, March, Oct weekdays 9.30–5.30 Sun 2.00–5.30, Nov–Feb weekdays 9.30–4.00 Sun 2.00–4.00.

Chatsworth: 'Palace of the Peak' built by Dukes of Devonshire. Full of masterpieces and curiosities, rooms suggest generations of inveterate collectors, but sixth Duke was 'had' when he bought the huge stone foot in the chapel corridor thinking it to be antique relic – it was a 19th c fake! Beautiful gardens (partly created by Paxton) with statues, fountains and famous cascade that tumbles down from temple. All set in acres of sheep-filled parkland, with fascinating farmyard and milking demonstration every afternoon at 3.30. Also farm shop at Pilsley village selling estate produce – legs of lamb, soft cheese, honey and Jacob wool, and excellent souvenir shop in house. A full day's entertainment. House open April–Oct Tues–Sun and bank hol 11.30–4.30, garden only Mon 11.30–5.00, Nov–Dec Sun 11.30–2.30. On B6012 four miles east of Bakewell.

Haddon Hall: romantic medieval manor house built around courtyard of castellated towers, turrets and gargoyles. Abandoned during 18th and 19th c by Dukes of Rutland in favour of Belvoir, it has survived unaltered. Restored by ninth Duke during 1920s. Rooms and galleries full of remarkable carved panelling, Tudor painted ceilings and tapestries. Medieval kitchen has unusual collection of dole cupboards with fancy fretwork doors to ventilate the food and keep the dogs out. Charming terraced gardens look down over grazing sheep and the River Wye. Open April–Sept Tue–Sat and Bank Hol Mon 11.00–6.00, Bank Hol Sun 2.00–6.00. Two miles southeast of Bakewell on A6.

Hardwick Hall: 'Hardwick Hall, more glass than wall', as the saying goes. Strange and beautiful house built by indomitable Bess of Hardwick who had a mania for building and knack of marrying well to finance it. A stone's throw from the Old Hall, started 1591 when Bess was in her 70s. Full of the finest examples of Elizabethan furniture and needlecraft. The High Great Chamber, unusually at top of house, was described by Sir Sacheverell Sitwell as 'the most beautiful room in the whole of Europe'. If not that, it certainly has the most extraordinary sense of light and grandeur. Elizabethan herb garden and herbaceous borders an inspiration for gardeners. Open April–Oct Wed, Thur, Sat, Sun, Bank Hol Mon 1.00–5.30 or dusk if earlier. Garden open from 12.00. Light lunches 12.00–2.00 and teas 2.15–5.00 in Great Kitchen. 6½ miles north-west of Mansfield, 9½ miles south-east of Chesterfield. National Trust.

Kedleston Hall: built for Sir Nathaniel Curzon, first Baron Scarsdale, c 1760, a fervent admirer of architecture of ancient Rome. Interior and domed south front designed by Robert Adam. Marble hall of classical splendour with fluted columns of pink alabaster, statues of gods and goddesses, Homeric scenes and magnificent coved ceiling. Original Adam furnishings and colours in other rooms – watery silks and pastel tinted ceilings. Indian museum in basement with oriental works of art collected by Lord Curzon while Viceroy of India. Garden dotted with statues, temple and domed summer house. Open Sun unly, last Sun in April to last in Sept, and Bank Hol Mon 2.00–6.00, park from 12.30. 4½ miles northwest of Derby (well signposted).

Wingfield Manor: wonderful ruins of great house built by Ralph, Lord Cromwell, c 1440 and destroyed during Civil War. In the middle of a farm, with farmhouse incorporated into it, incongruously jumbled up with bee-hives, fruit trees, peacock and cow yard. Mary Queen of Scots imprisoned here 1569 and 1584–5. In inner quadrangle among the runner beans is a walnut tree said to have grown from a nut dropped by Anthony Babbington who used to visit the Queen disguised as a gipsy, staining his skin with walnut juice. As long as they don't park in the way of tractors, farmer is happy to let visitors wander round the maze of rooms – don't miss dark stairway leading down to elegant vaulted crypt. At Manor Farm, South Wingfield village, nr Matlock.

Crich Tramway Museum: Edwardian street scene reconstructed in disused quarry railway cutting with gas lamps, ornate cast-iron tram stop, enamelled advertising signs for Brasso, Force Flakes, etc, and façade of Derby assembly rooms. Fleet of some 40 trams dating from 1873 to 1953, from Portugal to Leeds, takes you on a 20-minute ride down valley and back. On Aug Bank Hol there's usually a Grand Transport Extravaganza with flea market, when visitors arrive on anything on wheels – steam traction engines, vintage buses etc. For details tel Ambergate 2565. Staffed voluntarily by tram enthusiasts. Open April–Oct Sat, Sun, bank hol 10.30–5.00, June–Aug Tue, Wed, Thur as well 10.00–4.00. Near Matlock.

Riber Castle Wildlife Park: rare breeds' survival trust centre in hilltop setting around ruined castle. Splendid collection of domestic animals that have disappeared from the modern farm, including droopy-eared Nubian goats, long-snouted Gloucester Old Spot pigs, bagots imported by Crusaders; plus statuesque lynxes from all over world. In early summer lots of squealing young animals. Open all year, July–Aug 10.00–7.00 daily, closes earlier in winter. Off B614 just outside Matlock towards Tansley.

Caverns: several in area open to public. Castleton is good centre with four. Derbyshire Blue John deposits at Treak Cliff Cavern, open daily Easter–Oct 10.00–6.00, winter 10.00–4.00, and Blue John Cavern, open all year daily 9.30–6.00 or dusk. Peak cavern is Britain's largest natural limestone cave, open Easter–mid-Sept daily 10..0–5.00, Fri 1.00–5.00, and Speedwell Cavern is an old lead mine with mile-long underground boat ride, open all year daily 10.00–6.00. Good examples of Blue John at the Ollerenshaw Collection, Castleton, open all year daily 9.00–6.00.

Buxton Opera House: splendid Edwardian opera house re-opened 1979. Opera season part of annual summer Buxton international arts festival, but opera house open all year. Details of programme from box office or Tourist Information Centre, The Crescent.

Derbyshire Craft Centre: wide selection of local crafts – pottery, woodturning, weaving, hand-spun wool from Gritstone sheep – with demonstrations by craftsmen most weekends. Wholefood restaurant and play-room for children. Open daily. At Calver Bridge nr Baslow.

ACTIVITIES

Taking the waters: Buxton old baths closed now but spa water is sold bottled at Tourist Information Centre, in the Pump Room, The Crescent, and new swimming pool is fed with water from the thermal springs.

Industrial archaeology: this has been lead-mining area since Roman times.

Mining museum showing history at Matlock Bath Pavilion, open daily 11.00–4.00. Good examples of mining towns now no bigger than villages at Bonsall and Winster.

Cromford is interesting place to study beginnings of industrial revolution. One of Britain's earliest planned industrial communities with Arkwright's first water-powered cotton mill, 1771 (now a trout farm), just down Crich turning. On Matlock Rd, red brick Masson Mill – central block with Venetian windows

built 1783 by Arkwright now sandwiched between later additions but still making sewing thread. On the other side of A6 in Cromford village, North St – complete row of houses built by Arkwright for his workers, three-storeyed with large attics intended as framework knitting rooms. No 10 a Landmark Trust holiday house (details from Landmark Trust, Shottesbrooke, Maidenhead, Berks, tel Littlewick Green 3431).

At top of hill between Cromford and Wirksworth – Middleton Top Engine Winding House. Old steam winding engine built 1825–9 to haul wagons of Cromford and High Peak Railway up steep incline. This remarkable engineering project linked Cromford Canal and Peak Forest Canal, forming an important transport network. Open Sun 10.30–5.00 and in operation first Sat of each month.

Horse-drawn canal barges: trips in traditional narrowboats along canal from Cromford to Leawood Pump. April–end Sept boats leave Cromford Sat–Sun afternoons 2.00 and 4.00. Leawood Pump (1849 beam engine) in steam April–Oct monthly. Check dates and any other enquiries with Cromford Canal Soc, Old Wharf, Mill Lane, Cromford. Boats available for charter weekdays, tel Wirksworth 3727 or Winster 403.

Cycle hire: Peak Park and Derbyshire Council run three cycle hire centres in

area: at Parsley Hay, two miles south of Monyash, tel Hartington 493; Middleton Top, near old engine house off Cromford–Wirksworth road, tel Wirksworth 3204; Ashbourne, nr swimming pool, tel Ashbourne 3156. Privately owned centres at Monsal Head, four miles north-west of Bakewell on B6465, tel Great Longstone 505; and Dial-a-Bike at Parwich nr Ashbourne, tel Parwich 337. Leaflets from Park and Tourist offices.

Stagecoach tours: a dashing, but more costly, way of seeing Derbyshire – three-day stagecoach tours stopping off at old coaching inns, or day trips in stagecoach, landau, phaeton or Irish jaunting car. Also courses in driving singles, pairs, tandem and four in hand. Full details from Red House Stables, Darley School of Equitation, Darley Dale, nr Matlock, tel Darley Dale 3583.

Angling: mostly private fishing but permits available to residents of some hotels including Rutland Arms, Bakewell; Peacock Hotel, Rowsley; Marquis of Granby, Bamford; Izaak Walton Hotel, nr Thorpe. Speciality trout and grayling. Fly fishing only at Ladybower Reservoir – tickets from Fisheries office by reservoir at Bamford, tel Bamford 254.

Wallabies: walkers in south-west part of moors might be startled to see a

Trips in traditional horse-drawn barges operate along the canal from Cromford

One of the fleet of 40 working trams at Crich Tramway Museum

wallaby hop out in front of them. One of more bizarre escape stories: small colony has managed to breed and live here for many years, even through severe winters, but they are shy creatures and will survive only if left alone.

Tissington and High Peak trails: imaginative scheme that has made the most of miles of disused railway track running through some of most beautiful areas of Derbyshire. Grassed over, with convenient car parks and cycle hire centres, the trails provide easy walking, cycling and pony-trekking routes linking Ashbourne and Hartington and Cromford and Dowlow, nr Buxton. Further details from Peak Park information offices.

Fossils: look out for – but don't remove – remains of primeval creatures in the drystone walls. There are certainly some at Hope.

FOOD AND DRINK

Cat and Fiddle, at Wildboarclough on Macclesfield–Buxton road (A537) – the second highest pub in England, not always accessible in winter, with real beer from Robinsons Stockport brewery, restaurant and bar snacks.

Egon Ronay's Lucas Guide recommends **Cavendish Hotel Restaurant**, Baslow, tel Baslow 2311 – interesting and unusual dishes. **Peacock Hotel Restaurant**, Rowsley, tel Darley Dale 3518 – mainly English dishes, honestly cooked, generous portions. **New Bath Hotel Restaurant**, Matlock Bath, tel Matlock 3275 – international favourites, grills and roasts. **Izaak Walton Hotel Restaurant**, Dovedale, tel Thorpe Cloud 261 – good range of classic English and French dishes, well-cooked. **Ye Olde Nag's Head Restaurant**, Castleton, tel Hope Valley 20248 – English and Continental specialities in old stone inn.

TOURIST INFORMATION

Publications: *Derbyshire Times*, published on Fri, *Ashbourne News Telegraph* and *Buxton Advertiser*, Thur.

Peak National Park: useful calendar of walks and talks on dowsing, prehistory, bird-watching, plus details of well-dressings, sheepdog trials, etc, available in advance from National Park Office, Aldern House, Baslow Rd, Bakewell DE4 1AE, enclosing 9in × 4¾in sae.

Research: Pamela Brown.

The gritstone rocks of the Peak District

Skipton

There's a corner of the Yorkshire Dales so foreign-seeming and distinctive that its boundaries, although absent from any map, are instantly detectable. Surveyed as the village of Craven in the Domesday Book, it probably took its name from the ancient British word 'craig-ven', meaning stony place. At any rate, the district of Craven has never lost its association with the crescent of pure limestone that is the dominant gene, so to speak, in the ancestry of the landscape.

That a mere rock should inspire affection as well as admiration may seem surprising, but for centuries topographers, geologists, archaeologists, botanists, historians, poets, painters and people simply writing home on postcards have all tried to do justice to the character of the Great Scar Limestone. At its most ingratiating, it produces rounded contours neatly covered in short green turf, and lends itself to waterfalls; but now and then, like a great grey iceberg, light-reflecting, it rises through the scant soils in spectacular walls, the 'scars', or emerges in broad fissured terraces, the 'pavements', while its thicker depths are honeycombed with caves and passages that sheltered first packs of hyenas, then men.

This beautiful but stubborn rock, susceptible only to the scouring and gouging of ice or the wearing down of running water, is capped by coarser, darker, more malleable sandstone; the flat-topped pyramids of Ingleborough, Penyghent and Whernside – heights that dominate Craven but are wrenched apart by the Craven Fault which is seen to dramatic effect beside the A65 beyond Settle.

These, then, are the materials, quarried by hand, from which local stone buildings and drystone walls were built. Today, the people of Craven wince to see the lorries, like giant ants, bearing away their limestone load by load; from farmers to shopkeepers, from school-children to scientists, they know their underlying rocks by touch as well as eye, and have given them proprietorial names.

Coming down through the village of Upper Settle on the old packhorse trial from Malhamdale – and there are worse introductions to Craven topography – you pass Twistleton's Yard. A little farther on there is Twistleton's Scar. Twistleton was a Victorian farmer turned dialect poet (the tradition persists: wayside encounters can persuade the visitor that *all* Dales farmers are dialect poets). 'Such scenes as these, when seen in spring,' he wrote, 'Wad mak a Quaker dance and sing,' and sold his verses like hot cakes to the tourists.

By the mid-nineteenth century, hard-pressed cabhorses were hauling the bourgeoisie in their thousands up the steep hillsides above Settle, Clapham and Ingleton, to be overawed by the gothic grandeurs

Clapham, on the lower slopes of Ingleborough near the famous caves

of the scenery and – ladies having first removed their crinoline hoops – the sensation of the day, the newly opened show-caves. In these now world-famous chambers, local potholers had stumbled upon important remains, from extinct mammal bones in the pre-glacial hyena dens to a rich Romano-British hoard. In 1979, a collection of objects found around Settle was exhibited for the first time in the new Pig Yard Museum, so-called because, in the 1920s, a cavers' club met to discuss their finds in an old piggery.

Some pieces combine elegance, utility and rarity: a decorated lance over 12,000 years old made of reindeer antler is among the earliest evidence for man in the north of England. An on-site museum like this brings the past clearly into focus; on a bleak day, when the empty fells look like tundra, it is easy to visualize hunter and prey: he would surely have been an expert, confident of retrieving his fine weapon.

Visiting the self-sufficient Dales, with their vivid scenes and speech, their sweet-smelling hay-meadows, Victorian carriage-folk would have approved the neat and pleasant villages, the unpretentious solidity of the seventeenth-century houses, the number of Quaker meeting-houses and Methodist chapels, and the churches rebuilt and refurbished, most of them, in the style John Betjeman calls Craven regional Perp. Almost new then were the cotton mills still standing by the streams, and the multiple spans of Ribblehead viaduct that required a sprawl of shanty towns to house the 'foreign' labour.

Thomas Dunham Whitaker, the patrician vicar who published his *History of Craven* in 1801 – two absorbing volumes of insufferable opinions and fascinating domestic detail – despised these 'manufactories' as 'hot-beds of early immorality, premature marriage and unnatural population', complaining that one even polluted the Craven beauty-spot most admired by the Romantic Movement, Malham Cove. In order to understand the tributes paid to Malham and nearby Gordale Scar, one must visit them in weather so uncongenial that even the climbers are kept indoors. Under such conditions, the landscape has a black-and-white starkness, but the sweet greens of spring and summer are swamped, these days, by the primary plastic colours of the crowds.

Converging on Skipton and Settle are medieval tracks, the 'green roads' that make Craven uniquely accessible to the walker. Salt-ways, packhorse trails, drove roads, market roads, criss-cross the rugged exposed terrain like wrinkles on the palm of an old man's hand; one after another, they fell into disuse, isolating villages and hamlets. These communities preserve a genuine distinctiveness that continues to resist both banalization and self-consciousness. A visit to, say, Clapham, Austwick, Langcliffe, Stainforth, Horton-in-Ribblesdale, Thorpe and Linton – to name a mere sprinkling – will confirm that the very real pleasures of friendly people, all-purpose shops, good pubs, decent architecture (for some surprises, see Linton), set off by green spaces and clear streams, can still be enjoyed.

They are united by a local patriotism that the outsider immediately senses and can only envy. It saved the Skiptonians during the Civil

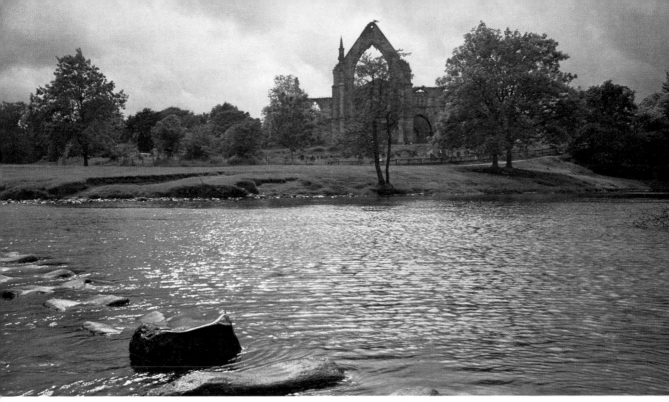

Bolton Abbey: the nave is still used
as a parish church

War, when the Royalist population within the castle was besieged – but
only in the most gentlemanly fashion – by another Skiptonian. It
supports two of the most conservative and successful publications in
England, the *Craven Herald and Pioneer*, a weekly broadsheet still
printed on machinery bought secondhand, 50 years ago, from the
Yorkshire Post, and *The Dalesman*, a sedate nostalgic monthly with a
healthy circulation which reaches Yorkshire exiles all over the world.

Yet the centres of Skipton and Settle, far from being smug rural
backwaters, have an almost European atmosphere. In the sunshine,
Settle looks like an Italian hill-town, with distinguished and eccentric
buildings and narrow backstreets, 'ginnels' and 'snickets', winding up
towards Castleberg crag which casts a shadow so long that it served as a
sundial. Skipton has a hidden eighteenth-century canal quarter and a
fine broad mall where market stalls recall the French provinces, a
confectioner's window has trays of elegant hand-made chocolates, and
a butcher sells 2000 home-made pork-pies a day, three hundredweight
at weekends, to discriminating residents. Banks, building societies and
accountants prosper: Skipton is the marketing centre for Craven livestock, and Dales farmers, as the saying goes, 'have wool on their backs'.

Perhaps because, at intervals in their history, the limestone has half
grudged them a living, the farmers appear as a group apart – a republic,
almost – ruled according to its own laws and mores. They were badly
treated, once, when the Enclosure Acts imposed a geometrical pattern
of drystone walls over their common land, driving out the weak. Today
they thrive, but they are also thrifty. More than anything else, it is their
independent character, *sui generis*, that dominates the region of Craven,
and the Dales.

JOANNA KILMARTIN

Skipton

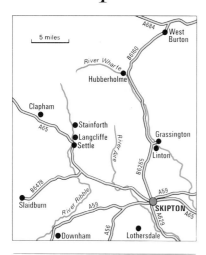

WHERE TO GO

High St: a thriving shopping centre with market stalls there most days. It is lined with a mixture of mainly 18th and 19th c stone and stucco buildings including several pubs. One house has a plaque reminding us that Edmund Kean acted here in the old theatre housed in the buildings behind. This is not the only interesting backview – there are arches in a lot of the buildings leading through to alleys and a covered market behind the Black Horse.

Holy Trinity Church: raised above the level of the High St it dominates one end of it. A long, low battlemented building typical of the area, it is mainly 14th and 15th c although restored in 17th c, after Civil War siege. Interesting bits and pieces inside include carved stone heads in nave, fine screen and font-cover, memorials to young men who died in 19th c colonial wars, Clifford family tombs, especially black marble slab for Queen Elizabeth I's champion and hand of death fresco nr door.

Castle: part of the building dates from 12th c. The splendid four-towered gateway through which you enter has the Clifford motto 'Desormais' cut in stone above it. This takes you into the spacious bailey. Castle keep has lovely central conduit court with ancient yew tree. Open all year round from 10.00 (Sun 2.00). Last admission 6.00 or sunset.

High Corn Mill at Mill Bridge: there has been a corn mill on this site since 13th c. Today two of the water wheels are re-stored and drive a variety of machinery – winnowers, oat rollers, straw choppers, turnip shredders – as well as stone-grinding flour. There is a collection of other old equipment including a black-smith's forge. The mill is open most Sun at 12.00.

Skipton Woods, behind High Corn Mill: with a fine view of the back of the castle on its formidable rock. Higher up in the woods is the dam that controls the flow of Eller Beck – water supply to the mill.

Canals: the Springs canal, which runs through the centre of town to Mill Bridge and the castle, is a branch of the Leeds–Liverpool canal which was opened here in 1770. It, and later the railway, gave the impetus to Skipton's industrial development.

Craven Museum in the High St: houses early remains found in the district, particularly those from the Iron Age settlements at Grassington and local Roman encampments, as well as a Bronze Age coffin. It also has a fine geological collection and equipment from the local lead-mining industry. Open April–Sept every day except Tue, week-days 11.00–5.00, Sat 10.00–12.00 and 1.00–5.00, Sun 2.00–5.00, Oct–March weekdays except Tue 2.00–5.00, Sat 10.00–12.00 and 1.30–4.30.

ACTIVITIES

Canal trips: Pennine Boats, Coach St, tel Skipton 60829, do hour-long canal trips. They also rent out their six cruisers. You can hire narrowboats at Silsden, tel Steeton 54552.

Yorkshire Dales Railway: at Embsay Station about a mile out of Skipton, off Bolton Abbey road. Has steam-train trips over a short distance of line. Its collection of 20 locomotives, vintage carriages, a miniature railway and shop is open every weekend, but the trains usually get steam up only on summer Sun and bank hol. Look in local press or tel for details – Skipton 4727.

SHOPPING

Market day: Sat, but there are stalls in the High St every weekday except Tue. Cattle market on Mon and alternate Wed.

Early closing: Tue.

Rackhams: famous northern department store has a branch here (with tea-room).

Stainforths Celebrated Pork Pie Shop: at Mill Bridge.

Whittakers, High St: hand-made chocolates, morning coffee, lunches and afternoon tea.

Skipton mill by the 18th-century canal that runs right through the town

Stainforths celebrated pork pies in Skipton

Castle Antiques, in the High St, and the shops around Mill Bridge have good expensive-looking antiques, but **The Curiosity Shop** in Belmont St is a junky one worth looking at. (Addingham, which is a village a few miles east of Skipton on the Ilkley road, is rapidly becoming the antique centre for the area.) **Craven Books**, Newmarket St: good antiquarian bookshop.
Skipton Potters, Raikes Rd: open during the week 10.00–5.00.
The Dales Outdoor Centre, Coach St: all the latest mountaineering and camping equipment.

FOOD AND DRINK

The Black Horse in the High St is the main hotel, It is reputed to have been Richard III's mews when he owned the castle. There is a big hotel bar with beams and huge old fireplace, where you can drink Youngers beer and have meals or bar snacks. **Albion Inn** in Otley St, **Castle Inn** in Mill Bridge, **Devonshire**

Hotel and **Vaults** all serve Tetleys beer. **Chews Bar** in Swadford St is a cosy one-room bar which serves Bass and lunch-time snacks (closed Sun). Out of the centre you might try the **Craven Hotel** or a small backstreet Tetleys house – **The Railway Inn** off Keighley Rd. In Coach St there is **The Rose and Crown** and **The Barge** which is a converted warehouse overlooking the canal with a freehouse pub, a restaurant and a discotheque.

WHERE TO STAY

Egon Ronay's Lucas Guide recommends the **Devonshire Arms Hotel** at nearby Bolton Abbey, tel Bolton Abbey 265.

TOURIST INFORMATION

In the car park behind the High St, open 10.00–5.00, Sun 2.00–5.00. Official guidebook to Skipton available here with lots of other useful leaflets, pamphlets, many of which are free.

Villages and country towns

Clapham

Built on the lower slopes of Ingleborough, one of the three famous peaks of Craven. The houses stand on either side of the beck, which is lined for the whole length of the village by splendid trees. As it flows between them, Clapham Beck appears thoroughly domesticated, but it starts life as the Fell Beck which disappears so sensationally into the pothole Gaping Gill, re-emerging in the show-caves of Ingleborough, before thundering into the village as a waterfall behind the church. 19 c St James stands at the top of the village nr Ingleborough Hall, where the Farrer family lived.

The botanist Reginald Farrer, expert on oriental plants, is commemorated in the nature trail through the grounds of the hall he laid out, along a lakeside path to the caves. Leaflets obtainable from National Park Information Centre, tel Clapham 419. The walk to the caves is about $1\frac{1}{4}$ miles, but for a less frequented walk try path under tunnel by church, which leads you via Long Lane to old packhorse 'green lane' over Sulber to Selside in Ribblesdale, and eventually to Hawes in Wensleydale if you're fit.

There is a post office with souvenirs, a food shop, a pottery, a café, and bed and breakfast at Brook House down by the beck. The New Inn, a free house, has a cocktail lounge, and does meals. At the Flying Horse Shoe, Clapham Station, you can hire bicycles some weekends.

Dalesman Publications are based in Clapham and you can buy books from their showroom here.

Downham

One of the ring of villages round the bottom of Pendle – the mysterious hill associated with a group of 17th c witches. Downham is built down a hill facing Pendle, which seems from this side to be always in shadow. The village itself is not at all sinister, with a small grassy banked stream at the bottom, crossed by an upright little bridge. A series of fine stone houses and farms build up to the Edwardian church, Downham House, the post office and pub, at the top of the hill. The Assheton Arms serves bar snacks and dinners on Saturday nights.

Grassington

Although not much bigger than neighbouring villages, Grassington has developed quite differently and now has a surprisingly smart shopping centre concentrated in its main street and cobbled market square. It began to develop as a tourist centre in 19th c, but it was already the main centre for lead-mining in the area. Grassington Moor is still riddled with dangerous mine shafts and has the remains of the old smelting-mill. Today Grassington looks remarkably prosperous and even the back alleys are pretty and trimmed with flowers.

Upper Wharfedale Museum, in a cottage on the Market Square, is a well-laid-out folk museum with tools for various trades such as a cow-doctor's horse gag. The tea-room has an open fire in the range. Open daily 2.00–4.30 and Tue 7.30–9.00 too. In winter shuts Mon, Wed and Fri.

At Lea Green, north of the village, there is a Bronze Age barrow and distinct traces of an Iron Age settlement.

Grass Wood, about a mile north of Grassington, is a nature reserve famous and protected for its flora. Bastow Wood, adjoining it, has wild rock roses in summer. No picking, but there are footpaths making it a very pleasant walk from the village.

The Black Horse Hotel and the Forresters Arms both have real ale and are pleasant-looking pubs.

Hubberholme

One of the peculiar tiny settlements you find at the very top of the Dales, still managing to sustain themselves through the harshest winters. Hubberholme is at the junction of Upper Wharfedale with Langstrothdale and has the attributes of a village – a pub and a church – but only a couple of houses are left.

St Michael's church is what brings people to Hubberholme, apart of course from the scenery. Inside, it has rough stone walls and extraordinary hand-hewn columns, contrasting with the delicacy of its pre-Reformation wooden rood loft. The church is actually enhanced by the modern pews from the workshop of Thompson of Kilburn (called the Mouseman because of his signature of a carved mouse). There have been times when fish swam in the nave, but normally St Michael's stands next to the River Wharfe.

Across the road is the George which, curiously enough, was owned by the church until 1965. The pub was originally the vicarage and the annual 'parliament' to negotiate the letting of the 'poor's pasture' still goes on there on New Year's Day. It is a free house and serves meals.

Linton

A monument on the village green says Linton won the Loveliest Village of the North Competition in 1949. The place does look like one of those wood-block illustrations they were so fond of in those days. It is very pretty indeed, with a beck running under a series of bridges through the village green. But, more than that, it has an unexpectedly metropolitan piece of architecture in the middle, Fountaine's Hospital, built in 1720s and attributed to Vanbrugh. An elaborate central clock tower houses a chapel and the symmetrical wings have three alms-houses each. This is a fine building in a marvellous setting. At the other end of the green is the Old Hall. In the architecture of the extensions here and at Linton House the influence of the hospital can be seen. The Fountaine Inn, a Whitbread pub, is also on the green.

The church is some distance away next to the river. On one of the columns in the nave is a Romanesque crucifix, found in the beck at Linton. It is well worth having a look at, though easy to miss as it is only hand-sized.

Lothersdale

Just south of Skipton the villages suddenly start becoming industrial. Lothersdale gives one an idea of how pleasant the surroundings of early industrialization could be before steam-power took over. The stone mill is bedded in beside the river in the centre of this long thin village. It contains the largest water-wheel in England, which can be seen by arrangement with James Wilson and Sons who make silk and rayon there. It was damaged by frost in 1962 so is no longer in use. Up behind the 19th c church is Stone Gappe, the house where Charlotte Brontë was governess and which she later used as the model for Gateshead Hall in *Jane Eyre*.

The seclusion of this lovely valley made it a good refuge from persecution for Quakers in the 17th c and their tiny meeting house still survives here. There

is a Websters pub, called the Hare and Hounds, used by people walking the Pennine Way, which runs through the village.

Settle

Even in the 18th c, Settle was described as a 'pretty great thoroughfare', and it still is, although discussions are now going on about where to put the bypass. The railway (carried on a viaduct over the town) and its position on the Leeds–Kendal road have affected Settle's recent character. But it remains primarily a shopping centre for the immediate district. On Tue the market square in the centre of town is full of stalls, including John Plant's Wholefood from Grassington and the Glanvilles selling pottery and rushwork. For visitors there are gift shops and antique shops with interesting jewellery as well as a promising junk shop. The Folly, a 17th c house, is by far the most bizarre – and interesting – building in town. The helpful tourist board information centre in the town hall has leaflets to help you find the most interesting corners of Settle, which are well worth exploring.

Up in Victoria St is the Museum of North Craven Life, open daily except Mon July–Sept 2.00–5.00, Sat only in winter.

The new Pig Yard Museum has remains from the different periods of occupation of the local caves – from hyena den to Romano-British squatters, as well as a remarkable piece of Celtic figure carving, Viking graffiti and lots of other fascinating objects. Open Oct–Easter Tues, Sat, Sun 2.00–5.00; Easter–Sept Mon, Tues, Thur, Fri 2.00–5.00, Sat, Sun 10.00–5.00. Parties by appointment, tel Settle 3664.

The Golden Lion Hotel in Duke St serves Thwaites beers and food, but it might be worth trying the Black Horse next to the church in Giggleswick. This village is Settle's old-fashioned twin on the other side of the Ribble – they almost join up but are entirely different in character. Giggleswick has a lovely old parish church and a public school.

Slaidburn

Originally one of the Craven villages, it is now in Lancashire in a remote hollow of the Forest of Bowland. The narrow streets which meet at the Hark To Bounty Inn contrast with the wide

Malham Cove, the beauty spot favoured by the Romantic Movement

grassy banks of the Hodder, which is joined by Croasdale Brook on the edge of the village. St Andrew's church has remarkable furnishings – an undisturbed arrangement of Georgian pews and triple-decker pulpit, an Elizabethan cover to the Norman font and a very fine Jacobean screen. The Hark To Bounty was the seat of the courts of the Forest of Bowland and surprisingly has the panelled courtroom preserved in it. *Egon Ronay's Pub Guide* recommends the grills and sandwiches here. In Slaidburn you feel that the village's remoteness has allowed all sorts of survivals which would have been tidied away long ago in somewhere more accessible, or more noticed.

You can drive from here on tortuous roads across the wild fell country to High Bentham or Clapham.

Stainforth and Langcliffe

Two villages next to each other in Ribblesdale, sheltering under the limestone scars. Stainforth loosely grouped around beck with stepping stones, Langcliffe more formal with narrow streets of terrace cottages leading to a big green dominated by the Methodist chapel and school. By the fountain is the house where Isaac Newton used to stay. Langcliffe has an industrial history and there are still mills down by the Ribble.

At Stainforth there is an elegant pack-horse bridge leading to Knight Stainforth and gaunt 17th c Stainforth Hall. This wooded stretch of the Ribble forms deep pools popular for swimming. Up behind Stainforth you can walk to the waterfall, Catrigg Force, or explore the moorland roads. The one to Halton Gill has splendid views of Penyghent. Behind Langcliffe is Attemire Scar with Attemire and Victoria Caves where important local prehistoric finds were made.

The Craven Heifer in the centre of Stainforth is a Thwaites pub, with several large comfortable bars and a garden overlooking the beck. It serves meals and snacks.

West Burton

More or less the first village you come to to if you drive over the pass at the head of Wharfedale, along Bishopdale to Wensleydale. An attractive, unspoilt place with a long uphill green. Most of the houses in the village are arranged along this green which has a strange spire-shaped market cross with a weathercock on top. On top of a barn dated 1707, at the corner of the Walden road, is another old weathercock. This one has holes in it to attach the ribbons with which it was decorated on Burton feast days, when it was carried from house to house by village children. The village has its own shop and butchers, as well as the Fox and Hounds – an inviting pub which serves a range of food and Camerons beer.

Just off the bottom of the green, past the old mill house, is a fine waterfall which takes its scale from the massive slab of rock over which it falls. This is Walden Beck, whose valley is well worth exploring.

Celtic carving from Pig Yard Museum, Settle

Places to visit

Brimham Rocks: nr Pateley Bridge, turning off B6265, is this extraordinary series of bulbous sandstone pinnacles weathered into grotesque shapes. They stand on the edge of a ridge with views across Nidderdale. The quantity of these rocks makes them unique in the British Isles and they are now owned by the National Trust, who have set up information centre and shop there.

Show-caves: there are caves to visit at Ingleborough (Clapham), White Scar (on B6255 nr Chapel-le-Dale) and at Stump Cross (on B6265 Grassington–Pateley Bridge road). They all have spectacular rock formations and underground rivers, but the lighting and walkways that make them accessible also rather destroy the romance. It is well worth visiting one of them, though. At Ingleborough there are tours on the half hour from 10.30–5.30. From end of Oct to beginning March caves only open at weekends. White Scar Caves are open daily 10.00–6.00 or dusk. Closed Dec–Jan. Stump Cross open daily from March to end Sept 10.00–6.00, then weekends 10.30–4.00. White Scar and Stump Cross are both near the road, there is a walk to Ingleborough (see Clapham). All opening times subject to weather conditions: caves cannot open when water levels are high.

Bolton Abbey: splendidly situated on the banks of the Wharfe, it is particularly interesting because it is not entirely ruined – the nave is still used as the parish church and the gatehouse is incorporated into Bolton Hall. From the abbey you can walk up-river through woods with six nature trails to the Strid, where the Wharfe is forced into a narrow rock channel. It looks jumpable but don't try: people have died in the attempt. Farther up the river is the lovely 17th c Barden Bridge and Barden Tower. This was originally built by Henry Clifford, 'the Shepherd Lord' brought up incognito by poor rustics to escape his family's enemies in Wars of Roses. He continued to prefer the simple life to worldy Skipton Castle and so built the tower as somewhere to escape to. All these free attractions make Bolton Abbey a very popular place to visit (small charge for car park and nature trails). About six miles from Skipton on B6160.

Fountains Abbey and Hall and Studley Royal: a superb complex – the 18th c water-gardens form an ideal complement to the grandeur of the abbey, which is the ruin at the bottom of the garden. The magnificent scale is sustained throughout, even to using Ripon Cathedral as the eye-catcher at the end of the avenue. You can leave your car in the grounds at Studley Royal and walk through the park to the abbey and Fountains Hall, a fine Jacobean house which can also be visited. This is the best-preserved of all the Cistercian abbeys – substantial remains of the monastic buildings allow you to imagine the quality of that life. There is also a sumptuous 19th c church designed by William Burges at Studley Royal. Abbey and gardens open daily all year round from 9.30; June–Aug till 9.00, May and Sept till 7.00, then progressively earlier. Nov–Feb also closed Sun till 2.00. Off B6265 about three miles west of Ripon.

Haworth Parsonage Bronte Museum: Georgian parsonage overlooking churchyard where Brontë family lived, now a museum with relics arranged in rooms, in an attempt to re-create atmosphere. You can walk across the moors to High Withens, the scene of *Wuthering Heights*. Haworth itself has become a great tourist centre full of craft shops, cafes (see also Worth Valley Railway). Parsonage open all year except three weeks in Dec, 11.00–5.30, Sun 2.00–5.30. Closes an hour earlier Oct–March. South of Keighley on A629.

Ripley Castle: built round a large courtyard, it has a 15th and 16th c gatehouse and tower, but the castellations are mainly 18th c. So there is a mixture of elegant interiors with fine portraits and furniture, contrasting with dark-panelled Jacobean rooms. The earlier rooms are seeped in the history of the Ingleby family, who have lived here since 14th c.

The grounds of the castle were laid out with a new lake by Capability Brown in the 1820s. In the mid-19th c Sir William Ingleby was so fond of villages in Alsace-Lorraine that he made his own look like one. Open bank hol only Easter–June and Sept 11.00–5.15, daily July–Aug 2.00–5.15, gardens Easter–end Sept daily 11.00–6.00.

Parcevall Hall Gardens: created in the 1930s to complement the hall's remarkable site above the dramatic limestone gorge of Trollers Ghyll. The woodland garden behind the hall changes imperceptibly from the lush and exotic to native plants. Reginald Farrer's knowledge of Himalayan and Oriental plants influenced Sir William Milner who made the garden with formal terraces in front of house and wild shrub and woodland gardens beyond. House not open to public but gardens open daily May–Sept 10.00–6.00. Turning to Skyreholme off Appletreewick–Pateley Bridge road.

Browsholme Hall: situated on the edge of Forest of Bowland and home of Parker family since 14th c. Reached through maze of lanes, the Hall is picturesque sandstone mixture of different periods from Tudor to Regency. Gardens were laid out in 18th c. Open mid-May–3 June, 18 Aug–2 Sept daily 2.00–5.00. Off B6243.

East Riddlesden Hall, on the outskirts of Keighley: small Jacobean stone house with a pond in front and a fine timber tithe barn, containing animal stalls and wagons. There are some good bits of contemporary furniture, paintings and some lovely pieces of stump work embroidery. National Trust. Open bank hol and daily except Mon and Tue from April–Oct 2.00–6.00, June–end Aug 10.30–6.00. On A650 one mile northeast of Keighley.

ACTIVITIES

Walking: the best way of seeing the countryside. The National Park produces a series of leaflets with suggested routes and information about points of interest on the way. They also have a programme of guided Dales walks, each of which starts from a National Park centre and should be booked. Others are open and are carefully designed to link up with Dales Rail and other public transport. For further information on both these schemes write to National Parks Officer, Colvend, Grassington, Skipton, North Yorks. Tel Grassington 752748. The Three Peaks Walk is for those who want something more strenuous. It entails climbing Penyghent, Whernside and Ingleborough in one day. The Penyghent Café in Horton-in-Ribblesdale makes it possible for you to time your walk by clocking in at the cafe at start and finish. They offer membership of Three Peaks Club and they will

Ribblehead viaduct: its foundations are stabilised on thousands of sheep fleeces

come and rescue you if you're not back in 12 hrs. Also have local weather forecast service, tel Horton-in Ribblesdale 333.

The Pennine Way stretches 250 miles from Derbyshire to Scottish border, linking all sorts of old tracks, packhorse routes, etc. There are pubs to stay in en route, although some of the gaps in between are long.

Potholing: Gaping Gill Winch is one of the best known potholes in this area famous for them. Here, a waterfall plunges 360ft from the surface into the main chamber. You can be winched down – if you have the nerve. You need boots, waterproof clothing and lighting. The potholing clubs who set the winch up say you can go down free, but there is a charge to come back up! It is usually set up on bank hols.

Whernside Manor Cave and Fell Centre, at Dent, Sedbergh, Cumbria, organizes a variety of residential courses on Pennine topics. It is the national centre for caving and potholing, so the best place to learn how to do it. They run an introductory caving day on request for parties of four or so, residential weekend introductory caving and potholing courses, and novice caving weeks. Tel warden for details, Dent 213.

Dales Rail: the building of the Settle–Carlisle Line was a heroic feat of engineering; during it 100 men died. The foundations of the Ribblehead viaduct were stabilized, when all else failed, on thousands of sheep fleeces. The viaduct

remains one of the most memorable sights of the Dales. It is still possible to travel along this spectacular line and when the Dales Rail scheme is in operation even the small stations are open. This enterprising scheme, which benefits people in the Dales as well as visitors, operates one weekend a month mid-April –mid-Oct. Details and dates from Settle Tourist Information office tel Settle 3617 (summer only). You can travel from Leeds or Carlisle right into the Dales and pick up bus links to Wensleydale, Teesdale or the Lakes. There are guided walks arranged to coincide. The trains run morning and evening and costs are very reasonable.

It is essential to book from relevant BR stations or by post from Dales Rail, Metro House, West Parade, Wakefield WF1 1NS. More information from BR or National Park Information Centre, tel Grassington 752748.

Worth Valley Railway: these steam trains run from Keighley to Haworth and Oxenhope. Service daily in July and Aug, weekends March–Oct. There are also some steam engines on view at Oxenhope. Talking timetable, tel Haworth 43629.

Weaving courses: Brontë Tapestries at Ponden Hall, Stanbury, nr Haworth, run residential weaving course for beginners. They also demonstrate weaving and at Ponden Mill they sell their handwoven goods. For details contact Haworth 44154.

Malham Tarn Field Centre: run week-long residential field courses. Tel Airton 331 for details.

Angling: see *Northern Anglers' Handbook* available direct from Dalesman Publications in Clapham.

Local rod licence available from tackle shops. Good quality trout fishing on Wharfe is expensive. Day tickets available Bolton Abbey Estate Office, the Red Lion at Burnsall and Devonshire Hotel, Grassington. Day tickets for Malham Tarn from the Field Centre. Some stretches of the Leeds–Liverpool canal are free, ask at Skipton tackle shop in Water St. Some pubs have their own fishing rights; for instance, guests who stay at the Falcon at Arncliffe or the New Inn at Clapham can fish in their waters.

FOOD AND DRINK

Local people recommend the **Game Cock** at Austwick for its roast duckling. *Egon Ronay's Lucas Guide* recommends the **Box Tree** at Ilkley, tel Ilkley 608484, a two-star restaurant which will give you a memorable evening. It has a very good wine list. **Devonshire Arms Hotel Restaurant**, Bolton Abbey, tel Bolton Abbey 265. Serves mainly traditional English food.

TOURIST INFORMATION

Publications: The *Dalesman* is a monthly full of local bits and pieces and they also produce an informative range of books on Dales topics and history. The *Craven Herald and Pioneer*, out on Fri, is worth watching for notices of sales, etc. The monthly leaflet, *What's On in The Yorkshire Dales National Park*, has useful list of events, and the Yorkshire Arts Association does a bi-monthly guide to films, theatres, music, and other events.

Tourist information offices: at Skipton, Settle, Burnsall, Haworth, Hebden Bridge and Oatley. The regional office is in York, tel York 707961.

National Park Centres: at Clapham, Grassington and Malham, and offices at Yorebridge House, Bainbridge, Leyburn, tel Bainbridge 0456, and at Colvend, Hebden Rd, Grassington, Skipton, North Yorks, tel Grassington 752748.

Research: Jessica York.

Helmsley

The North York Moors stand aloof as a plateau entire. No matter whether you approach that massive uplift from the smog of Teesside, or the last resorts of the East Coast, or the rich southern farmlands or, better still, from the sprawling Vale of York, the vistas everywhere are riven by little roads that seem to be making a determined effort to climb up into the sky. The approach from the west is not only by far the most spectacular; it eases you into the picture, slowly, with always the promise of more to come.

If you drive up the A1 towards Northallerton, the hazy walls of the plateau will loom up over your right shoulder soon after you pass the turn-off to Boroughbridge. The sheer rock face far ahead has been likened to those cliffs in *The Lost World* of Conan Doyle where Professor Challenger and his companion fought off ferocious attacks by a flock of pterodactyls, a fantasy enlivened today by the sight of gliders that share the thermals over Roulston Scar with black-headed gulls, buzzards and kindred fowl. Even that testy old trout Challenger would approve of the analogy, since you are climbing up onto the hundred-million-year-old remains of the Jurassic, the dynasty of the early dinosaurs. For centuries men have quarried that variable strata for stone, creamy-white, honey-coloured or reddish-brown, and from it built superb abbeys, townships and intimate villages that look what they are, a part of the rock floor on which they stand.

Glance at them as you hustle along the A170, skirting Thirsk. But after Sutton-under-Whitestone Cliff you will, if you are wise, adjust your seat belt, slip into second, watch out for two eyebrow-lifting bends and keep your sights only on that well-found, ever-mounting road to the very top of Sutton Bank which is one-in-three in places. There, with your back to a pretty good information bureau run by the National Park authority, you can look across what many of us consider to be the better half of England.

Some 500ft below lies Gormire, an almost circular lake left behind by a frustrated glacier when the cliffs were haunted by wolves, bears and big cats with canines the shape and size of bananas. However, the *pièce de résistance* is the incomparable view from the very rim of the cirque where, 40 miles away to the west, the flattened Pennine peaks of Great Whernside, Penhill and many more huddle like sheep in a mist. A shade more to the south the eye catches the pencil-thin TV transmitter on Holme Moss near Halifax and some curious egg-cups which turn out to be the cooling towers of Ferrybridge power station. Note, please, you are *looking at* what used to be called the Dales of the North

Helmsley: 'Spare what time you can here, for the heart of the moors lies immediately to the north'

and West Riding, but you are *standing on* an entirely different formation, the North York Moors.

Before returning to your car, take or turn your back on an exhilarating walk along a section of the Cleveland ('cliff-land') Way, and then
set off for the grandeur of Rievaulx, the greatest Cistercian house in
the north.

It nestles in the valley of the Rye ('Rievaulx') some six miles away,
via the first turn-off to the left, a mile beyond the top of Sutton Bank.
The switchback road is lined with the soft green larch of the Forestry
Commission that hide the racing stables of Jack Calvert and E. J. Carr.
You will notice the dry-built walls, the marvel of which is that such
permanence can be achieved so precariously, locked as they are only by
long slabs called 'throughs' laid transversely. You will notice, too, that
houses are built of the same stone, capped with rusty red pantiles, a
regional hallmark. And as for the abbey that lies across rather than
along the narrow ash-clad valley – 'so delicate, so beautiful it looks as
though a breath of wind might bring it down'.

With 12 monks well able to handle mallet, chisel and axe, in 1131
Abbot William, once secretary to the great St Bernard of Clairvaux,
began to build that enormous lacework of stone so vigorously that
hundreds came to help him. Two abbots later, that is in the days of the
Blessed St Aelred, there were said to have been at Rievaulx 150 white-
robed monks and at least 500 lay brothers, 'so that the church swarmed
with them like to a hive with bees.'

To the east of Rievaulx, plainly signposted, lies Helmsley, whose
long history can be read in the build and shape of the houses around its
cobbled market square. Its gaunt skeleton of a 12th-century keep
stands like a stone gibbet above the drive to the huge estate of the
Duncombes.

Spare what time you can here, for the heart of the moors lies
immediately to the north and, at its own request, one more village
demands to be inspected on the way. This is the self-conscious showplace of Hutton-le-Hole, a colony congealed in aspic for tourist con-
sumption: wrought-iron, beamy and coach-lamp lit, but beautiful still.
The putting-green-like village greens, all six of them, are cropped by
a resident flock of sheep, the bane of dozens of diesel coach drivers.
The folk museum next to the spacious pub is a local treasure house,
unquestionably one of the best in the country, and it's a privilege to
shake hands with its co-founder, Mr Bert Frank.

From here you may go to the wild daffodils of Farndale, the forests
of Cropton or the crypt of St Cedd's church at Lastingham, described
by Pevsner as 'unforgettable'. My immediate preference would be for
the moors. Ask for Rosedale by way of the Bank top and test your
brakes before you start. The route is down and down the prodigious
decline, through the workaday village of Rosedale, the home of the old
iron-miners, and then up and up over Egton High Moor, below which
lies the rippling more-green-than-green valley of the Whitby Esk.

The moors catch your breath. Stop and look around. From high places they seem to stretch out into something close to infinity. 'Everywhere peace, everywhere serenity and a marvellous freedom from the tumult of the world,' wrote the Blessed St Aelred. It matters to me not at all that heather in full bloom has become the symbol of the bad artist and manufacturer of postcards. The sight is one of placidity. The immense expanse offers no resistance to breezes which blow across it gently and steadily. In August and September, the commonest kind of heather, the ling as they call it locally, flares purple, with here and there the bright crimson flowers of bell heather that stand out like a splash of bright colour in the sett of a Highland plaid. It is here you will catch that most haunting of moorland signature tunes, the intermingled calls of curlew, peewits and golden plover. Music in miniature comes from the little ghylls or streamlets that feed the becks, while at dusk and at dawn the bark of a sheepdog or the triumphant notes of a missel-thrush far down in the dale might carry for a mile or more.

The marvel is that all you can see, including the cliffs on the rim, were once the silt of a huge prehistoric river that arose in what is now south-west Scotland and emptied into the sea along the east coast of Yorkshire.

Abbot William chose Rievaulx as the site for his great house of prayer and work because in that ravine-like valley he found solitude, noble patronage, stone, sweet water and grazing for his flocks. With the highly profitable addition of tourism, it's much the same today. On high ground you are rarely out of sight of black-faced 'moor-jocks' or Swaledales, a hardy breed of northern sheep. And rounded burial mounds or 'howes', the graves of Bronze and Iron Age folk, can be seen almost everywhere. There are about 10,000 in the region.

With one notable exception, all the rivers within the National Park flow south and spill out, eventually, into the Humber. The exception is the Esk, a fine salmon stream that gives the natural harbour of Whitby something of the character of a Scandinavian fjord. It is here that the hard floor of the moors crashes down into the sea, for the cliffs are the graveyard of long-extinct reptiles. The ruins of the abbey are of local stone, and jet – for which the town is famous – is fossilized wood borne down by that river of the lost world of the Jurassic.

JOHN HILLABY

Helmsley

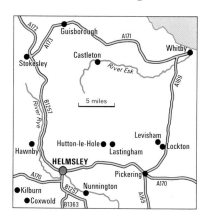

WHERE TO GO

Market Place: the centre of town. In the middle of this big square is a 19th c statue of Lord Feversham with a pinnacled canopy to keep his stone ermine dry. Around the square's edges are the town hall, the old police station turned cafe, a fine timber-frame house, Georgian houses and four inns of which the Crown and the Black Swan are old posting houses. The Bachelors' Quadrille Ball used to be held at the Crown. The Feathers is a new hotel but it incorporates one of the oldest buildings in Helmsley.

All Saints Church, High St, Castlegate: the parish church, just behind the Market Place, has a Norman porch and chancel arch but is mainly Victorian. Near the font are 15th c brasses of a knight and his wife and a yoke stick for leading slaves by the neck. The High St, behind the church, is a peaceful contrast to the Market Place. It has trees and a beck emerging from underground to run down its middle. Borough Beck continues flowing down one side of Castlegate with a bridge over it into the square. Castlegate has the Look Gallery with exhibitions of paintings, ceramics and sculpture.

The Castle: one of those 'gaping tooth' ruins with a splendid series of grassed earth ramparts, one complete wall of the keep, and a 16th c range of two-storey buildings still standing. Inside, it has mermaids in the heraldic plasterwork. Towards the end of its active life the castle passed by marriage

to James I's favourite, the Duke of Buckingham. It was later allowed to fall down after Duncombe Park was built next door. Open May–Sept daily 9.30–7.00, April daily 9.30–5.30, March, Oct weekdays 9.30–5.30 Sun 2.00–5.30, Nov–Feb weekdays 9.30–4.00 Sun 2.00–4.00.

Duncombe Park: 'Helmsley, once proud Buckingham's delight, Slides to a scrivener, or a city knight.' The city knight to whom Pope refers was Sir Charles Duncombe, Lord Mayor of London, who made his money in banking. His brother-in-law, Thomas Brown, inherited his estates and set about building Duncombe Park with the help of William Wakefield, an amateur architect much influenced by Vanbrugh, who was working on nearby Castle Howard at the time.

The house is now occupied by a school, but the park is open to the public. Its most interesting feature is the grand sweep of terraces near the house with a temple at either end, but these are raised tantalizingly out of reach on rusticated 'fortifications'. You can walk in the beautiful parklands along the River Rye. There are views of the castle with the town behind. Obtain permission from the estate office near the gate to the park.

Rievaulx Terrace: this terrace was built in the mid-18th c in response to the new taste for Gothic ruins. Rievaulx Abbey is in the valley below so, as you walk along the grassy terrace, you get glimpses of it through the trees. As at Duncombe there are two temples, one at either end of the terrace. The Ionic Temple is sumptuously furnished as a banqueting room, with a ceiling decorated with copies of Guido Reni and Caracci paintings. Downstairs in the rooms where the servants used to prepare the food there are now exhibitions about garden design and photographs of the Duncombe family, set up by the National Trust. Open April–Oct every day 10.30–6.00.

SHOPPING

Market day: Fri.
Early closing: Wed.
Winifred Fisher Antiques, Bridge St: furniture and china including some real bargains. There is also a junk shop in Church St with old buttons and bunches of home-grown flowers.
Bakery in Castlegate: has pasties and delicious date and walnut cakes.
Crofts of Harrogate: smart women's and children's clothes.

The tiled roofs of Helmsley with All Saints Church on the left

Ideas, Bridge St: honey, clothes, china, presents.
No 9 Bondgate: for patchwork cushions, Jacobs wool.
Helmsley Forge, Burogate: wrought iron work.

FOOD AND DRINK

Egon Ronay's Lucas Guide recommends the restaurants at the **Black Swan** and the **Feversham Arms**. The Black Swan for good English food with some local specialities; the Feversham Arms specializes in seafood. *Just a Bite* recommends the high teas at the **Crown** and the delicious home-baked goodies at **Nice Things** in the Market Place. Pubs include: the **Feathers** and the **Royal Oak**. The **Black Swan** serves teas.

WHERE TO STAY

Egon Ronay's Lucas Guide recommends the **Black Swan Hotel**, tel Helmsley 466, the **Feathers Hotel**, tel Helmsley 275, both in the Market Place, and the **Feversham Arms Hotel**, 1 High St, tel Helmsley 346.

TOURIST INFORMATION

The North York Moors National Park has an information service at The Old Vicarage, Bondgate, Helmsley, tel Helmsley 657.

Villages and country towns

Castleton

A gaunt upland township on the northern end of Castleton Rigg overlooking the Esk valley. The settlement originally grew up around a castle now gone, leaving only a mound and the plain village houses huddled tightly together along the High St. There are several pubs serving Camerons: the Downe Arms right in the centre and the Robin Hood and Little John. By the station, which is still functioning, is the Eskdale Hotel, a purpose-built railway hotel, and where the town meets the moors is the Moorland Hotel.

From Castleton there are marvellous drives or walks across the moors or along the meadowy dales. And in these remote parts it is worth knowing how good Champion's Garage is.

View from Sutton Bank – 'you can look across what many of us consider to be the better half of England'

In Sept the Castleton and Danby Horticultural Show is held here – one of the biggest in the area. And the sheep sales, advertised in the local press, are important local occasions.

Coxwold

Laurence Sterne described Coxwold as a 'delicious retreat'. It was while he was vicar here that he wrote *Tristram Shandy* and *A Sentimental Journey*, and Shandy Hall, the lovely rambling house where he lived, has conducted tours, June–Sept Wed 2.00–6.00.

The village is built evenly up a single street, neatly trimmed with wide grass verges. There are 17th c almshouses, the Old Hall (originally built as a grammar school in 1603 by a local lad who became Lord Mayor of London), and a good village shop. All the houses retain their long feudal strips of garden.

At the top of the hill is St Michael's, a fine perpendicular church with an unusual octagonal tower. Inside, it has box pews, a gallery and a strange elongated altar rail. There is a Breeches Bible open to show the controversial passage about the tailoring of Adam and Eve's fig leaves (could all those Renaissance painters be wrong?). In the chancel are tombs for the Bellasis family of Newburgh Priory (see Places to Visit). The finest of them is a wall monument by Grinling Gibbons.

At the bottom of the hill you can have home-made teas at the Old School House or visit Coxwold pottery where they make Uncle Toby jugs and kitchenware

in a woodfired kiln. Open 10.00–5.00 weekdays, 2.00–6.00 summer weekends. The Fauconberg Arms does excellent meals and sandwiches (not available on Mon).

Hawnby

The drive of a few miles from Helmsley leaves you quite unprepared for the scale or the remoteness of the valley containing this little village.

Some of the red-roofed houses and the village shop are at the bottom of the dale near the River Rye; the rest and the hotel are halfway up the steep hill to the moors. This hill is the end of one of the ridges which meet here to form a deep bowl – the bottom green and fertile, the rim purple moorland. Standing on its own next to the river, screened by trees, is the parish church of All Saints. It is basically Norman with a lot of later work, including a 17th c monument to two-year-old Ann Tankard showing a clock face, a rose bush, a woman and a baby in a cradle.

The Hawnby Hotel does morning coffee and bar snacks. You can get day tickets to trout fish here. There is a network of footpaths, either along the dale bottoms or across the moors, and a spectacular drive across the moors to Osmotherley.

Hutton-le-Hole

A well-known beauty spot with a beck running through the middle – worth a visit particularly for the superb Rydale

Folk Museum. The main building includes local crafts, trades, customs, and out in the grounds are many local buildings reconstructed and furnished with sufficient subtlety to give a realistic impression of rural life. There are surprises such as a witch's crystal ball and the magic books of another. Open from Easter–Oct daily 2.00–5.15 (in July, Aug 11.00–6.15). The village goes back possibly as far as neolithic times; there were certainly Bronze Age residents.

Since the 16th c Hutton has had a strong tradition of freeholders with no big landlord. They organized the village through a manor court – one of the very few that still exist. Nonconformism was strong here, particularly the Quakers. Though none of the chapels remain in use, it is significant that the parish church was built as late as the 1930s. The growth and decline of Hutton was tied in with the development of moorland coal and ironstone mines – almost exactly the same amount of land was farmed from Domesday to the Victorians.

The other major trade here was weaving but now tourism has taken over. There are several gift shops and a good pub called the Crown with Camerons beer and food available.

Kilburn

A pretty working village, with cottage gardens full of vegetables. On every other available space are piles of seasoning timber, adding a mellow colour to the place. The half-timbered house in the centre is the sale-room for Robert 'Mousey' Thompson and behind are the workshops where the famous domestic and church furniture is still made. The firm is run by his grandsons now, but they continue the tradition of oak craftsmanship and, of course, the carved church mouse with which he signed all his work. The showrooms sell a range of domestic furniture – at a price – most items cost hundreds of pounds.

The parish church is a lovely Norman building with two interesting tomb slabs, a Breeches Bible, and a chapel furnished as a memorial to Robert Thompson. Near the church is the Foresters Arms, a thriving pub which serves a good range of food for the village's many visitors. There is also a tea-room called the Singing Bird.

Kilburn is right underneath the escarpment where the North York Moors

suddenly begin. In the mid-19th c the village schoolmaster with the help of his pupils marked out a white horse on the hillside above Kilburn. There is a walk round the horse from Sutton Bank: leaflets from information centre at Sutton Bank.

Traditional wood carving in Robert Thompson's workshop at Kilburn

Lastingham

This village lies in a wooded hollow on the edge of the moors. There is a beck and a small green in the middle. Above the jumble of red-tiled roofs you can see the apse of the magnificent Norman parish church. This church has a venerable history, not only because Bede tells of the monastery that used to be here, but because it was founded and run by three saints, Cedd, Chad and Ovin. The original monastery was probably destroyed by Danish raids and the present church was begun about 1078. The splendid crypt with its stocky columns and massive capitals was built first to house the remains of St Cedd. The rest of the abbey was never finished – the monks moved to York. Today's church is only the chancel and crossing of the original conception. In the crypt are some fragments of stone carving that may date back to the days of the saints (7th c).

Up the hill near the church is the Blacksmiths Arms, which has low beams and a cast-iron kitchen range. They do good food and Theakstons and Tetleys beer. In the 18th c the local curate used to double as innkeeper here, inciting the locals to disorderly conduct by playing the fiddle. Now it's almost as restrained as the tea-room down the road by the village shop.

Levisham/Lockton

Two typical moorland villages of contrasting constructions: Lockton loosely grouped along several grassy streets; Levisham built around a long uphill green like a hayfield with donkeys grazing on it. On the map they stand right next to each other. When you get there you can look from one to the other, as they are on the same level, but there is a ravine to negotiate in between. These moors are full of extraordinary landscape surprises to which the rest of England offers no parallels. Levisham is not so remote as you might suppose, since beyond the village in another gully runs the North York Moors Railway. Lockton's centre is pleasant, with a bench under the horse-chestnuts by the churchyard. The plain little church has good 17th c woodwork. There are several Nonconformist chapels, some big farmyards, a post office, shop and many pretty cottage gardens: in fact all the ingredients of a quiet rural Yorkshire life. The walk to the pub must sometimes seem a bit long – you have to go either to the Horse Shoe, a free house at the top of Levisham green, or to the Fox and Rabbit, a Camerons pub about a mile out of Lockton on the Pickering–Whitby road.

At the bottom of the ravine next to Levisham Beck is St Mary's church, with a Saxon arch and a tombstone with a carved dragon from before the Norman Conquest.

Nunnington

An unassuming village built to a grid pattern on Caulkley's Bank, a ridge that extends from the moors into the Vale of Pickering. The three parallel roads of the grid have totally different characters. The first leads you into the village between a long avenue of sycamores to the 18th c bridge and Nunnington Hall, the manor house next to the River Rye. The second is a sunken lane leading down behind the church, through the village, to the Victorian school at the bottom. The third is lined with cottages up high grassy banks with the Royal Oak Inn, a free house, halfway up. In between are alleys to explore, with the chapel, the post office and farmyards.

Nunnington Hall is one of those pleasant houses where bits have been added and taken away over the years. The entrance front is late 16th c, but the most interesting interiors are 17th c – a

Smoking kippers: Mr Fortune's Whitby Smokehouse

fine staircase and room leading on to the garden. House, owned by National Trust, is open April–Oct Wed–Sun, Bank Hol Mon 2.00–6.00

You can get a very good meal at Rydale Lodge, about a mile out of Nunnington at the old railway station. Booking essential, tel Nunnington 246. It's also a lovely, peaceful place to stay.

The estate office of Nunnington Hall, or the keeper's cottage at weekends, have day tickets for various kinds of fishing.

Stokesley

A perfect Georgian market town in the plain of Cleveland, quite different in character from the moorland towns and villages. The number of handsome town houses suggests that for a long time Stokesley has been the centre of a prosperous agricultural community. Now it is near enough to Teesside to be a most desirable dormitory town. The houses and shops surround a large open space divided into squares and a tree-lined green. The townscape is vaguely Dutch, with bridges and tall, dark-pink brick buildings.

Near the church Sheila Kirk has a pottery at Manor Farm Studio, and there is a small market on Fri. Stokesley Show, one of the biggest in Yorkshire, held here in Sept. The Spread Eagle Hotel in the High St is a Camerons pub with a series of long bars.

Whitby

This town combines all that is best about the sea – a harbour in the river estuary of the Esk, busy quays, an early morning fish auction, white sands, cliffs, jetties, lighthouses and the famous lifeboat. There is a market square which has stalls on Saturdays and you can still buy Whitby jet in Church St. The Georgian terraces on West Hill were built at the height of Whitby's prosperity as a whaling port and shipper of alum.

The town has another, more ancient strand to its history. It was here that the pattern of religious life in England was decided at the Synod in 664, soon after St Hilda had founded the abbey. Its superbly weathered ruins stand fully exposed to the gales from the North Sea, on top of the east cliff. Visit the parish church, just down the hill from the abbey, which local ships' carpenters have fitted out as though it were below decks, with balconies, box pews and triple-decker pulpit.

Other places to visit are the Pannett Park Museum and Art Gallery, with a Captain Cook collection and lots of other seafaring items, a jet collection and some good paintings. Open May–Sept weekdays 9.30–5.30, Sun 2.00–5.00, Oct–April Mon, Tue, Thur, Fri 10.30–1.00, Wed and Sat 10.30–4.00, Sun 2.00–4.00. There is also a Lifeboat Museum at Scotch Head Pier Rd, open Easter–Sept daily 10.00–4.00. At 1 Flowergate is the studio of F. M. Sutcliffe, the famous photographer, with much of his work on show. Open Mon–Sat, except Wed, 9.00–5.00. Egon Ronay's *Just a Bite* awards a star to Magpie, 14 Pier Rd, for its excellent fish and chips. There are 14 real ale pubs, including the Plough, Baxtergate, which serves Sam Smiths.

—Places to visit—

Rievaulx Abbey: in secluded stretch of the Rye valley about three miles out of Helmsley, this was the first Cistercian house in the North of England, founded in 1131. The church was begun soon after and most of the monastery building was completed by the end of the century. By this time there were 150 monks and 500 lay brothers keeping 12,000 sheep on the moors at Bilsdale. They then set about altering the course of the Rye in order to take in the pastures of the valley bottom. The river was moved from the east side of the valley near the abbey church to a channel dug out on the far west side. Open daily, May–Sept 9.30–7.00, Oct to 5.30, Sun 2.00–5.30 or dusk.

Castle Howard: one of the most magnificent baroque mansions in England. It was Vanbrugh's first architectural job, and the view of the house from across the lake shows the full splendours of the design. Inside, the marble entrance hall and long corridor lined with statues are memorable. Otherwise, most of Vanbrugh has gone in subsequent redecorations and in the fire of 1940. There is a high Victorian chapel – an odd mixture of classical and Burne-Jones glass – and a long gallery with some very good portraits, including two Holbeins. The house also has paintings by Rubens, Tintoretto and Veronese. Probably the most celebrated features at Castle Howard are the garden buildings: obelisk, pyramid, temple of the four winds, bridge, but above all Hawksmoor's crumbling mausoleum standing on a ridge that makes it visible for miles around. Big costume collection in the stables. Open Easter to Oct daily 11.30–5.00, grounds from 11.00. 3 miles off A64 York–Malton road.

Ebberstone Hall: a tiny house, hardly more than a pavilion, designed by Colen Campbell in 1718. The idea was to link the house to its water gardens which stepped down the valley behind the hall in a series of pools and cascades; then the beck disappeared and re-emerged in two canals in front of the house. These canals have gone entirely, but there is just enough of the garden behind to suggest what it must have been like. Open Easter–mid-Sept Sat, Sun and bank hol 2.00–6.00. On A170.

Sutton Park: a plain early Georgian brick house in the pretty lowland village

Whitby: still a flourishing fishing port

of Sutton-on-the-Forest. The elegant pastel-coloured interiors are filled with flowers as well as very good quality furniture, china, portraits, plasterwork and panelling. Gardens laid out by present owners and park by Capability Brown. Tea-rooms. Open Easter and Sun in April, then May–Sept Tue, Wed, Thur, Sun and Bank Hol Mon 2.00–6.00.

Newby Hall: a happy blend of building from different periods. The main body of the house is 17th c, but in the 1760s Adam added a series of very successful rooms to hold William Wedell's collections – one specially to take a set of Gobelin tapestries with medallions designed by Boucher, another gallery to house his fine Roman marbles. The 19th c owners added a High Victorian billiard room, a collection of chamber pots and a church in the park by William Burges. More recently, the last owner laid out a series of lovely gardens down to the river Ure. Also adventure garden and miniature railway. Tea-rooms. Open Easter–Sept, gardens daily 11.00–6.00, house April, May and Sept Wed, Thur, Sat, Sun, June–Aug daily except Mon 2.00–6.00. Four miles south-east of Ripon on B6265.

Newburgh Priory: just outside Coxwold is this house standing next to a lake. It was converted from an Augustinian priory soon after the Dissolution by the Bellasis family, whose descendants have lived here ever since. One of Cromwell's daughters married into the family and she is said to have brought his bones here after the Restoration. But even Edward

VII was prevented from opening his sealed tomb, to check up. There is an unfinished haunted room. Any attempts to finish it are said to have disastrous effects on the heirs. There is an excellent Jacobean marble overmantle, lovely 18th c plasterwork, portraits etc. Outside is some very chunky topiary, and a small water-garden densely planted with rarities. Tea-rooms. Open 23 May–5 Sept Wed only, Bank hol Sun and Sun in Aug. House 2.00–5.00, grounds 2.00–6.00.

Byland Abbey and Mount Grace Priory: two splendid ruins. 12th c Byland stands just under the edge of the moors in a fine open site between Coxwold and Ampleforth. It was moved there from Old Byland, which was so near to Rievaulx that it led to disputes between the two Cistercian houses.

Mount Grace is under the western edge of the moors near Osmotherley. This is the best preserved charterhouse in England, built in the early years of the 15th c. The Carthusians with their vow of silence required a different layout to the Cistercians. Each monk had a separate two-storey house leading off the cloister. Each house had a garden behind with a lavatory at the bottom of it. Daily opening hours for both, May–Sept 9.30–7.00, earlier closing in winter.

Crosses and howes: one way of exploring the moor is to go and look for the many ancient crosses you will see marked on Ordnance Survey maps. Some seem to have marked boundaries of abbey lands, others show the way across the moors. As they have weathered and

broken over the years they have acquired distinct personalities and names. There is Lilla Cross, the Old Wife's Stone, the Wishing Chair (the base of a cross weathered into a stone armchair), Fat Betty and Ralph Cross, among others. Scattered across the moors there are thousands of 'howes', stone cairns marking prehistoric burial sites. You will sometimes find as many as 100 together, particularly on Danby High Moor. Near Goathland there is also a well-preserved stretch of Roman road.

Fylingdales: for a more modern sculptural presence on the moors, go and look at the early warning radar station near Goathland, affectionately known as the three balls. It may be the closest most of us will get to an encounter with the space age. Seen from A169 Pickering–Whitby road.

Flamingo Park Zoo: at Kirby Misperton outside Malton in wooded parkland. The animals are in large enclosures. Also, a variety of other attractions – funfair, jungle cruise, model railway, gnomeland, children's farm, adventure playground and pottery shop. Open Easter–Sept 10.00–4.00.

Beck Isle Museum, Pickering: Pickering is a good town to visit anyway for its castle and painted parish church. The museum makes an interesting comparison with the Rydale Folk Museum in Hutton-le-Hole. Rydale is primarily concerned with rural life whereas the Beck Isle's collection reflects life and commerce in a small town since the industrial revolution. Open daily Easter–mid-Oct 10.30–12.30 and 2.00–5.30, Aug 10.30–7.00.

Cropton and Dalby forest drives: through some of the extensive forest owned by the Forestry Commission. Both these are toll-roads which wind through some lovely stretches of woodland – they have picnic sites, viewpoints and forest trails. At Low Dalby, there is a small forest museum and a very helpful information centre. The Bridestones, sandstone outcrops owned by the National Trust and now in a nature reserve, can be reached from Dalby Forest drive. There is leafleted nature walk there. Toll charge per car.

Danby Lodge National Park Centre: has information, an exhibition, films, talks, a bookshop and buffet. Open daily April–Sept 10.00–6.00, Oct 10.00–5.00 and then weekends only until 5.00.

ACTIVITIES

Yorkshire Gliding Club, Sutton Bank: for pleasure trips in a twin-seater glider and five-day residential courses.

Hang-gliding at the Hole of Horcum, off the Pickering–Whitby road. Northern Hang-gliding Centre teaches hang-gliding in two-, four- or five-day courses (accommodation can be arranged). Contact them at Pickering Cottage, Staxton, tel Sherburn 333.

Boat trips: passenger boat *Girl Pat* runs hourly trips out to sea from the harbourside of Whitby. Also fishing trips.

Nature trails and wayfaring courses have been set out in the different forests of the Forestry Commission – pamphlets from the Information Centre. The wayfaring courses are simple introductions to orienteering. The North York Moors National Park also have a range of nature trails and trails relating to different areas of interest, eg geology, railways. There is a popular nature trail through the nature reserve of Garbutt Wood at Sutton Bank. Pamphlets available from Sutton Bank, Danby Lodge or Helmsley information centres.

Walking: pleasant walk from Helmsley High St to Rievaulx Abbey through fields and woods along the beginning of the Cleveland Way. About three miles. Waymarked walks are laid out by the Forestry Commission and the National Park, who do a series of 10 leaflets – mainly fairly short walks. Leaflets available from any of the information centres. Lyke Wake Walk and Cleveland Way, two long-distance walks. The first from Osmotherley to Ravenscar straight across the moors, including Westerdale Moor where souls go after death according to the Lyke Wake Dirge – hence the name. The second rounds the edge of the moors starting from Helmsley and finishing at Filey, having come all the way down the coast from Saltburn. The *Dalesman* has produced two books about them by Bill Cowley: if you want to do the walks, these will give you a lot of information. Available from The *Dalesman*, Clapham, North Yorks.

North York Moors Railway from Pickering to Grosmont was originally opened by Stephenson as a horse-drawn line in 1830s. It runs along the tremendous rocky gorge of Newtondale and passes Fen Bog nature reserve. Steam trains Sun, bank hol and high season; otherwise diesels most days Easter–early Nov. BR connections at Grosmont on Esk valley line Middlesbrough–Whitby. Information from Pickering station, tel 72508 or 73535.

Trotting races: at York Harkness Raceway, Pool Bridge Farm, Green Hamerton, off A59. There are fixtures here most Sat afternoons May–Oct.

Riding: the National Park produce a useful list of 24 different establishments which do riding and some pony-trekking in the moors. (See Information for National Park address).

Fishing: the National Park also produce a list of where you can get day tickets for a variety of fishing and refer you to *The Northern Anglers' Handbook* available direct from the *Dalesman* at Clapham, North Yorks. You need a rod licence for any fishing in this area, but they are easily obtainable from most tackle shops or from the water authority at Malton or Scarborough. In Helmsley rod licences available from George Cooper, ironmongers in Bridge St. Day tickets from Hawnby or Nunnington.

FOOD AND DRINK

Egon Ronay's Lucas Guide recommends the **Star Inn**, Harome, nr Helmsley, tel Helmsley 397, particularly the sauced veal and pork dishes. **Milburn Arms Restaurant**, Rosedale Abbey, nr Pickering, tel Lastingham 312, different dishes daily with huge helpings of good vegetables. **Dudley Arms Inn**, Ingleby Greenhow, nr Great Ayton, tel Great Ayton 2526, friendly village inn with minstrel gallery and small dance-floor. **Brompton Forge**, Brompton-by-Sawdon, tel Scarborough 85409, where skill and imagination and first-class ingredients produce delicious results. **Golden Lion Inn**, 27 High St, Stokesley, for well-cooked dishes.

TOURIST INFORMATION

Local paper: the *Darlington and Stockton Times*, published on Sat.

Guidebooks: CAMRA's guide to real ale pubs – *North Yorkshire Ale* – is excellent. The official guidebook to the Rydale District and *The Rydale Story* are both useful. Some of the *Dalesman's* publications relate to this area. The Yorkshire Arts Association publish a bimonthly guide to what's on in the arts.

Tourist information offices: the North York Moors National Park Information Service at The Old Vicarage, Bondgate, Helmsley, tel 657, or their centres at Sutton Bank and Pickering Station. The tourist board has a regional centre at Whitby, New Quay Rd, tel 2674.

Research: Jessica York.

Rievaulx Abbey – 'that enormous lacework of stone' – the first and the greatest of the Cistercian houses in the north

Barnard Castle

There are two routes you can take up Teesdale from Barnard Castle, the high road to the north or the low road to the south; they join forces for the final climb past the source of the Tees at 2900 feet on Cross Fell to Alston in the High Pennines and beyond. The southerly route passes through Lartington, Cotherstone, Romaldkirk and Mickleton, classic villages of northern England with symmetrical stone-built houses of the kind that children draw: typically, as in Romaldkirk, they face one another across a broad green, beside an inn that is a larger replica of themselves and a handsome square-towered church set at an angle.

The high road passes no habitation, but provides instead a panorama of rounded hills and meandering river like an idealized painted landscape. From east to west the eye travels from traditional pastures dotted with cattle and partitioned by neat hedgerows, where light and shadow betray the outlines of still older field-systems, to hay-meadows and copses, a glittering weir, white farmsteads and patches of sheep on green fells, then, finally, to stunted windbreaks of Scots pine and limitless purplish-brown moorland overhung by cloud. This broad, steep-sided, almost treeless valley, created by a single local glacier, is like an island whose vegetation and inhabitants, having evolved in near-isolation, are recognizably different.

At the entrance to Teesdale, the small market town of Barnard Castle – Barney to its friends and neighbours – shelters behind a frieze of fortifications that harmonize naturally with the 70ft cliffs along the riverbank from which they spring. Ruined by neglect rather than war, Bernard Baliol's Norman castle last heard a shot fired in anger in the mid-sixteenth century. Gradually, solid citizens built solid houses beside the steep lane rising from the riverside, and Barney prospered to become a nineteenth-century Liberal stronghold and the focus of Teesdale's agricultural, and increasingly important industrial, life.

The prolonged decline that followed this peak was not offset, as it was in the Lake District or the more southerly Yorkshire Dales, by a growth in tourism; even modernization of agriculture and communications was delayed. The lowland and hill-margins of the great Strathmore and Raby estates kept, and still keep, much of their pre-war rural tranquillity, while the desolate tundra of the uplands was sensibly neglected by everyone except botanists.

So things might have remained, had it not been for one small bright blue flower. In the 1960s a river-regulating reservoir was proposed on

'Barney' castle – ruined by neglect rather than war

Widdybank Fell where, against all the odds, a population of spring gentians had been thriving in undisturbed obscurity. During the subsequent much-publicized battle, conservationists were obliged to dwell on the gentians, as well as other Teesdale sites and specialities, and, by the time Cow Green Reservoir was full, Upper Teesdale found itself a tourist attraction. So much so that, last year, the inherent dangers caused the Countryside Commission to declare it an 'area of outstanding natural beauty' – to the relief of its admirers but the dismay of the residents most affected, its farmers.

No one could call Teesdale *privilégié* – as the French say of beauty-spots – where climate is concerned, and there are times when, to farmers and tourists alike, 'an area of outstanding natural bleakness' would seem a more appropriate designation: when the dark masses of the Pennines are piebald with lying snow, as though some landscape-wrapping artist had been trying to subdue them with sheets, chilling the notorious Helm Wind still further; when, below the ominous black scars of High Cup Nick and Falcon Clints, at Cauldron Snout and High Force, the swollen yellowish waters of the Tees boil with fury, pent up between the diamond-hard rocks of the Great Whin Sill.

The nature of this whinstone has done more for Teesdale than create dramatic scenic effects, however. As a molten fluid it baked the surrounding limestones to a coarse friable marble that weathered to the special crumbly 'sugar' so favourable to the famous gentian; mineralized, it provided the rich veins of ore mined in the lead dales for well over a thousand years. In the eighteenth and nineteenth centuries Teesdale was populated by miners who were also part-time farmers – it is their smallholdings that are responsible for the intricate, delicate pattern of drystone walls, so different from the rigid geometry prevalent elsewhere – and some of them, after the industry's collapse, clung on in scattered settlements to found the intensive farming economy of today. This legacy of hard life has formed the Teesdale character, as distinctive in its way as the local geography; while isolation has produced a marked clannishness and a particularly rich dialect whose most expert lexicographer, strange to relate, is a French academic.

Now Teesdale is being wrenched out of its privacy and calm, not only by the modern phenomena of television, mobility and comprehensive education, but also by a tourist drive engineered to take pressure off the Lake District and Yorkshire Dales. The vulnerable gentian has been adopted as an emblem, which may well seal its fate, and sites associated with painters and writers – Rokeby and Brignall Banks with Sir Walter Scott, Barnard Castle and Bowes with Dickens – are being promoted.

The great landscape artists, Turner, Cotman and Girtin – whose subjects were the lovely fourteenth-century castle at Raby and the ruins of Egglestone Abbey, High Force waterfall and the Meeting of the Waters at Greta Bridge – were presumably not indifferent either to the presence of two likely patrons: John Bowes, founder of the Bowes Museum, and J. B. S. Morritt, purchaser of the famous Velasquez known as the Rokeby (pronounced Rookby) Venus. 'I've bought a fine picture of Venus's backside,' he wrote to a friend, and he hung it in the saloon of Rokeby Hall, at a height permitting gentlemen an excellent view and ladies the possibility of averting their eyes.

Whereas Rokeby Hall (not open to the public) is a modest Palladian villa in scale with its surroundings, the ornate neo-Renaissance château John Bowes built to house his collection seems shockingly out of place. But the Bowes net gathered in some marvellous treasures – paintings (a fine El Greco was bought for £8 as part of a job-lot), furniture, porcelain, *objets d'art* – and the museum is rightly famous.

Although a local landowner and Barney's Liberal MP, Bowes married and spent much of his life in France. That he, like all exiles from this most individual of northern dales, suffered from nostalgia, we know from his purchase of 'View from Ornans' by Courbet when on a tour, and the contemporary entry in his diary: 'Aug 19. Entered the Jura mountains. . . . Parts like Teesdale magnified.'

JOANNA KILMARTIN

The silver swan at the Bowes Museum – some marvellous treasures

Barnard Castle,

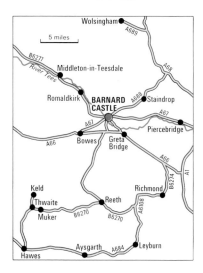

WHERE TO GO

The Castle: built by Bernard Baliol – long the home of the Nevilles, Earls of Warwick. This 12th c ruin stands above River Tees. From 16th c bridge follow winding path up around cliff base to castle gate. Archaeological excavations can be watched from distance. Open May–Sept daily 9.30–7.00, April daily 9.30–5.30, March, Oct weekdays 9.30–5.30 Sun 2.00–5.30, Nov–Feb. weekdays 9.30–4.00 Sun 2.00–4.00.

Bowes Museum: John Bowes, son of 10th Earl of Strathmore, and his wife Josephine built this French-style château. First view of high rooftops and ornate exterior is breathtaking. Collection includes paintings by Canaletto, El Greco, Goya, Gainsborough. Also Josephine's own highly competent work, French and English period rooms, costumes, outstanding porcelain and glassware, arms and armour, musical instruments. Lower galleries focus on local history, archaeology and natural history. Don't miss silver swan, an 18th c automaton, in action. Open weekdays March, April and Oct 10.00–5.00, May–Sept 10.00–5.30, Nov–Feb 10.00–4.00, Sun April–Sept 2.00–5.00, Oct–Feb 2.00–4.00.

Market Cross: unusual 18th c octagonal town hall in Market Place once served as jail, town council and market venue. Two bullet holes in its weathervane commemorate a private shooting match in 1804. Nearby plaque marks site of Thomas Humphrey, clockmaker, subject of Charles Dickens's *Master Humphrey's Clock.* Dickens stayed at the King's Head Hotel in Market Place while writing *Nicholas Nickleby.*

The Bank: below Market Cross, steep road running down to river is lined with antique shops. Perfect for long browsing stroll. Halfway down, Blagraves House, one of oldest Elizabethan houses among town's handsome 18th and 19th c buildings, was where Cromwell stayed in 1648. Recently renovated with popular restaurant. Some leaded windows, projecting four-storey bay crowned with steep gables.

Nearer river, well-renovated weavers' cottages past sycamore trees. Note long windows – a classic feature of weavers' cottages. Opposite, old weaving mill now turned to housing.

SHOPPING

Market day: Wed. Livestock market in Vane Rd – watch auctioneers selling sheep and cattle.

Early closing: Thur.

Barnard Castle Gallery and Cafe, The Bank: sells local crafts – watercolours, knitting, weaving, leatherwork, patchwork – and Third World baskets, carvings, necklaces, good teas, snacks with freshly ground coffee.

Mudlark Collectors Shop, 11 Galgate: intriguing collection of old books, maps, antique bottles. Cases full of cold cream pots, toothpaste jars bearing portraits of bearded Victorian gentlemen or ladies, dolls' heads and pipes.

Poppies, Galgate: wholefoods ranging from Tasmanian honey to wholewheat lasagne.

W. Kidd, 13 Market Place: a butcher selling (when available) the unique local Cotherstone cheese.

Partners: gourmet goods, many cooked in the local Cordon Bleu cookery school.

P. C. Sports, 17 Galgate, or **Dalesports,** Market Place: fishing, hunting gear, fishing permits.

FOOD AND DRINK

Pubs include: the **Red Well Inn,** serving elegant snacks and evening meals, free house with Theakstons; **Golden Lion Inn,** serving Bass and cheap meals – a down-to-earth local; **King's Head Hotel,** comfortable free house with dining room overlooking Market Place. *Egon Ronay's Lucas Guide* recommends **Blagraves House,** Teesdale 37668, enjoyable home cooking using fresh produce.

WHERE TO STAY

Egon Ronay's Lucas Guide recommends **Morritt Arms Hotel** at nearby Greta Bridge, tel Teesdale 27232, as a friendly well-run country hotel with lots of antiques, bric-à-brac, potted palms.

TOURIST INFORMATION

Teesdale District Council, Galgate, tel Teesdale 38481.

Villages and country towns

Aysgarth

Below main village is Aysgarth Falls where River Ure cascades spectacularly from High to Middle, Lower Force. Across 16th c bridge, originally built for packhorses but later widened, National Park Centre in old railway houses has cafe, offers advice on walks. Some along old railway bed, all through picturesque woods to falls. Beside bridge, old Yore Mill contains a carriage and coach museum and craft centre selling paintings, local weaving, quilts, pottery, bobbin-handled skipping ropes, yo-yos. Pottery, spinning-wheel demonstrations on Sun.

Follow stone stairs up to St Andrew's church – large, elegant, exquisitely set among trees. Base of west tower medieval, but rest rebuilt 1866 in unusual High Victorian style. Inside, see reading desk, two fine wooden screens originally from Jervaulx Abbey. George and Dragon is friendly village local.

Bowes

Village bisected by old Roman road, now A66, built by Agricola, 79 AD. Well-maintained ruined Norman keep, Bowes Castle sits within four-acre Roman fort. Superb views from keep of valley panorama and quaint little church, St Giles. Dotheboys Hall in Dickens's *Nicholas Nickleby* was based on Shaw's Academy

– now converted into three flats. Dickens stayed in 15th c coaching inn, Ancient Unicorn. Stables carefully renovated into modern motel rooms. Exterior retains much of original clean austerity. Initials carved on entryway beam, E.R. 1716, said to be those of Elisabeth Railton, innkeeper's daughter who died of broken heart a few hours after fiancé's death.

Hawes

Lively, crowded market town of proud greystone houses, cobbled streets and market square. Tourists mingle with farmers bringing milk from remote farms to Wensleydale Creameries – a tiny factory but town's largest employer. Watch cheese-making on summer Thur 1.15: book first at National Park Centre in Station Yard. Interesting mini-book, *Wensleydale Cheese* by Kit Calvert, also known for translating the Gospels into Yorkshire dialect. Old station house now the outstanding Upper Dales Folk Museum. Displays use poster-size black and white photos. Clear explanations cover oatcake-making, shepherd's skills, knitting, peat-cutting, butter/cheese-making, plus evil-looking veterinary tools. Open Easter–Sept Mon–Sat 11.00–1.00 and 2.00–5.00, Sun 1.00–5.00, Oct Tue, Sat, Sun only.

W. R. Outhwaite and Sons, ropemakers, weave ropes of all sizes and colours, making halters, plant holders, rope animals, dog leads, even bracelets, all in front of visitors.

Rose House, tucked between Fountain Hotel and Crown Inn, serves delicious carrot soup and dishes made with Blue Wensleydale cheese. Local paintings, embroidery on sale, country kitchen atmosphere.

Market day Tue. Sheepdog trials most weekends throughout area during June, July and Aug. List available at Hawes Tourist Information Centre.

Keld/Thwaite/Muker

Established by Norsemen, Keld is Swaledale's highest village. Pretty greystone cottages nestle in Swale's tree-lined gorge. The Pennine Way leads walkers from Keld to Thwaite. Several waterfalls – Catrake Force, Kisdon Force –worth short stroll for non-walkers. Tiny hamlet of Thwaite is hardly memorable, but two outstanding early naturalist photographers, the Kearton brothers, were born here. Farther on, Muker is a pretty village of tidy cottages with narrow interconnecting pathways stair-stepping hillside. Up path beside the Farmer's Arms is Swaledale Woollen Centre selling sturdy heavy wool sweaters. Knitting was once Swaledale's next biggest industry after mining. Everyone knitted, whether walking to market, herding sheep or sitting in a pub. East of Muker see Ivelet Bridge, said to be haunted by headless dog. This romantic tree-sheltered bridge arches high over rushing waters of young Swale.

Middleton-in-Teesdale

For 200 years, this attractive 'capital' of Upper Teesdale was dominated by mining. The Quaker-owned London Lead Mining Company built greystone houses, school, town hall, clocktower over gateway to Company Lead Yard. Now only great escarpments and rusting machines remain where lead was gouged from surrounding hills. A new wealth of Britain's rarest plants, including the famous gentians, has been found, a treasure carefully, and rightly, protected.

Behind village, there are trout in the River Tees. Salmon and sea trout once came here to spawn: today few dare brave Tees estuary pollution. J. Raine and Son, ironmongers, sell angling licences to those possessing Northumbria Water Authority permits. Addison's Fancy Goods Store stocks useful *Discover Teesdale* guide.

Cleveland Arms, handsome greystone coaching inn, with fine archway, recently renovated and renamed the Teesdale Hotel, serves lunches, teas, dinners. *Egon Ronay's Lucas Guide* recommends the Heather Brae Hotel and Restaurant, tel Middleton-in-Teesdale 4203. English and Continental dishes.

Piercebridge

Beneath this drowsy village of white cottages and tiny picket-fenced gardens circling spacious green lies Magis, a 4th c

Ropemaker at Outhwaites factory in Hawes

The River Swale at Richmond overlooked by the 11th century castle

Roman fort, extensively excavated. First settlements in 70 AD when Cerialis led campaign to control Brigantes entrenched in Stanwick Camp, Britain's largest Iron Age fort. In 300 AD, Constantius arrived to beat back Pict invasions and Piercebridge was rebuilt. These ruins are now being excavated by archaeologist Peter Scott and team behind eastern cottages. Villagers are accustomed to archaeologists poking in gardens or following Roman drains under their coal-sheds. Scott's team hospitably guide visitors when time allows. Across river, see Old Dere Street Bridge remains. Also visit nearby Stanwick Camp, 850 acres covered with four miles of ramparts, defensive ditches.

The George is a 250-year-old coaching inn, which serves Vaux beer. Menu includes wild boar, grouse, pheasant and pigeon. Dining-rooms almost close enough to Tees to paddle while eating.

Over bridge in pink house is Piercebridge Antiques – glass, porcelain, pottery in all colours, sizes, shapes. Wheatsheaf is popular local serving Camerons.

Reeth

Heather-covered fells and limestone cliffs of Feamington Edge dwarf this ancient Anglo-Saxon settlement, mentioned in Domesday Book as Rie. Greystone houses, shops, hotels with Georgian bay windows surround wide, sprawling green. Once centre of Swaledale lead-mining, Reeth is now a base for angling, grouse-shooting and walking. Swaledale Folk Museum in old Methodist Sunday school depicts history, lifestyle of Arkengarthdale and Swaledale: Methodism, population decline as mining died out, clogging, cheese-making. From Reeth, explore Dales of Arkengarth, Swale, Two spectacular drives to Richmond. Narrow, steep old road rides high ridges with vast panoramas while new road built by mining companies meanders along valley floor through lush glades past ruined priories of Marrick and Ellerton.

Old Butcher's Shop sells home-made Cumberland sausages, fresh pies, cooked, potted meats. The Pot Shop has interesting selection of Scottish woollens, locally made pottery. Reeth agriculture Show in Aug includes fell-running, horse-racing, brass band, fancy-dress parade. Buck Hotel has good bar meals and the Black Bull, with handsome Georgian façade, is another good stop for a pint.

Richmond

This former lead-marketing and military town is reminiscent of Italian hill towns. Richmond Castle's 11th c Norman keep and ruined walls shadow narrow lanes winding down to the banks of the Swale. These formidable battlements saw little more violence than Scottish raids. Legends claim that King Arthur and his knights sleep beneath castle in a vast hall – waiting until England needs them.

Since William I's day, curfew bells have rung from Holy Trinity church in steep, cobbled market-place. This odd 12th c church which served as a plague refuge, warehouse, school, assizes court, tobacconist, now houses the Green Howards Regimental Museum. Exhibits of early uniforms, medals, mess dress, details of battles from North-West Fronto Northern Ireland. Open April–Oct Mon–Sat 10.00–4.30, Sun 2.00–4.30, Nov, Feb, March Mon–Sat 10.00–4.30.

Town's architecture a delightful hodge-podge. Fleece Hotel's Victorian turrets, red-brick terracotta exterior could inspire a Gothic novel. Grey Friars Café, called after nearby 15th c tower, has a charming blue-grey Georgian exterior with bowed windows – Pevsner calls it 'an extravaganza in Norman Shaw motifs'. Walk down Newbiggin, gracious street with trees complementing an array of fine 18th c homes.

Beyond is Culloden Tower, a Georgian Folly no longer open to public for safety reasons. Small Georgian theatre, one of oldest and best-preserved in England, holds only 238. Museum on 191-year history recently opened with playbills and photos. Edmund Kean and Mrs Siddons both trod these boards. Dedicated volunteers enthusiastically guide visitors. Open daily, 30 May–30 Sept 2.30–5.00.

Colourful open-air market around obelisk plus Richmond Antiques, arts and crafts market in Ryders Wynd on Sat. Smaller market on Thur in Market Hall. Good secondhand bookshop – Archie Miles Ltd, 28 Victoria Rd. Joplings in Market Place has small delicatessen, canned drinks, wine. Castle Cabin, Castle Hill, sells Richmond rock, hand-dipped chocolates, home-baked Yorkshire biscuits, good local cheese including special hand-made Wensleydale. Upstairs the Pantry serves fresh coffee, cream teas, home-baked pastries, or visit Coffee Bean off Market Place for teas.

Pubs: Bishop's Blaize, Market Place, serves Camerons and bar snacks; Holy Hill, Sleagill, has Theakstons beer from the jug.

Romaldkirk

Exceptionally pretty village with stocks and water pump on green. Behind St Romald's church, named after a King of Northumbria's son, a narrow, tree-sheltered alley leads down toward Tees. St Romald's combines 12th, 13th, 14th c additions easily. Fine stained-glass windows. Massive, tower dominates entire building and village. Local brewery closed down long ago, but 18th c coaching inn, Rose and Crown Hotel, has Theakstons and Camerons beer in cosy old-fashioned surroundings. Food best in Teesdale, locals say.

Two good craftsmen further up Teesdale: Mickleton Pottery where Alastair Brookes sculpts local farmhouses and figures of farm-workers and blacksmiths. Pewtersmith Tom Neal in Egglestone designs unusual lights, dishes, wine glasses with spiralling stems, jewellery – keeps a small stock, so call first for appointment and directions to Eggleshope House, Egglestone, tel Teesdale 50235.

Staindrop

Life revolves around Raby Castle, Lord Barnard's majestic official seat. Built mainly in 14th c by Nevill family on site of an earlier castle of King Canute. Cicelly Nevill who lived here was the mother of Edward IV and Richard III. In 1616 passed to Vane family, Lord Barnard's ancestors who cannibalized nearby Barnard Castle to expand Raby – but not without public protest. 'O misery! Can £100 worth of lead, iron, wood and stone be worth more than a castle which might have been a receptacle for a King and his whole traine?' Raby's medieval splendour – proud battlements, towers, vast baron's hall, coach houses, gardens and parkland with deer – today seem well worth such sacrifices. Inside, see fine painting collections, ceramics, porcelains, very interesting medieval kitchen, Victorian octagonal drawing-room, coaches. Stables converted to tea-rooms. Open Easter–June Wed and Sun, July–Sept daily except Sat 2.00–5.00 and bank hol except Christmas.

Village church originally 8th c. Saxon windows and roofline still visible above nave arches. Nevill family effigies, especially tall, princely man carved in white alabaster, look eerie and beautiful in half-light of stained-glass windows. Old priest's vestry was once village jail. Pubs: Royal Oak – cosy, old world atmosphere – serves Bass, sandwiches; Black Swan has folk music evenings on Wed. Serves Camerons, like the recently-renovated Wheatsheaf.

Romaldkirk: the village pump and St Romald's church

Deer at Raby Castle, once owned by the Earls of Warwick

Places to visit

Bolton Castle: Pevsner describes ruined 14th c castle built by Richard de Scrope, a Lord Chancellor of England, as 'a climax of English military architecture'. Created to defend Wensleydale, it balanced harsh necessities of defence with comfort. Mary, Queen of Scots, was held here for seven months after Langside defeat of 1568. Restaurant serves meals, teas. Open daily except Mon May–Sept 10.00–6.00, other months closing at dusk. Off A684 north of Aysgarth, nr Redmire.

Bowlees Visitor Centre: outstanding ecological displays in Victorian chapel include rock collections marked 'Please Touch!' and sandbox with rubber stamps of wildlife tracks. Amusing and educational for all ages. Open Easter–Oct daily 11.00–5.00. Large parties tel Teesdale 22292. North of Middleton-in-Teesdale on B6277.

Greta Bridge: these serene woodlands, gentle vistas and noisy Greta River splashing from pool to pool inspired Turner, Sir Walter Scott and other artists and writers. Scott wrote epic poems *Brignall Banks* and *Rokeby* here. The Morritt Arms is a country hotel mentioned by Dickens in *Nicholas Nickleby*. Grand Rokeby Hall, built by Sir Thomas Robinson in 18th c, was original home of Rokeby Venus, now hanging in National Gallery. Remains of Roman fort can be seen in Morritt Arms gardens. Paradise Walk, on Yorkshire

Egglestone Abbey: idyllic ruins east of Bowes Museum. Founded in 1190 by Order of White Canons. Fine stonework in nave. Much of 13th c chancel remaining. Romanticized in Scott's *Rokeby*. Perfect for picnicking. Open May–Sept weekdays 9.30–7.00 Sun 2.00–7.00, March, April, Oct weekdays 9.30–5.30 Sun 2.00–5.30, Nov–Feb weekdays 9.30–4.00 Sun 2.00–4.00.

High Force: above Middleton-in-Teesdale, Tees drops over Great Whin Sill in 70ft cascade. Small parking and admission charges. Picnic, or snack at High Force Hotel.

Bow-topped gypsy caravan at the Aysgarth carriage museum

ACTIVITIES

Walking: the Pennine Way winds through wild, high fells. In Barnard Castle area, it runs from Cauldron Snout – a tumultuous waterfall – south through Middleton-in-Teesdale, Bowes Village, over Tan Hill to Keld, Thwaite, then from Swaledale it rambles over into Wensleydale to Hawes. Stop at Tan Hill Inn, highest pub in England at 1732 ft, for pint of Websters bitter and food. Stone walls three ft thick protect it from bitter Pennine winters. For fell-walking, take proper clothing, equipment, food supplies, since the weather can be treacherous. Keep to footpaths. Avoid damaging trees, wild plants, or disturbing birds and animals – carry guidebooks to identify many rare species here. For

information on organized day walks contact Barnard Castle Ramblers Association – Secretary Joan Martin, 8 Kirk View, Barnard Castle, tel Teesdale 37825.

Hamsterley Forest: of 5000 wooded acres more than 100 are open for picnics, nature walks, $4\frac{1}{2}$ mile forest drive. Watch for harriers, kestrels, deer, martens.

Stang Forest: from bleak fells above, Stang appears a luxuriant green blanket of 1600 acres, Norwegian, Sitka Spruce, larch, beeches, rhododendrons line forest edges. Walk to Hope Scar for fine views.

Angling: rod licences and daily or seasonal permits are available from most sport shops. Swale, Tees, Wear rivers fine for fly or worm fishing but many areas are private. Hury, Blackton, Balderhead, Cow Green reservoirs are stocked with brown trout, while Selset and Grasseholme both have rainbow trout.

Water sports: water skiing at Balderhead; rowing at Hury; sailing at Selset and Grasseholme.

FOOD AND DRINK

Egon Ronay's Lucas Guide recommends: **Three Tuns Inn**, Eggleston, tel Teesdale 50289 – wholesome, well-cooked food. **Black Bull Inn Restaurant**, Moulton, nr Richmond, tel Barton 289 – wide selection of dishes with emphasis on fish and shellfish and an outstanding wine list. **Hall Garth Hotel Restaurant**, Coatham Mundeville, nr Darlington, tel Aycliffe 313333 – set menus with choice of dishes such as cassoulet, roast duck and red mullet. **Newbus Arms Restaurant**, Neasham, tel Darlington 721071 – high standard of cooking.

TOURIST INFORMATION

Publications: local papers, *Darlington and Stockton Times*, Sat, *Teesdale Mercury*, Wed. *Discover Teesdale* part of the High Pennines Guide series available from the Information Centre, Barnard Castle. They also sell a *Walkabout* series of brochures for many of the villages, parks etc.

Tourist information: also at Richmond.

Research: Sue Morrow Lockwood.

side of bridge, is downriver to Meeting of The Waters where Greta joins Tees. See Mortham Tower (privately occupied), fine pele tower built in defence against Scots raiders. Or walk up to Brignall to romantic ruined church.

Killhope Wheel: high in Weardale, this giant iron wheel is all that remains of Park Head lead mine and crushing mill. Interesting picnic spot. Alongside A689 $2\frac{1}{2}$ miles west of Cowshill.

St Mary's Church, Wycliffe: has 9th c stones. South of Barnard Castle.

Hexham

From the bypass, zipping through the Tyne Gap, Hexham is easily dismissed. Pleasant little place. Quite picturesque, with the abbey lording it over the town. Clearly a would-be Durham. Pity, though, about the back end of that cinema, stuck out over the hillside.

But this is Hexham from the worst angle and at the wrong speed. You should explore from the centre, the Market Place, outwards. There aren't many signs of wilful commercial nastiness. The most attractive baker's shop had itself rationalized in plastic wood and orange trim last year, but perhaps they weren't to know that, in other parts of the country, great store is set by craft bakeries.

Yet at least Hexham hasn't been stricken with an Arndale Centre. Indeed, since the Scots stopped pillaging it some centuries ago, Hexham hasn't been greatly troubled by social or architectural upsets. The place is a model of snail's-pace adaptability. The jail is now a tourist information office. The abbey retains its Saxon crypt and seventh-century bishop's throne but, on the whole, isn't half as old as it looks. The east front was rebuilt in Early English manner by John Dobson, the man who proved, in Newcastle in the 1830s, that redevelopment was not necessarily a bad thing.

Hexham is made, as a place, by the abbey. Without it, the resemblance to Haltwhistle, the next market town along the Tyne, would be too strong. Its instincts, its allegiances, incline towards the east, towards the lowland farms, towards Newcastle, where so many of its inhabitants go every day to work. Hexham is pleasant, for sure, and unassuming. But, for the full character of the region, go higher up the Tyne and look to Allendale.

Just before midnight on New Year's Eve a troupe of what appear to be human torches – guizers they're known as – enters the square of Allendale Town to a brisk drumbeat. Dress is sort of Druidic Widow Twankey. The men encircle a towering woodpile, the half-barrels balanced on their heads flaming wildly.

At midnight precisely the drumbeat stops. Dead silence. Then, one after another, the guizers advance and duck, doff and tip their loads of fire into a dark mass of thorn and lumber. With a sizzle, a whoosh and a sudden gulping turmoil the bonfire catches. It billows frantically. Sparks flit over the rooftops. Anoraks and entranced faces show up in the vast glow. A moment later we come out with a roaring 'Auld Lang Syne'.

The other great annual event is the Allendale Show. This takes place on an August Saturday at Riding Haugh, a perfect natural showground below the village in a sheltered bend of the river. Whereas nowhere else has anything to match Allendale's New Year initiative, every decent-

Hadrian's Wall – 'farthest flung boundary of Roman Empire'

sized and self-respecting locality in the region has its own show. They have much in common: the Everest Double-Glazing promotion, the itinerant anorak vendors and certain avid competitors who go from show to show throughout the season. The passing of judgement on sheep, the ponyback antics, the wrestling, the stick-dressing, the best preserves and most admirable flower arrangement (under eight) are ubiquitous. Some connoisseurs, from north of the Tyne Gap, even go so far as to claim that the Bellingham Show surpasses Allendale's. But size isn't everything.

Much of Tynedale is covered by forest. England's biggest. The Upper North Tyne Valley is being scraped and dammed to serve as the new Kielder Reservoir, or 'Kielder Water' as they prefer to call it. Another biggest. The military use enormous amounts of the Cheviots for target practice. So, apart from recommending the forest trails and predicting a big future for watersports, the promoters of Tynedale tourism concentrate on the area with the most historic remains.

Things to see and do in these parts have a pronounced G. A. Henty ring to them. Possibilities include 'Walk the Pennine Way'; 'Along Hadrian's Wall' – be warned, though, the more spectacular stretches are more clamber than promenade; 'By Bus to Vindolanda' – watch out for hostiles from a replica wall-turret – and, when that palls, see History Unearthed daily in this major fort. For a jolly night out there's the phenomenal Langley Castle near Haydon Bridge where it's possible to feast right merrily, or I Claudiusly, or in hillbilly style.

The Wall itself needs no publicity, but I must recommend walking it in winter, when the distances are most sharply defined and the snow is liable to whirl up at you from the foot of Cuddy's Crag. And at Banks, beyond Greenhead going west, step aside to visit the museum, run in the most splendidly idiosyncratic fashion by Li Yuan Chia, who is not a native of these parts. He is the only person I know who has succeeded in bringing together, in peaceful co-existence, the antiquarian and the do-it-yourself, the avant-garde and the Women's Institute.

This part of the country isn't all frontier positions and defensive measures. Allendale, for instance, has an entire industrial history of its own. It began 1900 years ago, when the Romans started mining lead around Alston. By the sixteenth century Allendale was well on the way to becoming the centre of lead production. Of the two valleys (there's an East and a West Allendale) the East became the more elaborately developed, with a system of reservoirs to supply hydraulic power and supply the dressing floors. A $4\frac{1}{2}$-mile tunnel, the Blackett Level, was driven along the valley between 1854 and 1896.

Since then the industry has declined and virtually disappeared. Fluorspar, used as a flux in steelmaking and for non-stick surfacings, was extracted at Allenheads until last autumn when the British Steel Corporation declared the mine redundant.

Most of the population has gone. The schools have closed. Land that used to be worked, part-time, by the miners as crofts, is no longer workable on those terms. The walls collapse; the bracken encroaches.

Alston – England's highest market town

At well over a thousand feet above sea level, most of Allendale is good for nothing but grouse and sheep.

Two thousand or so feet up, at the head of the two Allendales, where Cumbria, Durham and Northumberland meet, you can look out over miles of oceanic fell and, on a bright day, see as far as the Cheviots and, to the west, Solway Firth. The carriers' ways, used for taking ore by packtrain, are now difficult to make out.

There are plenty of signs of old workings: hummocks, shaft tops and twisting, heathery gullies. Down below, beside the road linking the Allendales, you'll notice a group of derelict buildings. Quite deserted, apart from the odd browsing sheep. That's Coalcleugh, once remarkable for being the highest settlement in England. It's still marked on all the maps – only it no longer counts.

WILLIAM FEAVER

Hexham

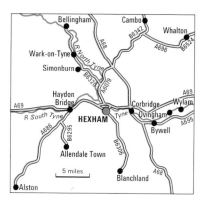

WHERE TO GO

Market Place: Hexham has been a major market town since 13th c and cattle still come from as far away as Ireland to be auctioned in Maiden's Walk.

Hexham Abbey: originally built by St Wilfred in 664 as Cathedral of St Andrews. After Norman-style reconstruction, Scots ravaged Hexham in 1296, burning much of the abbey and most of the town. The beautiful early 13th c north transept survived, along with Wilfred's apse, tiny barrel-vaulted crypt, stone frith stool where Northumbria's Saxon kings were crowned, and Saxon font with an elaborate Jacobean wooden cover. Small museum also contains Saxon hogbacks, Roman inscriptions, stone crosses.

Moot Hall: a sinister-looking 14th c tower house on the edge of the Market Place. Includes small gallery for visiting exhibitions. Open 11.00–1.00 and 2.00–5.00, Sun 2.00–5.00, closed Mon.

Manor Office: a stark ex-jail, possibly connected to Hexham Castle. Now it houses a tourist information office with a spiral staircase down to grim straw-filled dungeon with stocks. Reivers and Raiders summer exhibition relives Northumbria's bloody border history. Open Summer weekdays 9.00–6.00, Sun 2.00–6.00, winter weekdays 9.00–5.00. Extensive parking nearby – don't try to park in town centre.

Fore St: pedestrian precinct full of pretty Georgian façades. One especially attractive Victorian shop front, formerly Gibsons the chemist, is being preserved by new owner while its interior moves to the Science Museum in London.

EVENTS

Hexham Town Fair: last week in August.

SHOPPING

Market day: Tue; cattle and sheep market Tue/Fri.
Early closing: Thur.
Arthur Boadens, Market Place, and **David Boadens**, Market St: are the largest of the numerous antique shops.
Seasons Wholefoods, Hencotes: everything for health food fans.
H. A. B. Pyle, Hancotes: for shooting and fishing gear.
J. J. Cresswell, Priestpopple: sells sporting goods, hiking and biking supplies, and Northumbria Water Authority rod licences.

FOOD AND DRINK

Egon Ronay's Lucas Guide recommends **Abbey Flags**, 19 Market Place, tel Hexham 3252, for good quality dishes with a French bias on the short dinner menu. *Just a Bite* recommends **Country**

Kitchen, 23 Market Place, for outstanding home cooking. Pubs include: **Heart of All England**, a favourite with shoppers for light lunches; **Coach and Horses** – old coaching house with oak beams, leaded windows.

WHERE TO STAY

Egon Ronay's Lucas Guide recommends **Beaumont Hotel**, Beaumont St, tel Hexham 2331 – its imposing Georgian façade overlooks pretty abbey grounds.

TOURIST INFORMATION

Manor Office, Hallgates, tel Hexham 5555.

ACTIVITIES

Entertainments and interest in the arts gradually being revived with the Forum cinema now reopened and showing films six nights a week (also has sauna in the same building); and 400-seat theatre and arts complex to be opened in old Victorian Corn Exchange as soon as restoration work is complete.

Hexham Abbey: the crypt of the original Abbey

Hexham Abbey

Villages and country towns

Allendale Town
Village perched high above the River Allen among Pennine foothills. Odd central island of shops in broad square boxed by stone-roofed cottages.

Many fine walks with spectacular views of the Cheviots in nearby moorland. Drive up East Allen through small farming hamlets to Allenheads, where there is an active fluorspar mine. Occasional skiing in winter and, some say, best grouse-shooting in England. West Allen runs through beautiful Allen Gorge past Whitfield. Its church spire can be seen from top of gorge. At Cupola Bridge where banks become even steeper, woods lusher, walk down to Plankey Mill.

Crossed Keys Antiques fills a tiny white cottage with pottery and furniture, some restored by owner. Pubs: Hare and Hounds Inn, a tiny, cheerful local; Golden Lion Hotel, more formal country pub. Locals recommend its bar and restaurant meals.

Alston
England's highest market town at 1000 ft on a steep hillside with superb views. As well as cattle and sheep farming, there has been mining here for lead and silver since Roman days. Many houses were fortified with external staircases to first floors while animals occupied ground floors. Old station house at Town Foot contains tourist information office, with numerous booklets, black and white photos of old steam railway and new exhibition of railways and mining. Remaining foundry at Precision Products now provides lion's share of local employment. Visitors welcome. 10.00–11.30 and 2.30–4.30 weekdays. Best to tel first, Alston 228.

Fishing licences from D. W. Middleton, Front St (next to Post Office). Nent Hall Riding Centre for pony-trekking. Market day is Sat; early closing, Tue. Crowded with antique and junk shops.

Bellingham
Small market town of greystone cottages high among miles of empty fells. Once, when population was larger, a great wool fair took place here. St Cuthbert's, the 13th c towerless parish church, built for physical defence as much as spiritual solace. Extraordinary barrel-vaulted stone roof is supported by six-sided stone ribs. Hence, it was fire-proof against Scots raiders who had twice burnt previous wooden roof.

Perfect walking centre, directly on Pennine Way, with a hostel. Beautiful riverside walk behind church. Also up Hareshaw Burn to waterfall, Hareshaw Linn. Pubs: Black Bull – friendly local serving McEwans real ale; Cheviot – 17th c coaching inn with attractive bar full of copper collections, horse brasses, open fireplace.

Bellingham show – late August.

Blanchland
An enchanting village founded in 1165 by Premonstratensians, or White Canons, who built an abbey, corn mill, fish ponds and a silver refinery. Little survives of original abbey. Earls of Crewe laid out model estate village for local lead-miners on lines of the monastic settlement. Beyond monastery's castellated gatehouse, rows of terraced cottages surround a central gravelled square, a

Blanchland

university-like enclave. The present church is a handsome conglomerate of 13th, 15th and 18th c additions.

Parts of the abbot's lodge are incorporated in the Lord Crewe Arms Hotel. Visit its marvellous barrel-vaulted bar, heavy-beamed lounge with vast inglenook gaping open to the rooftop. Delicious food served; phone Blanchland 251 for a reservation.

Cambo

Don't miss this village if you visit nearby Wallington Estate. It has a modest church with interesting sepulchral slabs and post office was once a medieval pele tower. Capability Brown, born in nearby Kirkharle, went to school here.

Wallington was built by Blackett family in 17th c from coal/lead-mining and shipping fortunes. Later inherited by the Trevelyans. Over 100 acres of sprawling gardens rich with paths, lakes, bridges, an owl house, conservatory overflowing with magnificent fuchsias. Northern entrance houses National Trust shop, coaches, barouche, pony-cart, fire-engine. Interior of house sumptuous. Julia Blackett's embroidery-panelled needlework room and the saloon, with blue and white rococo plasterwork, are especially beautiful. Open daily April–Sept 1.00–6.00, except Tue, Oct Wed, Sat, Sun 2.00–5.00. Grounds open all year round.

Corbridge

Aptly described as 'the jewel of the Tyne Valley'. This gracious, historic town of dignified greystone houses hugs the Tyne slightly east of Corstopitum, once a vital Roman supply fort. Its medieval heyday ended when Scots burnt it down three times and Black Death caused populace to flee into countryside. In picturesque Market Place, visit Vicar's Pele Tower bordering St Andrew's churchyard, a fortified vicarage built of Roman stone for protection against the Scots. Pevsner calls nearby St Andrews with its Saxon tower and entire Roman arch in the nave 'most important surviving Saxon monument in Northumberland except for the Hexham crypt'.

Climbers and walkers should visit Watling St's odd knit shop, famed for its 'unwearoutable' socks which are exported worldwide. Studio Tea House, Hill St, offer teas and snacks. Forum Books and Crafts, Market Place, local

Cottage garden at Cambo: Capability Brown went to school in the village

pottery, wide choice of Northumberland guide books. Pubs include Angel Inn, Main St, oldest inn dating to 17th c. Serves bar snacks, evening meals. Black Bull, Middle St, 18th c Whitbread pub with restaurant, beamed ceilings and charm. Serves morning coffees. For real ale, the Wheatsheaf, Watling St.

Ovingham

Half old, half new, as tranquil as the Tyne bordering it. Dating from 11th c, St Mary's has the tallest tower on the Tyne. Here Thomas Bewick, the famous 19th c wood-engraver, is buried. As a boy, he sketched on gravestones and the church porch. Fine L-shaped vicarage was built in 14th and 17th c. Legends tell of a tunnel connecting it to Prudoe Castle on hillside above Ovingham.

Bridge End Inn, a quaint 300-year-old family-run pub, overlooks the tiny Packhorse Bridge – once used by pony trains carrying goods to coast.

Goose Fair mid-June with Northumbrian pipes and morris dancing.

Simonburn

Cluster of 18th c whitewashed cottages, sublime church among cedars and grand chestnut trees. Settlement given to Simon of Senlis by William the Con-

queror. Earliest human traces, mentioned by Pevsner, are four standing stones and Black Dyke, 'earthwork of uncertain age and purpose'. In St Mungo's, parallel arcades of Norman arches frame graceful lancet windows.

Imposing rectory with Georgian frontage. Early half was fortified tower to protect rector from reivers (robbers) and parishioners alike. Walk half a mile west through verdant woodlands to 12th c ruins of Simonburn Castle – good picnicking spot.

Wark-on-Tyne

The capital of Tynedale for 250 years under Scottish rule, ending in 1290. Ancient Saxon castle once stood on Mote Hill. Later, Robert the Bruce held court there when his 'great army' camped in Wark. Until late 18th c, lawlessness was rife. Every house was heavily fortified and attacks were so frequent that cottages were often roofed with upside-down turfs which were soaked with water when burning and pillaging seemed imminent. Today Wark is a picture of serenity. Simple greystone cottages circle village green and chestnut tree. For teas – Warksburn Guest House in lovely house on village edge. Home-made jams, scones, cakes served with fine hospitality.

Whalton

Looks less severe than most northern villages, with wide, tree-lined main street, grassy bank and verges. Originally Whalton was fortified castle-house village owned by the Lords Scrope, Wardens of the West March. The manor house is an adroit conversion from four cottages. Inside its pretty archway is Whalton Gallery which specializes in 18th, 19th and 20th c watercolours and drawings. Beresford Arms, a smart local covered in Virginia creeper, serves food and Vaux beer.

In July, Baal Fire Rite – jumping over the bonfire at village centre.

Wylam/Bywell

Wylam is an essential pilgrimage for railway devotees. Beyond the village, the National Trust has conserved the stone cottage where George Stephenson, the inventor of the railway engine, was born.

Pevsner waxes eloquent over Bywell snuggling beneath massive beeches in a bend of the Tyne, 'the most beautifully placed and the most picturesque and architecturally rewarding of all Tyneside villages'. It possesses a small castle, Bywell Hall, and two medieval churches, St Peter's and St Andrew's. The latter, owned by Blanchland's White Canons, has the county's best Saxon tower.

Wylam: George Stephenson's birthplace

—*Places to visit*—

Hadrian's Wall: farthest flung boundary of Roman empire stretching from Wallsend-on-Tyne to Bowness-on-Solway. Defensive line of 17 forts, with milecastles, turrets, ditches built in second c. It fell to Scots three times before Roman withdrawal in fourth c. Area can be very crowded, especially bad for cars on tiny lanes leading to forts. During the summer you can park at Once Brewed tourist information centre and catch special bus with taped commentary running circular route to major forts.

Best forts: Corbridge – key supply base on hilltop strategically overlooking Tyne at intersection of Dere St and Stanegate, Roman highway to Cumbria. Ruins have been well excavated. Fine little museum contains Roman sculptures, inscriptions, pottery, tools, military equipment. Chesters – housed 500-strong cavalry regiment. Fort projects north of wall for sorties into Scotland. Sophisticated baths with underfloor heating. Museum said to be one of most important collections of Roman relics in Britain, includes pottery, statuary, military equipment. Housesteads – classic Roman Wall photos taken here, with good reason. Superb walk along wall top. Vindolanda – one of original Stanegate forts rebuilt at least six times. Large civilian settlement. Recent excavations made important discoveries of writing tablets, leather sandals, textiles.

Corbridge, Chesters and Housesteads open May–Sept daily 9.30–7.00, April daily 9.30–5.30, March, Oct weekdays 9.30–5.30 Sun 2.00–5.30, Nov–Feb weekdays 9.30–4.00 Sun 2.00–4.00. Vindolanda open daily May–Sept 10.00–7.30, March, April, Oct 10.00–5.30, Nov–Feb 10.00–4.00.

Langley Castle: majestic 14th c tower house in romantic wooded setting. Unusual oblong building with four projecting towers. Used as family entertainment centre which holds medieval feasts, Henry VIII banquets, hillbilly evenings, carnivals, cabarets and Transylvanian nights. Lunches, teas, dinners – book well ahead for evenings, tel Haydon Bridge 481.

Beamish: regional open-air history museum spread over 200 acres. Ride working tram, visit farm, stocked with

Langley Castle, majestic 14th-century tower house

geese, chickens, cattle, and see station and cottages. Massive Victoriana collection (entire chemist shop) occupies Beamish Hall. Also includes tea-room and Bobby Shafto pub. Open April–Sept daily 10.00–5.00, Oct–March daily except Monday. Last admission is at 4.00.

Hunday National Farm and Tractor Museum: outstanding displays of over 130 beautifully restored antique tractors, steam engines and farm tools. Also new wagon collection, model dairy with livestock and working water-wheel. Open daily 10.00–6.00. Last admission 5.00. At Newton, nr Corbridge.

Li Yuan Chia Museum, Banks: permanent collection of avant garde art – new exhibition opens first weekend of each month. Arts room for visitor participation, do-it-yourself kitchen for Chinese and Indian tea or coffee. Picnic in sculpture garden. Open 9.00–7.00 daily all year. Tel Brampton 2328.

ACTIVITIES

Border Forest Park: Britain's largest man-made forest covers over 180 sq miles with over 2000 deer. Among rare species watch for wild goats on high fells, hen harriers, long-eared owls, ospreys, otters. Kielder Castle, once Duke of Northumberland's elaborate shooting lodge, offers picnic areas, toilets, parking, a playground, an outstanding forestry exhibition which sells tree seeds, with lots of walks and pony-trekking nearby. By 1982 Kielder Water's 2684 acres will be the 'largest man-made lake in western Europe'. For week-long programmes of fishing, kayaking, pony-trekking, natural and border history, contact the Reivers of Tarset, a licensed forest lodge outside Bellingham, tel Greenhaugh 40245. No hourly rates.

Walking: Pennine Way rambles down from north, round Border Forest to Bellingham, down along Hadrian's Wall then south via Roman road, Maiden's Way, through Slaggyford to Alston and beyond. Contains some of Britain's roughest and most beautiful walking. Short walks abound in this dramatically beautiful countryside. Hexham Tourist Information Centre has details.

Angling: mostly salmon, trout, eels in Tyne, Allen Rivers, Sweethope Lough, Whittle Dene Reservoir, Bolam Lake. Derwentwater reservoir is especially beautiful. Fine walks, picnicking. Northumbria Water Authority rod licences available from Gosforth Water Authority Headquarters, Hexham Tourist Information Centre and a scattering of small local shops. Acquire permits for individual waters locally. Boats for hire. Reserve in advance, tel Edrondbyers 55250.

FOOD AND DRINK

Egon Ronay's Lucas Guide recommends **Ramblers of Corbridge,** tel Corbridge 2424. German specialities. **Ashleigh Hotel Restaurant,** Allendale, tel Allendale 351 – Italian and French favourites in country-house setting. *Just a Bite* recommends **Watling Coffee House,** 11 Watling St, Corbridge, for teas, fluffy quiches and local preserves and crafts to take home. **Brownside Coach House,** Alston – especially good cheese scones, buttery shortbread.

TOURIST INFORMATION

Publications: *Hexham Courant*, Fri. Hexham Tourist Information offers pamphlets on pony-trekking, angling, antique and craft shops, camping and caravan sites, etc. Watch for *Passport to Northumbria*, useful free quarterly tourist guide.

Information centres: Kielder Water Authority Information Centre, overlooking reservoir site, tel Greenhaugh 40398. Kielder Castle Forestry Commission Information Centre, Kielder village. Open Easter–Sept 8.00–12.00, 1.00–4.00, weekends and holidays 12.00–6.00. Tel Kielder 50209.

Other tourist information centres at Bellingham, Corbridge and Haltwhistle.

Research: Sue Morrow Lockwood.

Ulverston

Most English market towns lie snugly at the centre of their own particular district. Ulverston, however, lies at the point where three quite different regions meet – Southern Lakeland, the Furness Plain and Morecambe Bay.

As you approach the town by road it seems to belong entirely to the hills. The soft, khaki-black rocks of High Furness loom close and almost tumble over it. On one side, houses and gardens scramble up the lower slopes of the Kirkby Moors, and it even has its own little mascot of a hill, called Hoad. But once you enter the streets you feel you have left the hills. For these houses are solid and urban. They have nothing of the happily haphazard improvization of Hawkshead or Ambleside. Above all, they are the wrong colour, not the almost black of slate but the near white of limestone.

Nearly all pre-1914 Ulverston is built of this cheerful stone. By now many of the houses and shops are blanketed over with stucco or rough-cast, but if you go to the car park behind Theatre Street, say, you can still see the old back-premises bare and un-plastered. One splendid warehouse rears a great rectangle of limestone, striped horizontally with window sills of the dark red sandstone of Furness Abbey.

Yet, oddly enough, it is the sea as much as the rock that has made Ulverston what it is. For Furness (pronounced with the accent on the first syllable) is the far-ness, the distant peninsula so cut off by the tides of Morecambe Bay as to be almost an island. The capital of medieval Furness, however, was not Ulverston but Dalton, because of the nearness of the rich and influential Furness Abbey.

It was not until after the Dissolution of the Monasteries that Ulverston began to grow and, of this period, the best building still to be seen stands just outside the town. Swarthmoor Hall, a beautiful but unostentatious Jacobean manor house, was once the home of Judge Thomas Fell. In June 1652, when the Judge was away from home, the young George Fox came there and, in a matter of hours, 'convinced' Margaret Fell of the truth of the Inner Light. After her husband's death, Margaret married Fox and made Swarthmoor into one of the nerve-centres of the Quaker movement. Later, in 1688, Fox bought a cottage and barn not far from the Hall and presented it to the Friends for their meeting house. It still stands, grey, modest, utterly self-contained, carrying on the Sunday meeting in an unbroken tradition of nearly 300 years.

The oldest remaining part of Ulverston town is mostly of the eighteenth century. Here the main streets take the shape of a wobbly capital T, of which the down-stroke, Market Street, splays out, at the top, like the arms of a catapult, to form the angular quirky and extremely

Hard Knott Pass, high above Eskdale

attractive Market Place. The left-hand of the upper stroke is now Queen Street, curving up towards the railway station, and the right-hand stroke is King Street, wriggling out of the Market Place through a gap so narrow as to seem like an unroofed gate-house. Here, and in the streets and alleys round about, is all the best of eighteenth-century and early nineteenth-century Ulverston. But you must not expect the elegance of Bath or Cheltenham. There are some handsome houses in Prince's Street but the rest of the old town is in the solid local vernacular style.

Much of the old Ulverston has been bulldozed to the ground and the new through road makes a horrid gash along the edge of it, though some good shop fronts remain here and there. But the prosperous, self-confident air of the early Victorian community still comes down to us in two highly individual buildings – the Savings Bank of 1845, at the corner of Market Street and Union Street, and the extraordinary memorial to Sir John Barrow. Sir John was a local man who became Secretary to the Admiralty and wrote the history of *The Mutiny on the Bounty*. His monument, appropriately, is in the form of a lighthouse which sticks up into the air from the top of the rounded Hoad Hill like the handle of a town-crier's bell.

That lighthouse brings us back to the sea. For, until the completion of the Furness Railway in 1857, the main approach to Ulverston was across the sands of Morecambe Bay when the tide was out. George Fox came by that route; so did John Wesley. Wordsworth was waiting to cross the Leven Sands when he heard of the death of Robespierre. Right up to about 1850, a regular over-sands coach service left the Sun Inn at Ulverston on Monday, Wednesday and Friday, returning from Lancaster on Tuesday, Thursday and Saturday. Ulverston was then at the top end of perhaps the most romantic and hazardous main road in England.

It was also, more surprisingly, a port. The villages of Morecambe Bay and the Cumbrian coast had long been supplied from small boats, but, in 1796, Ulverston became more ambitious and linked itself to the sea by what was claimed to be the shortest and straightest canal in England. Today, at Canal Foot, you can see the narrow and intricate windings of the channel that the small boats had to navigate.

By the time the canal was opened the main export from Ulverston was iron ore, for the limestone of Low Furness contained one of Britain's richest deposits of haematite. Even earlier, in the mid-eighteenth century, the water-powered, charcoal-burning blast furnaces of the south lakeland valleys were among the most advanced in the world, pioneering the Industrial Revolution. The Backbarrow furnace, set in the early Picasso landscape of the Blue Mills, was in continuous production for 200 years, closing down only after the Second World War; the Duddon furnace, established in 1736, still stands in ruins as big as a cathedral, hidden away in the woods beside Duddon Bridge.

Yet, when the new Iron Age came to Furness in the nineteenth century, and mine after mine was opened and Barrow boomed up into

The Ravenglass and Eskdale Railway – a seven-mile ride through the valley of the Esk

existence, Ulverston seemed, at first to have been left out. It was not until 1874, when the North Lonsdale Ironworks was set up, that prosperity came again to the town and saved it from declining into a mere dormitory for Barrow. In a way, that same development of the 1870s is saving the town even today, for, though the ironworks were closed down many years ago, the old site is occupied by the Glaxo pharmaceutical factory which has brought new employment and independence. The town can now look to the future more confidently than most in the area.

Ulverston has always been an essentially practical town. It is almost entirely free from the knick-knackery and gimcrackery that disfigure many of the tourist towns, yet it belongs to its district as much as they do. From Birkrigg Common you can see it lying comfortably at the foot of the friendly and unaggressive hills of High Furness – a country of little, tightly folded valleys and tucked-away villages which the main band of the tourists rarely discover. Move seawards, to the Quaker burial ground at Sunbrick, and you look across the bay – a great firth or in-shore sea when the tide is in, but, when it is out, a county-size acreage of sands, channels and shingle 'skears'.

On the far side of the water are the woods of Cartmel, with its delightful village and glorious priory church. On the near side, if you climb higher up, you can see the red-stained, worked-out iron-ore country around Lindal and Dalton, and, farther out, the cranes of Barrow-in-Furness. Walney Island, across its channel, shelters Barrow Docks like a cowl on a chimney-pot. Much of Walney is now a suburb, but the other 'Channel Isles' – Piel, Foulney and Sheep – remain quite remote.

You have the feeling that human occupation has gone on for a long time on these islands and all along the peninsula. Ulverston's antiquity is of a shorter time-scale, yet the past of the islands and the hills is the past that it grew out of. And, what is more, it is still growing.

NORMAN NICHOLSON

Ulverston

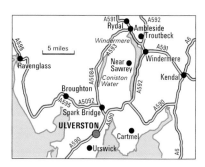

WHERE TO GO

Swarthmoor Hall: attractive manor house with mullioned windows and a balcony from which George Fox preached. Cosy dining hall and early 17th c furniture in the bedrooms upstairs. Open March–Oct Mon–Wed and Sat 10.00–12.00 and 2.00–5.00. On the A590 road to Barrow, not well signposted.

Cornishead Priory: set in 200-acre grounds on the site of a 12th c Augustinian Priory, this Gothic whimsy is rampant with towers, turrets and gables. A former owner embellished the sea view from the top window by building classical 'ruins' on Chapel Island. Now a centre of Buddhism called the Manjushri Institute, priory is open during summer Sat and Sun 2.00–5.00 or by appointment, tel Ulverston 54019. On the Barrow–Ulverston coast road.

Hoad Hill and Monument: 50ft landmark with extensive views of the Furness peninsula and Morecambe Bay. Monument is open whenever the flag is out, but view from the hill is almost as good. Especially impressive from the A590 and a reference point for miles.

Stan Laurel's birthplace, 3 Argyle St: the famous comedian was born in this small terraced house on 16 June 1890. Devotees can drink at the Stan Laurel pub around the corner, with posters, pictures and Stones bitter.

Furness Abbey: 12th c monastery with remnants of cloisters, refectory and dormitories. Built of beautiful rose-coloured sandstone with arches that reach to the sky. Tavern and bistro, standing between abbey and other monastic ruins, not as unsightly as it sounds. Abbey open May–Sept weekdays 9.30–7.00 Sun 2.00–7.00, March, April, Oct

Corner shop in Ulverston

weekdays 9.30–5.30 Sun 2.00–5.30, Nov–Feb weekdays 9.30–4.00 Sun 2.00–4.00.

SHOPPING

Market day: Cattle market, Thur; small general market, Sat.

Early closing: Wed.

Corn Mill Galleries, the Old Town Mill: one half devoted to 17th c working corn mill, the rest set aside for crafts. Ground floor has a selection of quality goods made by local artists; first floor has textiles and an exhibition gallery, while the skylit top floor is Wendy Todd's silk screen workshop. Everywhere whitewashed and airy, good place for gifts, café. Open Tue–Sat 9.30–5.30.

Cumbria Crystal, Lightburn Rd: in Ulverston's former cattle market, an

18th c octagonal building, the traditional skill of glass-blowing has been revived. Fascinating viewing, but not on a hot day. Goblets and decanters on sale in the shop. Glass-blowing factory open Mon–Fri 9.00–4.00, Sat 9.00–11.30. Shop open Mon–Fri 9.00–5.30, Sat 9.00–12.30, plus Sun 9.00–12.00. Small admission charge to factory.

Picnic fare: Parkinson's Butchers, Queen Street, for tasty pork pies. Or try Morecambe Bay shrimps from the stalls on market days. Several good bakeries for bread.

FOOD AND DRINK

In 1850 Ulverston had three breweries (including the Gill Breweries who brewed ginger beer in stone bottles), plus 58 public houses. Now there is one brewery and 28 pubs, almost all of which serve Hartley's, the local ale. All-day drinking on Thur – cattle market day.

Pubs include: **Railway Hotel**, opposite the station – cheerful and old-fashioned with smoked glass door, two bars, chilled wine by the glass; **Hope and Anchor**, Daltongate – low beams, round iron and wooden tables, cider on tap, very good lunchtime food including locally caught fish; **Rose and Crown**, King St – building dates from 1590, has been a pub for centuries.

WHERE TO STAY

Egon Ronay's Lucas Guide recommends **Lonsdale House Hotel**, Daltongate, tel Ulverston 53960. Georgian house with comfortable accommodation and friendly atmosphere.

TOURIST INFORMATION

The Renaissance Centre, 17 Fountain St: office open Mon–Sat 10.00–5.00 (closed winter Mon), tel Ulverston 52299. The Renaissance Theatre Trust was established over 20 years ago and presents shows and events throughout Cumbria. Watch local papers for venues.

Villages and country towns

Cartmel

Like a cathedral city in miniature on the banks of a river. Closely packed cluster of Georgian and Queen Anne houses with the odd medieval cottage, around a cobbled courtyard with an inn on either side. The King's Arms is in the *Good Beer Guide*; the Royal Oak has a heavy studded door and a bar of beer kegs. Both serve Whitbread.

Cathedral is actually a priory, elegant but small, founded in 1188 and according to the Baron of Cartmel 'never to be raised to the dignity of an abbey'. There is still a great community attitude, although village is increasingly popular due largely to the steeplechase racecourse bringing thousands every spring and summer bank hol. Priory has a large, mostly plain, glass window and a relatively new roof – some original bosses found their way to village fireplaces. Cromwell's troops once used the nave as a stable.

Up the stone steps of the Gatehouse is a National Trust gift shop, while tucked

behind the arch is the Anvil Gallery. In an old cruck barn is a collection of Michael Gibbon's large wooden sculptures, none for sale. Evocative, polished, with a texture like grainy silk, these sculptures are well worth a visit. Barn open 9.00–6.00 daily. Gatehouse open March–Dec. daily, Jan–March, Sat, Sun only.

Near Sawrey

Approached from the slopes of gleaming Esthwaite Water, Near Sawrey's buildings are bright and attractive. 200-year-old Tower Bank Arms stands at an angle of prominence with a clockface dominating its black-trimmed portico. This is the pub illustrated in Beatrix Potter's *Tale of Jemima Puddleduck*. Now preserved by the National Trust, interior has recently been restored with old framed pictures, exposed oak beams and lots of ancient clocks. Heritage keg bitter from hand pumps, accommodation upstairs. The garden path leads to Hilltop, Beatrix Potter's modest farmhouse where many of the Peter Rabbit books were written. Hilltop remains much as it was during the author's stay – no electric lights – with original drawings. The house suffers from a surfeit of visitors so devoted Potter fans only please. Many displays are high up and therefore not suitable for young children. National Trust. Open April–end Oct daily except Fri 10.00–5.30, Sun 2.00–5.30 or dusk if earlier.

Ravenglass

Much to see and do here with Muncaster Mill, with its working water-wheel, and freshly ground flour and bread for sale, the Ravenglass Nature Reserve, and Muncaster Castle, the seat of the Pennington family since the 13th c. Castle has a beautiful octagonal library with brass railings along the edge of a balcony, a rare collection of miniature furniture made as test pieces during the reign of Charles II, and a pale and spacious drawing-room with gracefully curving ceiling. Grounds are extensive, with splendid views of mountain, of Black Combe, and flamingoes. Ravenglass's prime attraction, however, is 'T'laal Ratty', the Ravenglass and Eskdale Railway, where visitors can ride for miles through a beautiful valley in a miniature 15in gauge train. Also Railway Museum. Ravenglass Information Centre open

Cartmel – cathedral city in miniature on the banks of the river Eea

Grasmere lake – an easy walk from Dove Cottage

May–Sept 11.00–6.00, tel Ravenglass 278.

Rydal

Stands peaceful and unhurried despite being bisected by the busiest road in Lakeland. Glen Rothay Hotel backs on to Dora's Field, which Wordsworth named after his daughter. Now owned by National Trust. White and rose-covered buildings mark the turning to Rydal Mount, the poet's home after he left Dove Cottage. Rooms contain both furniture and signed first editions from that period; also many portraits, including one of Coleridge and the only known painted image of Wordsworth's sister Dorothy. Little of the 4½ acres of sloping gardens has changed since his day; there's a lofty summerhouse, and a terrace with views of Rydal Water. Open daily 10.00–5.30, winter 10.00–4.00, closed Wed afternoon.

Troutbeck

Long, lovely dark-stone village strung along the top of a valley; almost every house has clear country views of the fells and grazing ponies. At one end is the attractive post office/public hall; at the other is the Mortal Man Hotel, recommended in *Egon Ronay's Lucas Guide* for its accommodation and generous portions of wholesome English food, tel Ambleside 3193. Just beyond the post office stands Townend, a National Trust owned yeoman's house, dated 1626. Lots of handsome carved oak furniture. Open March, Wed only; April–end Oct, daily except Sat and Mon but open Bank Hol Mon 2.00–6.00 or dusk. No electric lights, difficult to see on a dull day.

Church and school are at the bottom of the valley, on the main Windermere–Penrith road, simple church distinguished by its east window, the joint work of William Morris, Ford Madox Brown and Edward Burne-Jones. Around the corner is the Queen's Head, serving Youngers bitter from a bar which was a four-poster bed.

Urswick

Some say name stands for 'village of wild cattle'. Sheep, if not exactly wild, do graze Birkrigg Common, a lush plateau offering the best view of Urswick's grey stocky buildings on three sides of a tarn. Church contains a font with ornate sea serpents, fine brasses and much unusual wood carving; on one pew is carved a child with a monkey on an organ. Each autumn traditional rush-bearing takes place. Children in costume will leave Little Urswick (one mile away) and parade through the streets carrying flowers and rushes from the tarn, concluding with a special church service.

—Places to visit—

Holker Hall: 17th c stately home, partly rebuilt in 1873 after a fire. It is full of interesting objects: a Victorian double-seated children's rocking-chair, a Wedgwood fireplace and a self-portrait by Van Dyck. Open Easter–early Oct daily except Sat, 11.00–6.00. Eight miles south of Newby Bridge, four miles west of Grange-over-Sands.

Belle Isle: the only inhabited island on Windermere, with a romantic 18th c circular mansion accessible only by boat. Open end May–mid-Sept Sun–Tue, plus Thur, 10.30–5.00. Boat service behind Windermere Aquatic on Bowness Promenade. Café on island.

Sizergh Castle: 14th c pele tower is the oldest part of the castle and rises to 60 ft. The great hall was added later, as was the distinguished carved woodwork. Castle has been in possession of Strickland family since first half of 13th c – along the way they produced President George Washington of the USA – and many relics remain, including fine oak furniture, china, and a two-handed sword. Garden has an unusual amount of ferns. Rock garden with waterfall and pools. National Trust. Open April–end Sept Wed and Sun, also Thur in July, Aug 2.00–5.45. Garden Wed, Thur and Sun 2.00–5.45. Closed Bank Hol Mon. Three miles south of Kendal.

Dove Cottage, Grasmere: Dorothy and William Wordsworth spent nearly nine years here before leaving it to the tourist trade. Small low rooms, leaded light windows, little parking space. Wordsworth Museum in the barn across the road contains personal relics and original manuscripts. Open daily (except Sun) April–Sept 9.30–1.00, 2.00–5.00. Shorter hours in winter.

Brantwood: situated on beautiful Coniston Water. John Ruskin, the artist and critic, lived here for 30 years. Rooms contain 250 paintings, most by Ruskin, some by his contemporaries. Nature Trail. Open Easter–Oct Sun–Fri 11.00–5.30.

Ruskin Museum: pictures and archives relating to Ruskin and contemporaries. Also items detailing the growth of Coniston, plus a section on water-speed champion Donald Campbell. Open April–end Oct daily 9.30–8.00 or dusk. In Coniston village.

Millom Folk Museum: authentic full-scale model of a drift of the Hodbarrow Mine, complete with cage which could carry eight men. Open daily Easter–mid Sept 10.00–5.00. Millom village.

Holehird Gardens and Lakeland Horticultural Society's Gardens: landscaped grounds with spacious lawns, stream and pond, rockeries and splendid view across Windermere. Open any reasonable times, admission free. A592, three-quarters of a mile north of junction with A591.

Rusland Hall: sunny and informal Georgian mansion whose present owners have built up a collection of mechanical music and early photographic equipment. Open daily April–end Sept 11.00–5.30. Leave A590 $2\frac{1}{2}$ miles south of Newby Bridge at Haverthwaite crossroad.

Levens Hall: Elizabethan house filled with antiques, with Spanish leather wall coverings and fine plasterwork ceilings. Also topiary gardens designed by Guillaume Beaumont, James II's gardener at Hampton Court. The original shapes of the beds and borders have remained unchanged since 1692. Plants can be bought from the plant centre. Working

steam-engine collection, lunches and teas. Open Easter–end Sept. Tue–Thur, plus Sun and Bank Hol Mon 2.00–5.00. Garden and plant centre open daily 10.00–5.00, winter Mon–Fri only; lunches from noon. Five miles south of Kendal on A6.

Hawkshead Courthouse: once part of 15th c manorial buildings held by Furness Abbey; now only courthouse remains. Managed jointly by the National Trust and the Abbot Hall Gallery, Kendal, and used as a museum of rural life. Open Easter, May–mid-Oct daily including bank hol, except Mon, 2.00–5.00. Three miles east of Coniston, five miles south of Ambleside on B5286.

Windermere Steamboat Museum: distinctive collection of boats afloat, all in working order, including a 1780 yacht and Beatrix Potter's rowing boat. Open Easter–Oct weekdays 10.00–5.00, Sun 2.00–5.00. Off A592 on shore.

ACTIVITIES

Lakeside and Haverthwaite Railway: steam train rides along the Leven Valley. Haverthwaite Station has atmosphere reminiscent of the past. Several trains Easter, Sun in April, daily May–

early Oct. Can also be combined with a cruise on Windermere.

Grizedale Visitor and Wildlife Centre: lying in an 8000-acre forest of outstanding natural beauty, centre consists of two displays: the first is on the geology, soil structure and the history of the land use; the other has natural dioramas on a wide range of forest wildlife, using sound recordings to help identify the animals. Open daily Easter–Oct 9.00–5.00. Also forest trails and conservation nursery where trees are on sale. Situated between Hawkshead and Satterthwaite.

Theatre in the Forest: part of the Grizedale Forest complex, this intimate auditorium used to be a barn. Now it presents a wide range of quality events all year round, from chamber music to films and drama. Programmes available at most information centres or tel Satterthwaite 291.

National Park Centre: Brockhole: built in 1900 as a private home, Brockhole became Britain's first National Park Centre. With 32 acres of formal gardens extending to the lakeshore, centre has a multi-media exhibition which details the Lake District from prehistoric to modern times. Also putting green, café, informa-

Levens Hall: Elizabethan house with 17th-century garden

Public boat landings at Bowness on Windermere

tion centre. Open late March–early Nov daily from 10.00–5.30, closed earlier in spring and autumn. Between Ambleside and Windermere on A591.

Rusland Hall

Coniston Water: thought to be the gentlest of the Lakes, with fields of flowers near its shores, although Old Man is a popular peak for climbers. Best views are the fells around Tarn Hows. Coniston Boating Centre hires out a variety of boats, tel Coniston 366. Fishing permits from Shop 3, Lakeland House, Tilberthwaite Avenue, Coniston: perch, eels and trout if you're lucky.

Windermere: the largest lake in the whole of England – 10½ miles long – and no doubt the most popular; in the high season there can be 1500 people in boats. Best part for secluded walks is the west side, where the trees grow thick and close to the shore. Pamphlets on walks from tourist information offices, or buy a copy of *Lake District Walks for Motorists – Central Area* at local bookshops. Sealink offers cruises visiting Lake Side, Bowness and Ambleside, or a complete 'Around the Lake' trip, May–early Oct. Ski-boat hire from the Lakeland Sailing Centre, including free use of wet-suit and skis, tel Windermere 4366, open daily. Lessons in sailing from Nor'West Sailing, five-day courses in dinghy sailing and offshore cruising. Tel Newby Bridge 821.

FOOD AND DRINK

Egon Ronay's Lucas Guide recommends: **White Moss House Restaurant**, Grasmere, tel Grasmere 295 – five-course menu changes daily; **Michael's Nook Restaurant**, Grasmere, tel Grasmere 496 – skilled cooking of fresh ingredients; very good wine list; **Rothay Manor Restaurant**, Ambleside, tel Ambleside 3605 – elegant Georgian restaurant, home-made soups, unusual meat and poultry recipes; **Porthole Eating House**, Bowness-on-Windermere, tel Windermere 2793 – well-cooked Italian-influenced dishes; **Miller Howe Hotel Restaurant**, Windermere, tel Windermere 2536 – star-rating, excellent main course accompanied by impressive array of vegetables; superb views of the lake; **Tullythwaite House**, Underbarrow, tel Crosthwaite 397 – star-rating, the best in traditional English cooking. Unlicensed so take your own wine, and arrive punctually at 7pm; **Hodge Hill**, Cartmel Fell, tel Newby Bridge 480 – charming stone farmhouse in remote country setting; five-course set menu of mainly English dishes.

TOURIST INFORMATION

Publications: *Ulverston News*, published Fri, is good for films and galas. The *Lakeland Echo*, weekly, has information and features, particularly on the southern Lake District National Park, with daily 'What's on Guide'. The South Lakeland District Council Department of Tourism and Recreation puts out a monthly *Coming Events* bulletin available from information offices, while *Preview of Lakeland* is a colour quarterly which details shops, events, and places of interest.

Lake District Weather Service: tel Windermere 5151.

Tourist information centres: Barrow-in-Furness, Millom, Ravenglass, Grange-over-Sands, Bowness, Windermere, Hawkshead, Coniston, Brockhole, Grizedale.

Research: Martha Ellen Zenfell.

Dora's Field, named by Wordsworth, and Rydal Water

Penrith

It is no great commendation for a town to be dubbed 'gateway' – a way through rather than a stopping-place. This could easily befall Penrith, a small town on the north-eastern edge of the Lake District, its long history fogged over, its sombre aspect deriving from the red sandstone which gave it its name – Pen Rith, red town – being gradually overthrown by the bulldozers, bringing new architecture and materials.

In spite of its position inviting the gateway tag – half a mile from the M6 motorway; Northumberland and the Scottish border to the north; the peaks and waters of the Lake District west and south; and the long, uncompromising ridge of the Pennines to the east – Penrith emerges as an active market town on which local country folk converge with as much purpose as visitors who come to explore its surroundings.

It stands at the crossing of important routes leading in all directions, the modern ways superimposed with little deviation on the ancient. The Romans, advancing under Agricola, undaunted by the fearsome upheaval of the mountainous terrain, forged networks of roads inevitably leading to their final great fortification, Hadrian's Wall. Camps, forts, signal and staging posts punctuated the routes, many still visible.

At Old Penrith, four miles north of Penrith proper, the remains of a three-acre camp, Voreda, lie above the crazily twisting river Petteril, close to the A6, the modern version of the arrow-straight Roman road to Carlisle. Another fort, Brocavum, is a couple of miles south-east of the town at the junction of the B6260 with the A66.

Little remains of the Celtic era; but in St Andrew's churchyard, moved to form a group, stand the Giant's Grave and the Giant's Thumb, tall tenth-century wheel crosses, very weathered, their arms missing; while, between them hogback stones are romantically associated with the burial place of Owen Caesarius, Celtic King of Cumbria.

Caught by its strategic position, Penrith suffered constantly from invasion. At one time it even came under Scottish rule by means of some tenth-century swapping, though this loss of territory was hotly disputed by the Normans who drew their English boundary north of Penrith. With the Scottish border raids, destruction by fire was commonplace. Luckily, the narrow entrance roads and gates, leading to open spaces within, allowed inhabitants and cattle some protection.

In the late fourteenth century Ralph Neville, Bishop Strickland and first Earl of Westmorland, was granted permission to build a defensive castle, which he did with all speed. Subsequent illustrious owners included Warwick, the Kingmaker, and Duke Richard of Gloucester, before his crowning as Richard III. His castle survived a good deal longer than he did; but by the mid-sixteenth century it had fallen into

Fields near Kirkoswald: weeding turnips

total ruin, many of its stones carted off as handy building material. The castle still claims the attention of visitors, since it faces the railway station: a scant ruin, but protected, renovated and neat.

Penrith's higgledy-piggledy layout may not make exploration simple, but it provides the essentials for a flourishing country market town. There are ample pubs and parking places, jam-packed on market days; and the irregularly shaped open spaces are just what markets need: real markets, agricultural in essence, yet with a considerable overflow of stalls crammed with anything that may sell.

The parish church of St Andrew shows little of its Norman origins except in the thick-walled west tower; and fragments of old glass are set into some windows. Constant rebuilding has reduced any specific character, but it has emerged a lofty, galleried church of good proportions, once considered the finest in the county.

Old buildings have assumed new uses. Robinson's infant school, built in Middlegate around 1670, is now the tourist information office and small museum. In the narrow streets surrounding St Andrew's churchyard, where plaques tell of former notable occupants, a small bulging red sandstone building, part of the present Tudor Bar and Restaurant, was once Dame Birkett's school, which Wordsworth, his sister Dorothy, and future wife Mary Hutchinson attended.

Immediately to the north of Penrith is the Beacon, a 937-foot wooded hill topped by an eighteenth-century pyramidical structure, the Pike, which once flashed fires at the onset of national emergencies, and now flares on important ceremonial occasions. Paths wind to the top, but the superb views can well be seen from the Beacon Edge road – a mile-long promenade overlooking the town, with a panoramic view-finder to help you to sort out the mountains.

Gateway to the Lakes, Penrith is often called. Westwards, the A66 runs to Keswick and on to Cockermouth, and from it the main lakes can be reached by turning south, give or take a mountain pass or two. Ullswater is the nearest lake to Penrith, and easily one of the most beautiful. Branch off at Pooley Bridge at the head of the lake, and the main road runs down the western shore with dreamy views of the great fells rising on either side.

There's a National Trust car park, café and gift shop at the Dockray fork (the A5091, where it joins the A66), footpaths leading above clattering Aira Force, where the beck pitches over into a steep, narrow gorge; carry on, and you reach the upper falls. To the north lies Gowbarrow park and fell, where Wordsworth first saw his 'host of golden daffodils'; and, a bit to the south, tracks lead up through woods, passing a tiny village called Seldom Seen, now merely a line of little holiday cottages. When you turn to come back to water level across high sheep meadows, the views of the lake are totally bewitching. These are minimum-effort walks; plenty of tracks lead up the high fells for those who can and care to follow them.

The eastern road down Ullswater peters out at Howtown, one of the stops for lake cruisers. From this road are innumerable lovely walks:

along the shore, up to Martindale with its miniature thick-walled church, its paths beside hurrying becks. And from here, or from the Haweswater reservoir to the east, you can climb up to Roman High Street, and step out along it like a holidaying legionary.

Go east from Penrith and the countryside at once becomes more pastoral, rolling towards the distant ridge of the Pennines. The lovely River Eden, noted for salmon fishing, is swelled by the River Eamont near Penrith, and assumes majestic proportions as it flows towards Carlisle and the western end of Hadrian's Wall to spill into the head of the Solway Firth. A mile south of Penrith is once-proud Brougham Castle, above the River Eamont near its junction with the Lowther River, the earthworks of the Roman fort of Brocavum below it.

Follow the River Lowther south by minor roads and within a few more miles is the great Lowther estate, criss-crossed by public roads for motorists, signposts directing visitors to the wildlife park, and to the church with its Lowther memorials and mausoleum above the river. The Lowthers, Earls of Lonsdale, now live in the charming nearby village of Askham. As for the castle, busily turreted and pinnacled, it dominates the countryside and only on closer inspection do you realize that it is merely an empty shell. Follow the River Lowther southwards, and you reach Shap and its ruined abbey, tucked among the fells.

It's all too easy to be sidetracked by casual finds around Penrith. A few miles south-west is Dacre village, the lure provided by chance reading of notes on St Andrew's church. Here, in the churchyard, stand four very weathered stone bears, appearing to be in various stages of combat with a cat or lynx. The stones mark the corners of the original church. And barely a mile away, where the Dacre Beck meets the River Eamont, is Georgian Dalmain House, elegant in pinkish-grey stone, in gardens and deer park, its rooms beautifully proportioned, with a wealth of old oak panelling cut from estate trees.

The lovely Eden valley, full of pretty villages, old churches, and briskly flowing streams, seems almost threatened by the sometimes glowering and snow-streaked Pennines over to the east. But there's a quick way of getting a look at them at closer range by driving on the A686 from Penrith to Langwathby, and over the tops by the Hartside summit. The views are stupendous: the fells of Lakeland, and to the north, the Solway Firth and the mountains of Scotland.

Just north of Langwathby, a short diversion provides an excursion into prehistory. In high fields between Little Salkeld and Glassonby stand Long Meg and her daughters – a Bronze Age stone circle of 65 'daughters' and Long Meg herself, a slim 18-foot stone with ring markings. And a few hundred yards away is Little Meg with her smaller family of stones.

This whole region has the reputation of being among the wettest in England. Maybe so; but that mixture of rain and sunshine produces good green sheep country, exuberant rivers and waterfalls, and some fine local rainbows.

DIANA PETRY

Penrith

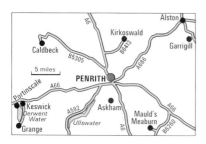

WHERE TO GO

St Andrew's Church: striking interior; the view from 18th c nave is of chandeliers, navy blue pillars and a balcony of turquoise columns. The ceiling is like a crimson draughts-board, squared and sectioned with elegant determination. On gallery steps are stone effigies of Anthony Hutton and his wife Elizabeth, who spent 30 years before her death having the tombs made. Occasional concerts held in the church.

Ancient Grammar School: 16th c building in St Andrew's churchyard which was used as a school up until 1915. Thought to have been originally founded as early as 1340 and re-established when existing building was constructed. Over the fireplace can be seen the Tudor royal arms.

Penrith Castle: red sandstone and roofless, castle was once the home of the Duke of Gloucester, later Richard III, now almost a total ruin. Grounds have been turned into a town park with tennis courts, a small aviary, bowls, putting-green and obstacle golf course. Good for picnics, with views of the wooded hillside and the Penrith Beacon.

Plague Stone, Bridge Lane: in the grounds of Greengarth Old People's home stands a rock with a hollowed-out centre. During the Great Plague in 1598, 2000 of Penrith's residents died. This stone was used for disinfecting money.

SHOPPING

Market Day: Tue.
Early closing: Wed.
Cumbrian Kitchen, 11 Market Square: wholefood store selling excellent picnic fare: home-made marmalade, mountain honey, take-away salads, haggis. Up the wooden stairs for beauty products, plus a restaurant for delicious snacks.
Old Smithy Crafts, Poet's Walk, Castlegate: goods include a selection of hand-knitted sweaters in local Herwick wool. Inexpensive wool on cones.

FOOD AND DRINK

Egon Ronay's Lucas Guide recommends **Leeming on Ullswater Restaurant**, Watermillock, tel Pooley Bridge 444 – elegantly laid tables, enterprising starters and outstanding wine list. *Just a Bite* recommends the **Tudor Bar**, 3 King's St, for snacks. Pubs include: **Two Lions**, Great Dockray. Building was once the

Penrith — 'its higgledy-piggledy layout may not make exploration simple'

Mike and Helen Eyre of the Fetherston Arms Hotel at Kirkoswald

home of Gerard Lowther, the son of the man who escorted Mary, Queen of Scots, from Workington to Carlisle. Present house replaces an earlier one, plaster-work in public bar might be Tudor. Whitbread, children welcome in the beer garden. **Gloucester Arms**, Great Dock-ray. Wood panelling, low beams, and lots of copper kitchen implements hanging from the ceiling. Richard, Duke of Gloucester, supposedly stayed here. Whitbread Trophy and draught cider. The **Woolpack**, Burrowgate, Lorimers Scotch ale, morning coffee, bar snacks. The grandparents of William and Dorothy Wordsworth lived next door.

WHERE TO STAY

Egon Ronay's Lucas Guide recommends **Leeming on Ullswater**, Watermillock, tel Pooley Bridge 444; **Sharrow Bay Country House Hotel**, Ullswater, tel Pooley Bridge 301.

TOURIST INFORMATION

Robinson's School, Middlegate, tel Penrith 64671, extension 33. Open June–30 Sept weekdays 10.00–1.00 and 2.00–8.00, Sun 1.00–6.00. Irregular opening hours in winter.

Villages and country towns

Askham
Ancient village on the edge of Lowther Park. Cottages grouped around a long green with narrow alleyways in between – remnants of a defence tactic used during the Scottish border raids. When the village was attacked, cattle and live-stock would be drven into the central space and small passages barricaded. On the banks of the river Lowther stands Askham Hall, the mellow sandstone home of the Earls of Lonsdale. The most colourful member of the family was the fifth Earl of Lonsdale, the first president of the Automobile Association, who was known as the 'yellow earl'. The Lons-dales formerly occupied Lowther Castle, now a ruin. The castle and its enchanting church stand in a 150-acre park which includes Lowther Wildlife Park. As well as the red deer, which have lived here for over 400 years, there are Chinese water deer, wolves and wild boar; also an adventure playground and a lake. Open April–Oct. Queen's Head Inn and Restaurant, tel Hackthorpe 225, is recommended in *Egon Ronay's Lucas Guide*

for traditional home cooking and bright, cosy bedrooms.

Caldbeck
Birthplace of huntsman John Peel and primarily a farming community. Grey stone houses surround the Oddfellows Arms inn, where 'D'You Ken John Peel?' was first sung, and Caldbeck church, where Peel was baptized, married and buried. A few years ago his grave was desecrated by anti-bloodsport supporters; now the tombstones rises like a ghostly beacon high above the others, pale and elaborately scrolled. You can buy a copy of *John Peel: The Man, The Myth and The Song*, with intro by that other local hero Melvyn Bragg, from the Old Smithy crafts shop, or buy a pair of wooden shoes by J. Strong & Son, clog-makers, who operate in the old blanket mill across the street. The house where Peel is thought to have been born is now Parkend restaurant, recommended in *Egon Ronay's Lucas Guide* for traditional English dishes, tel Caldbeck 442. Over the cattle grid lies Greenrigg, where Peel lived before his marriage. Not open to the public, but next house along is a pleasant pottery, especially good for large urns.

Garrigill
Perfect village for explorers, hikers or anyone with a penchant for wide open spaces: the Pennine Way passes nearby. Garrigill is snug, lying low in the hills and purpose-built for solid comfort – houses compact around a village green with thick walls for keeping out gales. George and Dragon pub serves Tetleys bitter and has a separate pool room. There is evidence of burials in the walled-in churchyard dating back to 1573; in church itself are brightly coloured rolls of honour by local artists. On the church a sign reads: 'Feel free to rest, picnic, even sleep here', and tents among the tombstones are a common sight.

Grange-in-Borrowdale
A bridge much loved by artists leads to tiny Grange, a secluded clutter of green stone cottages completely encircled by hills. The 200-year-old general store-cum-cafe sells local honey and ham. Holy Trinity church is a gem, its bell-tower a model of simplicity silhouetted against the fells; the absence of stained glass sets

Lowther Castle, near Askham – now in ruins

the whitewashed interior gleaming. Lakeland Rural Industries lies the other side of the bridge in an ivy-covered house, 95 per cent of its unusual stock made in the area. Hazelwood walking sticks, spoons made of horn and stainless steel and copper tableware hand-beaten on the premises. Open Easter–Oct daily 9.30–6.00, Nov–Dec 10.00–4.00. Closed Jan–Feb. Never enough parking space anywhere in village.

Kirkoswald

Elegant red sandstone village careful of its appearance: a few years ago residents had the power cables which criss-crossed its streets rerouted underground. 18th c buildings around a cobbled courtyard, many ivy-covered, quaint, with only a few paces separating the Crown Inn from the Black Bull. Next to the bow-faced general store is a Midland bank, handsome, imposing and even more remarkable for being open two mornings a week only. Kirkoswald takes its name from the church of St Oswald, a weathered, 13th c

structure at the foot of the hill. Its turreted bell-tower is some 200yds away, rising from a small mound and delightful to come across accidentally. Kirkoswald Castle, lying in a wooded copse across from the tower, was built 100 years ago. Overgrown and in ruins, castle still evidences a certain command: local animals get trapped in its dungeon.

Mauld's Maeburn

The early estate of Maeburn included this village and also one farther up the Lyvennet River. Held by the de Morville family, the manor was divided between two children, Mauld and Hugh. In 1170 Hugh was implicated in the murder of Thomas à Becket and his lands were confiscated by the Crown, resulting in the village of King's Maeburn. Mauld's Maeburn is little more than a hamlet, lying near the charming community of Crosby Ravensworth one mile south. Two narrow lanes of cottages follow the lines of the river – there are stone bridges to cross by, but sheep have the right of

way. Village green is actually well-worked grazing land; hordes of woolly animals come charging through at unexpected moments. Flass House is a Victorian mansion whose present owner has concentrated on the 18th–19th c trade between Britain and the Far East. An oriental figure stands sentry in the entrance hall, aggressive and colourful; there's a Mandarin Chinese bed with sitting space for concubines; and several opium weights and pipes. Incense on sale. Open Easter–Sept Thur, Sun 2.00–5.00.

Portinscale

Name is thought to mean 'prostitute's hut'. Sophisticated residential village on the edge of Derwent Water, the widest of the lakes and some say the most picturesque. Certainly this area is breathtaking; the drive from Grange to Portinscale includes views of the water's pretty islands with the fells in ever-changing colours. Cumbrian author Sir Hugh Walpole loved it here, his Rogue Herries stories give vivid pictures of life in the Borrowdale valley. Portinscale offers everything necessary for a short stay by the lake; large hotels almost hidden by glossy rhododendrons, Cumberland sausages on sale in the general store, and Jennings real bitter available in the Farmers Arms inn. From Nichol End Marine you can hire rowing-boats, motor-boats or sailing dinghies, or leave the driving to Keswick Launch, whose sightseeing launches pick up passengers from six different points. Lingholm Gardens, one mile south, grows interesting shrubs and flowers in a forest setting, with splendid views up the valley. Open April–end Oct Mon–Sat 10.00–5.00. Nichol End Marine, tel Keswick 73082. Keswick Launch, tel Keswick 72263.

The Moot Hall at Keswick

Aira Force Waterfall

—*Places to visit*—

Dalemain House: pink sandstone house dating from 12th c with Elizabethan and Georgian additions. Vivid Chinese drawing-room; once the room had been papered, individual figures and images were added to balance the design. Present courtyard derived from a medieval hamlet, next to Norman pele tower which houses a yeomanry museum and a tea-room. Sweet-smelling garden with summerhouses among a miniature orchard. Open Easter–end Sept daily except Fri 2.00–5.15. Off A592.

Hutton-in-the-Forest: some authorities maintain that on this site was once the castle of the Green Knight, to which Sir Gawain travelled from King Arthur's court. Pele tower built in 14th c as defence against the Scots; turrets are later, more romantic additions. Hutton-in-the-Forest has been owned by the Inglewood family since the early 17th c, with paintings and furniture acquired over the centuries. Note the Cupid staircase carved with foliage and cherubs, similar tapestry at the top. Open Thur May–mid-Sept, Bank Hol Mon April–Aug, 2.00–5.00. Off B5305.

Acorn Bank: owned by the National Trust, the gardens of Temple Sowerby Manor are open to the public every day except Mon from Easter Sun–31 Oct 10.00–5.30. Spring bulbs, walled garden, herb garden, no dogs.

Shap Abbey: one of three northern Premonstratensian abbeys in the care of the Department of the Environment. Dating mainly from 13th c, the ruins are slight but the view of the nearby fells is superb. Try to be there at sunset. Open May–Sept weekdays 9.30–7.00 Sun 2.00–7.00, Nov–Feb weekdays 9.30–4.00 Sun 2.00–4.00, March, April, Oct weekdays 9.30–5.30 Sun 2.00–5.30. Closed Christmas Eve, Christmas Day, Boxing Day and New Year's Day. Nominal admission. Minor road off the A6 at Shap village.

Brougham Castle: standing on seemingly flat ground but visible for miles, Brougham on the banks of the River Eamont is one of the most interesting castle ruins in northern England. The keep dates from about 1176. Department of the Environment. Open same hours as Shap but April–Sept also Sun mornings. $1\frac{1}{2}$ miles south-east of Penrith, off A66.

Wetheriggs Country Pottery: one of the last traditional earthenware potteries still making slipware using the old methods and equipment, including a blunger, a steam engine and a cow horn. 19th c beehive kiln was recently scheduled as an ancient monument. Three potters work in clean and spacious surroundings; in other rooms are a leather workshop and rugs being woven on handlooms. Visitors can wander freely or snack in the pleasant tea-room. Open daily 10.00–6.00. Take A6 towards village of Clifton, turn off at minor road marked Clifton Dykes. Difficult to find but persevere.

Aira Force Waterfall: Wordsworth used the legend of Aira Force in his poem *The Somnambulist*, about a girl named Emma who took to sleep-walking by the falls while her lover was away. On his return he tried to waken her, and she promptly fell into the water. Emma lived in a castle on the site of Lyulph's Tower, a privately owned Gothic folly, which can be seen by following footpaths east of Aira Force. Waterfall open any time, a 20-min walk from car park. By junction of A592 and A5091 roads along Ullswater.

The Watermill, Little Selkeld: a water-powered corn-mill producing stoneground flour the traditional way. See working water-wheel, mill-stones, sackhoist and other equipment. A tea-room sells scones and cakes baked from freshly ground flour, the shop sells organically grown grains. Open three afternoons a week Easter–Oct, five afternoons in Aug. Tel Langwathby 523 for details. One mile from Langwathby off A686.

ACTIVITIES

Sailing: Ullswater Sailing School – tuition for beginners, sailing craft for hire, plus log cabins, caravan sites, tent pitches and boat park. Tel Pooley Bridge 438.

Cruises: *Lady of the Lake* and *My Raven* sail three times daily April–Sept, then twice a day until end Oct. Trip lasts about an hour. Timetable from information centres or tel Kendal 21626.

Pony-trekking: 1½-hour trekking on the fells from Ellerslea Trekking Centre, Easter–Sept, tel Pooley Bridge 405, or

Ullswater, one of the most beautiful of the lakes

from Roe Head Trekking Centre. Easter –Sept, tel Pooley Bridge 459.

Fishing: fish for trout with fly, worm, spinner or maggot, for perch with maggot, minnow, worm or spinner. Try your luck and a permit from Armstrong and Stockdale, 4 Great Dockray, Penrith. Also available from Treetops in Pooley Bridge and the Glenridding Post Office. *The Northern Anglers' Handbook* is available from local booksellers.

Climbing: the most popular crags are Gowbarrow Crag and Thrang Crag. Sturdy shoes and a professional attitude required, climbing in the fells is serious business.

Walking: several pamphlets on sale at the Penrith Information Centre. Particularly good is the book *Lake District Walks for Motorists – Northern Area* by John Parker, published by Frederick Warne. Sheet 90 of the 1:50,000 Ordnance Survey series covers the Penrith to Keswick area.

FOOD AND DRINK

Egon Ronay's Lucas Guide recommends **Sharrow Bay Country House Hotel Restaurant**, Ullswater, tel Pooley Bridge 301. Star-rating, irresistible puddings. **Scafell Hotel Restaurant**, Rosthwaite, tel Borrowdale 208. Five-course table d'hôte menus and ambitious à la carte. *Just a Bite* recommends **Yan-Tyan Tethera**, 70 Main St, Keswick for substantial snacks.

TOURIST INFORMATION

Publications: the Cumbria Tourist Board publishes an excellent range of pamphlets on events, sporting activities, craft workshops and other activities, with grid references corresponding to their 'Leisure and Holiday Planning Map'. Recommended for anyone who wants more than a fell-walking trip. Available from booksellers, large hotels, tourist information offices. *Lakescene* is a monthly booklet which includes entertainment, shopping, sport and eating out, plus local features. From some hotels and most information centres.

Information centres: other centres at Alston, Appleby, Pooley Bridge, Glenridding, Keswick, Southwaite.

Research: Martha Ellen Zenfell.

Index

Useful guide and reference books

A list of local CAMRA beer guides and where to buy them appears each year in the *Good Beer Guide* published by Arrow Books and the Campaign for Real Ale, 34 Alma Rd, St Albans, Herts AL1 3BW. Local guides are comprehensive, the *Good Beer Guide* is a national selection of real ale pubs.

Historic Houses, Castles and Gardens in Gt Britain and Ireland, guide to those open to the public, published annually by ABC Historic Publications.

The National Trust Guide, Jonathan Cape.

Properties Open, booklet published annually by National Trust, 42 Queen Anne's Gate, London SW1.

AA Illustrated Guide to Britain, Drive Publications Ltd.

The Buildings of England, series edited by Nikolaus Pevsner (Penguin: hardback).

Houses in the Landscape, by John and Jane Penoyre (Faber).

Gardens Open to the Public, published annually by National Gardens Scheme, 57 Lower Belgrave St, London SW1 0LR.

The Shell Guide to Gardens, by Arthur Hellyer (Heinemann).

The Shell Guides, (Faber): *The Companion Guides*, (Collins); *Village* series (Robert Hale).

Craft Workshops in the English Countryside, published annually by CoSIRA, 35 Camp Rd, Wimbledon Common, London SW19 4UP.

Where to Ride, published annually by the British Horse Society, The National Equestrian Centre, Kenilworth, Warwickshire CV8 2LR.

Egon Ronay's Lucas Guide to Hotels and Restaurants; Egon Ronay's Raleigh Pub Guide; and *Just a Bite, Egon Ronay's Lucas Guide for Gourmets on a Family Budget*. All published annually (Penguin)

Photograph credits